1,000,000 Books

are available to read at

www.ForgottenBooks.com

Read online
Download PDF
Purchase in print

ISBN 978-0-259-54987-1
PIBN 10822850

1 MONTH OF
FREE
READING

at

www.ForgottenBooks.com

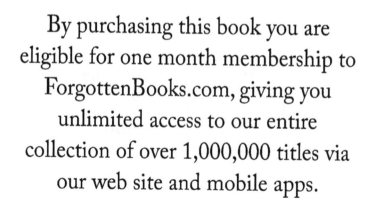

By purchasing this book you are eligible for one month membership to ForgottenBooks.com, giving you unlimited access to our entire collection of over 1,000,000 titles via our web site and mobile apps.

To claim your free month visit: www.forgottenbooks.com/free822850

English
Français
Deutsche
Italiano
Español
Português

www.forgottenbooks.com

Mythology Photography **Fiction**
Fishing Christianity **Art** Cooking
Essays Buddhism Freemasonry
Medicine **Biology** Music **Ancient**
Egypt Evolution Carpentry Physics
Dance Geology **Mathematics** Fitness
Shakespeare **Folklore** Yoga Marketing
Confidence Immortality Biographies
Poetry **Psychology** Witchcraft
Electronics Chemistry History **Law**
Accounting **Philosophy** Anthropology
Alchemy Drama Quantum Mechanics
Atheism Sexual Health **Ancient History**
Entrepreneurship Languages Sport
Paleontology Needlework Islam
Metaphysics Investment Archaeology
Parenting Statistics Criminology
Motivational

THE
LOVE LETTERS
OF
MARY QUEEN OF SCOTS,
TO
ES EARL OF BOTHWELL;

WITH HER

VE SONNETS AND MARRIAGE CONTRACTS,

(........................... FROM THE GILT CASKET.)

PAPERS, AND THE WRITINGS OF ...., GOODALL,
RTSON, HUME, LORD HAILES, LORD BUCHANAN, TYTLER,
ORACE WALPOLE, WHITAKER, LAING, CHALMERS,
BRANTOME, RONSARD, MISS BENGER, AND A
HOST OF AUTHORS.

FORMING A COMPLETE HISTORY OF THE ORIGIN OF

E SCOTTISH QUEEN'S WOES AND TRIALS,
BEFORE QUEEN ELIZABETH.

By HUGH CAMPBELL, LL.D. F.A.S.

ILLUSTRATOR OF ....

LONDON:
MAN, HURST, REES, ORME, BROWN, AND GREEN.

THE

LOVE LETTERS

OF

MARY QUEEN OF SCOTS,

TO

JAMES EARL OF BOTHWELL;

WITH HER

LOVE SONNETS AND MARRIAGE CONTRACTS,

(BEING THE LONG-MISSING ORIGINALS FROM THE GILT CASKET.)

EXPLAINED BY

STATE PAPERS, AND THE WRITINGS OF BUCHANAN, GOODALL,
ROBERTSON, HUME, LORD HAILES, LORD ELLIBANK, TYTLER,
HORACE WALPOLE, WHITAKER, LAING, CHALMERS,
BRANTOME, RONSARD, MISS BENGER, AND A
HOST OF AUTHORS.

FORMING A COMPLETE HISTORY OF THE ORIGIN OF

' THE SCOTTISH QUEEN'S WOES AND TRIALS,
BEFORE QUEEN ELIZABETH.

———◆———

BY HUGH CAMPBELL, LL.D. F.A.S.

ILLUSTRATOR OF OSSIAN'S POEMS.

———◆———

" If a story so authenticated as the Innocence of Mary is to be rejected, half the
history of mankind must be rejected with it."   WHITAKER.

" An English Whig, who asserts the reality of the Popish plot; an Irish Catholic,
who denies the massacre in 1641 ; and a Scotch jacobite, who maintains the innocence of Queen Mary, must be considered as men beyond the reach of argument or
reason."   HUME.

LONDON:
LONGMAN, HURST, REES, ORME, BROWN, AND GREEN.

Printed by T. DOLBY, 17, Catherine Street, Strand, London.

[*Entered at Stationers' Hall.*]

TO

Sir WALTER SCOTT, Bart.

OF ABBOTSFORD,

&c. &c. &c.

Sir,

Although I have been so much buffetted about the world, that I could almost enter on a defence of misanthropy, yet, I must confess, that amid the storms and clouds of life, I have occasionally experienced calms and sunshine, so that I am still inclined to side with humanity.

There are now but three persons in the world to whom I could feel disposed, or would condescend, to inscribe my labours: two of these are ladies, who in such a case as the present would naturally and properly shrink from publicity: consequently, the burthen falls on you, Sir Walter, and honest gratitude urges me to dedicate, without first consulting your feelings on the subject.

Some years before my long, laborious, and expensive inquiries into the authenticity of the Poems of Ossian introduced me to the literary world, you generously took sufficient time, from your numerous public and private avocations, to read my forthcoming poem—The Birth of Bruce — and to give me your valuable opinions on that work: now as such courtesy and kindness to an obscure stranger could only emanate from the best human feelings; so, in return, you must admit my plea of gratitude in the shape of a dedication, and not demur: and believe me, sir,

Your grateful servant,

HUGH CAMPBELL.

London, November, 1824.

PREFACE.

THE Letters which I now publish, in addition to those already given to the world by Buchanan in the 16th century, came into my hands by mere accident. The MS. appears to several judges to be upwards of one hundred years old, but I should take the language to be antecedent to the classical days of Addison. I am induced to publish the Letters with their present accompaniments, because I think they possess more internal marks of originality, and are more feminine than those ascribed to Mary in Buchanan's Detection of that Queen's actions.

A sort of history of the MS. has been given me, which represents the Letters to have been the property of a Nobleman who took an active part in the transactions of those times; and, that they are true copies of the Original Letters, which with seven of those already published, the Love Sonnet, and the two Marriage Contracts, composed

the twenty-one papers found in the Gilt
Casket of Bothwell; and, that they were
shown to the Commissioners of Elizabeth,
though unrecorded by Buchanan, the partizan of Murray, either because they were
not so absolutely criminal as those he recorded, or because it would have taken up
too much of that historian's time to have
translated them into Latin from the French.

Be that as it may, however, I am not fully
prepared to vouch for their authenticity, only
because I did not see the Queen write them;
but history and concurring details induce me
to feel almost confident that they are the
compositions of the unfortunate Queen of
Scots. Goodall says, and militates against
his own doctrine by so saying:

"To forge letters for Queen Mary, was no
easy matter. To her natural parts, which
were great, she had added more learning than
the half of her enemies put together could
pretend to. She spoke almost all the Euro-
pean languages, and possessed a great taste in
the fine arts. The French was as it were her
mother-tongue, which she spoke and wrote
in all the perfection that was to be found at
the court of France. Her hand-writing was

formed after what was commonly called Italic
print, which it much resembled both in
beauty and regularity, and not to be easily
imitated but by a fine writer. When such
a writer was found, he must write French
too, and that as well as the Queen, to which
few, even of the natives of France, could pretend: and not only so, but he must be acquainted with persons and transactions about
her court, so as to make proper allusions,
lest her Majesty should appear to write
quite out of character, which would have
spoiled all."

There has been so much said and written
about the guilt and innocence of this Princess, that I only aspire in this volume to give
the marrow of the opinions of the most celebrated advocates on either side.

Those who have more curiosity than this
work is calculated to satisfy, may consult
Jebb, who has digested the Life of Mary by
a host of Biographers, and other writers on
the same subject, in two vols. folio, Latin.
As some of the Letters appear to have been
written to Bothwell long before the Queen's
marriage with her cousin Darnley, so I give
them precedence accordingly to those of
Buchanan.

Superficial readers may object to my title, on the erring ground that Mary's woes and trials before Queen Elizabeth originated in her assuming a claim or right to the Arms and Crown of England, whilst she was Queen of Francis the Second, King of France. That foolish assumption of Mary was, most certainly, a great cause of offence to the English Queen; but she never would have had occasion, or an opportunity, to exceed the bounds of a neighbourly interchange of political or private matters, had it not been for the crimes which arose out of Mary's hapless love for Bothwell. That was the true source of her woes!

It remains for me to add, that the celebrated Gilt Casket, which to the lovely Queen of Scots had all the evils of the fabulous box of Pandora, without the solitary virtue at the bottom, is now to be seen at Hamilton Palace; but its regal literature has long since vanished: by what means has not been ascertained!

London, July, 1824.

P. S. Since writing the foregoing, I have received a letter from the ingenious antiquary and collector, Mr. David Laing, of Edinburgh, to whom I am indebted for the following information.

My Copy of Letters purports to be ' The genuine Letters of Mary Queen of Scots to James Earl of Bothwell, found in his secretary's closet after his decease, and now in the possession of a gentleman at Oxford. Translated from the French by Edward Simmons, late of Christ Church College, Oxford, 1726.'

It is now incumbent upon me to declare, in the most solemn manner, that when the MS. was placed in my hands about nine months since, I doubted the authenticity of the Letters; and, accordingly set about an inquiry to ascertain whether they had ever been published; but vain were all my inquiries. The London Institution, the British Museum, private Libraries, and all the old Book-shops, could produce nothing like the Letters in question. But my want of success, I admit, was no argument in favour of their authenticity ; no, the proving argument was in them. I then determined upon pub-

lishing the present volume, of which several
sheets had been printed, and a great expense
incurred, before I received Mr. Laing's letter.
The account, however, which I had with the
MS. differs widely from that of Mr. Laing.
I am told it belonged to some maiden ladies
named Maitland, descendants from the famous State Secretary of Mary Maitland of
Lethington; whose wife, both parties confess, copied the celebrated Letters for the
Queen of Scots, though some of her late partisans state that she neither could see the
originals nor procure copies, so as to make a
defence. Now if Maitland had the means
to enable his wife to take one copy, could
not that copy supply others? And was it not
natural that a copy should be kept in that
family? And if such was a matter of course,
may not the MS. now in my possession be
the same copy described, and the original
of that of Mr. Laing? The language of the
Letters seems to me to be the old Scotch
modernised to the reign of the second Charles;
and certainly not that of a member of Christ
Church College, Oxford, so late as 1726,
the days of Addison, Pope, and Swift.

There appears a want of coincidence or

discrepancy in the statement respecting the
Letters of Mr. Laing, and those of the MS.
Laing says they were found among the papers of Bothwell's secretary, a person I never
read or heard of, and the tradition leads
them to the celebrated Secretary of the Queen
of Scots. The reader may judge which is
the most probable of the two statements.
The difference is in the employer of the secretary.

It should also be observed that Mr. Laing's
title runs, " Genuine Letters;" that of the
MS. is Original Love Letters, &c. but no
translator's name or date is mentioned. I am
free to declare, however, that I should have
compiled this volume from the MS. even had
I possessed the information Mr. Laing has
since so kindly communicated; and should
these be the same Letters ascribed to Queen
Mary by Horace Walpole, in his Royal and
Noble Authors, I am fully justified in allowing the title of " Original" to remain, as his
opinion ran in favour of their authenticity.

All I claim then will be the credit due for
having again united the long-parted companions of the Gilt Casket, which formerly belonged to Francis the second King of France,

the quondam husband of Mary Queen of
Scots, and son of that nymph of hell, Catherine de Medicis! under whose superin-
tendance the lovely young Queen of Scots
could not fail to become inured to blood and
murder: when her mother-in-law, and former
companion, could instigate and urge to such
horrid massacres as those of St. Bartholo-
mew's Eve.

———◆———

To many readers of good sense and fine
feelings, the nature of the subject now treated
of will, I fear, place me before them as an
opponent of Queen Mary. I shall not blame
their feelings, nor anticipate a defence at
present: but, to complete the work, I have
began, and make it a sort of history: by way
of elucidation, I am determined, with God's
assistance, to publish another volume, in
which I shall endeavour to prove that Queen
Elizabeth was no better than she should
have been; and, much less merciful to her
cousin and sister, the lovely Queen of Scots,
than ninety women in a hundred would
have been to a fallen Queen in such un-

happy circumstances as those in which Mary, her heiress, was placed, in a great measure, by the snares laid for her by the jealous Queen of the golden days.

Temple, Nov. 30, 1824.

TABLE OF CONTENTS.

CONTENTS.

APPENDIX.

INTRODUCTION.

I THINK it was Dr. Radcliffe, who, on being pestered by some of the Physicians of his day, threatened, in case of farther annoyance, to leave the whole system of Physic on a half sheet of paper! In the case of Queen Mary Stuart, I cannot confine myself to such narrow limits; but I purpose to reduce and compress the immense volumes of stuff that have been transcribed, transposed, and transformed from the original history of facts, relating to the reign of that unfortunate Princess, into one volume; in which shall appear the principal arguments and statements for and against her participation in the murder of her husband, Lord Darnley, by the best advocates.

It is necessary to observe, that her unfortunate affection for Lord Bothwell was the guilty source of all her misfortunes—I say guilty source—for he was the husband of another, and in the unfortunate attachment originated the celebrated *letters* which were afterwards held forth to the world, as containing ample proofs of the guilt of Mary—whereon to ground a defence or justification of the Council, at the head of which was her natural Brother, Murray—for depriving her of her Crown and prerogatives of royalty.

From this act of the Scottish Faction Mary applied to Elizabeth of England, and it was subsequently agreed that her Commissioners should meet those of the Council before the Queen of England, who was thus called upon to arbitrate, and decide in favour of the injured Queen. The parties proceeded to England accordingly, and at York held their first conference before Commissioners appointed by Elizabeth, as her representatives, at the head of whom was the Duke of Norfolk, the secret friend and lover of Mary.

From York the Commissioners adjourned to Westmin-

ster, and subsequently to Hampton Court, at which place
the celebrated letters were produced and read by the Commissioners of the Council, to prove the guilt and criminality
of Mary in her own hand-writing!

It appears that two sets of letters were then presented as
proofs of guilt.—Eight were in French and ten in the Scottish language; however, seven only were admitted; but
Buchanan has published the eight*, in the appendix to his
history which he calls "The Detection of Mary," and the
others have been considered lost. The Letters published by
Buchanan have been held by some as forgeries, for the purpose of criminating Mary; and, the *eleven* which now appear to be really the composition of that hapless and accomplished Princess, were not quoted or preserved by the
celebrated scholar and historian,—to justify the Faction
against the Queen, of which Buchanan was a leader—because they did not go the whole length of proving her actually a party in the murder of her husband, but only gave
proofs of the fair writer's guilty attachment to Bothwell.

Had the eleven letters as *now* been published along with
the eight by Buchanan, the genuine would soon have been
distinguished from the spurious, if any were so, and the
curious reader would have been saved the trouble of reading
through massy volumes of tautological verbiage which—

" Leads to bewilder, and dazzles to blind."

From the publication of Buchanan's history about 1570,
until the year 1754, the literary world was almost silent on
the subject; and men generally took for granted, all that
had been written by that historian respecting the unhappy
reign of Mary. Her beauty, accomplishments, and misfortunes, however, continued through the long lapse of time to
excite that sympathy which is not diminished in our own
days, being characteristic of our national feelings, which are

* Cecil, Lord Burleigh, says it was lost with the others.—*Whitaker.*

generally biassed to the side of the unfortunate—forgetting their vices in their woe.

In the said year the world was surprized by an ingenious and creditable work in favour of Mary, and against the authenticity of the letters in Buchanan, from the pen of a Mr. Goodall, keeper of the Advocates' Library in Edinburgh— a source whence the able compiler had every advantage in his favour—the collection of that noble library being at that time equal to any other in the kingdom generally ; but certainly much better for the individual purpose of Mr. Goodall, on the subject at issue.

The redoubtable historian Hume, however, was not to be persuaded of Mary's innocence and the forgery of the Letters, by the opinions of Mr. Goodall ; and he has so expressed himself in his celebrated history*.

After Mr. Hume, came Mr. Tytler †, an advocate, a man of learning, taste, and ingenuity ; and, as far as he could, he advocated the cause of Mary, and endeavoured to establish the forgery of the letters. To Mr. Goodall succeeded the able and elegant historian Robertson, whose reasoning and observations on the guilt or innocence of Mary, form a masterpiece of historical and critical investigation. His history of the reign of Mary and her son James was more than sufficient to excite emulation ; and it is not to be wondered at, that Mr. Whitaker, a young clergyman who had been successful in writing the history of Manchester, should have stepped forward to augment his laurels in a field that had been previously won by two of the most correct and elegant historians that ever graced the annals of literature. —The writings of Mr. Whitaker bear upon them the stamp of an ardent, zealous, bold, and prejudiced mind.

He frequently gives fanciful positions and assertions as premises or facts, and argues upon them accordingly.

His conclusions are consequently favourable to his side

* Vide History of England, vol. 5, and Notes.

† I am not following the chronological order of their publications, but merely alluding to the pros and cons.

of the subject, and he would carry a superficial reader along
with the stream of his discourse, did not his citations from
the leading authors on the subject, induce one to pause in
the perusal, and judge for himself.

Dr. Robertson very prudently declined to answer his warm
and fastidious observations, for the best reason—because in
substance there was really nothing in his " Vindication" but
what was either known or written before, by those who
were in the least acquainted with the history of the times—
his irrelevant positions and assertions excepted.

After Mr. Whitaker, the love of fame called forth another champion to the field against Mary, whose discrimina-
tion and temperament might be considered as well matched
with those of the reverend vindicator. Mr. Malcolm Laing,
the anatomist of Ossian, and dissector of Macpherson, stood
forth, and avowed himself sufficiently strong in arguments
and facts to prove the unfortunate Mary guilty, and thence
to have her broken on the wheel of public opinion.   Much
of his reasoning is unanswerable, and he is only obscured by
the brilliancy of those who have gone before him.

The success of Laing against Mary called forth another
zealot in her favour, in the person of Mr. George Chalmers,
a clerk in the Treasury, who, consequently, had the means
and time on his hands to pursue literature.   This writer had
already published " Caledonia," a work grounded on, or
transposed from, " The Annals of Scotland," by Lord Hailes
—" The Beauties of Scotland," and the statistical account
of that country, collected by Sir John Sinclair, and other
descriptive publications.   He is a creditable compiler—I
would not have my judgment impugned, or offend Mr.
Chalmers, by styling him an historian.

His collation of the different papers of the preceding
writers and historians on the subject, proves that he clearly
understands the case against Mary; but, as an apologist,
like Whitaker, his master and leader, he is feeble, fails in
arguments, and flies to assertions.   Whitaker has written

octavo pages to prove that " Writings of espousal,"
are not synonimous with " Marriage Contracts ;" and there
are some of Chalmers, his echo's, pages almost as intelligibly
occupied. But book-making now-a-days is a sort of trade
acquired by rote, and not as formerly—the promptings of
large, expanded, and ingenious minds.

The public I think must be almost tired of the immense
volumes of trash that is annually poured upon it by trans-
posers of sentences, and see the value of Lindley Murray's
various modes of giving the same sense in different application of the words conveying it to the mind. It is much to be
regretted that my brave clansman, Sir Mathew Campbell,
who commanded the right wing of Mary's little army at the
battle of Langside, had not had one thousand such zealous,
knock-down, straight-forward, well-fed, sturdy fellows as
Mr. Chalmers on that memorable day, so fatal to Mary's interests. Had such champions been with my clansman he
would have saved the kingdom, and Elizabeth the subsequent trouble and disgrace which sprang from her jealous
cruelty. Though last not least forward steps the accomplished Miss Benger, and she has done more for her favourite Mary in her two small novel-like tomes, than her predecessor did in his three gigantic volumes*.

I need scarcely say any thing of the Scottish writers before the period of Goodall's vindication, or of Brantome,
and the other French writers who have defended the cause
of their Marie Stuart. I should gladly have embodied the
portion of Sir James Melville's Memoirs, which states his
successful flattery of Elizabeth, and embraces the time and
scene of action of this national tragedy, but it would out-
step the nutshell walls of the limits which I have prescribed
to myself as most eligible and agreeable to public taste,

---

* Mr. Chalmers, it is to be understood, does not confine himself to
Mary, although his title would lead one to believe so. His journal
contains memoirs of several other persons.

and I doubt not but that the epitome of arguments which *pro* and *con* I lay before the world, will satisfy all but the critically fastidious part of the community, whose appetites I do not aspire to gratify : these I leave to the catering of some or all of our book-makers, who—

Frown in folios, and in quartos rave.

But to the thinking part of society who can without violence to the delicacy of the sex conceive it not only possible, but probable for a woman—even though that woman should be a queen—and we have lived to see a queen as prodigal and accommodating in her choice of favourites as the Queen of Scots—for if Mary had her Chatelar, her Rizio, and her Bothwell ; report says, that Caroline had her S————, her M————, and her Bergami ; whilst, in each case, the Lazzaroni triumphed, and decency and virtue hung their heads.

To such then as think it not only possible but probable that such a woman could be so infatuated with a man as to urge him to sue for and obtain a divorce from his lawful wife, and afterwards to force that wretched dupe to her lusts to destroy her own husband and assume his rights*, I think I may fearlessly appeal for approbation of my views and efforts in placing all of the most prominent circumstances connected with these letters before them (as it has fallen to my lot to rescue them from oblivion and destruction) in a shape that will at once enable the reader to develope the whole accusation and defence—the whole guilt or innocence of Mary Queen of Scots of the murder of her husband, Lord Darnley.

In Hume's able and unanswerable note on the letters of Mary to Bothwell, he confidently and triumphantly asks in substance—" If these letters are now to be stigmatised as forgeries, why were they not so stamped when adduced be-

---

* It will be in the recollection of my readers, that within these three years a respectable farmer's wife was executed for instigating her partner in adultery to destroy her husband.

fore the Commmmissioners of Elizabeth, in the presence of Mary's best friend, the Bishop of Ross ?" The inference of the learned historian is not only just but natural.

. The Bishop and his fellow Commissioners well knew that they could not deny the fact of the letters being in the handwriting of Mary, for that was rendered impossible by the Duke of Norfolk, her secret friend and lover, and his fellow-representatives of the English queen, comparing the said letters with other well authenticated writings of the Queen of Scots.

The policy of James was natural and affectionate, after he succeeded to the English crown. To hide his mother's infamy, it is supposed that he had secretly brought before him the originals, notes and copies of all that had transpired before the Commissioners respecting his mother, and had the mass destroyed ; for it is beyond a doubt that not a relic of them remains in either the English or Scottish archives. Hence the absence of the originals, hence the doubts and volumes about the forgery of the letters, and hence the very slender grounds for the historian to build upon. The preservation of the corelative papers from those of the Duke of Norfolk, Sir Ralph Sadler, Cecil, and those brought forward by Mr. Goodall from the Advocates' Library, seems to have been more the result of chance, than the effect of relenting Vandalism in those that destroyed the principal papers.

But, as in other national causes, a copy escaped the general ruin, and it has been preserved in the family of an active nobleman in the transactions of those times. I have pleasure in giving it to the public as the only one known to be extant of the original letters produced at Hampton Court, and allowed to be genuine by Mary's best friends, in the presence of the English queen—the umpire between the Scottish queen and her nobles. In such a case I would—

" Nothing extenuate, nor set aught down in malice."

My object is to hold an open course: to keep, if possible,
between the Scylla and Charybdis of parties, and steer
round the Pelorus cape of independence. I shall be happy
to 'find that each reader will be able to judge for himself,
from the very conflicting testimony the nature of the subject
imposes upon me to adduce.

It is generally believed upon the authority of the accu-
rate historian, Robertson, that James Hepburn, Earl of
Bothwell, did not acquire the favours of Mary until 1566.
But Randolph's dispatches prove to the contrary.

The attachment of Mary to Bothwell, from his fidelity to
her mother and her, appears very early, and the honourable firmness of Bothwell, in adherence to his own principles, and in opposition to the Queen's, appears as early as
December the 7th, 1561. Randolph says of both, that " at
the *dirige* or mass upon Friday and Saturday last,—she observed the old manner in all her doings; yet she could not
perswade nor get one lord of her own to wear the *deule* for
that day, *nor so much as the Earl Bothwell.*"* But his
steady zeal for Protestantism, could not procure him the
good opinion of a Randolph; because he continued loyal to
his Sovereign, when he was averse to her religion. Randolph accordingly speaks of him on the 10th of April,
1563, with all the harshness of a man, who considered
the profession of Protestantism, as merely a long cloak to
hide the cloven-foot of treason. " The Queen," he says,
" knoweth now that the Earl Bothwell is sent for to London," when, on his flying out of Scotland by sea, he was
cast upon the shore of England:† I know that she thinketh much, that he is not sent into Scotland: it is yet greatly doubted, that if he were here, he would be reserved
for an evil instrument:—there come a vulture in this realm,
if ever that man comes again into credit ‡."   H. C.

---

* Keith, 207.   † Knox, 322.   ‡ Robertson, ii. 332, 333.

MEMORANDUM.

———◆———

THAT in the Castle of Edinburgh there was left by the Earl of Bothwell, befoir his fleing away, and was send for be ane George Daglische his servand, quha was takin by ye Erle of Mortoun, ane small gylt coffer, not fully a fute lang, being garnischit in sundrie places with the Romane Letter F. under ane Kingis crowne; quhairin wer certane letteris and wrytingis wel knawin, and be aithis affirmit to have bene writtin with the Quene of Scottis awin hand to the Erle Bothwell.

Besyde thay wrytings, thair was alswa extant a wryting writtin in Roman hand in French, avowit to be writtin be the said Quene of Scottis hirself, being ane promeis of marriage to the said Bothwell: Quhilk wryting being without dait, and thocht sum wordis thairin seme to the contrarie, zit is upon credibill groundis supposit to have bene maid and written be hir befoir the deith of hir husband.

Buchanan's Detection.

THE EARL OF MORTOUN'S RECEIPT OF THE BOX AND LET-
   TERS.   FROM THE ACTS OF LENNOX'S PRIVY COUNCIL,
   IN THE EARL OF HADDINGTON'S COLLECTIONS.

Apud Edinb. xxii. Januarii 1570-1.

The quhilk day, in presence of the richt honorabil Mat-
thew Erle of Levinox, Lord Darnlie, guidschir, lauchful
Tutor and Regent to our Soverane Lord, his realme and
lieges, and Lordis of Secreit counsal ; James Erle of Mortoun, Lord of Dalkeyth, Chancellar and greit Admiral of
Scotland, being in reddiness to pass to the Quenis Majesty
of Ingland, as ane of our Soverane Lordis Commissionaris,
for divers gryt and wechtie materis, concerning his Hienes
and his estait, grantit and confessit him to have ressavit
fra the said Lord Regent an silver box, overgilt with gold,
with the missive letteris, contractis or obligatiounis for marriage, sonnettis, or luif-ballettis, and utheris letteris thairin contenit, to the number of xxi*, send and past betwix
the Quene, our said Soverane Lordis moder, and James
sumtime Erle Bothville : Quhilk box, and haill pecis within
the samin, wer takin and fund with umquhile George Dal-
gleische, servand to the said Erle Bothville, upon the xx
day of Junii, the zeir of God MD. thré scoir sevin zeiris,
and were deliverit, be the said James Erle of Mortoun, to
umquhile James Erle of Murray, Lord Abirnethie, uncle
and Regent to our Soverane Lord for the time : Efter quhais
deceis, the samin box and letteris wer recoverit out of the
handis of his servandis, be the said Erle of Levinox, now
Regent.   Quhilkis letteris, being autentiklie copeit, and
subscrivit with the handis of his Grace and Lordis of Secreit
counsale, the samin copeis wer left to remane with his Grace

---

* It seems the box has been very prolific. for per Num. 20. they
were not near so many.—Goodall.

   Ten, and eight, and three, make twenty-one.—Goodall did not know
of the letters now published, and forgets the love sonnets, and
two contracts.—H. Campbell.

ad futuram rei memoriam : And als the said Erle of Mor
toun promeist and obleist him, to bring agane and deliver
the said box, and principal letteris, to the said Lord Regent, at his returning from this present legatioun.

A DECLARATION BY THE EARL OF MURRAY AND HIS COL-
LEAGUES, THAT THE LETTERS, AND OTHER PAPERS EX-
HIBITED BY THEM TO THE COUNCIL OF ENGLAND,
AGAINST QUEEN MARY, ARE ORIGINALS AND AUTHENTIC.

An original.

Quhairas, for verificatioun of the eik or additioun to our
answer, presentit be us aganis the accusatioun of our adversaries, concerning the murther of umquhil King Henry,
of gude memorie, our Soverane Lordis derrest fader, we
haif producit divers missive letteris, sonnettis, obligatiounis
or contractis for mariage betwix the Quene, moder to our
said Soverane, and James sometime Erle Bothwille, as
writtin or subscrivit be hir hand; quhilks were interceptit,
and cum to our handis, closit within a silver box, in sic
maner as is alredy manifestit and declarit: And we, be the
tenour heirof, testifies, avowis and affirmis, upon our honouris and consciences, that the saidis haill missive writingis, sonettis, and obligatiounis or contractis, are undoubtedly the said Quenis proper hand-write; except the
contract in Scottis, of the dait, at Seitoun the fift day of
Aprile 1567, written be the Erle of Huntly, quhilk alsua
we understand and perfectlie knawis to be subscrivit be hir,
and will tak the same upon our honours and consciences, as
is befoir said. In witness quhairof we haif subscrivit thir
presents with our hands, at Westminster the 10th day of
December, the zeir of God 1568 Zeirs.

JAMES, Regent.
MORTOUN.
AD. ORCHADEN.
PATRICK L. LINDSAY.
DUMFERMLING.

Whitaker has the following observations respecting the
Letters and Casket :—

The letters remained in Morton's possession to the day of
his death, June 2, 1581. They were then conveyed privately and clandestinely, by the bastard sons of Morton*,
to one of the original conspirators with him against Mary ;
even to that Lord Ruthven, now Earl of Gowrie, who was
heir to the principal assassin of Rizzio, and actually concerned himself in carrying the Queen to Lochlevin. They
were considered as the sacred palladium of rebellion ; as
the holy image, which was only to be seen by the priests
of anarchy, and on the keeping of which from the general
eye, depended the fate of the whole empire of mis-rule.
For this reason, Gowrie was unwilling to own that he had
them. He was still more unwilling to part with them.
He was urged by Elizabeth's embassadour. He was solicited
by James's prime minister. The minister had a curiosity to
see them. The Queen wanted to turn them again upon Mary.
And Gowrie would not part with them to either †.

At this period of their history, King James knew of their
existence, and of the hands in which they existed. Yet
he never offered to force them away ‡. He left them to
continue there unmolested. But they did not continue long
so. That busy period of plots would not suffer them. In
1584 Gowrie received the punishment from James, which
he had long merited from Mary. And the papers seem to
have been then transferred to a man, who was worthy to be
entrusted with the charge, who was nephew to Morton, and
had been recently a conspirator and a rebel with Gowrie—
the Earl of Angus §.

But the necessary season of concealment must now have
been nearly elapsed. All the great actors upon the scene
had successively disappeared from it ; and had gone to lodge

* Crawford, 371, and Moyse, 51.   † Robertson's Diss. 42—46.
‡ Robertson's Diss. 46.   § Goodall, i. 35, 36.

in the bosom of eternity, for that revisal of their actions, which Omniscience will execute, and Omnipotence will ratify, in the sight of all the world. The interests of survivors were less engaged in the spuriousness or the authenticity of the papers. And the care, which had incidentally preserved them hitherto, by taking pains to conceal them from the public, would now be relaxed, as the reason was removed. Accordingly, they appear to have been no longer transmitted from one hand to another; and, when the assassin or the executioner had cut short the life of their present proprietor, to have instantly migrated with the soul of rebellion, to some other child of election. At the death of Angus, they rested peaceably with the Douglases. The transferrible feud now settled into an inheritance. And the wandering paladium of Troy became stationary in the forum of Rome. "I find," says Mr. Goodall, "an anonymous historian, who wrote about the restoration of King Charles II. affirming, that the box and letters were at that time to be seen, with the Marquis of Douglas *."

Yet where are they at present? *Hic labor, hoc opus est.* In the recent days of Mr. Goodall, they were supposed by some to be still in the family of Douglas. But they were reported by others to have been seen at the Duke of Hamilton's †. The Hamiltons had then, by the termination of their line in an heiress, become Douglases. Yet the contradictoriness of the report and the suppositions, shews the uncertainty of both. And the non-appearance of them since, evinces both to be false. A contest has been since maintained concerning them with peculiar vivacity and vigour. The whole nation has stood by, attentive to the issue. The house of Hamilton, and the family of Douglas, have interested themselves, no doubt, equally with all the reading and historical part of the nation; and must have produced the papers, if they had them in their own posses-

---

* Goodall, i. 36.   † Ibid.

sion. No longer employed in the turbulence of war, the Douglases and the Hamiltons have leisure to superintend the contests of literature; to consider them as equally important now, with an inroad or an insurrection formerly; and to be as ready as ever to mingle in the fray. Indeed the papers are too singular in their nature, and too distinguished in their history, not to be known wherever they are found. And the casket, in which they were originally reposited, and with which, in all probability, they have always travelled; being " ane small gylt coffer, not fully ane fute lang," and " being garnischit in sindrie places, with the Romane letter F under ane Kingis crowne;" is an object impossible to lie unnoticed in any library.

They may, however, have been separated from their original vehicle. They may also be kept concealed by that spirit of party, which originally withheld them in England and in Scotland from the eye of examination, and of which the ghost is seen to haunt us still at times. Or they may have perished in that sweeping fire, which, in December, 1758, consumed the castle of Douglas, the seat of the Earl of Angus in 1581, the seat of the Marquis of Douglas in 1660; and consumed with it the greatest part of the furniture, paintings, and papers in it. But we need not be anxious for their appearance.

Were Whitaker alive he would doubtless be angry at seeing the whole contents of the casket in the following pages.   H. C.

ORIGINAL LOVE LETTERS OF MARY QUEEN OF SCOTS, TO JAMES EARL OF BOTHWELL.

LETTER THE FIRST.

This first Letter, as appears by Brantome's Memoirs, must be written when ye Earl of Bothwell was in Banishment, where he had been some time on an information given by the Lord Arran, that he had conspired against the Life of Murray, besides, the complaint she makes in it, how impossible it is for her to act as she would on having her power limited by two different Factions, perfectly agrees with Spotswood, Sir James Melvil, and almost all the authors who have written ye Histories of those times; the latter of them very confidently affirmed that she had never consented to marry with Lord Darnley, but that she hoped by that means to suppress the incroachments which the two Parties, headed by Hamilton and Murray, were daily making on her Prerogative.

You complain of me my dear Bothwell without cause; did you know what insurmountable difficulties attend a person of my station in the pursuit of an affair such as ours you would not blame but pity me, all my moments are taken up with consultations; the distractions of the times over whelm me—I ought to exchange this soft and gentle nature of mine for one all rough and masculine, to be able to cope with the oppositions I daily meet with—besides the Lord Darnley is perpetually with me, pretends to testifie his passion by his jealousy, and back'd by that assuming arbitress of my fate the English Queen, already takes

upon him the authority of an husband.—What can I do
torn and divided between different Factions, both equally
pernicious to their Sovereigns interest?—Yet in spite of
the contending storms, in spite of business cares, and all
my vast fatigues, still does my heart find room for love—
Yes I protest my ever dear Bothwell, that for an humble
life with you I gladly would exchange this load of greatness and throw it to those who seem ambitious of it, this
gaudy burthen of a crown; but even that is a priviledge
deny'd me; I must either continue to reign or cease to live;
my power is all that can protect my Bothwell; should I
relinquish that, or want the means of preserving you, it is
not the pretended friendship of the ever changing Murray
would afford you any shelter: do not therefore impute it to
the want of impatience to see you, that I stil delay your
coming to Edinburgh; 'tis for the future repose of us both
that I command you to tarry yet longer where you are; but
methinks I need not any arguments to convince you that it
is wholly yor interest I study.   Too precious have been the
proofs I have given you of my tenderness for you to doubt
the sincerity of it, nor do I believe you want sense or gratitude to acknowledge what I have done for you.   Time
however must be the touch-stone of the hearts of both—
write to me as usual; believe me, all the consolation your
unhappy Queen enjoys is in hearing from you; till fate
allows us the blessing of a nearer conversation, which I
hope and pray may be sooner than you expect, and as swift
as my desires—a legion of angels attend and be your guard
from all exteriour harms and keep you ever faithful to

M. R.

P. S. I had forgot to warn you of my Lord Herris; he
designs you a visit, it can be for no other reason than to
pry into your behaviour—be cautious of your self before
him, farewell.

LETTER THE SECOND.

This seems to be written a small time after the former, and both, according to Buchanan, must bear date about the middle of the year 1563. She was at that time greatly incommoded by the Faction of the Hamiltons, and was then beginning to contrive measures for their ruin, as appears by Castlenaw's Memoirs, Spotswood and Crawford.

———

It is in a transport proportionable to my late inquietudes that I now command the presence of my dear Bothwell—the greatest part of my anxietys are over. Elizabeth has changed her mind in favour of Lord Darnley, and I shall be persecuted no more with her menaces or persuasions on his score; Murray also declares himself an enemy to the match, and I shall have the double satisfaction of obliging my subjects and my self; but oh! there remains a greater felicity in store for me; I shall not only be eased of the solicitations of the man I hate, but enjoy with more security than ever the society of him I love; the council seems perfectly satisfied of your innocence as to the late troubles; you will have a publick mandate to recall you; but I cannot restrain my impatience from sending you this harbinger of our approaching happiness. Be secret, however, I conjure you; a too quick discovery of your contentment might yet ruin all—allways remember this, that the favourites of Princes have as many observers as eyes upon them—I learned this maxim from Katherine de Medicis, to wear a countenance the reverse of my heart—proposals frequently are made for no other reasons, than to sound the inclinations of ye persons to whom they are offered; that politick Queen therefore never discloses either the pleasure or discontent she conceives at what she hears, but leaving it to spring out of the reality, fathoms the whole of the design without giving, even those who think themselves at the very bottom of her secrets, liberty to know the least of her thoughts; it is

D

also by this means that Elizabeth circumvents all the plots
of her enemies; and this in fine is the onely security of a
great and envyed person. Dissemble therefore, my dear
Bothwell, with all the world but me, who, I do believe,
will be most pleas'd when most I know yor heart. See the
confidence which love inspires, jealousy and suspicion are
passions I am utterly a stranger to, but in the affairs of
state, I confess I have vanity enough to assure my self the
man I condescend to favour in the manner I have done you,
cannot but be mine; as for the divorce, you write to me
concerning, I would not have you think of it as yet; the
times are at present too much unsetled, and your wife has
powerful friends; strengthen first your own interest, which
may be a means to weaken hers, and leave to me and your
good friend the Bishop of Ross to manage that thereafter ;
we have already laid the scheme, and I am certain that
worthy man will not fail to perform the part enjoyn'd him,
to the satisfaction of both. In the mean time I would not
have you give the least hint of yor design : But of this we
shall have leisure to talk at yor arival. I have these three
days waited an opportunity to convey to you the tender
meanings of my soul, and must not waste the precious moment in dull narrations. No time is pleasing to me that is
not spent in giving you new demonstrations of my affections; well may I err in the rules of government and state,
when all my thoughts are taken up with love ; and yet perhaps I should be less capable than I am, if my concern for
the establishment of your happiness, did not make me now
and then apply my self to those maxims which alone can
have the power to fix it. The ambition I have to make
you great, keeps alive my desire of continuing so my self.

The scepter I am very certain would soon grow too unwieldy for the weakness of my hand, were it not for the
charming hope I should shortly have the means of transfer-
ring it into yours; 'tis there I wish to see it shine, and
took on myself but as the steward of a glorious relict. I do

believe however that there are joys in my power to bestow
infinitely more powerful to you than this, but I think not
my heart and person sufficient rewards for the merits of my
Bothwell, and long for the happy hour when I may give a
kingdom in dowry with my love; till then I cannot say
my joy is complete, nor will I ever rest till this, the supream-
est desire my soul can know, is accomplished. I am now
going to Council, where I have ordered it so that the Earl
of Hamilton, who I know yor enemy, shall be accused of
things, which, for a time at least, shall deprive him of the
Power of giving any interuption to happiness I propose to
myself in the enjoyment of my dear Bothwell's conversation; adieu—expect in a few days to be called to court and
to the impatient arms of

M. R.

LETTER THE THIRD.

This letter was written in the beginning of the year
1564, at which time Queen Elizabeth proposed the Earl of
Leicester to her for a husband, according to Camden, Hol-
lingshed, and almost all the historians, who mention that
affair with wonder; the greatest politicians of that age not
being able to fathom the secret motives which induced her
to so unexpected a behaviour.

What a sudden turn in our affairs! Good God! How
are the face of all things altered! Scarce have I courage
to report the story—but you, alas! are but too well acquainted with the misfortune in general, though the particulars
cannot yet have reached you: I am for ever doomed to be
the vassal of the English Queen, the tool of her cursed
policy, the property of her ambition, without a friend to
aid me. She writes me now that the reasons for breaking off
the match with Darnley were because she thinks Leicester
more worthy of my bed and crown! Leicester raised but
by her partial favour, and long the mirror of her loosest

wishes, must now be recompensed with the Scottish crown, but it shall perish first, though Murray and the faction again threaten to take up arms; though the remainder of the Gordon race rejoyce in this opportunity of revenge, and all I have endured nor all I can endure, shall frighten me to an act so loathed, so scorned, no, if not decreed for Bothwell, I will be for no other: in this world I will be mistress of myself, as for the rest let fate dispose. I am grown weary of the light, and almost would resign that life they make so wretched by perpetual troubles.

Attempt not to appear in Edinburgh, I intreat you, where all things being in confusion in this universal hurry, you may fall a victim to the malice of your enemies. I am now more than ever fearful of your betraying those secret practises he formerly intrusted to your care, and that he privately conspires against your life!

Hamilton gave me some hints of it the other day, and Douglas afterwards in heat of blood occasioned by a debate between them in my presence confirmed it: all are false! all are traytors to their Queen! Oh, Bothwell, where is one faithful friend to be chosen out among a thousand base designers? I aim not at encrease of power, oppress not my poor subjects by exorbitant taxations, nor envy the provinces my neighbours rule; all I desire is to possess in peace the little territories I was born to govern, and that is denyd me. Sure I was born to everlasting cares! like hydra heads, one no sooner disappears, than another rises in its room, and drives me from repose. I am in too much distraction to say much at present; but the person who brings you this has a commission to inform you of all the circumstances of this unexpected blow. I can only tell you that I am as ever wholly devoted to the interests of my dear Bothwell, and will yet some way or other compleat his happiness or sink in the attempt. If you have any advice, which may be of service in this exigence, let it be speedy, for never had I more need of consolation. 　　　　　Yours,　　　M. R.

P. S. Direct as your last under cover to the Nuncio, that man is faithful; but, beware of Seaton. He has a brother in the service of the Hamiltons, I more than fear he has already betrayed some things to your prejudice. My uncle of Corocin contributes to my persecution by proposing an alliance with the House of Austria : the bearer will inform you at full the contents of this letter, Farewell! pity me and continue to love me!

M. R.

LETTER THE FOURTH.

The contents of this letter make it evident to be written after her marriage with Lord Darnley, and not only Melville, but several of the historians also report, that the Earl of Bothwell was recalled to Court about that time. The reasons that she gives for her consent to the marriage are such as, whoever reads any of the treatises of her life, will find both natural and reasonable : all the writers concurring in this, that if she had continued single, the parties of Hamilton and Murray would in a short time have left her nothing but the name of Queen.

Cruel as your reproaches are, I pardon them; but oh, too little sensible of the pangs I feel, you ought rather to have applied balsams than corrosives to wounds like mine! 'tis true I am married and have given myself to another, and in that act have set aside the oft repeated promises I made you; but were self interests forgot and impartial justice had liberty to speak, you would, with the softest compassion, reflect on the sad necessity which forced me to it! France, Spain, England and Rome, were providing me husbands; Murray was depriving me of every thing but the name of Queen! How but by marriage could I put a stop to the solicitations of the one side, or have curbed the insolence of the other? Well you know it was not in my power to make choice of you, without I could have been content not onely to see my crown torn from me, but also resign both our lives to glut the implacable malice of our foes! You tell me Lord Darnley is handsome and well made! ungenerous Bothwell; well are you convinced I have no eyes for any charms but yours! What induced me to make choice of him rather than any other, was because I would avoid giving any umbrage to the contending Princes, whose equal pretensions might have expected equal favours; but in this marriage, which in the world's eye will seem wholly induced by inclination, neither Rome, nor France, nor Spain, can be disobliged; nor can Elizabeth with any show of justice blame me; because it was on her recommendation I first consented to listen to his suit; and in preferring him to Leicester, I cannot but have the approbation of the whole judging world! Think not that it was love that furnished me with arguments to justifie my choice; for I protest by the same dread power, by which I have so often swore, that Bothwell was the dearest thing on earth, that he is still so, and ever will be so, while I have life; and Darnley............ but the property of my revenge on Murray! Oh, Bothwell, did you but know what unparalleled tyranny I was treated with by that assuming traitor, you would not wonder I had recourse for shelter to this expedient. The haughty arrogance of both he and Hamilton is now reduced to low submissions, and though they murmur they dare not complain! Depend on this truth, that nothing less than what I have done could have secured the life of Bothwell.

The cruel and designing Murray had irretrievably made you the sacrifice of his ambition, and I think it needless to say, that motive was sufficient and perhaps the most weighty of any to influence me to this action; that, by making my person the victim of one's, I might preserve the more dearer part of me from falling one to the other's more destructive passion ! The first step I took was to inspire the new made King with notions to your advantage. By the time this reaches you, you will receive an order to return to court, where you will be encouraged and promoted. I shall see you, my dear Bothwell, though not as I could wish, yet I shall see you in safety, and while Heaven permits that blessing to me, I never can be truly miserable.

M. R.

LETTER THE FIFTH.

There can be no certainty of the date of this, any farther than that it was writ presently after the arrival of Bothwell, they having never, as the contents expressly state, seen each other in private, till this billet appointed the place of assignation.

The Lady Lusse, at whose house they met, was a near relation of the Earl's mother, and entirely in his interests ; as appears, not only in the trust the Queen reposed in her, but also by assisting her and assisting him with a large sum of money, when before his favour with the court party, his extravagancies had reduced him to great straits: this from Causin, who, to render it improbable that the Queen should love him, speaks of his person and behaviour with the utmost contempt, calling him a man of desperate fortune, and capable of the most mean and vile actions.

I believe you are now perfectly convinced that there was an absolute necessity for my marriage, though the regret with which you behold me in another's arms, will not permit you to acknowledge it. I lost nothing of the few words you spoke to me as you left the drawing-room. I have provided to gratifie the impatience you expressed for a renewal of those joys we have been so long deprived of! The Lady Lusse, who is in the secret of my heart, pretends an indisposition. A visit from me will not be wondered at, because the whole court knows how much she is in my favour. I will be at her apartment to-morrow by seven in the evening, but would have you prevent that hour, lest any of the pages or maids of honour who attend me should take notice of you being there. 'Tis easy for you to go incognito ; I wish to Heaven it were no greater difficulty for me. Our interviews would then be more frequent, and love make up for want of grandeur. But I shall defer giving you any testimony of the transports which the expectation of seeing you afford, till I am so blest in reality.

Adieu, my dear Bothwell. I have time to add no more than that I am, and ever shall be,

Yours, M. R.

LETTER THE SIXTH.

This was sent to Bothwell at the time when the animosities between the Queen and her husband were grown to such a height ; and proves, that if she was accessary to his death, it was, however, contrived and plotted by Murray, though Buchanan, with so much warmth, espouses his cause, contrary to all the other authors of that time, who clearly make manifest, that both he and Morton were the chief abettors of that horrid deed.

With a difficulty not to be imagined, not to be expressed, do I get an opportunity of writing this. My bodily indisposition, joyned to the troubles of my mind, render me incapable of invention. I suffer myself to endure the eternal presence of the persons I most hate, rather than be at the pains of making an excuse to be alone. That spirit, that courage which was used to bear me through the great-

est fatigues is now evaporated and extinct. A laziness of
soul possesses me. I cannot think, I cannot resolve on any
thing. Assist me in this perplexity, my dear Bothwell!

Advise me, comfort me, find some way for my relief!
I have no friend but you, and sure, if you are such,
you will not suffer me long to bear these insults. But what
is it I am asking? 'Tis dangerous to be loyal! Poor
Rizio! only because he loved his Queen, fell a sacrifice to
this injurious husband! My life is next—nor am I spared
but for the sake of the unborn heir of empire. Delivered
once of that dear burthen, my business in this world is
done, and Darnley will reign alone. I know that my
death alone can gratify the ambition of that ungrateful
man; or the unceasing malice of the English Queen. Yet
might a way be found to snatch me from the impending
ruin, had any one the boldness to attempt it. Murray, all
stern and fierce as he is by nature, expresses a concern for
my ill-treatment, and seemed to hint at some design on foot
for recovering that prerogative I so unadvisedly gave up.

But he, alas! has been so sullen already—so arbitrary and
insulting when in power, I dread to invest him with the
same again—I fear it would be exchanging one misfortune
for another. If he should communicate any of his intentions to you, answer him with caution. If he could be sincere, I know he has the means to serve me—fathom him,
if possible, and let me know your opinion directed under
cover to Lady Lusse.

The Bishop of Ross informs me that Morton is returning
from the North; if so, I may believe that Murray's working brain hath not been idle—but whether for mine or his
interest, Heaven only can resolve. Keep a fair correspondence with him, however, till we see the issue, which
a little time will soon determine. I would reward the
fidelity of La Ruch, by giving him some handsome post
about my person, but as affairs are it may be dangerous both

E

for him and me; assure him of my gratitude and favour, when once the times will permit me to make show of it. Farewell, keep me ever in your thoughts.

M. R.

P. S. Since I wrote this, Murray has been to visit me, and finding me all bathed in tears, the daily tribute which my griefs exact, bade me be of good comfort, for a blow would soon be given, which would restore all things to their proper order. I know not what he means, unless it be the death of the King, nor had I time to ask. Hamilton came in and broke off our conversation. I wish you would inform yourself and me with all convenient speed, but do it in a manner he may not think I am concerned in the enquiry. Once more adieu, my ever dear Bothwell. Pity me, pray for me, and never cease to love me.

LETTER THE SEVENTH.

There is little contained in this, any more than a confirmation of the foregoing one; viz. that Morton and Murray were the first proposers of the murder of the King, and that Bothwell was no more than their agent in the affair, as indeed is manifest enough in their being the persons who make a kind of mock-accusation, that they might have a better opportunity of clearing him by a form of judicature.

That I answered yours no sooner was owing to the struggles in my mind occasioned by proposals so shocking to a woman of my gentle nature. Heaven knows I love not blood, and the thoughts of having that of a husband is terrible to reflection; yet self-preservation is the first of laws, and if there remain no other means, I must submit to this. I could wish either that Murray was not engaged in the

design, or that he did not know I was acquainted with it.
You, my dear Bothwell, are too liable to give credit to his
insinuations, but I both fear and hate him. Who knows
what use he may hereafter make of the guilt he makes me
to become a sharer in? But it is now past remedy, and I
must make a show of confidence. Never was a soul more
hurried than mine has been this dreadful night! A thousand horrible ideas have run through my distracted brain;
sometimes I thought I saw the King all covered over with
wounds, and with his dying breath imploring vengeance
on his inhuman murderers! At others, wild imagination
presented the conspiracy unravelled, and Morton, yourself
and Murray, already fallen victims of his revenge; while
he, exulting in his cruelty, held a drawn dagger at my
breast! Oh, what variety of horrors has this design involved me in! Why was I endued with a soul so little capable of cruelty, yet urged to acts that have so much the
appearance of it? I never loved this Darnley, and his in-
gratitude has made me hate him. Yet could I with pleasure
part with some of my blood to ransom his, were there a
possibility of avoiding it. How am I then guilty? 'Tis
he himself that brings on his own fate. He forces me, he
drives me to this abhorred extremity; and his must be the
blame. Oh, that I could always retain this thought! That
I could wholly banish a softness prejudicial to my peace!
  But 'twill not be, in spite of all my efforts, and all my
monstrous wrongs. Pity returns, and overwhelms my soul!
Cure me of this weakness, and inspire me with notions
suitable to the enterprise in hand; the very idea will otherwise distract me, and in the moment of the execution, I
shall cry out, Forbear! and all betray! Exert, then, my
dear Bothwell, that all-prevailing wit and eloquence of
yours to furnish me with arguments to overcome so unsea-
sonable tenderness. 'Tis in your power to make me almost
any thing. Represent the injuries I have received from this
tyrannic husband, the vast indignities, the dangers, which

nothing but his death can free me from ; but above all, make me remember, that while he lives I am deprived of the power to make my Bothwell happy. That last remonstrance, perhaps, may arm my feeble resolution, and while that glorious image is in view, I could, methinks, with unrelenting hands, myself perform that deed. I expect a letter from you this night, with a further account of the whole plan of this design, which, while in agitation, will never suffer me to know a moment's peace. Afford me all the satisfaction you are able in this tempest of my divided thoughts, and know, what I do, I do for you.

M. R.

LETTER THE EIGHTH.

This plainly appears to have been written soon after the murder of the King, which happening on the 10th of February, 1567, and the process of divorce between the Earl and Lady Jane Gordon, his wife, being issued the 26th of April, the same year, makes it evident that this must be sent before he had solicited the court upon it. Concerning the times of these two transactions there is no need to quote any particular author, all historians agreeing as to this.

By Darnley's death I am indeed once more a Queen, again enjoy those pleasures which power affords, and have the means of punishing and rewarding indifferent persons, and in trifling causes, yet am still circumscribed. The more material business of my life remains unfinished. I am a Queen, but you are not a King; till I accomplish that, the work is not complete, nor can I taste the sweets of royalty.

I begin to think Murray at last sincere, and approve of your design in engaging him to favour your divorce, which the Bishop seems to make a light matter of, but I am afraid will not be so easily attained as he or you may imagine. The apology you make for your long stay at Dumbarton is altogether needless. I am so far from resenting it, that I look on this self-denial as the most prudent thing you ever did. There are at this time many eyes upon our actions, and to be too frequently seen together at present might be a means of preventing of our being for ever together hereafter. Send me a copy of what you write to Murray, enclosed in your next, and if possible make an interest with Lansford, in whose power it is to be serviceable to you on this account. Let my secretary know what sums are wanting to carry it on, and they shall be remitted to you. Morton and some others attend to speak with me, and I have time to say no more, but that I am ever, my dear Bothwell,

M. R.

P. S. The Bishop of Ross intends you a long letter of instruction, which I would have you observe in every thing. You have not a better, or a more sincere friend on earth.

LETTER THE NINTH.

It was in the utmost transports of impatient and expecting love that this epistle was dictated, and seems to be immediately after the Earl had obtained the divorce from his wife, which, according to Castlenau, Melvill, and Buchanan, was on the 11th or 12th of May, 1567.

———

Fortune, grown weary of persecuting me, at length grows as extravagant in her blessings as she was in the former part of my life in her cruelty ; and your divorce being looked upon as good as completed, Murray himself proposed you to me as an husband, nay, seemed eager in his pressures that I would give him my promise that you should become so immediately you were in condition.

Scarce could I contain the joy of my exulting soul—scarce keep my tongue from letting him know how much my heart took part in his persuasions. Never did I so much as then assume the politician. Had any other discoursed to me in the manner, sure I am I had not been able to conceal the pleasure it gave me ! But the often-experienced falsehood of that Earl secured my caution, and made me reply no otherwise than that I would be advised by him in every thing. 'Tis possible that he may in this be cordial ; but to apprehend the worst is certainly the most safe. He cannot, however, recede from what he has sayd, and Morton, and several others, have of late spoke of you with that respect, that I am sensible he has communicated to them his intentions of uniting us.

Though I know you are to be in Edinburgh in so short a time, I could not delay making you the partaker of those transports you are the author of. There is a delicacy in such a love as mine, which will not suffer me to be blessed alone, and when I think this happy news has reached you, I shall indulge myself in sympathy with those ecstasies which I flatter myself you will feel at the receipt of so unexpected an information. Make all the convenient speed you can to town ; I now long with double impatience for your presence; it is not Bothwell, a man whose freedom with me love alone could authorise—but my intended husband and future king, that I shall now embrace. Haste then to the arms, though ever present to the heart, of

M. R.

LETTER THE TENTH.

This was occasioned on the first contrivance of the pretended ravishment, as Buchanan terms it, and discovers also that Murray and Morton had a hand in this, as well as in the murder of the King, though Murray made this action appear wholly the Queen's own act, when the affair was examined into by the delegates of Queen Elizabeth at York.

I received yours at a time when I was overwhelmed in grief that scarce the flowing tears would give me leave to read it. Need had I, my dear Bothwell, of all that consolation which this new stratagem affords; yet am I not convinced (plausible as it seems) of its success; we are so much accustomed to treachery, that methinks there is nothing to be depended on. Should this pretended rebellion you have on hand be detected or betrayed by any one you confide in, by what pretence can I screen you from the sword of justice?

Should I not be obliged to give you up to law, and hear you condemned for this imaginary crime? However, as our case is desperate, I will not confine you from making use of all the methods ingenious love can form for our common felicity.

This brings a summ large enough to raise more men than you will have occasion for, and depend, that I will come attended by as few as possible.   Hamilton is the person I most fear, both for his courage, and the interest he has in those parts.   I cannot think it was well advised that Murray should not be in the way.   His presence would have been of infinitively more service than that of Morton, but that is now past recall!   But if he has engaged so many hands as he pretends to you, for the signing the articles of our marriage, I do not indeed foresee that it will be in the power of the contrary party to oppose it.   I must, however, appear all along refractory to that which is the only wish of my desiring soul.   How shall I so greatly dissemble?   How appear at the head of an army, animating them to pursue to death the man I love far more than life!   How seem to represent that as a rape, which to embrace I would run through the most imminent dangers?   Assist me, all the artifices of my sex!   For all will be too little in such a circumstance.   The Bishop of Ross smiles at my fears, and is assured of success.   I know his integrity; and I find Murray has been perfectly sincere in this affair—doubt not but that he has left emissaries capable of bringing it about: yet doubts and anxieties are ever the inseparable companions of love while in pursuit.   Heaven send ours once completed, and give some period to this distracting suspence!   Adieu.

M. R.

P. S. Once more I warn you to be careful whom you trust in this affair.   Remember tis our last stake, and if that fails, farewell to all hopes of happiness hereafter.

LETTER THE ELEVENTH.

Though Buchanan so very strenuously takes upon him the vindication of Murray, 'tis evident by this and the preceding letter, that he was the promoter of this design, and that before he left Edinburgh he had engaged most of the nobility to set their hands to the articles of marriage between the Queen and Bothwell. It is remarked by Castlenau, Melville, Causin, and even by Camden himself, that when there was any sinister affair in hand, that subtile politician, Murray, always took care to be absent, leaving his under engines to work out the schemes he had formed, and by that means reaped all the profit of his designs, and threw all the odium on the Queen.

I write to you with infinitively more tranquillity of mind than that with which my last was dictated. Murray has well retrieved his character, and more contributed to my felicity than heretofore to my vexation. The Bishop of Orkney, from whom I least expected it, is wholly on our side; and 'tis the Earl to whom we are indebted for this change in his behaviour: I put myself among the obliged, because I am really so, though they who serve me most believe at the same time they are acting the reverse of my inclinations. See by this how very necessary dissimulation is. My very enemies, by immagining they undo me, make the happiness of my life; and those who wish to see me most wretched, unite to make me most completely blest! Did Morton, Orkney, and the rest of that turbulent faction, know the perfect attachment we have to each other, would they plot to joyn us? No! they would sever us for ever! Thus, by a concealment of our mutual tenderness, do we disappoint all the stratagems which would otherwise be formed to the ruin of it, and triumph in security. I ex-

F

pect not to hear from you any more, neither do I desire it. The great design grows now so near the point of being executed, that I would have your thoughts wholly taken up with managing to the best advantage this last and only trial of our fortune. I am now of opinion that it cannot fail, and feed my fond imagination with a thousand glorious ideas of your approaching greatness! It will be a joy unspeakable to see you on the Scottish throne ; but, to reflect you are seated there by me, a pride and pleasure which it is not in language to represent, and can only be reached by thought.

Oh, my Bothwell, my heart beats high with expectation, and every faculty of my soul's on fire with the impatient hope. 'Tis but three days before the grand catastrophe arrives, yet do they seem so many ages! Be you more cool to attend the longed for issue, or you will be little able to carry on the charge entrusted to your care, and on which depends not only our lives, but fortune and fame! Indulge in secret the swelling rapture ; but let no outward sign of joy appear, till you are past prevention in the arms of

M. R.

Here end the MS. letters, ascribed to Mary. I have taken no liberties with the orthography or style. If they are from the pen of the Scottish Queen, they were written in French,—for she did not generally write in Scotch,—and are nothing indebted to the translator. They seem vulgar in parts—but perhaps we form too high notions of the delicacy and refined accomplishments of that age! The celebrated and lovely Anna Boleyn wrote to her cousin in the country, from London. "Don't forget to feed the chickens! You know when I was in the country I could eat my loaf of bread, my pound of bacon, and drink my tankard of ale, but here the half serves me! My good mother went to Cheapside the other day, and bought me two Holland smocks at eightpence per ell, &c. &c."* From this specimen of exalted rank in those days, and language and sentiments which we now call vulgar and indecorous, I think it would be straining the point too far, to judge of the elegance of our progenitors by our more refined and accomplished epistolary modes of communication. I might urge another argument in favour of the letters and sonnets.

Women in love are not always limited by the cold and frigid rules which custom on other occasions has imposed on their sex. Hence I think it within the pale of reason that these letters and sonnets should not be considered spurious, on the ground that they are not so elegant and delicate as might be expected from a young lady of high rank in our days.

To fortify my position I might triumphantly cite the malignant letter of Mary Queen of Scots to Queen Elizabeth, when the former was a prisoner, detailing the slanderous gossip of her keeper's wife, the Countess of Shrewsbury. The beastly scandal related solely to the private life of the English Queen; and, the very generous, accomplished, and delicate, Queen of Scots, in that letter, uses language at

---

* Original letters of Anna Boleyn, in the British Museum.

once so base, obscene, and filthy, that I would not run the
risk of offending my readers by reprinting it in this volume,
had not Whitaker attempted to justify its purport—namely, to annoy Elizabeth—and the lovely and accomplished
Mademoiselle de Keralio inserted it in her life of Mary.—
Vide the Appendix.   H. C.

[These are the letters which Buchanan has given to the
world as those publicly sent to Elizabeth; but it should
be recollected, that the whole contents of the casket were
privately laid before the English Queen.]

A Letter written by her from Glasgow to BOTHWELL,
proving her hate to her husband, and some suspicions of
practising his death: which Letter was written in French,
and here ensueth, translated word for word.

It appears, that with your absence there is also joyned
forgetfulness, seeing that at your departing you promised
to make me advertisement of your news from time to time.
The waiting upon them yesterday, caused me to be almost
in such joy as I will be at your returning, which you have
delayed longer than your promise was. As to me, howbeit
I have no further news from you according to my commission. I bring the man with me to Cragmillar upon Monday, where he will be all Wednesday, and I will go to Edinburgh, to draw blood of me, if in the mean time I get no
news to the contrary from you. He is more gay than ever
you saw him; he puts me in remembrance of all things that
may make me believe he loves me. Perhaps you will say,
that he makes love to me: of the which I take so great

pleasure, that I enter never where he is, but incontinent I take the sickness of my sore side, I am so troubled with it. If Pareis brings me that which I send him for, I trust it shall amend me. I pray you advertise me of your news at length, and what I shall do, in case you be not returned when I am come there; for in case you work not wisely, I see that the whole burden of this will fall upon my shoulders. Provide for all things, and discourse upon it first with yourself. I send this by Betoun, who goes to one day of law of the Lord of Balfours. I will say no further, saving I pray you to send me good news of your voyage. From Glascow this Saturday in the morning.

ANOTHER LETTER TO BOTHWELL, CONCERNING THE HATE OF HER HUSBAND; AND PRACTICE OF HIS MURDER.

Being departed from the place where I left my heart, it is easy to be judged what was my countenance, seeing that I was even as much as one body without a heart, which was the occasion that while dinner time I held purpose to no body, nor yet durst any present themselves unto me, judging that it was not good so to do. Four miles ere I came to the town, one gentleman of the Earl of Lenox came and made his commendations unto me, and excused him that he came not to meet me, by reason that he durst not enterprize the same, because of the rude words that I had spoken to Cunningham, and he desired that he should come to the inquisition of the matter that I suspected him of. This last speaking was of his own head, without any commission. I answered to him, that there was no receit could serve against fear, and that he would not be afraid in case he were not culpable, and that I answered but rudely to the doubts that were in his letters: So that I made him hold his tongue; the rest were too long to write. Sir

James Hamilton met me, who shewed that the other time,
when he heard of my coming, he departed away, and sent
Houston to shew him that he would never have believed
that he would have pursued him, nor yet accompanied him
with the Hamiltons. He answered that he was only come
but to see me, and that he would neither accompany Stew-
art nor Hamilton but by my commandment. He desired
that he would come and speak with him, he refused it. The
Lord of Luse, Houston and Cauldwallis son, with forty
horse or thereabout, came and met me. The Lord of Luse
said that he was charged to one day of law, by the king's
father, which should be this day, against his own hand
writing, which he has. And yet notwithstanding, knowing
of my coming it is delayed, he was inquired to come to
him, which he refused, and swears that he will endure nothing of him.

Never one of that town came to speak to me, which
causes me to think that they are his, and nevertheless he
speaks good, at the least his son. I see no other gentleman,
but they of my company. The king sent for Joachim yesternight, and asked of him, why I lodged not beside him,
and that he would rise the sooner if that were, and wherefore I come, if it was for good appointment, and if you were
there in particular, and if I had made my estate, if I had
taken Pareis and Gilbert to write to me, and that I would
send Joseph away. I am abashed who has shewn him so
far, yea he spake even of the marriage of Bastian. I inquired him of his letters, whereunto he complained of the
cruelty of some, answered that he was astonished, and
that he was so glad to see me, that he believed to die for
gladness; he found great fault that I was pensive, I departed to supper, this bearer will tell you of my arriving,
he prayed me to return, the which I did, he declared unto
me his sickness, and that he would make no testament but
only leave all things to me, and that I was the cause of his
malady, because of the regret that he had that I was so

strange unto him. And thus he said, you ask me what I
mean by the cruelty contained in my letter, it is of you
alone that will not accept of my offers and repentance. I
confess that I have failed, but not into that which I ever
denied, and such like has fallen to sundry of your subjects
which you have forgiven. I am young. You will say, that
you have forgiven me oftentimes, and yet that I return to my
faults. May not any man of my age for lack of counsel
fall twice or thrice, or in lack of his promise, and at last repent himself, and be chastised by experience? If I may obtain pardon, I protest I shall never make fault again. And
I crave no other thing but that we may be at bed and board
together as husband and wife, and if you will not consent
hereunto, I will never rise out of this bed, I pray you tell
me your resolution. God knows how I am punished for
making my God of you, and for having no other thought
but on you, and if at any time I offend you, you are the
cause, because when any offends me, if for my refuge I
might complain unto you, I would speak it unto no other
body; but when I hear any thing, not being familiar with
you, necessity constrains me to keep it in my breast: and
that causes me to try my wit for very anger.

I answered straight unto him, but that would be overlong to write at length. I asked why he would pass away
in the English ship, he denies it, and swears thereunto, but
he grants that he spake with the men. After this I inquired of the inquisition of Highgate, he denied the same,
while I shewed him the very words was spoken. At which
time he said, that Minto had advertised him that it was said
that some of the counsel had brought one letter to me to be
subscribed to put him in prison, and to slay him if he made
resistance. And he asked the same of Minto himself, who
answered, that he believed the same to be true. In the
morning I will speak to him upon this point. As to the
rest, William Highgates he confessed it, but it was the
morning after my coming ere he did it. He would very

fain that I should lodge in his lodging, I refused it,
and said to him, that he behoved to be purged, and that
could not be done here; he said to me, I hear say you have
brought one letter with you, but I had rather have passed
with you. I think he believed that he would have sent him
away prisoner; I answered that I would take him with me
to Cragmillar, where the physician and I might help him,
and not be far from my son; he answered, that he was ready
when I pleased, so I would assure him of his request: he
desires no body to see him, he is angry when I speak of
Walcar, and says, that he shall pluck the ears from off his
head, and that he lies: for I inquired him upon that, and
that he was angry with some of the Lords, and would
threaten them; he denies that, and says, he loves them all,
and prays me to give trust to nothing against him; as to me
he would rather give his life ere he did any displeasure to
me. And after this he shewed me of so many little flatteries, so coldly, and so wisely, that you will be ashamed
thereat. I had almost forgot that he said he could not
doubt of me in this purpose of Highgates, for he would never
believe that I, who was his proper flesh, would do him
any evil, as well it was shewn that I refused to subscribe
the same; but as to any others that would pursue him at
least he should sell his life dear enough, but he suspected
no body, nor yet would not, but would love all that I loved.
he would not let me depart from him, but desired that I
should wake with him, I make it seem that I believe that
all is true, and takes heed thereto, and excused my self for
this night that I could not wake; he says, he sleeps not
well, you saw him not better, nor speak more humble.
And if I had not a proof of his heart of wax, and that mine
were not of a diamond, whereinto no shot can make breach,
but that which comes forth of your hand, I would have
almost had pity of him. But fear not, the place shall hold
unto the death. Remember in recompence thereof that ye
suffer not yours to be won by that false race that will travel

no less with you for the same. I believe they have been at
school together, he has ever the tear in his eye, he salutes
every body, yea unto the least, and makes piteous moan
unto them to make them have pity on him. This day his
father bled at the mouth and nose, guess what presage that
is. I have not yet seen him, he keeps his chamber.

The King desires that I should give him meat with mine
own hands. But give no more trust where you are then I
shall do here. This is my first journey, I shall send the
same tomorrow. I write all things, howbeit they be of
little weight, to the end that ye may take the best of all to
judge upon. I am in doing of a work here that I hate
greatly. Have you not a desire to laugh to see me lie so
well, at the least to dissemble so well, and to tell
him truth betwixt hands. He shewed me almost all
that is in the name of the Bishop and Sunderland,
and yet I have never touched one word of that you shewed
me, but only by force flattering, and to pray him to assure
himself of me. And by complaining on the Bishop I have
drawn it all out of him. You have heard the rest. We are
coupled with two false races, the devil sunder us, and God
knit us together for the most faithful couple that ever
he united. This is my faith, I will die in it. Excuse it, I
write evil, you may guess the half of it, but I cannot mend
it, because I am not well at ease, and very glad to write
unto you when the rest are asleep, sith I cannot sleep as
they do, and as I would desire, that is, in your arms my
dear love, whom I pray God to preserve from all evil, and
send you repose ; I am going to seek mine till the morning
when I shall end my Bille ; but I am vexed that it stops me
to write news of my self unto you, because it is so long.

Advertise me what you have deliberated to do in the matter,
you know upon this point, to the end that we may understand each other well, that nothing thereof be spilt. I am
weary, and going to sleep, and yet I cease not to scrible all
this paper in so much as remains thereof. Wearied might
this pocky man be, that causes me to have so much pain ;

for without him I should have a far pleasanter subject to
discourse upon. He is not overmuch deformed, yet he has
received very much. He has almost slain me with his
breath, it is worse than your uncles, and yet I come no
nearer unto him but in a chair at the bed's feet, and being
at the other end thereof.

[The message of the father in the gate.

The purpose of Sir James Hamilton.

Of that the L. of Lusse shewed me of the delay.

Of the demands that she asked of Jaochim.

Of my estate, of my company, of the occasion of my
coming, and of Joseph.

Item, The purpose that he and I had together.

Of the desire he has to plese me, and of his repentance.

Of the interpretation of his letter.

Of William Highgate's matter of his departing.

Of Monsieur de Levingston.]

I had almost forgot that Monsieur de Levingston said in
the Lady Rerese's ear at supper, that he would drink to the
folk I wist of, if I would pledge them. And after supper
he said to me when I was leaning upon him warming me at
the fire; you have fair going to see such folk, yet you cannot be so welcome unto them, as you left some body this
day in sadness, that will never be merry while he see you
again. I asked of him, who that was? With that he thrust
my body and said, that some of his folks had seen you in
faschery, you may guess at the rest. I wrought this day
while it was two hours upon this bracelet, for to put the
key of it within the lock thereof, which is coupled underneath with two cordwins. I have had so little time that it
is evil made; but I shall make one fairer in the mean
time.

Take heed that none that is here see it, for all the world
will know it; because for haste it was made in their presence. I am now passing to my intended purpose. You
make me dissemble so far that I have horror thereat; and
you cause me to do almost the office of a traitour. Remem-

ber how if it were not to obey you, I had rather be dead
ere I did it; my heart bleeds at it. So that, he will not
come with me except upon condition that I will promise to
him that I shall be at bed and board with him as before,
and that I shall leave him not after; and doing this upon
my word he will do all things that I please, and come with
me; but he prayed me to remain with him while another
morning. He spake very bravely at the beginning, as this
bearer will shew you, upon the purpose of the Englishmen,
and of his departing; but in the end he returned again to
his humility. He shewed amongst other purposes that he
knew well enough, that my brother had shewed me that
thing which he had spoken in Scriveling; of which he denies the one half, and above all, that ever he came in his
chamber. For to make him trust me, it behoved me to fain
in some things with him; therefore when he requested me
to promise unto him, that when he was whole we should
have both one bed, I said to him, fainingly and making me
believe his promises, that if he changed not purposes betwixt this and that time, I would be content therewith; but
in the meantime I bad him take heed that he let no body
know thereof; because to speak amongst our selves the
Lords could not be offended, nor will evil therefore. But
they would fear in respect of the boasting he made of them,
that if ever we agreed together, he should make them know
the little account they took of him; and that he counselled me not to purchase some of them by him, they for
this cause would be in jealousie, if attains without their
knowledge, I should break the play set up in the contrary
in their presence. He said very joyfully; and think you
they will esteem you the more for that? but I am very glad
that you speak to me of the Lords, for I believe at this time
you desire that we should live together in quietness; for if
it were otherways, greater inconveniency might come to
us both then we are aware of; but now I will do what ever
you will do, and will love all that you love, and desires

you to make them love in like manner; for since they seek·
not my life, I love them all equally. Upon this point the
bearer will shew you many small things. Because I have
over much to write, and it is late, I give trust unto him
upon your word. So that he will go upon my word to all
places. Alas, I never deceived any body; but I remit me
altogether to your will.

Send me advertisement what I shall do, and whatsoever
thing shall come thereof I shall obey you. Advise to with
your self if you can find out any more secret invention by
medicine: for he should take medicine and the bath at
Cragmillar. He may not come forth of the house this long
time. So that by all that I can learn, he is in great suspition; and yet notwithstanding he gives credit to my word;
but yet not so far as that he will shew any thing to me.

But nevertheless I shall draw it out of him, if you will that
I avow all unto him. But I will never rejoyce to defame
any body that trusts in me; yet notwithstanding you may
command me in all things. Have no evil opinion of me for
that cause, by reason you are the occasion of it your self,
because for mine own particular revenge I would not do it to
him. He gives me some checks of that which I feared, yea,
even in the quick, he says thus far, that his faults were pub-
lisht, but there is that commits faults that believe they will
never be spoken of, and yet they will speak of great and
small. As towards the Lady Rerese he said, I pray God
that she may serve you for your honour. And said, it is
thought, and he believes it to be true, that I have not the
power of my self over my self, and that because of the refuse I made of his offers. So that, for certainty he suspects
of the thing you know, and of his life. But as to the last,
how soon that I spake two or three good words unto him,
he rejoices, and is out of doubt.

I saw him not this evening to end your bracelet, to the
which I can get no locks, it is ready for them, and yet I
hear it will bring some evil, and may be seen if you chance

to be hurt. Advertise me if you will have it, and if you will have more silver, and when I shall return, and how far I may speak. He inrages when he hears of Lethington or of you, or of my brother, of your brother he speaks nothing, he speaks of the Earl of Argyle. I am in fear when I hear him speak; for he assures himself that he has not one evil opinion of him. He speaks nothing of them that is ought neither good or evil, but flies that point. His father keeps his chamber, I have not seen him. All the Hamiltons are here, that accompanies me very honourably. All the friends of the other conveys me when I go to see him. He desires me to come, and see him rise the morn betime. For to make short, this bearer will tell you the rest. And if I learn any thing here, I will make you a memorial at even. He will tell you the occasion of my remaining.

Burn this letter, for it is over dangerous, and nothing well said in it; for I am thinking upon nothing but fraud. If you be in Edinburgh at the receit of it, send me word soon. Be not offended, for I give not over great credit. Now seeing to obey you, my dear love, I spare neither honour, conscience, hazard, nor greatness whatsoever, take it I pray in good part; and not after the interpretation of your false good brother *, to whom I pray you give no credit, against the most faithful lover that ever you had, or ever shall have.

See not her whose faint tears should not be so much praised nor esteemed, as the true and faithful travels which I sustain for to merit her place†. For obtaining of the which against my nature, I betray them that may impeach me. God forgive me, and God give you, my only love, the hap and prosperity which your humble and faithful love desires of you, who hopes to be shortly another thing to you for the reward of my irksome travels. It is late, I desire never to cease from writing unto you, yet now after the

---

* Huntly.   † Lady Bothwell.

kissing of your hands, I will end my letter. Excuse my
evil writing, and read it twice over. Excuse that thing
that is scribbled, for I had no paper yesterday when I writ
that of the memorial. Remember your love, and write unto her, and that very oft. Love me as I shall do you. Remember you of the purpose of the Lady Rerese, of the
Englishmen, of his mother, of the Earl of Argyle, of the
Earl Bothwell, of the lodging in Edinburgh.

ANOTHER LETTER TO BOTHWELL, CONCERNING CERTAIN TOKENS THAT SHE SENT HIM.

My Lord, if the displeasure of your absence, of your
forgetfulness, the fear of danger so promised by every one
to your so loved person, may give me consolation, I leave
it to you to judge, seeing the mishap that my cruel lot and
continual misadventure, has hitherto promised me following
the misfortunes and fears as well of late as of a long time
by past, the which you do know. But for all that I will in
no wise accuse you, neither of your little remembrance,
neither of your little care, and least of all your promise
broken, or of the coldness of your writing, since I am else
so far made yours, that that which pleases you is acceptable
to me, and my thoughts are so willingly subdued unto yours,
that I suppose that all that cometh of you, proceeds not of
any of the causes aforesaid, but rather for such as be just and
reasonable, and such as I desire my self. Which is the
final order that you promised to take, for the surety and honourable service of the only supporter of my life. For which
alone I will preserve the same, and without the which I desire not but suddain death. And to testifie unto you how
lowly I submit me under your commandments, I have sent
you in sign of homage by Pareis the ornament of the head,

which is the chief guide of the other members. Inferring thereby, that by the seising of you in the possession of the spoil of that which is principal, the remnant cannot be but subject unto you, and with consenting of the heart.

In place whereof since I have else left it unto you, I send unto you one sepulture of hard stone coloured with black, sawin with tears and bones. The stone I compare to my heart, that as it is carved in one sure sepulture or harbour of your commandments, and above all of your name and memory, that are therein incl⸗ed, as is my heart in this ring never to come forth, while death grant unto you to one trophie of victory of my bones, as the ring is filled, in sign you have made one full conquest of me, of mine heart, and unto that my bones are left unto you, in remembrance of your victory, and my acceptable love and willingness, for to be better bestowed than I merit. The ameling that is about is black, which signifies the stedfastness of her that sendeth the same. The tears are without number, so are the fears to displease you, the tears for your absence, the disdain that I cannot be in outward effect yours, as I am without faintness of heart and spirit, and of good reason, though my merits were much greater than that of the most profit that ever was, and such as I desire to be, and shall take pains in conditions to imitate, for to be bestowed worthily under your regiment. My only wealth receive therefore in as good part the same, as I have received your marriage with extreme joy, that which shall not part forth of my bosome while that marriage of our bodies be made in publick, as a sign of all that I either hope or desire of bliss in this world.

Yet my heart, fearing to displease you, as much in the reading hereof, as it delights me in the writing, I will make an end, after that I have kissed your hand, with as great affection as I pray God (O, the only supporter of my life) to give you long and blessed life, and to me your good favour, as the only good that I desire, and to the which I pretend. I have shewn unto this bearer that which I have learned, to whom I remit me, knowing the credit that you give him; as she. doth, that will be for ever unto you an humble and obedient lawful wife, that for ever dedicates unto you her heart, her body, without any change as unto him that I have made possessor of my heart, of which you may hold you assured, that unto death shall no ways be changed, for evil nor good shall never make me go from it.

ANOTHER LETTER TO BOTHWELL OF HER LOVE TO HIM.

I have waked later there up then I would have done, if it had not been to draw something out of him, which this bearer will shew you, which is the fairest commodity, that can be offered to excuse your affairs. I have promised to bring him to him in the morn. Put order to it if you find it good. Now sir, I have broken my promise, because you commanded me nether to write nor send unto you; yet I have not done this to offend you. And if you knew the fear that I have presently, you would not have so many contrary suspitions in your thought, which notwithstanding I treat and cherish as proceeding from the thing in the world that I most desire and seek fastest to have, which is your good grace. Of the which my behaviour shall assure me; as to me I shall never despair of it. And prays you according to your promise to discharge your heart unto me; otherwise I will think that my evil and the good handling of her that has not a third part of the faithful nor willing obedience unto you that I bear, has won against my will that advantage over me, which the second love of Jason won. Not that I will compare you to one so unhappy as he was, nor yet my self to one so unpitiful a woman as she.

Howbeit you cause me to be somewhat like unto her in any thing that touches you, or that may preserve and keep you unto her, to whom only you appertain : If it be so that I may appropriate that which is won through faithful, yea only loving of you, as I do and shall do all the days of my life, for pain or evil that can come thereof. In recompence of the which, and of all the evils which you have been cause of to me, remember you upon the place here beside. I crave with that you keep promise to me in the morn, but that we may meet together, and that you give no faith to suspicions without the certainty of them. And I crave no other thing of God, but that you may know that thing that is in my heart, which is yours, and that he may preserve you from all evil, at least so long as I have life, which I repute not precious unto me, except in so far as it and I both are agreeable unto you. I am going to bed, and will bid you good night. Advertise me timely in the morning how you have fared, for I will be in pain until I get word. Make good watch; if the bird get out of the cage, or without her mate as the turtle. I shall remain alone to lament your absence, how short that soever it be. This letter will do, with a good heart, that thing which I cannot do myself, if it be not that I have fear that you are in sleeping. I durst not write this before Joseph, Bastian, and Joachim, that did but depart even when I began to write.

ANOTHER LETTER TO BOTHWELL CONCERNING THE DE-PARTURE OF MARGARET CURWOOD, WHO WAS PRIVY, AND HELPER OF ALL THEIR LOVE.

My heart, alas, must the folly of a woman, whose unthankfulness toward me you do sufficiently know, be occasion of displeasure unto you? considering that I could not have remedied thereunto without knowing it? And since that I perceive it, I could not tell it you, for that I knew not how to govern myself therein. For neither in that, nor in any other thing, will I take upon me to do any thing without knowledge of your will: which I beseech you let

H

me understand; for I will follow it all my life, more willingly than you shall declare it to me. And if do not send me word this night what you will that I shall do, I will rid myself of it, and hazard to cause it to be enterprized and taken in hand; which might be hurtful unto that whereunto both we do tend. And when she shall be married, I beseech you give me one, or else I will take such as shall content you, for their conditions, but as for their tongues or faithfulness towards you, I will not answer. I beseech you, that an opinion of another person be not hurtful in your mind to my constancy. Mistrust me, but then I will put you out of doubt and clear my self. Refuse it not, my dear life, and suffer me to make you some proof by my obedience, my faithfulness, constancy and voluntary subjection, which I take for the pleasantest good that I might receive, if you will accept it, and make no ceremony at it, for you could do me no greater outrage, nor give more mortal grief.

ANOTHER LETTER SENT FROM STERLING TO BOTHWELL, CONCERNING THE PRACTICE FOR HER RAVISHMENT.

Alas! my Lord, why is your trust put in a person so unworthy, to mistrust that which is wholly yours? I am mad. You had promised me that you would resolve all, and that you would send me word every day what I should do, you have done nothing thereof. I advertised you well to take heed of your false brother-in-law; he came to me, and without shewing me any thing from you, told me that you had willed him to write to you that that I should say, and where and when you should come to me, and that that you should do touching him, and thereupon hath preached unto me that it was a foolish enterprize, and that with mine honour I could never marry you, seeing that being married, you did carry me away, and that his folks would not suffer it, and that the Lords would unsay themselves, and would deny that they had said. To be short, he is all contrary. I told him, that seeing I was come so far, if you not withdraw yourself of yourself, that no perswasion, nor death itself, should make me fail of my promise. As touching the place, you are too negligent (pardon me) to remit yourself thereof unto me. Chuse it yourself, and send me word of it. And in the mean time I am sick, I will differ, as touching the matter it is too late. It was not long of me that you have not thought thereupon in time. And if you had not more changed your mind since mine absence than I have, you should not be now to ask such resolving.

Well, there wanteth nothing on my part; and seeing that your negligence doth put us both in the danger of a false brother, if it succeed not well, I will never rise again. I send this bearer unto you, for I dare not trust your brother with these letters, nor with the business. He shall tell you in what state I am, and judge you what amendment these new ceremonies have brought unto me. I would I were dead, for I see all goeth ill. You promised other manner of matter of your foreseeing, but absence hath power over you, who have two strings to your bow. Dispatch the answer, that I fail not, and put no trust in your brother for this enterprize, for he hath told it, and is also quite against it. God give you good night.

ANOTHER LETTER· TO BOTHWELL; FOR THE PRACTICE AND
DEVICE TO EXCUSE THE RAVISHING.

Of the place and the time, I remit my self to your brother and to you. I will follow him, and will fail in nothing of my part. He findeth many difficulties: I think he
doth advertise you thereof; and what he doth advertise
you for the handling of himself. As for the handling of
myself, I heard it once well devised. Methinks that your
services, and the long amity, having the good will of the
Lords, do well deserve a pardon, if above the duty of a
subject you advance yourself, not to constrain me, but to
assure yourself of such place nigh unto me, that other admonitions or foreign perswasions may not let me from consenting to that that you hope your service shall make you
one day to attain: and to be short, to make yourself sure of
the Lords, and free to marry: and that you are constrained
for your surety, and to be able to serve me faithfully, to use
an humble request, joyned to an importune action. And to
be short, excuse yourself, and perswade them the most you
can, that you are constrained to make pursuit against your
enemies. You shall say enough, if the matter or ground do
like you, and many fair words to Ledinton. If you like not
the deed, send me word, and leave not the blame of all
unto me.

ANOTHER LETTER TO BOTHWELL, OF THE PRACTICE FOR
HER RAVISHMENT, AND TO ADVISE HIM TO BE STRANGE
TO DO IT.

My Lord, since my letter written, your brother-in-law
that was, came to me very sad, and both asked me my coun-
cel, what he should do after to-morrow, because there be
many folks here, and among others the Earl of Souther-
land, who would rather die, considering the good they
have so lately received of me, than suffer me to be carried
away, they conducting me ; and that he feared there should
some trouble happen of it : of the other side, that it should
be said that he were unthankful to have betrayed me. I
told him, that he should have resolved with you upon all
that; and that he should avoid, if he could, those that
were most mistrusted. He hath resolved to write thereof
to you of my opinion : for he hath abashed me to see him
so unresolved at the need. I assure myself, he will play
the part of an honest man. But I have thought good to advertise you of the fear he hath, that he should be charged and
accused of treason, to the end that without mistrusting him,
you may be the more circumspect, and that you may have the
more power. For we had yesterday more than three hundred
horse of his, and of Leniston. For the honour of God be
accompanied rather with more than less; for that is the
principal of my care. I go to write my dispatch, and pray
God to send us a happy interview shortly. I write in haste,
to the end you may be advised in time.

NOTE.

THAT amazing miracle of impudence, in showing the same letters one day in Scotch and the next in French, and pretending them to be different in themselves, and both in Mary's hand-writing, accounts very well by itself for the conduct of Murray, in not entrusting the commissioners at Westminster with even copies of the ten, though he did with copies of the eight. Those were professedly adduced as proofs against Mary, equally with these. " As they had yesternight produced and shewed sundry wrytings, tending to prove the hatred," &c. says Murray ; " so, for the further satisfaction both of the Quene's Majestie and theyr lordships, they were ready to produce and shew a great number of other letters," &c. Yet these alone staid with the commissioners, even in copies. Those were instantly withdrawn, both in copies and in originals. And what seems plainly to intimate that the commissioners were privy to the whole system of illusion, in secretary Cecil at least, who altered and interlined the journal, as he pleased, and must therefore be supposed to have directed the clerks too, as he thought proper; the journal of the day before, takes no notice of those Letters being either produced or withdrawn. But, had they not been withdrawn, in what a happy state would the epistolary evidence against Mary have then stood.

There would have been sundry letters in Scotch, pretending to be her hand-writing. There would have been several of them also in French, equally pretending to be her writing too. They were both the same. Yet one asserted, she had written them in Scotch. The other affirmed, she had written them in French. Each in effect called the other an impostor. Each proved the other to be so.

The Sonnets are plainly one letter, written and sent to one period of time. This appears from some of them running into the others, from the general connection that spreads through many or most of them, and from the last of them forming obviously a conclusion to all. And the rebels accordingly instructed the commissioners at Westminster to consider them all as one sonnet.

I have pursued this ridiculous argument at a greater expense of time and words, than it had a right to claim at my hands; in order to show it ridiculous, in every principle and particle of it.—*Whitaker.*

LOVE SONNET OF MARY QUEEN OF SCOTS TO JAMES EARL OF BOTHWELL,

CONSIDERED BY THE COMMISSIONERS AS ONE DOCUMENT.

O Dieux, ayez de moy compassion,
Et m'enseignez quelle preuve certaine
Je puis donner, qui ne luy semble vaine,
De mon amour et ferme affection.

Las n'est-il pas ja en possession
Du corps, du cœur, qui ne refuse peine,
Ny deshonneur en la vie incertaine,
Offence de parens, ne pire affliction?

Pour luy tous mes amis j'estime moins que rien,
Et de mes ennemis je veux esperer bien.
J'ay hazardé pour luy et nom et conscience;
Je veus pour luy au monde renoncer;

Je veux mourir pour le faire avancer:
Que reste plus pour prouver ma constance?
Entre ses mains, et en son plein pouvoir,
Je mets mon fils, mon honneur, et ma vie,

Mon païs, mes subjets; mon ame assubjettie
Est toute a luy, et n'ay autre vouloir
Pour mon objet, que sans le decevoir
Suivre je veux, malgré toute l'envie

Qu'issir en peut.   Car je n'ay autre envie,
Que de ma foy luy faire appercevoir:
Que pour tempeste, ou bonasse, qu'il face,
Jamais ne veut changer demeure ou place.

THE SONNETS

I have attempted to freely translate in the elegiac stanza
of Hammond and Shenstone, because I think it most ex-
pressive for love poetry.   How far I have succeeded, my
readers may judge.   H. C.

Ye Gods, upon your suppliant pity take,
And me inform—that from my soul may flow—
What proofs of sweet affection, for his sake,
Shall prompt my pen to paint my bosom's glow !

Alas, does he already not possess
My heart, my person, that declines not pain,
Nor yet dishonour, nay, nor wretchedness,
Could I his love ensure, nor sue in vain !

Friends may withdraw—afflictions dire may come,
But these are nothing to my ardent mind—
With him, in hope, through enemies I'll roam,
And hazard all, to fame and honour blind.

For his sweet sake I will renounce the world ;
To make him great, even death itself were dear:
Reft of a crown, or into exile hurled,
Were nought to me, so Bothwell, lov'd, be near.

Placed in his power, my son, my honour, life,
My country, subjects, soul, all, all subdued
By him, the conqueror of my will, in strife
Of sweet emotions, that my love pursued.

Without deceit, in spite of envy, aye,
And all her votaries, this is all my aim—
That he may see my faithfulness, and sigh,
And haply feel my soul's consuming flame.

Bref, je feray de ma foy telle preuve,
Qu'il cognoistra, sans faute, ma constance ;
Non par mes pleurs, ou feinte obeïssance,
Comme autres sont, mais par diverse espreuve

Elle, pour son honneur, vous doit obeïssance :
Moy vous obeïssant, j'en puis recevoir blasme,
N'estant, a mon regret, comme elle, vostre femme
Et si n'aura pourtant en ce point préminence.

Pour son proufit elle use de constance,
Car ce n'est peu d'honneur d'estre de vos biens dame :
Et moy, pour vous aimer, j'en puis recevoir blasme,
Et ne luy veux ceder en toute l'observance.

Elle de vostre mal n'a l'apprehension ;
Moy je n'ay nul repos, tant je crain l'apperrence.
Par l'advis des parens ille eust votre accointance ;
Moy, malgré tous les miens, vous porte affection.

[Et neantmoins, mon cœur, vous doutez de ma con-
     stance],
Et de sa loyauté prenez ferme asseurance.
Par vous, mon cœur, et par vostre alliance,
Elle a remis sa maison en honneur ;

Elle a joüy par vous de la grandeur,
Dont tous les siens n'avoient nulle asseurance.
De vous, mon bien, elle a eu la constance,
Et a gaigné pour un temps vostre cœur ;

Par vous elle a eu plaisir en bon heur,
Et pour vous a honneur et reverence ;
Et n'a perdu, sinon la joüissance
D'un fascheux sot, qu'elle avoit cherement.

Je ne la plain d'aimer donc ardement
Celuy, qui n'a en sens, ny en vaillance,
Ny en beauté, en bonté, ny constance,
Point de second.   Je vy en ceste foy.

Fix'd as it is, nor calms nor storms shall move
Its fervent dwelling—where, to interests blind—
It blazes, hallow'd, at thy altar, love,
And sighs in flame, oh, were my Bothwell kind!

But soon he shall such proofs receive of me,
As, without fiction, shall pourtray the truth:
Nor yet by weeping, nor despondency,
Nor feigned obedience to the noble youth.

So others did—but stranger practice now,
From dear experience, shall my thoughts engage—
She, for her honour, does her lord avow,
But my obedience fills dishonour's page.

Alas, I am not Bothwell's wife—yet she
By that sad right shall not precede in love ;
Her constancy's her interest! as for me,
No sordid interest can my passion move.

To be the mistress of yourself and wealth,
Is no small honour to her, so possest ;
While blame is mine, for loving you by stealth,
I'm not less true in loving, though unblest!

She has no fears, no bodings of the woes
May happen Bothwell, whilst my breast is torn—
I fear for all that may occur—repose
Oft flies my pillow from the night till morn.

Blest in your friendship by her willing friends,
Against their wills do my affections flow !
You doubt my faith, and hence my spirit bends,
Whilst well assured *her* faithfulness you know !

By you, my heart, ah, she has now restored
Her house to honour, and to lasting fame ;
By you, in greatness, she is now adored,
To which her friends had never any claim.

Quant vous l'aimiez, elle usoit de froideur,
Si vous souffriez pour s'amour passion,
Qui vient d'aimer de trop d'affection :
Son doight monstroit la tristesse du cœur.

N'aiant plaisir en vostre grand ardeur,
En ses habits monstroit sans fiction,
Qu' elle n'avoit paour, qu' imperfection
Peust l'effacer hors de ce loyal cœur.

De vostre mort je ne vis la peaur,
Que meritoit tel mary et seigneur.
Somme, de vous elle a eu tout son bien ;
Et n'a prisé, n'y jamais estimé,

Une si grand heur, sinon puis qu'il n'est sien ;
Et maintenant dit l'avoir tant aimé.
Et maintenant elle commence a voir,
Qu'elle estoit bien de mauvais jugement,

De n'estimer l'amour d'un tel amant ;
Et voudroit bien mon amy decevoir
Par les escrits tous fardez de scavoir
Qui pourtant n'est en son esprit croissant,

Ains emprunté de quelque auteur luisant,
A faint tres-bien un envoy sans l'avoir.
Et toutesfois ses paroles fardéez,
Ses pleurs, ses plaincts, remplis de fictions,

Et ses hautz cris, et lamentations,
On tant gaigné, que par vous sont gardéez
Ses lettres escrites ; ausquels vous donnez foy,
Et si l'aimez, et croiez plus que moy.

Vous la croyez, las ! trop je l'appercoy,
Et vous doutez de ma ferme constance,
O mon seul bien, et ma seule esperance,
Et ne vous puis asseurer de ma foy.

From you, my wealth, her happiness she draws,
Acquaintance first, then conqueror of your heart,
For all her wealth and pleasure—you the cause —
She made no sacrifice, she felt no smart !

For 'tis no sacrifice to lose a fool—
Such as she dearly loved, ere you appeared ;
Unpleasant he—brought up in Folly's school ;
Hence what enjoyment had such lout endeared !

But I mourn not, though she may ardent love
The source of all my hope, my love, my joy !
Second to none in manhood will he prove !
Nor yet in beauty, truth, nor constancy !

Such is my faith—in such my hopes feel rest ;
With coldness Lady Bothwell met your love !
If passion then you suffer—that confest,
Is love and confidence that nought may move.

Her doubting shows the picture of her heart,
Nor in your ardent love she pleasure knows ;
Her manner shows her fear shall not impart,
Nor imperfections spoil your love's repose !

When dangers circumvolved my Bothwell round,
Where were her fears ?—I saw them not in place—
She show'd no symptoms of that grief profound,
Which speak the fond and feeling wife's best grace.

Yours is her wealth, and all she can esteem ;
But she had not the sense to weigh its worth ;
On happiness so pure she ne'er could dream,
Till now, not hers, she owns you best on earth.

And now her erring judgment she can see,
That such a lover's love she should possess,
And well she may dissemble courteously,
By soft accomplishments and sweet address !

.Vous m'estimez legiere, qui je voy,
Et si n'avez en moy nulle asseurance,
Et soupçonnez mon cœur sans apparence,
Vous meffiant a trop grand tort de moy.

Vous ignorez l'amour que je vous porte,
Vous soupçonnez qu' autre amour me transporte.
Vous estimez des paroles du vent,
Vous despeignez de cire mon las cœur,

Vous me pensez femme sans jugement;
Et tout cela augmente mon ardeur.
Mon amour croist, et plus en plus croistra,
Tant que vivray; et tiendray a grand heur,

Tant seulement d'avoir part en ce cœur;
Vers qui enfin mon amour paroistra
Si tres-clair, que' jamais n'en doutera.
[Pour luy je veux tacher contre malheur],

Pour luy je veux rechercher la grandeur;
Et feray tant, que de vray congnoistra.
Que je n'ay bien, heur, ne contentement,
Qu'a l'obeyïr et servir loyaument.

Pour luy j'attendz toute bonne fortune,
Pour luy je veux garder santé et vie,
Pour luy tout vertu de suivre j'ay envie,
Et sans changer me trouvera tout' une.

Pour luy aussi j'ay jetté mainte larme,
Premier qu'il fust de ce corps possesseur,
Duquel alors il n'avoit pas de cœur;
Puis me donna un autre dur alarme,

Quand il versa de son sang mainte dragme;
Dont de grief me vint laisser douleur,
Qui m'en pensa oster la vie, et frayeur
De perdre las! le seul rampart qui m'arme.

By writings elegant, that paint the soul,
And learning, not her own, acquired by time—
From authors who have run to glory's goal—
With not one sentence of her own sublime.

But oh, I mourn her painted words and tears,
Her plaints dissembling, and her feeling sighs,
Have won your heart, hence thrill'd my chord of fears;
And, now I seem a true love's sacrifice!

For her accomplishments, and writings clear,
Which you approve, ah, more than all I say,
Or now can write, you love your lady dear,
And hold in doubt my stedfast constancy.

But oh, mine only wealth, and hope that's mine!
Soul of my soul, that will not mind my love,
I know that you esteem me frail, nor find
The plan that would your weak suspicion move.

Ah, did you know the love I bear my dear,
Whilst you think other love transporteth me,
And deem my words but wind, and heart of fear,
Like wax, that melteth, and my heart is free.

You think me without judgment, and my pain
Is hence increased, and love burns forth anew,
Increasing, still increasing, though in vain,
For Bothwell still, my dearest lord, for you.

Oh, to possess one portion of your heart,
To which at length my love shall yet appear
So purely, that thy doubts shall act the part
Of kind interpreters of love so clear.

A world in arms I'd combat for my love,
For him all princely greatness I'd resign;
And prove content, nor happiness shall move
The soft affections of my fervent mind.

Pour luy depuis j'ay meprisé l'honneur,
Ce qui nous peult seul pourvoir de bonheur.
Pour luy j'ay hazardé grandeur et conscience,
Pour luy tous mes parens j'ay quitté et amis,

Et tous autres respectz sont a part mis ;
Brief, de vous seul je cherche l'alliance.
De vous je dis seul soustein de ma vie
Tant seulement je cerche m' asseurer,

Et si ose de moy tant presumer
De vous gaigner maugre toute l'envie.
Car c'est le seul desir de vostre chere amie,
De vous servir et loyaument aymer,

Et tous malheurs moins qui rien estimer,
Et vostre volonte de la mien ne sujure,
Vous cognostrez avecques obeyssance
De mon loyal devoir n' omittant lascience

A quoy je estudieray pour tousiours vous complaire
Sans aymer rien que vous, soubz la subjection.
De qui je veux sans nulle fiction
Vivre et mourir et à ce j'obtempere.

Mon cœur, mon sang, mon ame, et mon soucy
Las, vous m'avez promis qu'aurons ce plaisir
De deviser avecques vous à loysir,
Toute la nuict, ou je languis jey,

Ayant le cœur d'extreme paour transy,
Pour voir absent le but de mon desir
Crainte d'oublier un coup me vient à saisir :
Et l'autre fois je crains que rendurcie

Soit contre moy voystre amiable cœur
Par quelque dit d'un meschant ramporteur.
Un autre fois je crains quelque aventure
Qui par chemin detou ne mon amant,

Him to obey and serve, I will attend,
And seize good fortune, and preserve my life;
Courage I claim, and faith shall stand my friend,
For oh, I sigh to be my Bothwell's wife!

When first this person he possess'd, my tears
Flow'd forth on cheeks now pale and wan with care,
Nor did he then possess my heart—my fears
Had told him love did not his passion share.

Then when the villain drew my Bothwell's blood,
What were my thoughts—my feelings, what were they?
I felt as if my breast had lost the flood
That nurtures life—and in the grave I lay!

For him even honours since I have despised,
The source, 'tis said, whence springs felicity!
Friends in the wreck, and greatness were comprised,
And love renounced their dear society.

Hence, soon I'll claim the hand of you, my friend!
Of you, my love, upholder of my life!
Assure me of your faith, and then I bend
Before you, conscious I shall be your wife!

To serve and love you truly is my aim;
All my aspirings are to you confin'd;
I deem misfortunes but an empty name,
And meet your will with all a lover's mind!

Nor once omit my duty, which shall still
Be my fond study, how I most may please,
In love for Bothwell I shall form my will,
Till death itself shall bid affections cease.

My heart, my blood, my soul, my care, and all
I own, and all I claim as mine, content
I render to him, and shall wait his call,
To yield those blessings which kind Heaven has lent!

Par un fascheux et nouveau accident.
Dieu detourne touté malheureux augure.
Ne vous voyant selon qu' avez promis
J' ay mis la main au papier our escrire

D' un different que je voulu transcrire.
Je ne scay pas quel sera vestre advis
Mais je scay bien qui mieux aymer scaura,
Vous diriez bien que plus y gaignera.

———

Of Mary's poetry it has been said:—

" Elle composoit de vers,' dont j'en ay veu aucun de beaux et tres bien faits, et nullement resemblant a ceux qu'on lui a mis sus avoir fait sur l'amour du Comte de Both-uel. Ils son trop grossiers et mal polis pour etre sortis d'ele."

Brantome, vol. i.

That the reader may judge for himself on a comparison, we give from Brantome the following stanzas of an Elegy, made by Queen Mary on the death of her husband, King Francis II.

Alas! you pleasure promised me, your slave,
And said our leisure hours we should enjoy;
Oh, hasten then, and precious moments save,
For all night long I languish, sob, and sigh!

Fear whelms my heart, and absence cools desire,
I sometimes think you have forgotten me;
At other times, I fear your love—on fire—
Has other causes for its sympathy.

Perhaps some slanderer, worthy of the name,
Has cleared the way to coldness and neglect,
Or some adventure, yet unknown to fame,
Has check'd your ardour, and my love thrown back.

Oh, God, prevent the bodings of my mind—
You promised I should see you, but forgot—
Hence do I scrawl—with tears mine eyes are blind,
I cannot copy, and I must not blot.

Nor can I tell what shall your judgment be;
But well I know who most does dearly love!
And you can tell who most shall win—not me—
Then come, my soul, my life, my lover—prove.

STANZAS,

BY MARY QUEEN OF SCOTS, ON THE DEATH OF HER
HUSBAND, KING FRANCIS II.

———

Ce que m'estoit plaisant
Ores m'est peine dure,
Le jour le plus luisant
M'est nuit noire et obscure,
Et n'est rien si exquis
Qui de moy foit requis.

Pour mon mal estranger
Je ne m'arreste en place,
Mais j'en ay beau changer
Si ma douleur n'efface,
Car mon pis, et mon mieux,
Sont les plus deserts lieux.

Si en quelque sejour
Soit en bois, ou en prée,
Soit vers l'aube de jour
Ou soit sur la vesprée,
Sans cesse mon cœur sent
Le regret dun absent.

Si par fois vers les cieux
Viens adresser ma vue,
Le doux trait de ses yeux
Je vois en une nue,
Soudain le voys en l'eau
Comme dans tombeau*.

* In illustration of this stanza, it may be proper to observe, that in
Queen Mary's time, and at this day, embellished fountains and canals
were the chief ornaments of gardens in France. Every palace was
ornamented with a piece of water.—*Lord Elibank.*

THE STANZAS TRANSLATED.

What formerly was pleasant to my eyes
Now gives me pain.
The brightest day,
To me, seems dark and obscure night.
For the most exquisite delights
I now have neither relish or desire.

As a relief for my singular misfortune
I wander from place to place;
But 'tis in vain to think of change,
Which effaces not my grief;
For scenes which formerly gave me delight
Are now become frightful solitudes to me.

If in some solitary retreat
Amidst the wood, or in the plain;
Whether in the morning's dawn,
Or in the evening's shade,
Without ceasing,
Still my heart feels its irreparable loss.

If I lift my eyes to heaven,
I figure to myself his sweet features
In the clouds;
Soon casting my eyes
On the wat'ry scene below,
I see him, as in his grave.

Si je suis en repos
Sommeillant sur ma couche
J'oy qui me tient propos
Je le sens qui me touche,
En labeur en recoy
Toujours est près demoy.

Mets chanson ici fin,
A si triste complainte,
Dont sera le refrin,
' Amour vraye, et non feinte,
' Pour la separation
' N'aura diminution.'

' Lord Hailes seems to have a mean opinion of Queen Mary's poetry. He quotes the fourth stanza with this remark:—
" This I suppose is what Brantome reckoned *beau et gentil.*"
And on the last stanza he remarks, " This may serve to show what sort of poetry it was which Mary indeed wrote."

I am loth to dissent from the opinion of so able a critic. But in a matter of mere taste, of which I know no fixed standard, every one is at liberty to judge of what pleases himself. In my humble opinion, the poem taken altogether is a fine composition. Ronsard, one of the first poets of that age, thought it so. The thoughts are natural, and simple, well conducted, and elegantly expressed. The fourth stanza appears to me, particularly, to be beautiful and poetical.

When I lay myself to rest,
If slumbering on my couch,
I think I hear his sweet voice
In conversation with me,
I dream as if I felt him by my side.
Restless, or at ease,
He still is present with me.

Here let me put an end
To my sad complaint,
Of which the theme shall be,
' Sincere and unfeigned love
' Shall never by separation
' Suffer any diminution."

TRANSLATION OF QUEEN MARY'S ELEGY ON THE DEATH OF HER HUSBAND, KING FRANCIS II.

BY MR. PYE, MEMBER OF PARLIAMENT FOR BERKS.

In melting strains that sweetly flow,
Tun'd to the plaintive notes of woe,
My eyes survey, with anguish fraught,
A loss beyond the reach of thought,
While pass away life's fairest years
In heaving sighs and mournful tears.

Did cruel destiny e'er shed
Such horror on a wretched head?
Did e'er once happy woman know
So sad a scene of heartfelt woe?
For ah! behold on yonder bier
All that my heart and eyes held dear!

Alas! even in my blooming hours,
'Mid opening youth's resplendent flowers,
I'm doom'd each cruel pang to share,
Th' extremest sorrows of despair,
Nor other joy nor bliss can prove
Than grief, and disappointed love.

The sweet delights of happier days
New anguish in my bosom raise;
Of shining day the purest light
To me is drear and gloomy night;
Nor is there aught so good and fair
As now to claim my slightest care.

In my full heart and streaming eyes,
Pourtray'd by woe, an image lies,
Which sable robes but faintly speak,
Or the pale languor of my cheek,
Pale as the violet's faded leaf,
The tint of love's despairing grief.

Perplex'd by this unwonted pain,
No place my steps can long detain;
Yet change of scene no comfort gives,
Where sorrow's form for ever lives;
My worst, my happiest, state of mind
In solitude alone I find.

If chance my listless footsteps leads
Through shady groves, or flowery meads,
Whether at dawn of rising day,
Or silent evening's setting ray,
Each grief that absence can impart
Incessant rends my tortured heart.

If to the Heavens, in rapt'rous trance,
I hap'ly throw a wistful glance,
His visionary form I see,
Pictur'd in orient clouds to me;
Sudden it flies, and he appears
Drown'd in a wat'ry tomb of tears.

Nous Marie, par la grace de Dieu, Royne d'Escosse, doua-
ryere de France, &c. promettons fidellement, et de bonne
foy, et sans contraynte, à Jaques Hepburn Conte de Boduel,
de n'avoir jamays autre espoulx et mary que luy, et de le
prendre pour tel toute et quant fois qu'il m'en requerira, quoy
que parents, amys ou autres, y soient contrayres. Et puis
que Dieu a pris mon feu mary Henry Stuart dit Darnlay, et
que par ce moin je sois libre, n'estant soubs obeïssance de
pere, ni de mere, des mayntenant je proteste que, lui estant
en mesme liberté, je seray preste, et d'accomplir les ceremonies requises au mariage : que je lui promets devant Dieu,
que j'en prantz à tesmoignasge, et la presente, signée de
ma mayn : ecrit ce ———

                                        MARIE R.

There is also another writing in Scottish, avowed to be
wholly written by the Earl of Huntley, dated the fifth of
April, 1567, containing a form of contract of marriage betwixt the said Queen and Earl Bothwell, subscribed Mary,
which is avowed to be the proper hand of the said Queen ;
and underneath it, James Earl Bothwell, which also is
avowed to be the proper hand of the Earl Bothwell, at which
time he was commonly defamed of the King's slaughter,
and not cleansed or acquit thereof before the thirteenth of
April following. The tenor of which contract here
ensueth.

THE SECOND CONTRACT.

At Seyton, the fifth day of April, in the year of God, 1567. The right excellent, right high and mighty Princess Mary, by the grace of God Queen of Scots, considering the place and estate wherein Almighty God hath constituted her Highness, and how by the decease of the King her husband, her Majesty is now destitute of a husband, living solitary in the state of widowhood. In the which kind of life her Majesty most willingly would continue, if the will of her realm and subjects would permit it. But on the other part, considering the in conveniencies may follow, and the necessity which the Realm hath, that her Majesty be coupled with an husband, her highness hath an inclination to marry. And seeing what incommodity may come to this Realm, in case her Majesty should join in marriage with any foreign Prince of a strange nation, her Highness has thought rather to yield unto one of her own subjects. Amongst whom, her Majesty finds none more able, nor endued with better qualities, than the right noble, and her dear cousin James, Earl Bothwell, &c. Of whose thankful and true service, her Highness in all the times by-past has had large proof, and infallible experience. And seeing not only the same good mind constantly persevering in him, but with that an inward affection, and hearty love towards her Majesty, her highness amongst the rest, hath made her choice of him.

And therefore, in the presence of the eternal God, faithfully, and in the word of a Prince, by these presents takes the said James Earl Bothwell as her lawful husband. And promises and obliges her Highness, that as soon as the process of divorce intended betwixt the said Earl Bothwell and Dame Jane Gordon, now his pretended spouse, be ended by the order of the laws, her Majesty shall, God willing, thereafter shortly marry, and take the said Earl to her husband, and compleat the band of matrimony with him in the face of Holy Church. And shall never marry any other husband but him only during his life-time. And as her Majesty of her gracious humanity, and proper motive, without deserving of the said Earl, hath thus inclined her favour and affection towards him, he humbly and reverently acknowledging the same, according to his bounden duty, and being as free and able to make promise of marriage, in respect of the said process of divorce intended for divers reasonable causes, and that the said pretended spouse hath thereunto consented, he presently takes her Majesty as his lawful spouse, in the presence of God. And promises and obligeth him, as he will answer to God, and upon his fidelity and honour, that in all diligence possible, he shall prosecute and set forward the said process of divorce already began and intended betwixt him and the said Dame Jane Gordon his pretended spouse, unto the final end of a decree and declaration therein.

And incontinent thereafter, at her Majesties good will and pleasure, and when her Highness thinks convenient shall compleat and solemnise in face of holy church, the said band of matrimony with her Majesty, and love, honour, and serve her Highness, according to the place and honour that it have pleased her Majesty to accept him unto, and never to have any other to his wife during her Majesty's life time. In faith and witnessing whereof, her Highness and the said Earl hath subscribed this present faithful promise, with their hands, as followeth, day, year, and place aforesaid, before these witnesses; George Earl Huntly, and Master Thomas Hepburn, Parson of Old Hanstock, &c.

Sic subscribitur,   MARY R.

James Earl Bothwell.

Here note, that this contract was made the 5th of April, within eight weeks after the murder of the King, which was slain the 10th of February before. Also it was made seven days before that Bothwell was acquitted by corrupt judgment of the said murder.

Also it appeareth by the words of the contract itself, that it was made before sentence of divorce between Bothwell and his former wife: And also, in very truth, was made before any suit of divorce intended or begun between him and his former wife, though some words in this contract seem to say otherwise. Which is thus proved. For this contract is dated the 5th of April; and it plainly appeareth by the judicial acts before the two several ecclesiastical ordinary judges, wherein is contained the whole process of the divorce between the said Earl and Dame Jane Gordon his wife, that one of the same processes was intended and begun on the 26th and the other on the 27th day of April.

NOTE.

I think it necessary, in order to make this volume a complete history of the origin of the Scottish Queen's misfortunes, to give the accurate and indisputable account of Hume, as an opening to the case, before I cite the opinion of Buchannan and the other advocates for and against her criminality and participation in the murder of her husband. With that able historian I shall also close the inquiry on the letters.

MURDER OF DARNLEY.

The Earl of Bothwell was of a considerable family and power in Scotland; and though not distinguished by any talents either of a civil or military nature, he had made a figure in that party, which opposed the greatness of the Earl of Murray, and the more rigid reformers. He was a man of profligate manners; had involved his opulent fortune in great debts, and even reduced himself to beggary by his profuse expenses; and seemed to have no resource but in desperate councils and enterprises. He had been accused more than once of an attempt to assassinate Murray; and though the frequency of these accusations on all sides diminish somewhat the credit due to any particular imputation, they prove sufficiently the prevalence of that detestable practice in Scotland, and may in that view serve to render such rumours the more credible.

This man had of late acquired the favour and entire confidence of Mary; and all her measures were directed by his advice and authority. Reports were spread of more particular intimacies between them; and these reports gained ground from the continuance or rather increase of her hatred towards her husband. That young prince was reduced to such a state of desperation, by the neglects which he underwent from his Queen and the courtiers, that he had once resolved to fly secretly into France or Spain, and had even provided a vessel for that purpose.

Some of the most considerable nobility, on the other hand, observing her rooted aversion to him, had proposed some expedients for a divorce; and though Mary is said to have spoken honourably on the occasion, and to have embraced the proposal no farther than it should be found consistent with her own honour and her son's legitimacy, men were inclined to believe that the difficulty of finding proper means for effecting that purpose, was the real cause of laying aside all farther thoughts of it. So far were the suspicions against her carried, that when Henry, discouraged with the continual proofs of her hatred, left the court, and retired to Glasgow, an illness of an extraordinary nature, with which he was seized immediately on his arrival in that place, was universally ascribed by her enemies to a dose of poison, which, it was pretended, she had administered to him.

While affairs were in this situation, all those who wished well to her character, or to public tranquillity, were extremely pleased, and somewhat surprised, to hear, that a friendship was again conciliated between them ; that she had taken a journey to Glasgow on purpose to visit him during his sickness ; that she behaved toward him with great tenderness ; that she had brought him along with her ; and that she appeared thenceforth determined to live with him on a footing more suitable to the connections between them. Henry, naturally uxorious, and not distrusting this sudden reconciliation, put himself implicitly into her hands, and attended her to Edinburgh.

She lived in the palace of Holyrood House ; but as the situation of the place was low, and the concourse of people about the court was necessarily attended with noise, which might disturb him in his present infirm state of health, these reasons were assigned for fitting up an apartment for him in a solitary house, at some distance, called the Kirk of Field.

Mary here gave him marks of kindness and attachment ; she conversed cordially with him ; and she lay some nights in a room below his ; but on the ninth of February, she told him, that she would pass that night in the palace, because the marriage of one of her servants was there to be celebrated in her presence. About two o'clock in the morning the whole town was much alarmed at hearing a great noise ; and was still more astonished, when it was discovered that the noise came from the King's house, which was blown up

by gunpowder; that his dead body was found at some distance in a neighbouring field; and that no marks either of
fire, contusion, or violence, appeared upon it.

- No doubt could be entertained but Henry was murdered;
and general conjecture soon pointed towards the Earl of
Bothwell as the author of the crime. But as his favour with
Mary was visible, and his power great, no one ventured to
declare openly his sentiments; and all men remained in
silence and mute astonishment. Voices, however, were
heard in the streets, during the darkness of the night, pro-
claiming Bothwell, and even Mary herself, to be the murderers of the King; bills were secretly affixed on the walls
to the same purpose; offers were made, that, upon giving
proper securities, his guilt should be openly proved. But
after one proclamation from the court, offering a reward
and indemnity to any one that would discover the author of
that villainy, greater vigilance was employed in searching
out the spreaders of the libels and reports against Bothwell
and the Queen, than in tracing the contrivers of the King's
assassination, or detecting the regicides.

The Earl of Lenox, who lived at a distance from court,
in poverty and contempt, was roused by the report of his
son's murder, and wrote to the Queen, imploring speedy
justice against the assassins; among whom he named the
Earl of Bothwell, Sir James Balfour, and Gilbert Balfour,
his brother, David Chalmers, and four others of the Queen's
household; all of them persons who had been mentioned
in the bills affixed to the walls at Edinburgh. Mary took
his demand of speedy justice in a very literal sense; and
allowing only fifteen days for the examination of this important affair, she sent a citation to Lenox, requiring him
to appear in court, and prove his charge against Bothwell.
This nobleman, meanwhile, and all the other persons accused by Lenox, enjoyed their full liberty; Bothwell himself was continually surrounded with armed men; took his
place in council; lived during some time in the house with

M

Mary; and seemed to possess all his wonted confidence and familiarity with her. Even the castle of Edinburgh, a place of great consequence in this critical time, was intrusted to him, and under him, to his creature, Sir James Balfour, who had himself been publicly charged as an accomplice in the King's murder. Lenox, who had come as far as Stirling, with a view of appearing at the trial, was informed of all these circumstances; and reflecting on the small train which attended him, he began to entertain very just apprehensions from the power, insolence, and temerity of his enemy. He wrote to Mary, desiring that the day of trial might be prorogued: and conjured her, by all the regard which she bore to her own honour, to employ more leisure and deliberation in determining a question of such extreme moment. No regard was paid to his application: the jury was enclosed, of which the Earl of Caithness was chancellor; and though Lenox, foreseeing this precipitation, had ordered Cunningham, one of his retinue, to appear in court, and protest, in his name, against the acquittal of the criminal, the jury proceeded to a verdict. The verdict was such as it behoved them to give, where neither accuser nor witness appeared; and Bothwell was absolved from the King's murder (April 12). The jury, however, apprehensive that their verdict would give great scandal, and perhaps expose them afterward to some danger, entered a protest, in which they represented the necessity of their proceedings. It is remarkable, that the indictment was laid against Bothwell for committing the crime on the 9th of February, not the 10th, the real day on which Henry was assassinated. The interpretation generally put upon this error, too gross it was thought to have proceeded from mistake, was, that the secret council, by whom Mary was governed, not trusting entirely to precipitation, violence, and authority, had provided this plea, by which they ensured, at all adventures, a plausible pretence for acquitting Bothwell.

Two days after this extraordinary transaction, a parliament was held: and though the verdict in favour of Bothwell was attended with such circumstances as strongly confirmed, rather than diminished, the general opinion of his
guilt, he was the person chosen to carry the royal sceptre
on the first meeting of the national assembly. In this parliament, a rigorous act was made against those who set up
defamatory bills; but no notice was taken of the King's
murder.

The favour which Mary openly bore to Bothwell kept
every one in awe; and the effects of this terror appeared
more plainly in another transaction, which ensued immediately upon the dissolution of the parliament. A bond or
association was framed; in which the subscribers, after relating the acquittal of Bothwell by a legal trial, and mentioning a farther-offer which he had made to prove his innocence by single combat, obliged themselves, in case any
person should afterward impute to him the King's murder,
to defend him with their whole power against such calum-
niators. After this promise, which implied no great assurance in Bothwell of his own innocence, the subscribers
mentioned the necessity of their Queen's marriage, in order
to support the government; and they recommended Bothwell to her as a husband. This paper was subscribed
(April 14) by all the considerable nobility there present.
In a country divided by violent factions, such a concurrence
in favour of one nobleman, nowise distinguished above the
rest, except by his flagitious conduct, could never have been
obtained, had not every one been certain, at least firmly
persuaded, that Mary was fully determined on this measure. Nor would such a motive have sufficed to influence
men, commonly so stubborn and intractable, had they not been
taken by surprise, been ignorant of each other's sentiments,
and overawed by the present power of the court, and by the
apprehensions of farther violence, from persons so little
governed by any principles of honour and humanity. Even

with all these circumstances, the subscription to this paper
may justly be regarded as a reproach to the nation.

The subsequent measures of Bothwell were equally precipitate and audacious. Mary having gone to Stirling to pay
a visit to her son, he assembled a body of eight hundred
horse, on pretence of pursuing some robbers on the borders, and having waylaid her on her return, he seized her person near Edinburgh (April 24), and carried her to Dunbar,
with an avowed design of forcing her to yield to his purpose. Sir James Melvil, one of her retinue, was carried
along with her, and says not that he saw any signs of reluctance or constraint; he was even informed, as he tells
us, by Bothwell's officers, that the whole transaction was
managed in concert with her. A woman, indeed, of that
spirit and resolution which is acknowledged to belong to
Mary, does not usually, on these occasions, give such marks
of opposition to real violence, as can appear anywise
doubtful or ambiguous. Some of the nobility, however, in
order to put matters to further trial, sent her a private message; in which they told her, that if, in reality, she lay
under force, they would use all their efforts to rescue her.
Her answer was, that she had indeed been carried to Dunbar by violence, but ever since her arrival had been so well
treated, that she willingly remained with Bothwell. No
one gave himself thenceforth any concern to relieve her
from her captivity, which was believed to proceed entirely
from her own approbation and connivance.

This unusual conduct was at first ascribed to Mary's sense
of the infamy attending her proposed marriage; and her
desire of finding some colour to gloss over the irregularity
of her conduct. But a pardon given to Bothwell a few days
after, made the public carry their conjectures somewhat farther. In this deed, Bothwell received a pardon for the violence committed on the queen's person; and for all other
crimes; a clause, by which the murder of the King was indirectly forgiven. The rape was then conjectured to have

een only a contrivance, in order to afford a pretence for in-
irectly remitting a crime, of which it would have appeared
andalous to make openly any mention.

These events passed with such rapidity, that men had no
isure to admire sufficiently one incident, when they were
urprised with a new one equally rare and uncommon.
There still, however, remained one difficulty, which it was
ot easy to foresee how the Queen and Bothwell, deter-
ained as they were to execute their shameful purpose, could
nd expedients to overcome. The man who had procured
he subscription of the nobility, recommending him as a
usband to the Queen, and who had acted this seeming vio-
ence on her person in order to force her consent, had been
aarried two years before to another woman; to a woman
f merit, of a noble family, sister to the Earl of Huntley.
But persons blinded by passion, and infatuated with crimes,
oon shake off all appearances of decency. A suit was com-
nenced for a divorce between Bothwell and his wife; and
his suit was opened at the same instant in two different, or
rather opposite, courts: in the court of the Archbishop of
St. Andrew's, which was Popish, and governed itself
by the canon law; and in the new consistorial or commis-
sariat court, which was Protestant, and was regulated by
the principles of the reformed teachers. The plea advanced
n each court was so calculated as to suit the principles
which there prevailed: in the Archbishop's court, the pretence of consanguinity was employed, because Bothwell
was related to his wife in the fourth degree; in the com-
missariat court, the accusation of adultery was made use of
against him. The parties, too, who applied for the divorce, were different in the different courts: Bothwell was
the person who sued in the former; his wife in the latter.
And the suit to both courts was opened, pleaded, examined,
and decided, with the utmost precipitation; and a sentence
of divorce was pronounced in four days.

The divorce being thus obtained, it was thought proper
that Mary should be conducted to Edinburgh, and should
there appear before the courts of judicature, and should acknowledge herself restored to entire freedom. This was
understood to be contrived in a view of obviating all doubts
with regard to the validity of her marriage. Orders were
then given to publish in the church the banns between the
Queen and the Duke of Orkney; for that was the title
which he now bore; and Craig, a minister of Edinburgh,
was applied to for that purpose. This clergyman, not content with having refused compliance, publicly in his ser-
mons condemned the marriage, and exhorted all who had
access to the Queen, to give her their advice against so
scandalous an alliance. Being called before the council to
answer for this liberty, he shewed a courage which might
cover all the nobles with shame on account of their tameness
and servility. He said that, by the rules of the church, the
Earl of Bothwell, being convicted of adultery, could not be
permitted to marry; that the divorce between him and his
former wife was plainly procured by collusion, as appeared
by the precipitation of the sentence, and the sudden conclusion of the marriage with the Queen; and that all the
suspicions which prevailed, with regard to the King's murder, and the Queen's concurrence in the former rape, would
thence receive undoubted confirmation. He therefore exhorted Bothwell, who was present, no longer to persevere
in his present criminal enterprises; and turning his discourse to the other counsellors, he charged them to employ
all their influence with the Queen, in order to divert her
from a measure which would load her with eternal infamy
and dishonour. Not satisfied even with this admonition, he
took the first opportunity of informing the public, from the
pulpit, of the whole transaction, and expressed to them his
fears, that notwithstanding all remonstrances, their sovereign was still obstinately bent on her fatal purpose : " For

mself (he said), he had already discharged his conscience,
d yet again would take heaven and earth to witness, that
abhorred and detested that marriage, as scandalous and
teful in the sight of mankind; but since the great, as he
rceived, either by their flattery or silence, gave counte-
nce to the measure, he besought the faithful to pray fer-
ntly to the Almighty, that a resolution, taken contrary
all law, reason, and good conscience, might, by the di-
ne blessing, be turned to the comfort and benefit of the
urch and kingdom." These speeches offended the court
tremely; and Craig was anew summoned before the
uncil, to answer for his temerity in thus passing the
unds of his commission. But he told them that the
unds of his commission were, the word of God, good
ws, and natural reason; and were the Queen's marriage
ed by any of these standards, it would appear infamous
d dishonourable, and would be so esteemed by the whole
orld. The council were so overawed by this heroic be-
viour in a private clergyman, that they dismissed him
thout farther censure or punishment.

But though this transaction might have recalled Bothwell
d the Queen of Scots from their infatuation, and might
ve instructed them in the dispositions of the people, as
ell as in their own inability to oppose them; they were
ll resolute to rush forward to their own manifest destruc-
n. The marriage was solemnized by the bishop of Ork-
y (May 15), a Protestant, who was afterward deposed
the church for this scandalous compliance. Few of the
bility appeared at the ceremony; they had most of them,
her from shame or fear, retired to their own houses. The
ench ambassador, Le Croc, an aged gentleman of honour
d character, could not be prevailed on, though a depen-
nt of the house of Guise, to countenance the marriage by
s presence. Elizabeth remonstrated, by friendly letters
d messages, against the marriage: the court of France
ade like opposition; but Mary, though on all other occa-

sions she was extremely óbsequious to the advice of her relations in that country, was here determined to pay no regard to their opinion.

The news of these transactions being carried to forei-
countries, filled Europe with amazement, and threw 'in-
my not only on the principal actors in them, but also a-
the whole nation, who seemed by their submission a-
silence, and even by their declared approbation, to give
their sanction to these scandalous practices.   The Scots,
who resided abroad, met with such reproaches, that they
durst no where appear in public; and they earnestly exhorted their countrymen at home to free them from the
public òdium, by bringing to condign punishment the authors of such atrocious crimes.   This intelligence, with a
little more leisure for reflection, roused men from their
lethargy; and the rumours which, from the very beginning, had been spread against Mary, as if she had concurred in the king's murder, seemed now, by the subsequent transactions, to have received a strong confirmation
and authority.

It was every where said, that even though no particular
and direct proofs had as yet been pronounced of the Queen's
guilt, the whole tenor of her late conduct was sufficient,
not only to beget suspicion, but to produce entire conviction against her: that her sudden resolution of being reconciled to her husband, whom before she had long and justly
hated; her bringing him to court, from which she had banished him by neglects and rigours; her fitting up separate
apartments for him; were all of them circumstances which,
though trivial in themselves, yet being compared with the
subsequent events, bore a very unfavourable aspect for her:
that the least which, after the king's murder, might have
been expected in her situation, was a more than usual caution in her measures, and an extreme anxiety to punish the
real assassins, in order to free herself from all reproach and
suspicion: that no woman, who had any regard to her cha-

racter, would allow a man, publicly accused of her husband's murder, so much as to approach her presence, far less give him a share in her councils, and endow him with favour and authority: that an acquittal, merely in the absence of accusers, was very ill fitted to satisfy the public; especially if that absence proceeded from a designed precipitation of the sentence, from the terror of which her known friendship for the criminal had infused into every one: that the very mention of her marriage to such a person, in such circumstances, was horrible; and the contrivances of extorting a consent from the nobility, and of concerting a rape, were gross artifices, more proper to discover her guilt than prove her innocence: that where a woman shews a consciousness of merited reproach, and instead of correcting, provides only thin glosses to cover her exceptionable conduct, she betrays a neglect of fame, which must either be the effect or the cause of the most shameful enormities: that to espouse a man, who had, a few days before, been so scandalously divorced from his wife; who, to say the least, was believed to have, a few months before, assassinated her husband, was so contrary to the plainest rules of behaviour, that no pretence of indiscretion or imprudence could account for such a conduct: that a woman, who, so soon after her husband's death, though not attended with any extraordinary circumstances, contracts a marriage, which might in itself be the most blameless, cannot escape severe censure; but one who overlooks, for her pleasure, so many other weighty considerations, was equally capable, in gratifying her appetites, to neglect every regard to honour and to humanity: that Mary was not ignorant of the prevailing opinion of the public, with regard to her own guilt, and of the inferences which would every where be drawn from her conduct; and therefore, if she still continue to pursue measures which gave such just offence, she ratified, by her actions, as much as she could by the most formal confession, all the surmises and imputations of her enemies: that a prince

N

was here murdered in the face of the world; Bothwell
·alone was suspected and accused; if he were innocent,
nothing could absolve him, either in Mary's eyes or those
of the public, but the detection and conviction of the real
assassin; yet no inquiry was made to that purpose, though
a parliament had been assembled; the sovereign and wife
were here plainly silent from guilt, the people from terror.

That the only circumstance which opposed all these presumptions, or rather proofs, was, the benignity and goodness of her preceding behaviour, which seemed to remove
her from all suspicions of such atrocious inhumanity; but
that the characters of men were extremely variable, and
persons guilty of the worst actions were not always of the
worst and most criminal dispositions: that a woman who,
in a critical and dangerous moment, had sacrificed her honour to a man of abandoned principle, might thenceforth be
led blindfold by him to the commission of the most enormous crimes, and was in reality no longer at her own disposal; and that, though one supposition was still left to
alleviate her blame, namely, that Bothwell, presuming on
her affection towards him, had of himself committed the
crime, and had never communicated it to her, yet such a
sudden and passionate love to a man, whom she had long
known, could not easily be accounted for, without supposing some degree of preceding guilt; and as it appeared
that she was not afterward restrained, either by shame or
prudence, from incurring the highest reproach and danger,
it was not likely that a sense of duty or humanity would
have a more powerful influence over her.

These were the sentiments which prevailed throughout
Scotland; and as the protestant teachers, who had great
authority, had long borne an animosity to Mary, the opinion
of her guilt was, by that means, the more widely diffused,
and made the deeper impression on the people. Some attempts made by Bothwell, and, as is pretended, with her
consent, to get the young Prince into his power, excited

the most serious attention ; and the principal nobility, even many of those who had formerly been constrained to sign the application in favour of Bothwell's marriage, met at Stirling, and formed an association for protecting the Prince, and punishing the King's murderers.

The Earl of Athole himself, a known Catholic, was the first author of this confederacy ; the Earls of Argyle, Morton, Marre, Glencairne, the Lords Boyd, Lindsey, Hume, Semple, Kirkaldy of Grange, Tulibardine, and Secretary Lidington, entered zealously into it. The Earl of Murray, foreseeing such turbulent times, and being desirous to keep free of these dangerous factions, had, some time before, desired and obtained Mary's permission to retire into France.

Lord Hume was first in arms; and, leading a body of eight hundred horse, suddenly environed the Queen of Scots and Bothwell in the castle of Borthwick. They found means of making their escape to Dunbar ; while the confederate Lords were assembling their troops at Edinburgh, and taking measures to effect their purpose. Had Bothwell been so prudent as to keep within the fortress of Dunbar, his enemies must have dispersed for want of pay and subsistence ; but hearing that the associated Lords were fallen into distress, he was so rash as to take the field (June 15), and advance towards them.

The armies met at Carberry-hill, about six miles from Edinburgh; and Mary soon became sensible that her own troops disapproved of her cause, and were averse to spill their blood in her quarrel. After some bravadoes of Bothwell, where he discovered very little courage, she saw no resource but that of holding a conference with Kirkaldy of Grange, and of putting herself, upon some general promises, into the hands of the confederates. She was conducted to Edinburgh, amidst the insults of the populace ; who reproached her with her crimes; and even held before her eyes, which way soever she turned, a banner, on which were painted the murder of her husband, and the distress of her infant son.

Mary, overwhelmed with her calamities, had recourse to tears and lamentations. Meanwhile Bothwell, during her conference with Grange, fled unattended to Dunbar; and fitting out a few small ships, set sail for the Orkneys, where he subsisted during some time by piracy. He was pursued thither by Grange, and his ship was taken, with several of his servants, who afterward discovered all the circumstances of the King's murder, and were punished for the crime. Bothwell himself escaped in a boat, and found means to get a passage to Denmark, where he was thrown into prison, lost his senses, and died miserably about ten years after—an end worthy of his flagitious conduct and behaviour.

The Queen of Scots, now in the hands of an enraged faction, met with such treatment as a sovereign may naturally expect from subjects who have their future security to provide for, as well as their present animosity to gratify. It is pretended, that she behaved with a spirit very little suitable to her condition, avowed her inviolable attachment to Bothwell, and even wrote him a letter, which the Lords intercepted, wherein she declared, that she would endure any extremity, nay, resign her dignity and crown itself, rather than relinquish his affections. The malcontents, finding the danger to which they were exposed, in case Mary should finally prevail, thought themselves obliged to proceed with rigour against her; and they sent her next day under a guard to the castle of Lochlevin, situated in a lake of that name. The mistress of the house was mother to the Earl of Murray; and as she pretended to have been lawfully married to the late King of Scots, she naturally bore an animosity to Mary, and treated her with the utmost harshness and severity.

Elizabeth, who was fully informed of all these incidents, seemed touched with compassion towards the unfortunate queen; and all her fears and jealousies being now laid asleep, by the consideration of that ruin and infamy in which Mary's conduct had involved her, she began to reflect on the instability of human affairs, the precarious state of royal grandeur, the danger of encouraging rebellious subjects; and she resolved to employ her authority for alleviating the calamities of her unhappy kinswoman. She sent Sir Nicholas Throgmorton ambassador to Scotland, in order to remonstrate both with Mary and the associated Lords ; and she gave him instructions, which, though mixed with some lofty pretensions, were full of that good sense which was so natural to her, and of that generosity which the present interesting conjuncture had called forth. She empowered him to declare in her name to Mary, that the late conduct of that princess, so enormous and in every respect so unjustifiable, had given her the highest offence: and though she felt the movements of pity towards her, she had once determined never to interpose in her affairs, either by advice or assistance, but to abandon her entirely, as a person whose condition was totally desperate, and honour irretrievable: that she was well assured that other foreign princes, Mary's near relations, had embraced the same resolution; but for her part, the late events had touched her heart with more tender sympathy, and had made her adopt measures more favourable to the liberty and interests of the unhappy Queen: that she was determined not to see her oppressed by her rebellious subjects, but would employ all her good offices, and even her power, to redeem her from captivity, and place her in such a condition as would at once be compatible with her dignity, and the safety of her subjects: that she conjured her to lay aside all thoughts of revenge, except against the murderers of her husband; and as she herself was his near relation, she was better entitled than the subjects of Mary to interpose her authority on that head ; and she therefore besought that princess, if she had any regard to her own honour and safety, not to oppose so just and reasonable a demand : that after those two points were provided for, her own liberty, and the punishment of her husband's assassins, the safety of her infant son was

next to be considered: and there seemed no expedient more
proper for that purpose, than sending him to be educated
in England: and that, besides the security which would
attend his removal from a scene of faction and convulsions,
there were many other beneficial consequences, which it
was easy to foresee, as the result of his education in that
country.

 ˊThe remonstrances which Throgmorton was instructed
to make to the associated Lords, were entirely conform-
able to those sentiments which Elizabeth entertained in
Mary's favour. She empowered him to tell them, that
whatever blame she might throw on Mary's conduct, any
opposition to their sovereign was totally unjustifiable, and
incompatible with all order and good government: that it
belonged not to them to reform, much less to punish, the
mal-administration of their Prince: and the only arms
which subjects could in any case lawfully employ against
the supreme authority, were, entreaties, counsels, and re-
presentations: that if these expedients failed, they were
next to appeal by their prayers to Heaven; and to wait
with patience till the Almighty, in whose hands are the
hearts of princes, should be pleased to turn them to justice
and to mercy; that she inculcated not this doctrine, because she herself was interested in its observance; but because it was universally received in all well-governed states,
and was essential to the preservation of civil society; that
she required them to restore their Queen to liberty; and
promised, in that case, to concur with them in all proper
expedients for regulating the government, for punishing the
king's murderers, and for guarding the life and liberty of
the infant Prince: and that if the services which she had
lately rendered the Scottish nation, in protecting them from
foreign usurpation, were duly considered by them, they-
would repose confidence in her good offices, and would
esteem themselves blameworthy in having hitherto made no
application to her.

Elizabeth, besides these remonstrances, sent, by Throgmorton, some articles of accommodation, which he was to
propose to both parties, as expedients for the settlement of
public affairs; and though these articles contained some important restraints on the sovereign power, they were in the
main calculated for Mary's advantage, and were sufficiently
indulgent to her. The associated Lords, who determined
to proceed with greater severity, were apprehensive of Elizabeth's partiality; and being sensible that Mary would take
courage from the protection of that powerful princess, they
thought proper, after several affected delays, to refuse the
English Ambassador all access to her.

There were four different schemes proposed in Scotland
for the treatment of the captive Queen: one, that she should
be restored to her authority under very strict limitations:
he second, that she should be obliged to resign her crown
to the Prince, be banished the kingdom, and be confined
either to France or England; with assurances from the Sovereign in whose dominions she should reside, that she
should make no attempts to the disturbance of the established government: the third, that she should be publicly
tried for her crimes, of which her enemies pretended to
have undoubted proof, and be sentenced to perpetual imprisonment: the fourth was still more severe, and required,
that, after her trial and condemnation, capital punishment
should be inflicted upon her. Throgmorton supported the
mildest proposal; but though he promised his mistress's gua-
rantee for the performance of articles, threatened the ruling
party with immediate vengeance, in case of refusal, and
warned them not to draw on themselves, by their violence,
the public reproach which now lay upon their Queen; he
found that, excepting Secretary Lidington, he had not the
good fortune to convince any of the leaders. All counsels
seemed to tend towards the more severe expedients; and
the preachers, in particular, drawing their examples from

the rigorous maxims of the Old Testament, which can
only be warranted by particular revelations, inflamed the
minds of the people against their unhappy sovereign.

There were several pretenders to the regency of the
young Prince after the intended deposition of Mary. The
Earl of Lenox claimed that authority as grandfather to the
Prince: the Duke of Chatelrault, who was absent in France,
had pretensions as next heir to the crown: but the greatest
number of the associated Lords inclined to the Earl of Murray,
in whose capacity they had entire trust, and who possessed
the confidence of the preachers, and more zealous reformers.
All measures being therefore concerted, three instruments
were sent to Mary, by the hands of Lord Lindesey and Sir
Robert Melvil; by one of which she was to resign the
crown in favour of her son; by another to appoint Murray
Regent; by the third to make a council, which should admi-
nister the government until his arrival in Scotland. The
Queen of Scots, seeing no prospect of relief, lying justly
under apprehensions for her life, and believing that no deed,
which she executed during her captivity, could be valid,
was prevailed on, after a plentiful effusion of tears, to sign
these three instruments; and she took not the trouble of
inspecting any one of them.

In consequence of this forced resignation, the young
Prince was proclaimed King (July 29), by the name of
James VI. He was soon after crowned at Stirling, and the
Earl of Morton took, in his name, the coronation-oath; in
which a promise to extirpate heresy was not forgotten.
Some republican pretensions in favour of the people's power
were countenanced in this ceremony; and a coin was soon
after struck, on which the famous-saying of Trajan was in-
scribed, *Pro me; si merear, in me:* For me; if I deserve
it, against me. Throgmorton had orders from his mistress
not to assist at the coronation of the King of Scots.

The Council of Regency had not long occasion to exer-

cise their authority. The Earl of. Murray arrived from
France, and took possession of his high office. He paid a
visit to the captive Queen; and spoke to her in a manner
which better suited her past conduct than her present condition. This harsh treatment quite extinguished in her
breast any remains of affection towards him.

Murray proceeded afterward to break, in a more public
manner, all terms of decency with her. He summoned a
parliament (Dec. 15); and that assembly, after voting that
she was undoubtedly an accomplice in her husband's murder,
condemned her to imprisonment, ratified her demission of
the crown, and acknowledged her son for King, and Murray
for Regent. The Regent, a man of vigour and abilities,
employed himself successfully in reducing the kingdom.
He bribed Sir James Balfour to surrender the Castle of
Edinburgh; he constrained the Garrison of Dunbar to open
their gates; and he demolished that fortress.

But though every thing thus bore a favourable aspect to
the new government, and all men seemed to acquiesce in
Murray's authority; a violent revolution, however necessary, can never be effected without great discontents; and
it was not likely that, in a country where the government
in its most settled state possessed a very disjointed authority,
a new establishment should meet with no interruption or
disturbance. Few considerable men of the nation seemed
willing to support Mary, so long as Bothwell was present;
but the removal of that obnoxious nobleman had altered the
sentiments of many. The Duke of Chatelrault being disappointed of the regency, bore no good-will to Murray;
and the same sentiments were embraced by all his numerous retainers. Several of the nobility, finding that others
had taken the lead among the associators, formed a faction
apart, and opposed the prevailing power; and besides their
being moved by some remains of duty and affection towards
Mary, the malcontent Lords, observing every thing carried to extremity against her, were naturally led to embrace

her cause, and shelter themselves under her authority.   All
who retained any propensity to the Catholic religion, were
induced to join this party; and even the people in general,
though they had formerly either detested Mary's crimes,
or blamed her imprudence, were now inclined to compas-
sionate her present situation, and lamented that a person
possessed of so many amiable accomplishments, joined to
such high dignity, should be treated with such extreme severity.   Animated by all these motives, many of the principal nobility, now adherents to the Queen of Scots, met
at Hamilton, and concerted measures for supporting the
cause of that Princess.

While these humours were in fermentation, Mary was
employed in contrivances for effecting her escape; and she
engaged, by her charms and caresses, a young gentleman,
George Douglas, brother to the Laird of Lochleven, to
assist her in that enterprise.   She even went so far as to
give him hopes of espousing her, after her marriage with
Bothwell should be dissolved on the plea of force; and she
proposed this expedient to the Regent, who rejected it.
Douglas, however, persevered in his endeavours to free her
from captivity; and having all opportunities of access to the
house, he was at last successful in the undertaking.   He
conveyed her in disguise into a small boat (May 2), and
himself rowed her ashore.   She hastened to Hamilton; and
the news of her arrival in that place being immediately
spread abroad, many of the nobility flocked to her with their
forces.   A bond of association for her defence was signed
by the Earls of Argyle, Huntley, Eglington, Crawford,
Cassillis, Rothes, Montrose, Sutherland, Errol, nine Bishops,
and nine Barons, besides many of the most considerable
gentry.   And in a few days an army, to the number of
six thousand men, was assembled under her standard.

Elizabeth was no sooner informed of Mary's escape, than
she discovered her resolution of persevering in the same generous and friendly measures which she had hitherto pur-

sued. If she had not employed force against the Regent,
during the imprisonment of that Princess, she had been
chiefly withheld by the fear of pushing him to greater extremities against her; but she had proposed to the court of
France an expedient, which, though less violent, would
have been no less effectual for her service: she desired that
France and England should by concert cut off all commerce with the Scots, till they should do justice to their
injured sovereign.   She now dispatched Leighton into
Scotland to offer both her good offices, and the assistance of
her forces, to Mary; but as she apprehended the entrance
of the French troops into the kingdom, she desired that the
controversy between the Queen of Scots and her subjects
might by that Princess be referred entirely to her arbitration, and that no foreign succours should be introduced into
Scotland.

But Elizabeth had not leisure to exert fully her efforts in
favour of Mary.   The Regent made haste to assemble forces;
and notwithstanding that his army was inferior in number
to that of the Queen of Scots, he took the field against her.
A battle was fought at Langside (May 15), near Glasgow,
which was entirely decisive in favour of the Regent; and
though Murray, after his victory, stopped the bloodshed,
yet was the action followed by a total dispersion of the
Queen's party.   That unhappy Princess fled southwards
from the field of battle with great precipitation, and came,
with a few attendants, to the borders of England.   She
here deliberated concerning her next measures, which
would probably prove so important to her future happiness
or misery.   She found it impossible to remain in her own
kingdom; she had an aversion, in her present wretched condition, to return into France, where she had formerly appeared with so much splendour; and she was not, besides,
provided with a vessel which could safely convey her thither:
the late generous behaviour of Elizabeth made her hope for
protection, and even assistance, from that quarter; and as

the present fears from her domestic enemies were the most urgent, she overlooked all other considerations, and embraced the resolution of taking shelter in England. She embarked on board a fishing boat, in Galloway, and landed the same day at Workington in Cumberland, about thirty miles from Carlisle; whence she immediately dispatched a messenger to London, notifying her arrival, desiring leave to visit Elizabeth, and craving her protection, in consequence of former professions of friendship made her by that Princess.

Elizabeth now found herself in a situation when it was become necessary to take some decisive resolution with regard to her treatment of the Queen of Scots; and as she had hitherto, contrary to the opinion of Cecil, attended more to the motives of generosity than of policy, she was engaged by that prudent minister to weigh anew all the considerations which occurred in this critical conjuncture. He represented, that the party which had dethroned Mary, and had at present assumed the government of Scotland, was always attached to the English alliance, and was engaged, by all the motives of religion and of interest, to persevere in their connection with Elizabeth; and though Murray and his friends might complain of some unkind usage during their banishment in England, they would easily forget these grounds of quarrel, when they reflected that Elizabeth was the only ally on whom they could safely rely, and that their own Queen, by her attachment to the Catholic faith, and by her other connections, excluded them entirely from the friendship of France, and even from that of Spain; that Mary, on the other hand, even before her violent breach with her Protestant subjects, was in secret entirely governed by the counsels of the house of Guise; much more would she implicitly comply with their views, when, by her own ill conduct, the power of that family and of the zealous Catholics was become her sole resource and security: that her pretensions to the English crown

would render her a dangerous instrument in their hands;
and, were she once able to suppress the Protestants in her
own kingdom, she would unite the Scottish and English
Catholics with those of all foreign states in a confederacy
against the religion and government of England: that it
behoved Elizabeth, therefore, to proceed with caution in
the design of restoring her rival to the throne; and to take
care, both that this enterprise, if undertaken, should be
effected by English forces alone, and that full securities
should beforehand be provided for the reformers and the reformation in Scotland; that, above all, it was necessary to
guard carefully the person of that Princess; lest, finding this unexpected reserve in the English friendship,
she should suddenly take the resolution of flying into France,
and should attempt, by foreign force, to recover possession
of her authority: that her desperate fortunes and broken reputation fitted her for any attempt; and her resentment,
when she should find herself thus deserted by the Queen,
would concur with her ambition and her bigotry, and
render her an unrelenting, as well as powerful, enemy
to the English government: that if she were once abroad,
in the hands of enterprising Catholics, the attack on
England would appear to her as easy as that on Scotland; and the only method, she must imagine, of recovering her native kingdom, would be to acquire that crown to
which she would deem herself equally entitled; that a neutrality in such interesting situations, though it might be
pretended, could never, without the most extreme danger,
be upheld by the Queen; and the detention of Mary was
equally requisite, whether the power of England were to
be employed in her favour, or against her; that nothing,
indeed, was more becoming a great prince than generosity;
yet the suggestions of this noble principle could never,
without imprudence, be consulted in such delicate circumstances as those in which the Queen was at present placed:
where her own safety and the interests of her people were

intimately concerned in every resolution which she embraced; and though the example of successful rebellion,
especially in a neighbouring country, could nowise be
agreeable to any sovereign, yet Mary's imprudence had
been so great, perhaps her crimes so enormous, that the insurrection of subjects, after such provocation, could . no
longer be regarded as a precedent against other princes;
that it was first necessary for Elizabeth to ascertain, in a regular and satisfactory manner, the extent of Mary's guilt,
and thence to determine the degree of protection which she
ought to afford her against her discontented subjects; that
as no glory could surpass that of defending oppressed innocence, it was equally infamous to patronise vice and murder
on the throne; and the contagion of such dishonour would
extend itself to all who countenanced or supported it; and
that, if the crimes of the Scottish princes should, on inquiry, appear as great and certain as was affirmed and believed, every measure against her, which policy should
dictate, would thence be justified; or if she should be found
innocent, every enterprise, which friendship should inspire
would be acknowledged laudable and glorious.

Agreeably to these views, Elizabeth resolved to proceed
in a seemingly generous, but really cautious, manner with
the Queen of Scots; and she immediately sent orders to
Lady Scrope, sister to the Duke of Norfolk, a lady who
lived in the neighbourhood, to attend on that princess.
Soon after, she dispatched to her Lord Scrope himself,
warden of the marches, and Sir Francis Knolles, vice-
chamberlain. They found Mary already lodged in the castle of Carlisle; and, after expressing the Queen's sympathy with her in her late misfortunes, they told her, that
her request of being allowed to visit their sovereign, and of
being admitted to her presence, could not at present be
complied with: till she had cleared herself of her husband's murder, of which she was so strongly accused.
Elizabeth could not, without dishonour, show her any

countenance, or appear indifferent to the assassination of so
near a kinsman. So unexpected a check threw Mary into
tears; and the necessity of her situation extorted from her
a declaration, that she would willingly justify herself to
her sister from all imputations, and would submit her cause
to the arbitration of so good a friend. Two days after she
sent Lord Herries to London, with a letter to the same purpose.

This concession, which Mary could scarcely avoid without an acknowledgment of guilt, was the point expected
and desired by Elizabeth: she immediately dispatched
Midlemore to the Regent of Scotland; requiring him both
to desist from the farther prosecution of his Queen's party,
and send some persons to London to justify his conduct
with regard to her. Murray might justly be startled at
receiving a message so violent and imperious: but as his
domestic enemies were numerous and powerful, and England was the sole ally which he could expect among foreign nations, he was resolved rather to digest the affront,
than provoke Elizabeth by a refusal. He also considered,
that though that Queen had hitherto appeared partial to
Mary, many political motives evidently engaged her to support the king's cause in Scotland; and it was not to be
doubted but so penetrating a Princess, would in the end discover this interest, and would at least afford him a patient
and equitable hearing. He therefore replied, that he would
himself take a journey to England, attended by other commissioners; and would willingly submit the determination
of his cause to Elizabeth.

Lord Herries now perceived that his mistress had advanced too far in her concessions; he endeavoured to maintain, that Mary could not, without diminution of her royal
dignity, submit to a contest with her rebellious subjects
before a foreign prince; and he required either present aid
from England, or liberty for his queen to pass over into
France. Being pressed, however, with the former agree-

ment before the English council, he again renewed his
consent; but in a few days he began anew to recoil; and
it was with some difficulty he was brought to acquiesce in
the first determination. These fluctuations, which were
incessantly renewed, shewed his visible reluctance to the
measures pursued by the court of England.

The Queen of Scots discovered no less aversion to the
trial proposed; and it required all the artifice and prudence
of Elizabeth to make her persevere in the agreement to
which she at first consented. This latter princess still said to
her, that she desired not, without Mary's consent or approbation, to enter into the question, and pretended only, as a friend,
to hear her justification: that she was confident there would
be found no difficulty in refuting all the calumnies of her
enemies; and even if her apology should fall short of
full conviction, Elizabeth was determined to support her
cause, and procure her some reasonable terms of accommodation; and that it was never meant that she should be
cited to a trial on the accusation of her rebellious subjects;
but, on the contrary, that they should be summoned to
appear, and to justify themselves for their conduct towards
her. Allured by these plausible professions, the Queen of
Scots agreed to vindicate herself by her own commissioners,
before commissioners appointed by Elizabeth.

During these transactions, Lord Scrope and Sir Francis
Knolles, who resided with Mary at Carlisle, had leisure to
study her character, and make report of it to Elizabeth.
Unbroken by her misfortunes, resolute in her purpose,
active in her enterprises, she aspired to nothing but victory; and was determined to endure any extremity, to undergo any difficulty, and to try every fortune, rather than
abandon her cause, or yield the superiority to her enemies.
Eloquent, insinuating, affable; she had already convinced
all those who approached her, of the innocence of her past
conduct; and as she declared her fixed purpose to require
aid of her friends all over Europe, and even to have recourse

to infidels and barbarians, rather than fail of vengeance
against her persecutors, it was easy to foresee the danger to
which her charms, her spirit, her address, if allowed to ope-
rate with their full force, would expose them.   The court of
England, therefore, who, under pretence of guarding her,
had already, in effect, detained her prisoner, was determined to watch her with greater vigilance.   As Carlisle,
by its situation on the borders, afforded her great opportunities of contriving her escape, they removed her to Bolton,
a seat of Lord Scrope's, in Yorkshire; and the issue of the
controversy between her and the Scottish nation was
regarded as a subject more momentous to Elizabeth's
security and interests than it had hitherto been apprehended.

NOTE.

FROM the foregoing relation of Hume, the reader will perceive, that Elizabeth was inadvertently, and really in self defence, compelled to detain Mary prisoner. It should be recollected, that the fires at Smithfield were scarcely extinguished when she mounted the throne—thousands of Papists only waited for a rallying point to overthrow her and the Protestant religion. The streets of Paris were yet drenched with the blood of Protestants; and Mary's hopes centred in the assistance she expected from the bloody house of Guise. How then could the Queen of England be censurable for using the means which Providence placed at her disposal for averting the plans of her vengeful enemies?

But let us look at Mary now at the bar, charged with the murder of her husband. As Buchanan was living in the verge of the court, at the period now written of, I allow that eminent scholar to open the case with his work, named, a Detection of the Actions of Mary Queen of Scots.

WHEREAS of things judicially determined within a dominion, to have an account demanded by strangers, is, to such as are not subject to foreign jurisdiction, both strange, and also for the strangeness displeasant. To us, above all other, it ought to be most grievous, who are driven to this strait of necessity, that whose faults we desire to cover, their lives we are forced to accuse, unless we ourselves will be accounted the most wicked persons that live*. But a great part of this grief is relieved by your equity (most excellent queen!) who take it no less displeasantly to see your kinswoman, than we to see our Queen thus in speech of all men to be so dishonourably reported of; who also are for your part no less desirous to understand the truth, than we for ours to avoid slander. Therefore we will knit up the matter as briefly as possibly may be, and declare it with such shortness, as we may rather seem to have lightly run over the chief points, than to have largely expressed them, beginning at the Queen's first inconstancy. For as in making of her marriage, her lightness was very headlong and rash, so suddainly followed either inward repentance, or at least outward tokens of change of her affection, without any causes appearing. For whereas the King in former time was not only neglected, but also unworthily used, at length began open hatred to break out against him, especially in that winter, when he went to Peble with a small train, even too mean for a private man, not being sent thither a hawking, but commanded away into a corner, far from counsel, or knowledge of public affairs. Neither is it necessary to put in writing those things, which as they were then a spectacle noted of all men's eyes; so now, as a fresh image, they remain imprinted in all men's hearts. And though this were the beginning of all the evils that fol-

* It is to be understood, that Buchanan drew up this Detection under the auspices, and at the request, of the Lords and Murray, with whom Buchanan had acted against the Queen.—Editor.

low'd, yet at the first their practices were secret, so as not
only the common people, but also such as were right familiar and present at the doing of many matters, could not
understand throughly, what thing the Queen then chiefly
intended.

At the last, about the month of April, in the year 1566,
when the Queen was returned from Dunbar to Edinburgh,
and lodged in the castle, she kept there till the time of her
travail of child. After her deliverance, immediately the
secret counsels of the intended mischief began to break out,
the effect whereof was this, To dispatch away the King by
one means or other howsoever, and to marry with Bothwell;
and, that herself should not be touched with suspicion of
the murder, she began secretly, by little and little, to sow
seeds of dissention between the King and the Lords that
were then at court, still more and more inflaming them to
bring the matter to deadly feud. And if at any time she
espied the suspicions of the one against the other to languish, immediately, with new reports to both parts, she
whetted them on again to fresh displeasures, persuading the
nobility against the King, and the King against the nobility, that each intended others destruction. And she thought
nothing so long as to see the matter come to strokes, not
caring whether of them obtain'd the victory; for she accounted the loss on either side for her advantage, as hoping
thereby to advance forward one degree nearer to that which
she intended. Finally, In short time she so filled their
hearts with mutual jealousies one against another, that
there was not a man of any reputation in the court, but was
driven to this necessity, either with dishonour to yield to
rumours feigned against him, or to enter into combat with
the reporters, or to withdraw him home. And though we
shall pass over the rest, having desire to haste to the chief
point of the matter, yet this one notable slanderous practice at that time, is not to be omitted: for on a time when
the King had been in talk with the Queen, till the night

was far spent; the sum, in a manner, of all her communication was, that almost all the nobility had conspired his death, and were devising how to dispatch him. After the King's departure from her, she sent forthwith for the Earl of Murray her brother, who after was Regent, with this message, That the matter was heinous, and necessarily requiring his presence without delay. He being awak'd out of sound sleep, in great fear, cast a night-gown over his shirt, and as he was half-naked, ran to her in haste. To him she used even the like talk as she had then before to the King, informing him, That the King boiled in such deadly hatred against him, and took it so displeasantly that he stood so highly in her grace, that he was fully determined, so soon as any possible opportunity served, to murder him. So, as much as in her lay, she left no means unassay'd to set them together by the ears; and, without all doubt, had done it indeed, if it had not been God's good pleasure to deliver the innocent persons from so perilous treasons, and to disclose her wicked treachery.

When this attempt failed her, she assay'd the young and unexperienced gentleman with a new subtil practice. She earnestly laboured with him, that while she was great with child, he should chuse him some young gentlewoman, whereof there was great store. whose company he might use in the mean time. She promised him her assent and furtherance, with pardon and leave to commit the offence. She named to him the Earl of Murray's wife; not for that she esteemed that most noble Lady most apt for such a villainy, but because she thought by that way to be revenged of three enemies at once, the King, the Earl, and his wife, and therewithal to win a colour and cause of divorce, to make empty bed-room for Bothwell. After she was delivered of child, though she courteously entertained all others, yet as oft as word was brought her that the King was come to see her, both she and her company so framed their speech and countenance, as if they seemed to fear nothing more

than that the King should not perceive that they loath'd
him, and that his coming and presence was displeasant to
them all. On the other side, Bothwell alone was all in all;
he alone was governour of all her counsels, and all her affairs: and so desirous was the Queen to have her hearty
affection towards him understood of all men, that if any
suit were to be made towards her, there was no way of
speeding for any man, but by Bothwell, to obtain it.

Not long after her deliverance, on a day very early, accompanied with very few that were privy of her counsel,
she went down to the water-side, at the place called the
New Haven; and while all marvelled whither she went in
such haste, she suddenly entered into a ship there prepared for her: which ship was provided by William Blacater, Edmond Blacater, Leonard Robertson, and Thomas
Dickson, Bothwell's servants, and famous robbers and py-
rates. With this train of thieves, all honest men wondering
at it, she betook herself to sea, taking not any other with
her, no not of her gentlemen, nor necessary attendants for
common honesty. In Aloe-Castle, where the ship arrived,
how she behaved herself, I had rather every man should
with himself imagine it, than hear me declare it. This one
thing I dare affirm, that in all her words and doings, she
never kept any regard, I will not say of Queen-like majesty, but not of matron-like modesty.

The King, when he heard of this sudden departure of
the Queen, followed her with all the haste that he possibly
could by land, and there overtook her, in purpose and
hoping there to be in her company, and to enjoy the mutual loving fellowship of marriage. But how lovingly he
was received of her, both all they that were present, and
such as have heard them report it, can well remember: for
being scarcely suffered to tarry there a few hours, while his
men and horses baited, he was enforced to get him away in
haste again, on pain of further peril. As for herself, she
pastimed there certain days, if not in princely magnificence,

yet in more than princely, or rather unprincely licentiousness. There went she a hunting, once at a river of Magat,
another time at the forest of Glenartus. There how coyly,
yea how loftily and disdainfully she behaved herself to the
King, what need it be rehearsed, for the thing was openly
done in all men's sight, and continueth imprinted in all
men's memories.

When she was returned to Edinburgh, she took not her
lodging in her own palace, but in a private house next ad-
joining to John Balfours. Thence she removed into another house, where the yearly court, which they call the
Exchequer, was then kept: for this house was larger, and
had pleasant gardens to it, and next to the garden, all along,
a solitary vacant room. But there was another matter
which, more than all these things, specially allured her
thither. There dwelt hard by, one David Chambers, Bothwell's servant, whose back-door adjoyn'd to the garden of
the Queen's lodging. The rest, who guesseth not? for the
Queen herself confessed the matter, both to many others,
and also, namely, to the Regent and his mother. But she
laid all the blame upon my Lady Rerese, a woman of the
most vile unchastity, who had sometime been one of Bothwell's harlots, and then was one of the chief of the Queen's
privy-chamber. By this woman, who now in her age had,
from the gain of whoredom, betaken herself to the craft of
bawdry, was the Queen, as herself said, betray'd: for
Bothwell was brought through the garden into the Queen's
chamber, and there forced her against her will forsooth.
But how much against her will, Dame Rerese betrayed
her, time, the mother of truth, hath disclos'd; for within
few days after, the Queen intending, as I suppose; to requite
force with force, and to ravish him again, sent Dame Rerese (who had herself also before made trial of the man's
strength) to bring him captive unto her highness.

The Queen, with Margaret Carwood, a woman privy to
all her secrets, did let her down by a string over an old wall

into the next garden. But in such warlike affairs, all things
cannot ever be so well foreseen, but that some incommodious chance may overthwartly happen: behold, the string
suddenly broke, and down with a great noise fell Dame.
Rerese, a woman very heavy, both by unwieldy age, and
massy substance. But she, an old beaten soldier, nothing
dismay'd with the darkness of the night, the height of the
wall, nor with the suddenness of the fall, up she getteth
and running to Bothwell's chamber, she gate the door
open, and out of his bed, even out of his wife's arms, half
asleep, half naked, she forcibly brings the man to the
Queen. This manner and circumstances of the deed, not
only the most part of them that then were with the Queen
have confessed, but also George Daglish, Bothwell's chamberlain, a little before he was executed, plainly declared
the same, which his confession still remaineth upon record.

In the mean time, the King being commanded out of
sight, and with injuries and miseries banish'd from her,
kept himself close, with a few of-his-servants, at Sterlin.
For, alas! what should he else do? He could not creep into
any piece of grace with the Queen, nor could get so much
as to maintain his daily necessary expences to maintain his
few servants and horses; and finally, with brawlings, lightly
arising from every small trifle, and by quarrels, usually
pick'd, he was chased out of her presence: yet his heart,
obstinately fixed in loving her, could not be restrained, but
he must needs come back to Edinburgh, on purpose, with
all kind of serviceable humbleness, to get some entry into
her former favour, and to recover the kind society of marriage. Who once again being with most dishonourable disdain excluded, returned from whence he came, there to be-
wail his woful miseries, as in a solitary desart.

Within few days after, when the Queen determined to
go to Jedworth, to the assizes there to be holden, about
the beginning of October, Bothwell maketh his journey

into Liddesdale. There behaving himself neither according to the place whereto he was called, nor according to his nobility of race and estimation, he was wounded by a poor thief, that was himself ready to die, and carried into the Castle called the Hermitage, with great uncertainty of his recovery. When news hereof was brought to Borthwick to the Queen, she flingeth away in haste like a mad woman, by great journeys in post, in the sharp time of winter, first to Melrose, and then to Jedworth. There, though she heard sure news of his life, yet her affection, impatient of delay, could not temper itself, but needs she must bewray her outrageous lust, and in an inconvenient time of the year, despising all discommodities of the way and weather, and all dangers of thieves, she betook herself headlong to her journey, with such a company as no man of any honest degree would have adventured his life and his goods among them. Thence she returned again to Jedworth, and with most earnest care and diligence, provideth and prepareth all things to remove Bothwell thither. When he was once brought thither, their company and familiar haunt together, was such as was smally agreeing with both their honours. There, whether it were by their nightly and daily travels, dishonourable to themselves, and infamous among the people, or by some secret providence of God, the Queen fell into such a sore and dangerous sickness, that scarcely there remained any hope of her life.

When the king heard thereof, he hasted in post to Jedworth, to visit the Queen, to comfort her in her weakness, and by all the gentle services that he possibly could, to declare his affection and hearty desire to do her pleasure: So far was it off, that his lodging, and things necessary, were provided for him against his coming (as were wont to be for mean persons) that he found not any one token toward him of a friendly mind. But this was a point of most barbarous inhumanity used against him, that the nobility, and all the officers of the court, that were present, were specially forbidden to do him any reverence at all at his coming, nor to yield him their lodging, nor to harbour him so much as for one night.   And whereas the Queen suspected that the Earl of Murray, which afterward was Regent, would shew him courtesy, she practised with his wife to go home in haste, and feign herself sick, and keep her bed, that at least by this colour, under pretence of her sickness, the King might be shut out of doors.   Being thus denied all duties of civil kindness, the next day, with great grief of heart, he returned to his old solitary corner.   In the mean time, while the King in that want of all things, and forsaken of all friends, scarce with begging findeth room in a cottage, Bothwell, out of the house where he was lodged before, as it were in triumph over the King, was gloriously removed, in sight of the people, into the Queen's own lodging, and there laid in a lower parlour, directly under the chamber where the Queen herself lay sick.   There, while they both were yet feeble and unhealed, she of her disease, and he of his wound, the Queen being very weak of her body, yet visited him daily.   And when they were both a little recovered, and their strengths not yet fully settled, they returned to their old pastime again, and that so openly, as they seemed to fear nothing more, than lest their wickedness should be unknown.

About the 5th day of November, being removed from Jedworth to a town called Calco, there she received letters from the King: which when she had read in presence of the Regent, the Earl of Huntley, and the Secretary, she cast a piteous look, and miserably tormented herself, as if she would have immediately fallen down again into her former sickness; and she plainly and expressly protested, that unless she might, by some means or other, be dispatched of the King, she should never have one good day: and if by no other way she could attain it, rather than she would abide to live in such sorrow, she would slay herself.

Within few days after, while in her return through

Marchland she lay at Coldingham, Dame Rerese passed through the watch, and was known, and let go. What company she had, and whither she went at that time of the night, it was not unknown to the Queen. From thence, about the end of November, she came to Cragmiller, a castle about two miles from Edinburgh, there, in the presence of the Earl of Murray (who afterward was Regent, and now is himself also slain) and of the Earls of Huntley 'and Argyle, and the Secretary, she fell into her said former discourse, and also added the most commodious way, as she thought, how it might be brought to pass, that is, to sue a divorce against the King. And she doubted not but that it might be easily obtained, forasmuch as they were the one to the other in such degree of consanguinity, as by the Pope's law might not marry together, especially (which was easy for her to do) the Bull being conveyed away, whereby the same law was dispensed with. Here when one had cast a doubt, that if she should go that way to work, their son should be made a bastard, being born out of lawful wedlock, especially, sith neither of his parents were ignorant of the causes whereby the marriage should be void.

When she had tossed this answer a while in her mind, and knew that he said truth, and that she durst not as yet disclose her purpose to make away her son, she gave over that devise of divorce, and yet from that day forward, she never ceased to pursue her intention of murdering the King, as may easily be perceived by that which followed.

The King being returned from Sterline to Cragmillar, when he hoped to have found her more gentle toward him, and her displeasure by process of time somewhat appeased, he so found no token of change of her affection, that he was not allowed any thing for his daily sustenance, unless he kept him still at Sterline. Which thing exceedingly increased the people's suspicion, otherwise of itself already

enough inclined to that judgment, of the unchast company
of the Queen with Bothwell.

About the beginning of December, when there were
embassadours came out of France and England, to the
christening of the King that now is: that Bothwell might
be seen gorgiously arrayed among the nobility, she herself
laid out the money to buy him apparel, and some she bought
herself of the merchants for him, and she so applied herself, with such diligence in overseeing the making thereof,
as if she had been, I will not say his wife, but even his
servant.   In the mean time, her lawful husband, at the
christning of his own child, not only wanted all her maintenance for his necessary expences, but also was commanded
not once to come in the embassadours sight; his ordinary
servants were removed from him; the nobility were en-
joyned not once to attend on him, nor to do him honour,
nor in a manner to know him: the foreign embassadours
were warned not to talk with him, when as the most part
of the day they were in the castle where he was.

The young gentleman, thus contemptuously and unkindly
used, fell in such despair, that he departed from Sterline
and went to Glasgow to his father.   At his departure, the
Queen still pursued him with her wonted hatred.   All his
silver plate, wherewith he was served from his marriage till
that day, she took it away every whit, and appointed pew-
ter in the stead thereof.   But let this serve only to prove her
contempt of him: the rest that followed are evident arguments of outragious cruelty and unappeasable hatred.   Before he had passed a mile from Sterline, all the parts of his
body were taken with such a sore ach, as it might easily
appear, that the same proceeded not of the force of any
sickness, but by plain treachery.   The tokens of which
treachery, certain black pimples, so soon as he was come
to Glasgow, brake out over all his whole body, with so
great ach and such pain throughout all his limbs, that he

lingered out his life with very small hope of escape: and yet all this while, the Queen would not suffer so much as a physician once to come at him.

After the ceremonies of the christening ended, she practised with her brother, the Earl of Murray, that when he should go to conduct the Earl of Bedford, the Queen of England's embassadour, to St. Andrewes, he should require Bothwell also to bear him company: who, indeed, freely promised so to do; howbeit, both he and the Queen, the deviser of that dissimulation, thought nothing less, as the success showed. For so soon as the King was gone to Glasgow, and the rest towards St. Andrewes, she with her Bothwell got her to Drumen, and from thence to Tylebarn. In which houses, they so passed the time about eight days, in every corner, and in familiar haunting together, as all (saving themselves alone, that had thrown away all shame) were highly offended with their contempt and vile regard of public fame, seeing them now not once to seek to cover their filthy wickedness.

When about the beginning of January, they were returned to Sterline, she began to find fault with the house wherein her son was nursed, as incommodious, because it stood in a cold and moist place, dangerous for bringing the child to a rheume. But it shall easily appear, that this was done for other purpose, forasmuch as all these faults, that she pretended were not in that house, but were indeed in the other house to which the child was removed, being set in a low place, being a very marsh. The child being scarcely above six months old, in the deep of a sharp winter, was conveyed to Edinburgh. There, because the first attempt prevailed not, and the force of the poyson was overcome by strength of nature, that at length yet she might bring forth that wherewith she had so long travailed, she entreth into new devises for the murder of the King.

Herself goeth to Glasgow, she pretendeth the cause of her journey to be to see the King alive, whose death she had continually gaped for the whole moneth before. But what was indeed the true cause of that journey, each man may plainly perceive by her letters to Bothwell. Being now out of care of her son, whom she had in her own ward, bending herself to the slaughter of her husband, to Glasgow she goeth, accompanied with the Hamiltons, and other the King's natural enemies.

Bothwell (as it was agreed on between them before) provideth all things ready, that were needful to accomplish that hainous act; first of all, a house not commodious for a sick man, nor comely for a King, for it was both torn and ruinous, and had stood empty without any dweller for divers years before; in a place of small resort, between the old fallen walls of two churches, near a few alms-houses for poor beggars. And that no commodious means for committing that mischief might be wanting, there was a postern door in the town-wall hard by the house, whereby they easily might pass away into the fields. In chusing of the place, she would needs have it thought, that they had respect to the wholesomeness thereof. And to avoid suspicion, that this was a fegined pretence, herself, the two nights next before the day of the murder, lay there in a lower room under the King's chamber. And as she did curiously put off the shews of suspicion from herself, so the execution of the slaughter, she was content to have committed to others. ·

About three days before the King was slain, she practised to set her brother Robert and him at deadly enmity, making account that it should be gain to her, which soever of them both had perished. For matter to ground their dissention, she made rehearsal of the speech the King had had with her, that concerning her brother. And when they both so grew in talk, as the one seemed to charge the other with the lie; at last they were in a manner come from words to blows. But while they were both laying their hands on their weapons, the Queen, feigning as though she had been marvellously afraid of that which she so earnestly desired, calleth the Earl of Murray, her other brother, to the parting, to this intent, that she might either presently bring him in danger to be slain himself, or in time to come to bear the blame of such mischief as then might have happened. When this way the success fell not out as she desired, she devised a new way to transfer the suspicion from herself.

While the Earl of Murray did willingly keep himself from the court, and had reasonable excuse for his absence, for that his wife being near her time, was besides that always very sick: at the same time there was an ambassa-. dor come from the Duke of Savoy. This the Queen took for a convenient colour to send for her brother: but the true cause of her sending for him was, that she had a desire to throw the suspicion of the King's murder upon him, and upon the Earl Moreton, and therewithal also at once to procure the destruction of those two, being men acceptable to the peril, and likewise adversaries to her practice, who intended to set up a tyrannical government: but God's good clemency, that had oft before delivered the Earl of Murray from many treasons of his enemies, did then also manifestly succour him; for upon the Sunday, which was the ninth day of February, when he was going to church, to hear a sermon, a letter was brought him, that his wife was delivered before her time, and in very small hope of life. When he, being dismayed at this sudden news, desired leave of the Queen to depart; she answered, that if the cause were so, it were a superfluous journey for him to go to her, being not able to do her any good in her sickness. But he being still the more importunate, she prayed him, that he would yet tarry but that one night, and take his journey the next day to his wife. But the mercy of God now, as at many other times, did deliver that innocent gentleman from the present peril, and also took away the occasion of slander against him for the time to come. Howbeit for all this, though there were no cause of suspicion, yet he escaped not free from slander: for Huntley and Bothwell, though they could not justly charge him, yet laboured, by infamous libels, which they spread abroad, to distein him with the most foul spot of that shameful act. And whereas the murder was committed after midnight, they had before day-light caused (by special fore-appointed messengers) rumours to be spread in England, that the Earls of Murray and Moreton were acters of that slaughter. But that rumour, so soon as the light of the truth once brake forth, suddenly vanished away, as other falsehoods are commonly wont to do.

When all things were ready prepared for performing this cruel fact, and yet all occasions cut off to divert the blame thereof, the partners of the conspiracy, fearing lest long delay should either bring some impediment to their purpose, or disclose their counsels, determined to dispatch it in all haste. The Queen therefore for manners sake after supper, goeth up to the King's lodgings. There, being determined to shew him all the tokens of reconciled good will, she spent certain hours in his company, with countenance and talk much more familiar than she had used in six or seven months before. At the coming in of Paris, she broke off her talk, and prepared to depart. This Paris was a young man born in France, and had lived certain years in the houses of Bothwell and Seton, and afterward with the Queen. Whereas the other keys of that lodging were in custody of the King's servants; Paris, by feigning certain fond and slender causes, had in keeping the keys, which Bothwell kept back, of the back gate and the postern. He was in special trust with Bothwell and the Queen, touching their secret affairs. His coming (as it was before agreed among them) was a watchword, that all was ready for the matter. As soon as the Queen saw him, she rose up immediately, and feigning another cause to depart, she said, alas! I have much offended toward Sebastian this day, that I appeared not in a mask at his marriage. This Sebastian was an Arvernois, a man in great favour with the Queen for his cunning in music, and his merry jesting, and was married the same day. The King thus left, in a manner, alone in a desolate place, the Queen departeth, accompanied with the Earls of Argyle, Huntley, and Cassilis, that attended upon her. After that she was come into her chamber after midnight, she was in long talk with Bothwell, none being present but the captain of her guard. And when he also withdrew himself, Bothwell was there left alone without other company, and shortly after retired into his own chamber. He changed his apparel, because he would be unknown of such as met him; and put on a loose cloak, such as the Swartrytters wear, and so went forward through the watch, to execute his intended traiterous fact. The whole order of the doing thereof, may be easily understood by their confessions, which were put to death for it.

Bothwell, after the deed was ended that he went about, returned, and as if he had been ignorant of all that was done, he got him to bed. The Queen in the mean time, in great expectation of the success, how finely she played her part (as she thought) it is marvel to tell. For she not once stirred at the noise of the fall of the house, which shook the whole town ; nor at the fearful outcries that followed, and confused cries of the people, (for I think there happened to her not any new thing unlooked for) till Bothwell feigning himself afraid, rose again out of his bed, and came to her with the Earls of Argyle, Huntley, and Athole ; and with the wives of the Earls of Athole and Murray, and with the Secretary. There, while the monstrous chance was in telling, while every one wondered at the thing, that the King's lodgings was even from the very foundation blown up into the air, and the King himself slain. In this amazedness and confused fear of all sorts of persons, only that same heroic heart of the Queen maintained itself so far from casting herself down into base lamentations and tears, unbeseeming the royal name, blood, and estate; that she marched, or rather far surmounted all credit of the constancy of any in former times. This also proceeded of the same nobility of courage, that she set out the greater part of them that were about her, to inquire out the manner of the doing, and commanded the souldiers that watched to follow, and she herself, settled herself to rest, with a countenance so quiet, and mind so untroubled, that she sweetly slept till the next day at noon. But lest she should appear void of all naturalness at the death of her husband, by little and little, at length she kept her close, and proclaimed a mourning not long to endure.

The common people, not certainly knowing whether she laughed or lamented, were divided into sundry imaginations, sith it was perilous dealing with the disguising of the court, either in knowing it to seem to mock it, or in not cunningly dissembling to seem to know it. While some talked of one sort, some of another, in the mean time, of any enquiry to be had of the murder, there was no mention made at all. At length, the day following, in the afternoon, when both shame and fear constrained them thereto, Bothwell, the principal doer of the vile act, with certain others that were privy to the same, assembled together with the Earl of Argyle, for that he is by inheritance the Justice to deal with crimes punishable by death. First, as though they had been utterly ignorant of all that ever was done, they begin to wonder at the strangeness of the matter, such as never was heard of, and incredible. Then they begin a little to be busy about their enquiry, they sent for a few poor silly women that dwelt thereabout. Which, poor souls, standing in doubt whether it were better for them to tell, or hold their peace, though they daintily tempered their speech, yet when they had blabbed out somewhat more than the Judges looked for, they were dismissed again as fools that had but undiscretly prated. For their testimonies, though they touched some folks shrewdly, yet they were such as they might easily set light by.

Then were called and examined the King's servants, that were of his houshold, such as were left undestroyed by that cruel chance. They denyed that they had the keys in keeping. Being examined who had them, they said, the Queen. So the enquiry (for manners sake) was adjourned, but indeed suppressed, for fear lest if they proceeded further, the secrets of the court might hap to be disclosed. Yet lest the matter should seem not to be regarded, out goeth a Proclamation with rewards promised to him that could give information of it. But who durst accuse the Queen? or (which was in manner more perilous) who durst detect Bothwell of such an horrible offence? Especially when he himself was both doer, judge, inquirer, and examiner? Yet this fear, which stopped the mouths of every man in particular, could not restrain the whole multitude in general. For both by books set out, and by pictures, and by cries in the dark night, it was so handled, that the doers of that mischievous fact might easily understand, that those secrets of theirs were come abroad. And when every man was now out of doubt, who did the murder, and who gave furtherance unto it, the more that they laboured to keep their own names undisclosed, so much the more the people's grudge, (being restrained) broke out the more openly.

Though they took upon them, as if they regarded not these things, yet, sometime the rumours so inwardly pricked them to the quick, that they could by no means hide their anger. Therefore, discontinuing their searching for the King's death, they begin a new enquiry, far more earnest, against the authors of books, and the slanders of Bothwell, as they themselves termed them. These examinations were so rigorously put in execution, as neither money, nor labour of men nor horses was spared about it. All the painters were called together, all that earned their living by writing, were assembled, to judge of the pictures and books that had been set out. And if any painter had not of his own accord confessed, that it was he of whose work they

enquired, another that was not guilty thereof, but touched
a little with a slight suspition, had suffered for it. There
was published a Proclamation agreeable with the manner
of the Inquisition, wherein it was made death, not only to
set out any such matter, but also to read it, being set out
by another. But these persons, that with threatening of
death practised to stop the speech of the people, yet not satisfied with the most cruel murder of the King, ceased not
their hatred against him when he was dead. All his goods,
armour, horses, apparel, and other furniture of his house,
the Queen divided, some to them that slew him, and some
to his father's ancient deadly foes, as if they had upon at-
tainder come to her by forfeiture, and his father's tenants,
as though they had been also part of our conquered booty,
she so scraped, till she brought them in a manner to extream
beggary.

But this was a strange example of cruelty, and such as
never was heard of before, that as she had satisfied her
heart with his slaughter, so she would needs feed her eyes
with the sight of his body slain. For she long beheld, and
not only without grief, but also with greedy eyes, his dead
corpse, the goodliest corpse of any gentleman that ever
lived in this age. And then suddenly, without any funeral
honour, in the night-time, by common carriers of dead bodies, upon a vile bier, she caused him to be buried hard by
David Rizo. When these doings were known abroad, and
that the indignation of the people had overcome the threat-
enings of penalties, and the frankness of sorrow surmounted
fear, by little and little she began to set her face, and with
counterfeiting of mourning, she laboured to appease the
hearts of the grudging people. For where the ancient
manner hath been for Queens, after the death of their husbands, by the space of forty days, not only to forbear the
company of men, but also from looking on the open light,
she attempted a disguised manner of mourning. But the
mirth of heart far passing the feigned sorrow, she shut the

doors indeed, but she set open the windows, and within four days she threw away her wailing weed, and began to behold both sun and open sky again.   But this one thing fell very overthwartly.   For when Henry Killegree was come from the Queen of England to comfort her, as the manner is, this gentleman strangers hap was to mar the play, and unvizor all the disguising.   For when he was, by the Queen's commandment, come to the court, though he being an old courtier, and a good discreet gentleman, did nothing hastily, yet he came in so unseasonably, ere the stage was prepared and furnished, that he found the windows open, the candles not yet lighted, and all the provision for the play out of order.   When of the forty days that are appointed for the mourning, scarce twelve were yet fully past and the counterfeiting would not frame half handsomely, and to disclose her true affections so soon she was somewhat ashamed, at length taking heart of grace unto her, and neglecting such trifles, she cometh to her own bias, and openly sheweth her own natural conditions.

She posteth to Seton's house, with a very few, and those not all of the saddest company.   There Bothwell, though it seemed, that for the great favour he then had in court, and for the nobility of his birth, and other respects of honour, he should have been, next after the Queen, most honourably received, yet was lodged in a chamber hard by the kitchen.   Howbeit the same was a place not altogether unfit to assuage their sorrows, for it was directly under the Queen's chamber: and if any sudden qualm of grief should have happened to come over her heart, there was a pair of stairs, though somewhat narrow, yet wide enough for Bothwell to get up to comfort her.

In the mean time, after the rumour hereof was spread into France, Monsieur de Croc, who had often before been Ambassador in Scotland, came in suddenly upon them, God wot, full unseasonably.   By his advice she returned to Edinburgh, out of that den which, even as far as France, was

infamous. But in Seton's house were so many commodious
opportunities for her purpose, that howsoever her good name
were thereby impaired, needs she must go thither again.
There were counsels holden of the great affairs of the realm.
The end of the consultation was, that Bothwell should be
arrained of the murder, and acquit by judges thereto chosen
for the purpose, and constrained. It was concluded, That
the meaner sort of the judges might with favour and fair
promises be led, and the rest of the greater and graver sort
(whom for fashion's sake they were driven to call to the
matter) might be drawn with fear to acquit him. For beside libels thereof commonly thrown abroad, the King's father, the Earl of Lennox, did openly accuse him for principal author of the murder.

The assembly of the States in Parliament was at hand,
which was to be holden the thirteenth of April, before
which day they would needs have the arraignment dispatched. That great haste was the cause why, in that
proceeding and trial, nothing has been done according to
the form of law, nothing in order, nothing after the ancient
usage. There ought to have been public summons of the
accusers, the next of the kin, the wife, the father, and the
son, either to be present themselves, or to send their proc-
tors. The law also gave them time of forty days. But
here the father was commanded to come within thirteen
days, and that without any assembly of his friends, with
his own houshold retinue only, which by reason of his
great poverty, was now brought to a few: while in
the mean time Bothwell, with great bands of men, daily
mustered about the town. And because he verily believed that in so assured peril, no man would take upon him
to be his accuser, he grew to such a negligence, and such contempt of law and judicial proceedings, that the indictment
was framed of a murder supposed to be done the ninth day
of February, when indeed the King was slain the tenth day.
In choosing and refusing of the judges, the like severity

was used, for the murderers themselves made the choice of the judges, when there was no man to take exception against them. The Earl of Cassiles, willing rather to pay his amercement, as the manner is, than to be a judge in the matter, when he had stood in it awhile, and would not appear at the Queen's request and menacing, yea, though she sent her ring for credit both of her earnest prayer and threatening, at length, constrained with fear of exile and punishment, he yielded. There sate the judges, not chosen to judge, but picked out to acquit: the cause proceeded without any adversary: a trial in matter of life and death, when there was never an accuser, but subborned by the party accused: so as a man might well think it not the trial of a cause in a court, but the playing of an enterlude upon a stage.

In all this fearlessness of all things, yet behold, I pray you, of what force is the testimony of conscience on either side. Suddainly, unlooked for, there starteth up a young man of the Earl of Lennox house, in whom the respect of duty vanquished the fear of danger. This young man made an open protestation, that the same assembly of judges was not lawful, because in their proceeding there was nothing done according to law nor order. At this saying the judges were all stricken in such a fear, that they all, by and by, with one accord made protestation, with proviso, that it should not hereafter be prejudicial to them, in that they had acquitted a prisoner whom no man accused, and that they had acquitted him of a murder alledged to be committed on the ninth day of February, when the King was slain the tenth day. This is that same noble tryal and judgment, whereby Bothwell was not cleansed of the crime, but as it were washed with Sowter's blacking, and so more comly prepared to go a wooing to wed the Queen, and so to become a husband to her greater shame, than when he was before an adulterer. To make up yet the full perfection and encrease of this jolly acquital, there was set up a writing in the most notorious place of the court, that though Bothwell had by just trial and judgment been lawfully cleared and acquitted of the murder, whereof he had been falsely accused, yet for more manifest declaration of his innocency to the whole world, he was ready to try it in combat, if any man of good fame, and a gentleman born, would charge him with the murder of the King.

The next day after, there was one that set up a bill in open place, and offered to accept the combat, so that there might for the battel be such a place appointed, wherein the party might safely without fear disclose his name.

While matters and mens affections were in this stir, the parliament assembled. Thereafter they had for eight days together, in manner done nothing but treated of reversing the judgment, whereby the Earl Huntley's father had been attainted of treason, and for restoring the son to his father's possessions and honours: there were also certain plausible things granted to please the people, and specially for the church, namely, the repealing of certain laws of Popish tyranny, made for punishing of such as durst once mutter against the decree of the see of Rome.

Though these things were acceptable among the commonalty, yet there remained one thing which no less vexed the Queen, than offended the people, that is to say, her company with Bothwell, not altogether so openly as she would fain have had it, and yet not so secretly, but that the people perceived it, for that all men's eyes were gaping upon them. For whereas Bothwell had a wife of his own, and to tarry for a divorce, was thought an overlong delay, and in the mean time the Queen could neither openly avow to have him, nor secretly enjoy him, and yet in no wise could be without him: some shift, though not an honest one, yet a shift, forsooth, must be devised; and when they could not think upon a better, it seemed to them a marvellous fine invention, God wot, that Bothwell should ravish and take away the Queen by force, and so save her honour.

So within a few days after, as the Queen was returning from Sterline, Bothwell forceably took her by the way, and carried her to Dunbar; whether with her will, or against her will, every man may easily perceive by her own letters, that she wrote to him by the way as she was in her journey. But howsoever it were, that the wrong of the ravishment might be defaced with honest colour of marriage, Bothwell's wife was compelled in two courts to sue a divorce against her husband.

Before judges delegate, appointed by the Queen's authority to have jurisdiction in such causes, the wife accuseth the husband of adultery, which with them was a just cause of divorce. Before Popish judges, who indeed by law were forbidden, yet by special dispensation of the Bishop of St. Andrew, were for the hearing of this cause only permitted: Bothwell was accused, that before his marriage with his wife, he had committed fornication with his wife's near kinswoman: howbeit all this while they kept close the Pope's bull, by which the same offence was dispensed with. The divorce was posted forward without any slackness either in the witnesses, or in the judges. Within the space of ten days, the matter was taken in hand, began, and intended, joyned unto, tryed, and judged, before both the companies of judges. When the sentence of divorce was given, and sent to Dunbar, Bothwell by and by assembleth together from all parts, all his friends, his servants, and retainers, to convey to Edinburgh the Queen, who would then needs take upon her to be a prisoner.

When that they were thus gathered together, the most part of them in armour, by the way, as they were conducting the Queen, many of them were suddenly stricken in some fear, lest, in time to come, they might be charged for holding the Queen as prisoner; and although there were no other evidence, yet this one thing would be proof enough against them, that in time of peace they were found armed about her. While they were in this doubt, in the midst of

their journey, they all threw away their launces, and in
mcre peaceable array, at least in shew, they conveyed her
to the Castle of Edinburgh, which castle was also the
same time at Bothwell's commandment. There she tarried
with Bothwell while the banes were publishing. Then
she came down out of the castle into the town, to the common assembly of the judges, and there pronounced herself
to be free at her own liberty. And so at length, within
eight days, she finished that unmatrimonial matrimony, all
good men so far detesting, or at least grudgingly forejudging
the unlucky end thereof, that Monsieur de Croc, the French
King's embassadour, a man very well affectioned to the
Queen, one of the faction of the house of Guise, and so-
journing very near to the place, though he were earnestly
required, yet he thought he could not with his honour be
present at the feast.

These things were done about the 25th of May, in the
year of our Lord 1567. The 25th day of June following,
Bothwell, being either dismaid with a guilty conscience of
the vile fact, or sent away by the Queen, she came herself
to the Lords of the realm, who earnestly required the public King-murderer to be brought forth to due execution.
What hath been done since pertaineth not much to the present matter. And though my speech have been, perhaps,
longer than you looked for, yet I plainly perceive in myself, that, while I seek to make an end of my tale, I have
omitted, and many things for haste I have but lightly
touched; and nothing have I, according to the heinousness
of the offence, fully expressed.

SEEING these things are by writings and witnesses so
probable, and stick so fast imprinted in the knowledge of
all the people, that such as would have them most hidden,
cannot deny them: what place is here left for cunning, or

what need can be of diligence, to prove or reprove a thing
so plain and évident? For all things are so clear, so manifest, and so mutually knit together, each part to strength-
en each other, that there is no need of foreign probations;
and all things so fully witnessed, that there is no necessity
of other arguments. For if any will ask me, as in other
matters is used to be ask'd, the causes of so foul a fact, I
might also likewise ask of him, sith the time, the place,
the deed, and the author is sufficiently known, to what purpose is it to stand upon searching the causes, or to
enquire by what means it was atchieved? Again, when
there be extant so many causes of hatred, and so many
tokens thereof, which do offer themselves to knowledge,
as may well be able to bring even things uncertain to
be believed, surely so far-fetched an explication of the
act committed may right well seem superfluous. Nevertheless, for as much as so great is the impudence of the vile
offenders in denying, and so confident the boldness of im-
pudent persons in lying, let us assay to see with what weapons truth is able to defend innocency against those wicked
monsters. If then they demand the cause of so heinous a
deed, I answer, it was unappeasable hatred: I demand of
them again, if they can deny that such hatred was, or that
the same hatred was so great, as without blood could not
be satisfied? If they can deny that such hatred was, then
let them answer me, why she, a young woman, rich, noble, and finally a Queen, thrust away from her, in a manner, the young gentleman into exile, he being beautiful,
near of her kin, of the blood royal, and (that which is
greatest) entirely loving her, in the deep of sharp winter,
into places neither fruitful of things necessary, nor replen-
ished with inhabitants, and commonly perilous, being
haunted with thieves? Why sent she him away into desart
and craggy mountains, without provision, into open perils,
and in a manner without any company? What could she
more have done, if she had most deadly hated him, and

covenanted to have him dispatched? But I trow, she feared
no such thing. But that voidness of fear, I construe to be
a note of most obstinate hatred, especially sith she both
knew the places, and was not ignorant of the dangers.
That husband, therefore, to whom she was but lately married, against the liking of her subjects, against the will of
their friends on both sides, without whom she could not
endure, whom she scarcely durst suffer out of her sight;
him, I say, she thrust forth to uncertain death, and most
certain perils.

. Will ye ask of me the causes of the change of her affection? What if I say, I knew them not? It sufficeth for
my purpose to prove that she hated him. What if I ask
again, why she so extremely loved the young man whom
she never saw before? Why she so hastily married him,
and so unmeasurably honoured him? Such are the natures
of some women, especially such as cannot brook the
greatness of their own good fortune; they have vehement affections both ways; they love with excess, and
hate without measure; and to what side soever they bend,
they are not governed by advised reason, but carried by
violent motion. I could, out of the monuments of antiquity, rehearse innumerable examples; but of herself, I
had rather believe herself.

Call to mind that part of her letters to Bothwell, wherein
she maketh herself Medea, that is a woman that neither in
love nor hatred can keep any mean. I could also alledge
other causes of her hatred, although indeed not reasonable
causes, yet such as are able to shove forward, and to push
headlong an outrageous heart which is not able to govern
itself.

But herein I will forbear: and, if herself will suffer me,
howsoever she hath deserved of her subjects, yet, so much
as the common cause will permit, I will spare her honour; yea, I will spare it more than the cause will allow
me.

†Therefore I omit her other causes of hatred, and return this; that she hated, and not meanly hated him.

Will you see also another proof of her hatred? The tender wife, forsooth, so loving and fond of him, when she could not do him the duty of a wife, offereth to do him the service of a bawd: she made choice of her own brother's wife to put to him in her place.

What shall we think to be the cause of this so sudden change? She that of late gapingly sought for every small breath of suspicion against her husband, and, where true causes were not to be found, she invented such as were manifestly false; and this she curiously did, not when she loved him, but when she had begun to hate him; and while she was fishing for occasions to be divorced from him, even she, I say, of her own accord, offereth him a lover; declareth her own contentation therewith, and promiseth her furtherance.

What can we imagine to be the cause hereof? Was it to please her husband? No, for she hated him; and although she loved him, yet such manner of doing in a woman is uncredible. Was it that he, knowing himself likewise guilty of adultery on his part, might the more willingly bear with a partner in use of his wife? No, for he bare with all perforce against his will. Was it to find cause of divorce, and so to drive him to leave his bed empty for Bothwell? Yea, that it was indeed that she sought for, but yet not that alone; for in this woman you must imagine no single mischief. She hated the Earl Murray's wife, even with such hatred as all unhonest persons hate the honest. The differences of their two fames much vexed her, and therewithal also she coveted to set the good Lady's husband, and the King together by the ears, and so rid herself of two troubles at once.

Thus you see how many and how great things she practised to dispatch, with one labour, her paramour's enemy, the bridler of her licentiousness, and her own

hated husband, she hopeth to rid all at once; while, by
such sundry sorts of wicked doings, she maketh haste to
her most wicked wedding.

To what end tended that fearful hasty calling for the
Earl of Murray, at midnight? Could she not tarry till
day-light? What was the occasion of so sudden fear? The
good woman, God wot, careful for the concord of the nobility, dearly loving her brother, and most dearly loving
her husband, was afraid, forsooth, lest her brother should,
in the night, have been assaulted by the King, whom she
herself had disarmed. Disarmed, said I? yea, she had
disfurnished him of all convenient company for his estate,
and made him to be shaken up with a woman's scolding,
and that by one of her own train, one who was past all
shame, and of prostitute unchastity.

She feared much, lest the young Man, destitute of
friends, beset with all sorts of miseries, should make as-
sault in the night-time. Upon what person? The Queen's
brother, a man of great reputation and power, and in
highest favour with all estates. And where should he
have assaulted him? In a most strong castle; whereupon
the deed being done, neither was way for him to flee, nor
means of refuge to the Queen's mercy. For what cause
should he assail him? there was no enmity between them,
but such as she had sowed. What say you, if she coveted that thing most, which she most feigned herself to
fear: for to what purpose else sent she for her brother to
come to her in the night-time, unarmed? Why did she
not advise him of this one thing at least, that because he
was to pass by, and hard by the King's door, he should
in any wise put on his armour? Why did she not either
forewarn him of the danger, or defer the calling of him
till next morning? No; no, she had a more subtil purpose
in hand. She had but newly sent the King away, inflamed
(as she hoped) with hatred of the Earl of Murray.

So thought she it not unlikely, but that the King,

kindled with fresh displeasure, rash by fervour of youth,
lightly believing her by excess of love, would have adventured to slay his supposed enemy, naked, unaccompanied, and unarmed. So sent she the King, raging in
anger, to commit the slaughter, and practised to draw
the Earl of Murray naked, unaccompanied, unwarned, to
be suddenly trapped in treason. This was her meaning,
this was her desire. But wicked counsels, how subtil
soever they be, are not always prosperous.

What meant this, that after her deliverance of child, at
which time other women do chiefly comfort themselves in
the lovingness of their husbands, and confess that they
find some ease of pain by sight of them, she at the same
time driveth her husband away? What else shall we say
she meant thereby; but, as the Poet saith, for pure love,
God wot, she shut him out of doors. But this tender creature, that either shutteth out her husband, or as soon as he
is come chaseth him away again, whose stomach turned at
the sight of him, who is suddenly taken with pangs at his
presence, when she was in the pinnace amongst pirates and
thieves, she could abide at the poop, and be content to
handle the boisterous cables. Now ask I whom she loved,
and whom she hated? For that at Aloes he drove away the
cumbersome interrupter of her pastime; that again, when
he came to her at Edinburgh, she rejected him, I blame her
not. I am content to believe she did it not for hate to her
husband, but for her fancy's sake; that again at Jedworth
she suffered him not to come at her, let it be borne withal:
for not without cause she feared, lest the force of her sickness would increase at sight of him, whose death she so
earnestly desired. That she gave special commandment
that no man should lodge him, no man should relieve him
with meat or drink, that she in a manner forbad him the
use of fire and water: this is undoubtedly a token of outrageous hatred. But it seemeth she feared the very infection
of her husband, if he were in any place near her.

That she sent him back from Cragmillar to Sterline, I
complain not.   But that she bereaved him of all his neces-
saries, that she took him from his servants, that she abated
the allowance of his expences, that she alienated the nobility from him, that she forbade all strangers the sight of
him, and (as much as in her lay) took from him, even
while he lived, the use of heaven, earth, and air: this, I
say, I know not what to call it, unnaturalness, hatred,
barbarous fierceness, or outrageous cruelty? That when
he went from Sterline, she took away all his plate, let it
be pardoned, for what need had he of silver, that carried
with him present death in his bosom? But this I beseech
you to consider, what great indignation of all men it hath
kindled, that when the King, poor soul, made hard shift
to live in desolation, sorrow, and beggary, whilst that
Bothwell, like an ape in purple, was triumphantly shewed
to the embassadours of foreign nations, even that same
partner of her husband's bed, not so much for the love of
himself, as for despight of her husband, was carried abroad,
set out with all kind of ornaments, even that adulterous
partner, I say, that neither in birth, nor in beauty, nor in
any honest quality, was in anywise comparable with her
disdained husband.   Now let them deny that here were
tokens of hatred.

But how great, and how unappeasable this hatred was,
even by this, ye may gather.   Her husband so oft shut out,
so oft sent away with despight, driven to extreme poverty,
banished into a desolate corner, far from the court, far
from the presence of men, spoiled of his servants and household furniture, bereaved, in a manner, of his daily necessary
sustenance, yet by no injuries can be shaken from her, by
no fear of death can be withdrawn, but with serviceableness and patience he assayeth, if not to overcome, yet at
least somewhat to assuage the violent cruelty of her unkind
courage.   In the meantime, what doth this good gentle-
wife, this merciful Queen, that is at the beholding of men's

miseries so kind and pitiful? Neither is she once moved with the loving doings, nor with the wretched plight, nor with the miserable wofulness of her husband, nor appeased by time, nor satisfied with torments, but rather with his serviceableness she is irritated, with his humble prayers she is more inflamed, and at every time of his coming she deviseth some new increase of spightful dishonour: wherein, when she had spent the uttermost of all her force, wit, and bitterness of nature, when she saw the poor young gentleman, neither to give over by fainting, being oppressed with poverty; and though he were despised of all men, and so often thrown into open peril, neither to despair, nor otherwise, more cruelly, to make away himself; at length, as it were, glutted with the sight of his miseries and torments, she determined presently to rid him of his calamities, herself of irksomeness, and her adulterer from fear, and so, by certain special persons thereto appointed, she caused him to be poysoned, that being absent from her, he might so die with less suspicion. But of the poyson I will say more in another place.

When this practice framed not fully to her desire, she goeth herself to Glasgow, that whom being absent she could not kill, she might herself in presence satisfy both her cruel heart and her eyes with sight of his present miseries. And, as if herself alone were not sufficient to execute the cruel tormenting of him, she bringeth into his sight ministers of her heinous doings, and his ancient natural enemies, and with these outrages travelled to vex his soul at his last breath. But wherefore gather we arguments, as in a doubtful case, when she herself will not suffer us to doubt at all? She, the Queen herself, I say, openly protested, not to her lover in bed, not among her confederates in secret chambers, nor before few and mean persons of estate, apt to flattery, constrained by poverty, or of purpose affectioned; she herself, I say, openly confessed, that she could not live one good day, if she were not rid of the

King; and that not once, nor unadvisedly, but in presence of those personages whom she used to call to counsel in the weightiest affairs.   For it cannot be said, unadvisedly slipped from her, that was so oft spoken, in so many, so far distant places, with tears always added, to move credit, before men notable, both for their nobility, wealth and wisdom, and wherein she declared her own opinion, practised to win their assent, and hearkened for their advices.   But be it that she forged all these things; be it that her tears were feigned; let them not believe it that heard it; let the greatness of the outrage make the report uncredible.   I myself also would gladly be one of that number, to think these things uttered by her, rather to groap the minds of others, than that she herself so thought in her heart, if it were not so, that the thing itself confirmeth the report, that the outragiousness of the doings far surmounteth all bitterness of utterance.

When he was preparing to depart from Glasgow, she caused poison to be given him.   You will ask, by whom? In what manner? What kind of poison? Where had she it? Ask you these questions? As though wicked Princes ever wanted ministers of their wicked treacheries. But still you press me perhaps, and still you ask me who be these ministers? First, that poisoned he was, it is certainly known: for though the shamelessness of men would not stick to deny a thing so manifest, yet the kind of disease, strange, unknown to the people, unacquainted with physicians, especially such as had not been in Italy and Spain, black pimples breaking out over all his body, grievous aches in all his limbs, and intolerable stink disclosed it.   If this cause were to be pleaded before grave Cato the Censor, all this were easy for us to prove before him that was perswaded, that there is no adultress, but the same is also a poisoner.   Need we seek for a more substantial witness than Cato, every of whose sentences antiquity esteemed as so many oracles? Shall we not in a manifest thing believe him whose credit hath in things doubtful so oft prevailed? Lo here a man of singular uprightness, and of the most notable faithfulness and credit, beareth witness against a woman burning in hatred of her husband, and in love with an adulterer, and in both these diseases of corrupt affections unbridled, untemperable by her estate, raging by her power, and indulgently following the wantonness of her wealth.

But let us omit old and discussed things, and let us sever the credit of inconstant multitudes from the ease of Princes. Let us in so great a matter admit no witness, in whom either his estate may be suspected, or his manners may be blamed. What witnesses then shall we use? For by this condition, we may bring forth none under the royal degree of a King or a Queen.

But such vile acts are not wont to be committed by noble and good men, but by lewd and wicked Ministers. Howbeit that herein also the most precise may be satisfied, go to, let us bring forth a royal witness. Read her own letter; her letter (I say) written with her own hand.

What mean these words? " He is not much deformed, and yet he hath received much." Whereof hath he " received much?" The thing itself, the disease, the pimples, the savor do tell you. Even that much he received, that brought deformity, forsooth, very poison. But her letters name not poison. This is sufficient for me, that it is there said, that " though he received much, he is not much deformed," or, " though he be not much deformed, yet he received much." What meaneth this word " yet?" What else but this, that whatsoever it was that he received, the same was the cause of his deformity, which though it were much, yet was it not so much as to work such deformity as was desired. But be it, it were not poison. What then was it else? You can find nothing that can with convenience of reason be named in place of it. Finally, whatsoever it be that is meant by this word " much," it is such, as she herself, in so secret and familiar a letter, dare not call by the right name. Yea, and though we would shift it off by cavillous expounding, yet she herself will not suffer us. Compare that which went before with that which followeth, and by her device and purpose for time to come, ye shall easily understand, what it is that she hath done in time past. First she saith, it is needful that he be "purged;" then she determineth to carry him to Cragmillar, where both the pnysicians, and (which is more dangerous than any physician) she herself may be present. Finally, she asketh counsel of Bothwell, whether he can devise any secreter way by medicine, than that at Cragmillar, and after a bath. See how all things hang together. "He hath received much, he must be purged," and at Cragmillar; that is, in a desolate corner, in a place, by reason of small resort, very apt for a mischief to be committed. "And medicine he must use," and what, forsooth? Even the same whereof he had before received much. How shall that appear? She will have the manner of ministring the medicine to be secret. If it be to heal him, what needs that secrecy? Why is it not administred openly, in a known and populous place? Now he is eased of his sickness, lusty and healthy, why is he purged in an unusual manner, and in an uninhabited corner? But perhaps it was a strange kind of disease, it had need of strange remedies.

What physicians then called she to counsel? To whom is this charge committed to seek out a medicine and curing for the King? Forsooth, to the King's enemy, to the Queen's adulterer, the vilest of all two-footed beasts, whose house was in France defamed for poisoning, and whose servants were there for the same cause, some tortured, some imprisoned, and all suspected. When was he appointed to receive this noble medicine? Either at his bathing, where he should wash alone, or after his bathing where he should sup alone, So forsooth are medicines accustomed to be provided by enemies, in a secret place, without witnesses. That therefore while an adulterer, an adulteress, and the partner of his wife's body, curiously prepareth, and secretly ministreth; what medicine this is, let every man with himself weigh and consider.

By this time, I suppose, you see the hatred of the Queen, how unappeaseable, how outrageously cruel, how obstinate it was against her husband, whom she thrust among thieves, whom she practised to match in feud and battle with the nobility and with her brethren, who were both naked and poor, loden with despights, vexed with railings, assailed with poison, she drove him away into a solitary corner, there to die with the extremest torment. Now let us proceed to the other causes.

This hatred itself was of itself sufficient to prick her forward to her enemies slaughter, often sought, once attempted, and almost atchieved. Yet was there besides, a stronger enforcement, itself able to enflame her hatred, I mean the love wherewith she intemperately fancied Bothwell: Which love, whosoever saw not, and yet hath seen him, will, perhaps, think it incredible. For what was there in him, that was of a woman of any honest countenance to be desired? Was there any gift of eloquence, or grace of beauty, or virtue of mind, garnished with the benefits, which we call, of fortune? As for his eloquence and beauty, we need not say much, sith they that have seen him can well remember both his countenance, his gate, and the whole form of his body, how gay it was: they that have heard him, are not ignorant of his rude utterance and blockishness. But you will say, he was in executing attempts, wise and politic; in adventuring of perils, hardy and valiant; in free-giving, liberal; in use of pleasures, temperate. For wisdom, even they that be most affectionate unto him, dare not charge him with it. Of valiantness indeed he laboured to win some estimation, but among horsemen, on a swift steed well mounted, well provided for his own safety; a beholder of other men's fighting, sometime hardly chasing them that fled; but his face toward him near at hand, he never durst abide. —Will ye have an example of his excellent valiantness! Of a thief, a notable coward, whom being yielding, and unawares he had deadly wounded, he was thrown down to the ground, hurt, bruised with dry strokes, and had been quite slain, if the poor thief's strength, being ready to die, had not failed him. I could rehearse his glorious vain braggeries in France, I could tell of his last fearful flight as far as to Denmark; but I had rather rub up the remembrance of that day, when the Queen forsaking him, came to the nobility; that protested to revenge the slaughter of the King. The armies stood ready in array, Bothwell in number of men was equal, in place had the advantage; there stood before him, to be his reward, being vanquisher, a Queen much fancying, and entirely loving him; a kingdom, wealth, and honour, for him and his posterity; moreover, impunity for his offences past, extream liberty to do what he list for time to come; ability to advance his friends, and be revenged of his enemies: and on the other side, if he were vanquished, dishonour, poverty, and banishment; finally, all things that thereafter happen'd, or hereafter may happen, were then before his eyes. There were also present, beside the two armies, beholders and witnesses of each man's valiantness and cowardice, the Queen the price of the battel, and Monsieur de Crock, the embassador of France. Now you look to hear how this magnifical boaster of valiantness did acquit himself. First being mounted upon an excellent horse, he came bravely before the army. There the man, forsooth, very sparing of his countrymen's blood, and lavish of his own, calleth for one to try it with him by combat, man to man; and when there were many on the other side, of honourable birth and estates, that offered to accept the combat, by and by his violent heat cool'd, and his glorious speech quailed and had it not been that the Queen, as it were some god out of a ginn in a tragedy, had by her authority taken up the matter, and forbidden her pretty venerous pigeon to give battel, he had fail'd to find, not only a mean, but also an honest colour to refuse to fight, and so the combat was interrupted; yet in the joyned battel he behaved himself so valiantly. Forsooth, the first man, almost at the beginning, and alone, he ran his way, and so at length drew the rest of his part to flee after him.

But his defaults in martial feats, perhaps the man was supplied with civil virtues: alas! what were they? or what virtues could be looked for in him? A man for the most part brought up in the Bishop Murray's palace, to wit, a most wicked corrupt house, in drunkenness and whoredoms, amongst other vile ministers of dissolute misorder. After that he was grown towards man's estate, at dice, and among harlots, he so wasted a most goodly large revenue of his inheritance, that (as the poet saith) at his need he had not left wherewith to buy him a halter to hang himself. He, I say, that defiled not only other men's houses with cuckoldry, but also his own with incestuous villainy.

This man, therefore, when I say to have been beloved of the Queen, and not only loved, but also outrageously and intemperately loved, they that know it not, will, peradventure, think, that I tell wonders. But some man, perhaps, will say, was there none other in all the troop of the youth of nobility, beside him, more worthy to be beloved? Certainly, there were very many. And one there was, in all things that were wont to allure love, of all other most excellent, even her own husband. What was it then that joyned so unequal love, and so far against reason? If I shall say it was likeness of conditions, I shall name a likely cause of love, though to some men, perchance, it may seem an untrue cause of their love. Neither am I willing to enter into that discourse. Neither do I affirm the rumours spread of her in France, in time of her first marriage: howbeit the wickednesses of the rest of her life make some proof that they rose not all of nothing. And

many things that have been noised of her since her return
into Scotland, I have no mind to believe. As for my
part, I am content they be buried in forgetfulness, or if
that cannot be, let them be taken for false and feigned.
Neither is it necessary over-curiously to examine causes in
love, which is usually so carried with a rash violent motion of
a muddy and troubled mind, that for the most part it endeth in
madness, which if ye labour to govern by discreet advice,
ye do nothing else but as if ye should endeavour to be mad
with reason. But yet here there want no causes, for there
was in them both a likeness, if not of beauty, nor outward things, nor of virtues, yet of most extream vices. She
a young woman, suddenly advanced to the highest degree
of authority, when she had never seen with her eyes,
heard with her ears, nor considered in her heart, the form
of a kingdom governed by law, and thereto was furnished
with the untemperate counsels of her kinsmen, who themselves practised to set up a tyrannous rule in France, endeavoured to draw right, equity, laws, and customs of ancestors to her only beck and pleasure.

Of this immoderate desire, there burst out from her
many times, many words disclosing it. This she studied day
and night; but against this desire, there withstood the custom of the country, the laws and statutes, and principally
the consent of the nobility, who remaining safe, she could
never attain it. To the end therefore that she might be
able violently to atchieve it, she determined by force to remove all that stood in her way. But she wist not well by
what means, or by whose help to attempt it.

Fraud was the way to work it, for otherwise it was not
possible to be obtained. For this purpose, therefore,
Bothwell only seemed the fittest man, a man in extream
poverty, doubtful whether he were more vile or wicked,
and who between factions of sundry religions, despising
both sides, counterfeited a love of them both. He, when
he had once before offered the Hamiltons his service to mur-

der the Earl Murray, gave thereby a likelihood, that upon
hope of greater gain, he would not stick to adventure some
greater enterprise, being one whom the ruin of his own
decay'd family prick'd forward headlong to mischief, and
whom no respect of Godliness or honesty restrained from
ungracious actions. As for excessive and immoderate use
of lechery, he therein no less sought to be famous, than
other men do shun dishonour and infamy. She, therefore,
a woman greedily coveting untempered authority, who esteem'd the laws her prison, and the bridle of justice her
bondage, when she saw in her husband not metal enough
to trouble the state, she picked out a man for her purpose,
who neither had wealth to lose, nor fame to be stained,
even such an one as she might easily overthrow again, if
she should once grow weary of him; such a one as she
might easily snare his incontinence with wanton allure-
ments, satisfy his need with money, and bind his assured-
ness to her with a guilty conscience, confederate in mischiefs. These be the fountains of that same, not unmeasurable, but mad love, infamous adultery, and vile patri-
cide, wherewith, as with a pledge, that bloody marriage
was plighted. These therefore were the causes of enter-
prizing that heinous act, to wit, unappeasable hatred of her
husband, and intemperate love of her adulterer. There
was, moreover, a hope, that the crime might be diverted
from them to other, and the execution for it might be laid
upon the poor lives of their enemies, and that men most
guiltless of the fault might be thrust in their place, as sacrifices to appease the people's displeasure: if not, to what
end then served that battel which was almost begun to be
fought between the King and the Lord Robert, her brother? To what end tended those seeds of discord that were
scattered between the King and the nobility? Wherefore
did she so curiously intreat the Earl Murray to stay with
her the day before the murder was committed? Or what
cause was there to send for him? There was an embassa-

U

our come out of Savoy. For what cause? Surely it must needs be a great cause, and such as could not be ended without the assembly of the nobility. No, God wot. The embassadour of Savoy, being bidden to late to the christening, came when all was ended, not for an embassadour to the christening, but as one sent to excuse the neglecting of doing that kindness, when both he liked not to send so far for so small a matter, and he was somewhat ashamed to have failed in presence, when the Frenchmen and Englishmen had already done it. For the more honourable dismissing of him, the Earl Murray was sent for, and that with sundry messengers, to come from his wife that lay a-dying. What need was there then of his presence? To draw him to be a party in conspiracy of the slaughter? Why was it never attempted before? Thought they it best then at the last point, at the very instant when the murder should be committed, to joyn him to their fellowship, as a light man, inconstant, and shifting his purposes at every moment of time, infamous in his former life, and not well assured in his present estate? No, there is none of these things that yet dare say of him.

Seeing then they cannot immagine a false cause to stay him, what was the true cause indeed every man may easily gather; even the same that caused first the Earl of Athol, and afterwards him to depart from the court; the same that so brought him in danger of death; the same that had slander'd him with false rumours scatter'd in England; the same that persecuted him with infamous libels of the murderers themselves; the same that made him to chuse rather to go into banishment, than to remain in court among ruffians' weapons, with great peril of his life.

But what availeth this equity of the cause before hearers, either utterly ignorant of the matter how it was done, or of themselves dissevouring this part; are envious, or apt to be carried away with feigned rumours; which esteem the slanders of most lewd slight persons for true testimonies, and give credit to these men, who boasting at home, that they are able to do what they list, yet neither dare commit their cause to the sentence of the judges, nor were able to defend themselves in battel? And as by a guilty conscience of offences they feared judgment; so by rage, grown of their guiltiness, they run headlong to battel, and from battel run cowardly away: And now again, when standing upon the advantage that they have both in number and wealth, they scorn the wisdom of their adversaries, and despise their power in comparison of their own; yet distrusting to prevail by true manhood, they fall to robbery, and turn their ungracious minds to slandering, cavelling, and lying, whom but yet for the good will that I bear to my countrymen, I would advise to cease from this folly, or fury, or disease of evil speaking, lest in time to come, when truth shall shine out, they shut up and stop with hatred of them those persons' ears to their petitions, whom now they fill and load with false rumours, for there will not always be place for forgiveness; but as darkness at the sun shining; so lies at the light of truth must vanish away.

As for the commodious means for committing that vile fact, and the hope of hiding it, I need not to pursue the declaring of them in many words, sith both the easiness to do it, the opportunities of places, and all advancements of occasions and seasons were in their own power: and to hide the fact, what needed they? When they feared no punishment although it were published; for what punishment could they fear in so strong a conspiracy, when both the force of laws, whereof themselves were governors, was utterly extinguished, and the minds of the most part of men were either snared with partnership of the mischievous fact, or carried with hope, or forestalled with rewards, or discouraged and bridled with fear of so great a power on the other part? But howsoever this be, yet it will be good to see throughly both the order of the doing, the unadvisedness, inconstancy, and end of their devises. For thereby

shall ye perceive, that there wanted not desire to hide the
fact, but that the fury of a distracted mind overthrew all
the order of their counsels, while sometime, as desirous to
beguile public fame, they endeavoured to keep close their,
intended mischief, yet they dealt therein so openly, as careless of their estimation, they seemed to make small account
how men judged of their doings. · For at his preparing to,
go to Glasgow, the poison was given him secretly, and they,
thought they had sufficiently well provided that he should.
in his absence from them, be consumed with pining sickness.

But the rest of their dealings towards him were so cruelly
handled, that though his disease should have happened to
be natural, yet it would have been suspected for poisoning.
For he, her husband, the father of her only and first-born
child; the father, I say, of that son, whose christning was,
solemnised with that great pomp and glory, being escaped
away, in a manner, naked out of his house flaming in fire,
tormented by the way with grievous pain, when he lay at
Glasgow, of a dangerous sickness, likely to die, what- did
his excellent good wife the while? What did she? At the
first news of it did she haste to him in post? Doth she with
her presence, with her friendly familiar speech, or with her
loving countenance comfort him in sickness? When she
cannot stay him in life, cometh she to receive his last breath?
Closeth she his eyes at his dying? Doth she the other kind
duties of honest matrons? No. But she that had now let
him escape to go and die, and hoped that he could not,
linger out his unhappy life much longer, she goeth a quite
contrary way into another country in progress, and, with
her fair Adonis, she visiteth noblemen's houses, and staineth
the houses that harboured them with the spots of their un-
chastities; and just about the time of her husband's death
(as she guessed by the strength and working of the poyson)
she returns to Sterlin.

When the matter wrought not so fast as she expected,

(for the strength of his youth had wrestled with the sore-
ness of his pain) lest she should seem to have altogether
forsaken her duty, she daily prepares to go to Glasgow, but
never goeth. At the last, disappointed of the hope that
she had conceived in her heart, she taketh herself to other
devices. She cometh to Edinburgh, and there calleth to
counsel her adulterer, and a few other, privy of those secrets; there they decree, that in any wise the King must
be slain. Yet were they not fully advised with what kind
of death he should be murdered; which may easily be gathered by her letter, wherein she partly compareth herself
to Medea, a bloody woman, and a poysoning witch. Also
by another of her letters, wherein she asketh advise about
the poysoning of him. The King, who had already tasted
of her lovely cup, doubting whether he were better any
more to believe her flattering speeches, or to fear the shrewd-
ness of her nature, though sometimes he despaired not of
her reconciliation, yet was evermore fearful and suspicious.
But when he saw that neither his life nor his death were in
his power, he was constrained to purse up his past injuries,
to dissemble his present fear, and to feign himself some
hopes for time to come. So was he led out, not as a husband, but carried out as a corpse, or rather drawn, as it
were, to the shambles. The Queen, gloriously shewing
herself in pompous manner, goeth before in triumph over
the young gentleman vexed with all kind of miseries, tormented with poyson, entrapped with treasons, and drawn
to execution. There follows after the triumphant car, the
ancient enemies to his father's house, brought thither on
purpose, that they also might feed their eyes with that
woful spectacle; and whose death, at hand, they looked
for, they might in the meantime take pleasure of the sorrow
of his heart. And, that no ceremony of solemn sacrifices
might be wanting, John Hamilton, Archbishop of St. Andrews, was present as their priest, a man before defiled with
all kind of wickedness, pampered with the spoils and mur-

ders of his countrymen, an old conqueror of many murdering victories. The people all along the way, looking pi-
teously, shewed a foretelling of no good luck to come.
The Queen's companions could neither tell their sadness,
nor hide their gladness; when the heinous outrage of the
vile fact intended, held their unmeasurable joy in suspence, upon expectation of the success. Thus led they
him to Edinburgh, not into the Queen's palace. Why so?
Lest the infection of the pestilent disease, forsooth, might
hurt her young son; as though they that be poysoned were
also to be shunned for fear of infection. But the truer
cause was this, lest his presence should trouble them, in
interrupting their free enjoying their pleasures, and their
consultations about his murder. Whither then is he led?
Into the most desolate part of the town, sometime inhabited,
while the popish priest's kingdom lasted, but for certain
years past without any dweller; in such a house, as of itself
would have fallen down, if it had not been botched up for
the time to serve the turn of this night's sacrifice. Why
was this place chiefly chosen? They pretended the wholesomeness of the air. O good God! going about to murder
her husband, seeketh she for a wholesome air? To what
use? Not to preserve his life, but to reserve his body to
torment. Hereto tend her wifely, diligent attendance, and
her last care of her husband's life. She feareth lest he
should, by preventing death, be delivered from pain, she
would fain have him feel himself die. But let us see what
manner of wholesomeness of air it is. Is it among dead
men's graves to seek the preserving of life? For hard by
there were the ruins of two churches: on the east side a
monastry of Dominic fryars: on the west a church of our
lady; which, for the desolateness of the place, is called
" The church in the field:" on the south-side the town-
wall; and in the same, for commodious passage every way,
is a postern-door: on the north-side are a few beggars' cottages, ready to fall, which sometime served for stews for

certain priests and monks, the name of which, place doth
plainly disclose the form and nature thereof, for it is commonly called " Thieve's Lane." There is never another
house near, but the Hamilton's house, which is about a
stone's cast distant, and that also stood void. Thither re-
moveth the Archbishop of St. Andrews, who always before was used to lodge in the most populous parts of the
town: He also watched all that night that the King was
slain. Now I beseech you, sith you cannot with your eyes,
yet at least with your minds, behold a house lately of old
priests, among graves, between the ruins of two temples,
itself also ruinous, near to the thieve's haunt, and itself a re-
ceiver of thieves, not far from the fort and garrison of his
enemies, that stood right over-against the door; by which,
if any man should flee out, he could not escape their traiterous ambushment. The very shape of this place, when
you consider it in your mind, when you hear of the ruins of
churches, graves of dead men, lurking corners of thieves,
brothel-houses of harlots; doth not, I say, not the house
only, but also every part near about it, seem to proclaim
mischief and treachery? Seemeth here a King to have gone
into a house for lodging, or to be thrust into a den of thieves?
Was not that desolate wasteness, that unhabited place, able
of itself to put simple men in fear, to make wiser men suspi-
tious, and to give wicked men shrewd ocasions? What
meant his enemies, unwonted repair into those parts, and
watching all night, in manner, hard at his gate? Why
chose he now this place for his lodging against his former
usage? the house ye will say was empty, and his brother's
house, and near to the King' lodging. It was empty long
before; why lodged you never there before? Why forsook you the populous places in the heart of the city, and
nearness to the court, and thrust yourself into a desolate
corner? What profit, what commodity, what pleasure herein
respect you? Was it your meaning, that you, being one
that ever had been a greedy coveter of popular fame, and

catcher of courtiers with baits of good chear, now would of your own accord go hide yourself in a blind hole out of all company and resort? that you, rather overwhelmed than laden with plenty of benefices, went thither to delight your heart in the ruine of temples? . But be it that your coming thither was but by chance, and that you had some causes to go thither, though not true, yet somewhat likely.

What meant your unwonted watching all night? What meant the fearful murmurings of your servants that night, whom yet in that public tumult you commanded not once to stir out of doors? But what cause had they to go out? Was it to have understanding of the matter whereof yourself were an author and deviser? . No, for out of your own watch-tower you heard with your ears the noise of the ruin, you saw the smoak and ashes with your eyes, you drank up the joy thereof in your heart, and the savour of the gunpowder you in a manner snuffed up at your nose. Perhaps you meant to send out some to receive them that fled; but you saw no men flee. And therefore the lights that were seen out of the highest part of your house all the night long; were, as upon the lucky ending of the thing that you looked for, even then suddenly put out.

But let us return to the King. They thought it not enough to have set open the postern in the wall, to let in thieves thereat, not to have set an ambush before the door, that none should escape, but also they kept with themselves the keys of two doors, the one of the lower room, where they had undermined the wall, and filled the holes with gunpowder, and the other of the upper room, that the murderers might come to the King in his bed. Then of those few servants that he had, they withdrew the greater number, being such as were before set about him, not so much to do him service, as to be spies of his secrets, and carry news to the Queen. The last that was left, one Alexander Durain, when he could find no reasonable excuse to depart was thrust out by the Queen herself. She in the mean time, meaning not to fail in playing her part, while Bothwell is in preparing the tragical stage for the murder, daily visiteth the King, his heart passioned with love, sometimes she comforteth with sweet promises, sometimes she vexeth with brawlings, and still keepeth his wit occupied with suspicions, and rightly representeth in action the poet's fable, wherein is feigned, that Prometheus his liver daily growing to invent new torment, is daily knawn and preyed upon by an eagle. For after the very same manner, sometimes she cherisheth and refresheth the silly young gentleman, to no other end, but that he may have life remaining to suffer more sorrows.

Now, I beseech you every one, think with yourselves upon the fresh doing of the fact, how men's hearts were moved, when even now these things cannot be heard reported without indignation. There was provided by the most wicked man in the world, by his enemy, by his wife's adulterer, a house, in manner severed from all concourse of people, fitter for a slaughter-house, than for man's dwelling: it is provided for a young gentleman, unprovident by youth, easie to be trapped in treason by love, spoiled of his servants, forsaken of his friends: a house (I say) torn, solitary on every side, not also unclose, but open to pass through, the keys thereof in his enemies custody, no man left within but a young man, not yet recovered of sickness, and an old man feeble by age, and two strangers unacquainted with the places, matter and persons, no man dwelling near but his enemies and thieves. But as for danger of thieves, the good fore-casting woman had well provided, for she had left him nothing to allure a thief withal and as for his enemies, she had appointed them to be but lookers-on, and not part-players in this tragedy; but the glory of the fact she reserved to herself and Bothwell.

What in the mean time doth the Queen's great careful-

x

ness? What meaneth her unwonted resort? What her malicious, and not obsequious diligence? She visiteth him daily, she prolongeth her talk with him many hours together, two nights she resteth in a lower chamber under him, (if guilty conscience of most heinous doings can from torments of furies suffer that outrageous heart to rest at all). She feared much, lest if the lower place of the house were left empty, the noise of the underminers working, and of the bringers-in of the powder, should bring some of the servants into some suspition of the treachery. Beside, she had a mind to see the thing done herself, rather than to commit it to the trust of any other. She had a desire to take a foretaste of the joy to come, and when she could not with her ears, yet at least with her heart, to conceive aforehand the fire, the smoak, the powder, the crack of the house falling, the fearful trouble, the tumult, the confused dismaidness of the doers, the thieves, and the people. All things thus prepared for that doleful night, then entreth she into the last care of her good fame: she endeavoureth to divert all suspicions from her, she goeth to her husband, she kisseth him, she giveth him a ring for a pledge of her love, she talketh with him more lovingly than she was wont to do, and promiseth more largely, she feineth that she had a great care of his health, and yet her companying with her adulterer she surceaseth not.

They that more nearly noted these things, prognosticated no good thing to come. For how much greater tokens that the Queen shewed of reconciled affection, so much the more cruelty did every man in his heart fore-conceive of all her intentions. For else, whence cometh that sudden change, so great care for him whom she had poysoned the month before, whom even lately she not only wished dead, but desired to see him die; whose death she set her brother, yea, both her brethren to procure: and she, like a master of mischief, thrust forth the King to fight, and herself in

the mean time prepared for his burial? Not past a few
months before, she herself was desirous to die, because
she loathed to see the King alive. Whence cometh now
this sudden care of his health? I looked she should say she
was reconciled to him. Were you reconciled to your husband, whom you sent away into that desart, that camp of furies, as the poet calleth it? For whom among brothel-
houses of harlots, among beggars' cottages, among thieves'
lurking-holes, you prepared a house so open to pass through,
that you left therein more entries than men to shut them!
You that allured and assembled ruffians to his slaughter, and
thieves to his spoil? You that drove away his servants that
should have defended his life? You that thrust him out
naked, alone, unarmed, among thieves, in danger to be
slain? When in all this miserable state of your husband,
your adulterer in the meantime dwelt in your palace, daily
haunted your chamber, day and night all doors were open
for him, whilst your poor husband, debarred all company of
the nobility, his servants forbidden to come at him, or sent
away from him, was forsaken and thrust away into a solitary desart, for a mocking stock, and I would to God it had
been for a mocking stock only? Of his other servants
I enquire not. I do not curiously question why they went
away, why they then especially forsook the King, when
he chiefly needed their help and service, when he was newly recovered? When he began to go abroad, and had no
other company. Of Alexander Duram, I cannot keep
silence, whom you had for his keeper, and your spy.
What was there for him to espy? Was there any thing for
him to bring news of to an honest matron, loving to her
husband, faithful in wedlock, and fearful of a partner of
his love? Feared she lest he, a young gentleman, beautiful, and a king, should cast wanton eyes upon some other
woman in her absence? No, God wot. For that was it
that she most desired. For she herself had practised to allure him thereto before, she herself had offered him the

occasions, and of herself shewed him the means.   This
was it that most grieved her, while she was seeking
causes of divorce, that she could not find in him so much
as any slender suspition of adultery.   Why then were
spies set about him to watch him? Was it not that none
of the nobility, none of his servants, nor any stranger at
all should come at him, that no man should speak with
him, that might disclose the treason, and forewarn him
of his danger? This same very Alexander, how carefully she saveth, when she goeth about to kill her
husband? How late she sendeth him away, when the
rest were gone, even at the very point of her husband's death, when she had now no more need of
espials? For the day before the murder was committed,
there was none of the ministers that were privy to her secret counsels left behind, but only Alexander. He, when
he saw that night, no less doleful than shameful, to approach, prepareth, as himself thought, a fine subtle excuse
to be absent, so as rather chance might seem to have
driven him out, than he himself willing to have forsaken
his master. He putteth fire in his own bed-straw, and
when the flame spread further, he made an out-cry, and
threw his bedding, half singed, out of the King's chamber. But the next day, when that excuse served not so
handsomely as he desired, for that in the Queen's hearing,
the King very sweetly entreated him not to leave him
alone that night, and also desired him to lie with himself,
as he had often used to do, for the King entirely loved him
above all the rest; Alexander in perplexity, wanting what
to answer, added to his first excuse, fear of sickness, and
pretended, that for commodious taking of physic for his
health, he would lie in the town. When this would not
yet serve him, the Queen added authority, and told the
King, that he did not well to keep the young man with him
against the order of his health, and therewithal she
turned to Alexander, and bade him go where was best for

him: and forthwith, as soon as the word was spoken, he
went his way. I will not here precisely trace out all
the footings of these wicked doings; neither will I curiously enquire, whether that former days fire were happened by casualty, or kindled by fraud. Neither will I
ask why he that had so often been received to lie in the
King's own bed, doth now this only night specially refuse
it. Let us suppose that sickness was the cause thereof.
This only one thing I ask, what kind of sickness it was,
that came upon him at that very instant, and before morning left him again, without any physician's help, and
whereof neither before, nor since, nor at that present,
there ever appeared any token? But I trust, though he
hold his peace, ye all sufficiently understand it. In the
man guilty in conscience of the mischievous intention, fear
of death overcame regard of duty. Had it not been that
Alexander, before-time a spy and tale-bearer, now a
forsaker and betrayer of his master, was joyned to her in
privity of all these wicked doings, would not the Queen,
so cruel in all the rest, have found in her heart to bestow
that one sacrifice upon her husband's funerals? While these
things were in doing, the night was far past, and my
Lady Rerese, a lusty valiant souldieress, before sign given,
cometh forth into the field out of array, abroad she goeth,
getteth her to horse-back, and though she were somewhat
afraid, as one that foreknew the storm to come, yet she
sate still upon her horse, tarrying for the Queen, but yet a
good pretty way from the house. In the mean time Paris
cometh. Then the communication brake, and they rose
to depart. For, by and by, upon sight of him came to
her remembrance that heinous offence, that without great
propitiation could not be purged; forsooth, that the Queen
had not danced at the wedding-feast of Sebastian the
minstrel and vile jester, that she sate by her husband,
who had not yet fully recovered his health, that at the
banquet of her domestical parasite, she had not played

the dancing skit.   A matter surely worthy of excuse.   But
what should she else do?   She must needs go, as soon as
she saw Paris; for so it was agreed, and somewhat must
needs be pretended.   How happened it that the other
nights before, when she went away earlier, she made no
excuse at all, and now her departure about midnight,
must needs have an excuse alledged?   But be it so, could
she remember no better excuse than Sebastian's wedding?
No, no, I say to the contrary, that if she had left the
wedding of her own natural brother, or her sister, to visit
her husband, though but a little crased, she had had a
just excuse before all men so to do.   What if she had
done the same kindness for the King, being not her husband, or for any other of the nobility.   Is Sebastian's wedding of such a value, that a masking dance thereat is to be
preferred before a wife's duty and love?   But surely in this
curious excusing and pretended sorrow of neglected duty,
somewhat lieth hidden, and yet not so hidden, but that it
appeareth through the closure.

   This overmuch preciseness of diligence, excusing where
no need is, hath some suspicion of some secret mischief that
you are loath to have disclosed, and the slightness of the excuse, encreaseth the suspicion, especially when there
were other matters enough that she might better have
alledged: but let us admit the excuse, since the Queen
herself hath thought it reasonable; whither then goeth
she? straight into her chamber.   What doth she next?
wearied with the day's travel, and the night's watching,
goeth she to bed?   No; but she falleth to talking with
Bothwell first almost alone, and afterward alone, altogether.   What talk she had, the matter itself declareth: for
Bothwell, after that he had put off his cloaths, as if he
would have gone to bed, by and by putteth on other apparel.   Going to do the deed, he would not be known.   I
like well the man's policy.   But his way was to go
through the watch.   Here I marvel at his madness.   But

men's wits beset with guiltiness of mischiefs, do commonly
bewray themselves by their own inconstancy, and blind to
all other things, do see only that which they have bent
their mind unto. What he did, the King's death, his own
running away, the confessions of the guilty persons, and
other things that followed the murder, do declare. After
the great uproar in the town about it, he, as one utterly ignorant of all, returneth through the same watch to bed.
When noise of the ruin had filled all men's ears, and the
crack of it had shaken all the houses, only the Queen inten-
tive to expectation of the chance, and broad awake, heareth
nothing at all, and Bothwell heareth nothing. O marvellous
deafness! All other throughout the town, as many as were
awake were afraid, and as many as slept were awaked. At the
last, Bothwell riseth again, and in the self-same enterlude, by
suddenly shifting from the poet, becometh a messenger, he
runneth to the Queen, and thither resorted many others also
that lodged in the palace. To some the matter seemed true,
to some feigned, to some marvellous. What doth the Queen
the whilst? What should she do? She temperately broodeth
good luck, she resteth sweetly till the next day at noon:
yet, the day following, to observe decorum, and comely
convenience on her part, without marring the play, she
counterfeiteth a mourning; which yet neither her joy-
fulness dwelling withal in heart suffereth long to be feigned,
nor shame permitteth to be wholly neglected. These things
thus lying open before your eyes, thus palpable with hands,
thus fast imprinted in men's ears and knowledge, stand we
yet enquiring for the author of the murder, as though it
were doubtful? But ye say, the Queen denieth it. What
denieth she? forsooth, that she did the murder: as though
there were so great a difference, if one should be the author,
or the executioner; yet he commands it, and commits it:
she gave her counsel, her furtherance, her power and authority to the doing of it. Neither is the cause unknown
why she did it; even that the same filthy marriage with

Bothwell might be accomplished. Though all which arguments, and so many witnesses of them that were privy to it failed; yet by her own testimony, by her own letters, it must needs be confessed. And though all other things wanted, these things that followed the murder do plainly declare the doer, namely, that at the slaughter of her husband she sorroweth not, but quietly rested, as after a gay enterprize well atchieved; that she mourned not, but in manner openly joyed; that she could abide, not only to look upon his dead body, but also greedily beheld it; that she secretly in the night buried him without funeral pomp, or rather hid him like a thief: for that same so inconstant counterfeiting or mourning did plainly bewray itself. For what meant that removing to Seton's? Why shunned she the town's resort, and people's eyes? Was it because she was ashamed to mourn openly? or because she could not well cloak her joy? or secretly to give herself all to sorrow? No, for at Seton's she threw away all her disguised personage of mourning; she went daily into the fields among ruffians; and not only resorted to her former custom, but also affected to exercise manly pastimes, and that among men, and openly. So lightly she despised the opinion and speech of her country. But I beshrew that same Killegree, and that same Monsieur de Croc, that came upon her so unseasonably, and shewed to others her counterfeited person unvizzored. For had not they been, many things that were done might have been denied, many things might have been handsomely feigned, and much of the matter might have been helped by forged rumours.

But they will say, there was a solemn enquiry for the murder. Forsooth, by Bothwell himself principally, and by some other that then laboured, and yet at this day do labour to deliver the persons guilty thereof, from punishment of law, and do now plainly shew what they then secretly meant. But with what diligence, with what upright severity was that enquiry handled? A few poor souls, the next dwelling neighbours to the King's lodging, being called, neither durst tell what they had seen and heard, and if they touched any thing near the matter, either they were with fear put to silence, or despised as of no credit: the wiser sort of them durst not offend Bothwell, that sate among the judges. One or two of the King's servants that escaped the mischance, were examined which way the murderers came in. Forsooth, say they, we had not the keys: who then had them? It was answered, that the Queen had them. So began the secrets of the court to break out. Then was that enquiry adjourned, and never recontinued. What can be more severe and upright than this enquiry? and yet they prevailed nothing by it: for what the examiners would have had kept secret, that the people cried out openly; that which they suppressed, burst forth; and that which they cloaked in secret, it breaketh out into broad light. But there was a proclamation set forth, with pardon of the fact, and promise of reward to him that would utter it? Why? who had been so mad, that he durst, in so manifest peril of his life, bear witness, or give information against the judges themselves, in whose power lay his life and death? It was likely, forsooth, that they which had murdered a King, would spare him that should disclose the murderer, especially when all men saw that the enquiry of the King's slaughter was quite omitted, and the other enquiry severely pursued concerning books accusing the slaughter. What manner of judgment it was, whereby Bothwell was acquitted, you have heard. Forsooth by himself procured, the judges by himself chosen, the accusers by himself suborned, lawful accusers forbidden to be present, unless they would yield their throats to their enemies weapons; the assizes appointed neither to a day, according to the law of the land, nor after the manner of the country; nor to enquire of the murder of the King, but of such a murder as was alledged to be committed the day before that the King was slain. Here, when Bothwell by

his friendship and power, and the Queen by prayer and
threatening travailing with the judges, do you now expect
what sentence men, chosen against law, and against the
custom of the land, have pronounced? In their judgment,
they touched the matter nothing at all; only this they have
declared, that it was no lawful judgment, in this, that with
a special protestation they provided, that it should not be
prejudicial to them in time to come. Then, that all men
might understand what it was that they sought by sword,
fire and poyson, they jumble up marriages; one is divorced,
another is coupled, and that in such posting speed, as they
might scant have hasted to furnish a triumph of some noble
victory. Yet, that in these unlawful weddings some shew
of lawful order might be observed, the goodly banes were
openly proclaimed. For publishing whereof, though the
minister of the church was threatened with death if he did it
not, yet, at the time of his publishing, himself openly protested, that he knew cause of exception, why that marriage
was not lawful. But in such a multitude assembled, how
few were they that knew it not? sith all could well remember that Bothwell had then alive two wives already
not yet divorced, and the third neither lawfully married,
nor orderly divorced. But that was not it that was intended,
to observe the ceremonies of lawful order; but (as they do
use in enterludes) they provided a certain shew, or disguised counterfeiting of common usage. For he that hath
oft broken all human laws, and hath cast away all conscience and religion, could easily neglect the course of God's
law.

Now, I suppose, I have briefly declared (in respect of
the greatness of the matter) and yet perhaps in more words
than needed (the plainness of the proofs considered) of
what purpose, by what counsel, and upon what hope, that
heinous murder was attempted, with what cruelty it was
executed, by what tokens, advertisements, testimonies, and
letters of the Queen herself, the whole matter is proved,

and so plainly proved, that it may be as openly seen, as if it lay before your eyes; yet will I shew forth the testimony of the whole people, which I think worthy not to be neglected: for several men do commonly deceive, and are deceived by others, but no man deceiveth all men, nor is deceived by all. The testimony of the people is this. When at the Queen's going abroad among the people, the greatest part of the commons were wont to make acclamations, wishing her well and happily, with such speeches as either love enforceth, or flattery inventeth: now at her going after the King's slaughter to the castle, through the chief and most populous street of the town, there was all the way a sad glooming silence. And when any woman alone of the multitude had cryed, God save the Queen, another by and by so cryed out, as all men might hear her; So be it to every one as they have deserved.

Albeit these things were thus done as I have declared, yet there are some that stick not to say, that the Queen was not only hardly, but also cruelly dealt with, that after so detestable a fact, she was removed from her regency; and when they could not deny the fact, they complained of the punishment. I do not think there will be any man so shameless to think that so horrible a fact ought to have no punishment at all. But if they complain of the grievousness of the penalty, I fear least, to all good men, we may seem not to have done so gently and temperately, as loosly and negligently, that have laid so light a penalty upon an offence so heinous, and such as was never heard of before. For what can be done cruelly against the author of so outrageous a deed, wherein all laws of God and man are violated, despised, and in a manner wholly extinguished? Every several offence hath his punishment both by God and man appointed: and as there be certain degrees of evil deeds, so are there also encreases in the quantities of punishments. If one have killed a man, it is a deed of itself very heinous. What if he have killed his familiar friend?

What·if his father? · What if in one foul fact he hath
joyned all these offences together? Surely of such a one,
neither can his life suffice for imposing, nor his body for
bearing, nor the judges policy for inventing pain enough
for him? Which of these faults is not comprised in this
offence? I omit the mean common matters, the murdering
of a young gentleman, an innocent, her countryman, her
kinsman, her familiar, and her cousin german. Let us also
excuse the fact, if it be possible. She unadvisedly, a
young woman, angry, offended, and one of great innocency of life till this time, hath slain a lewd young man, and
adulterer, and unkind husband, and a cruel King.

If not any one, but all these respects together, were in
this matter, they ought not to avail to shift off all punishment, but to raise some pity of the case. · But what say
you that none of these things can so much as be falsly pretended? The fact itself, of itself is odious: in a woman it
is monstrous: in a wife not only excessively loved, but also
most zealously honoured, it is uncredible. And being
committed against him whose age craved pardon, whose
hearty affection required love, whose nighness of kindred
asked reverence, whose innocency might have deserved favour, upon that young man I say, in whom there is not so
much as alledged any just cause of offence, thus to execute
and spend, yea, to exceed all torments due to all offences,
in what degree of cruelty shall we account it? · But let
these things avail in other persons to raise hatred, to bring
punishment, and to make examples to posterity. · But in
this case let us bear much with her youth, much with her
nobility, much with the name of a Princess. · As for mine
own part, I am not one that thinks it always good to use
extream strictness of law, no not in private, mean, and
common persons. · But in a most heinous misdeed, to dis-
solve all force of law, and where is no measure of ill doing,
there to descend beneath all measure in punishing,
were the way to the undoing of all laws, and the over-

throw of all humane society. But in this one horrible act is such a hotchpotch of all abominable doings, such an eagerness of all outrageous crueltie, such a forgetfulness of all natural affection, as nothing more can be feigned or imagined. I omit all former matters.

I will not curiously inquire upon Prince's doings, I will not weigh them by the common beam, I will not restrain them to common degrees of duties. If there be any thing that without great offence may be passed over, I will gladly leave it unspoken of; if there be any thing that may receive excuse, either by respect of age, or of woman kind, yea, or of unadvisedness, I will not urge it. And to pass over all the rest, two heinous offences there be, that neither according to their greatness be fully expressed, nor according to their outrage be sufficiently punished. I mean the violating of matrimony, and of royal majesty. For matrimony (as the Apostle saith) doth truly contain a great mystery. For, as being observed, it compriseth within it all inferiour kinds of duties, so being broken, it overthroweth them all. Whoso hath misused his father, seemeth to cast out of his heart all natural reverence, but for the husband's sake, one shall love both father and mother. Of all other duties, the degrees, or like observances, either are not at all in brute creatures, or not so plain to be discerned: but of matrimonial love, there is almost no living creature that hath not some feeling. This mystery, therefore, whoso not only violateth, but also despiseth, he doth not only overthrow all the foundations of human fellowship; but, as much as in him lyeth, dissolveth and confoundeth all order of nature. Whosoever (I do not say) hurteth the King, that is the true image of God in earth, but slayeth him with strange and unwonted sort of cruelty, so as the untemperate and incredible outragiousness is not contented with simple torment, seemeth he not, as much as in him lieth, to have a desire to pull God out of Heaven? What refuge have they then left themselves to mercy, that in satisfying their lust of unjust hatred, have exceeded, not only all measure of cruelty, but also all likelihood, that it can be credible.

But they will say, we ought to bear with, and spare her nobility, dignity, and age. Be it so, if she have spared him in whom all these respects were greater, or at least equal. Let the majesty of royal name avail her. How much it ought to avail to her preserving, herself hath shewed the example. May we commit our safety to her, who, a sister, hath butcherly slaughtered her brother, a wife her husband, a Queen her King? May we commit our safety to her, whom never shame restrained from unchastity, woman-kind from cruelty, nor religion from impiety? Shall we bear with her age, sex, and unadvisedness, that without all just causes of hatred, despised all these things in her kinsman, her King, her husband? She that hath sought such execution of her wrongful wrath, what shall we think she will do being provoked by reproaches to men not knit to her by kindred, subject to her pleasure, not matched with her in equal fellowship of life, but yielded to her governance, and enthralled to her tormenting cruelty? When rage for interrupting her pleasure, and outrage of nature, strengthened with armour of licentious power, shall ragingly triumph upon the goods and blood of poor subjects? What is then the fault whereof we are accused, what cruelties have we shewed? That a woman raging without measure or modesty, and abusing to all her subjects destruction, the force of her power, that she had received for their safety, we have kept under governance of her kinsmen and well-willing friends : and whom by right we might for her heinous deeds have executed, her we have touched with no other punishment, but only restrained her from doing more mischief. For we deprived her not of liberty, but of unbridled licentiousness of evil doing. Wherein we have more fear among all good men, the blame of too much lenity, than among evil men the slander of cruelty.

ıs I have given all that is necessary from Buchanan,
though doubtless prejudiced, must be considered the
thority—he being one of the courtiers of the day,
ell informed of all that was going on ; and, subse-
y one of the King's Commissioners who went before
glish Queen.

THE INTRODUCTION.

AMONGST all the controverted histories in the world,
that of Mary Queen of-Scots hath now, for many years,
been reckoned the most amazingly intricate and perplexed,
and continues to be so esteemed to this very day. Yea to
one who will curiously weigh the opposite and contra-
dictory accounts, given by different persons of the same
facts, it would seem as if this were not of the like nature
with any other history, either ancient or modern. Other
histories, for the most part, have become disputable, through
the scarcity, or destruction, of monuments relating to their
several times, to the want of capacity in those who wrote
them, or some obvious disadvantage under which they
laboured for attaining to sure means of knowledge, by
living either at too great distance of time after the
transactions themselves, or of place from the theatre of
action. But none of these things can be alledged in
Queen Mary's story. It had become a subject of high
dispute in her own time; and hath been treated ever
since, as a point of the deepest concern in all modern
history, by the ablest writers abroad and at home. Many
have made it their peculiar care to search out and preserve
whatever monuments or documents they thought could be
of use for clearing any doubts and objections that fell
in their way; while others have laid themselves out to
collect, publish and preserve all the scandalous libels, or
stories, that had ever been trumped up, either by them
who dethroned her, or those who murdered her, to screen

their own wickedness. Hence it happens, that we are rather overwhelmed with memoirs and vouchers of the several particular events during that period, than defective therein: yet nevertheless the history itself, by this multiplicity of jarring and inconsistent evidence, is become rather more involved, especially that part of it relating to the murder of her second husband, and whether she was herself innocent, or guilty, of that fact. Some have always absolved her, while others passionately condemn her, and spare not to bestow the most opprobrious language upon all who presume to differ from their opinion, uncharitable as it is.

The truth of the matter is, the Queen's enemies took the start of her friends. They not only invented and spread abroad this calumny upon her, but also in the presence of Queen Elizabeth and her Commissioners in England, they proved, so far as their positive oaths could go, two main points against her, namely, " That she was in the foreknowledge, counsel, device, and persuaded and commanded that her husband should be murdered; and after that was done, fortified and maintained the murderers:" As also, " That the Earl of Bothwell seized her person with her own consent, and by a stratagem of her own contrivance." Both which points they did verify by some French letters which they exhibited upon oath as written with her own hand to the Earl of Bothwell: which letters were received by the English Commissioners, examined and compared, once and again, with other letters unquestionably written by Queen Mary, and likewise with a translation of them into English, that had been sent up by Murray to England in the month of June that year; and no difference being by them found, the letters to Bothwell were all ingrossed in the memorials of the Sessions of these Commissioners, excepting one, of which afterwards.

Was not this a very cautious and solemn procedure?

z

Behold with what scrupulous nicety, and critical exactness, these letters were admitted, and so patiently collated once and again, before they were recorded! But this being once done in such a court, where Queen Elizabeth herself, that bright occidental star, presided in person; at the sight too of an unusual number of the nobility of Old England, convened for that very purpose; their whole acts being drawn up by the direction and assistance of honest Secretary Cecil; and all the fundamentals so well secured by the repeated oaths, and solemn protestations, of these godly worthies, the Earls of Murray and Morton, the first Protestant Bishop of Orknay, the Lord Lindsay, and the titular Abbot of Dunfermling; the business seems to have been almost over: for if fortifications so impregnable could be taken by storm, and such solid foundations blown in the air, what other safe refuge could the persons concerned expect to find! The Earl of Murray was so certain of the truth of all that he had laid to Queen Mary's charge, that he thought Queen Elizabeth bound by God's ordinance to put her to death for the murder of her husband, because he was Elizabeth's near kinsman, and born her subject. And Cecil was of the same opinion, even " that Queen Elizabeth was bound in conscience to answer the petitions of her subjects, in matters of blood, upon her subjects ;" that is, upon Queen Mary, for, in Cecil's language, she and all the people of Scotland were subjects to Elizabeth, by reason of her superiority over that kingdom. Is it to be imagined that the one would have petitioned, or the other so soon resolved, that a sovereign Queen should be put to death, had not the force of conviction pressed very hard upon their tender consciences?

If the reader shall desire to know, as it is likely he will, how Queen Mary's Commissioners could be employed all this time, that they did not either refute these letters, or, at least, give in their objections against them, as they certainly always esteemed them forgeries; he may find in the appendix, that they were not idle; and in the following brief account of these conferences, the manner in which they were employed, is narrated in few words, and to these he is referred. But to refute the letters was altogether impossible for them, because they could never obtain either a sight of the pretended originals, or copies of them, although they often demanded them, at the Queen of England's hands. Nay, Elizabeth declared that she would receive proof of Murray's accusation of the Queen, his Sovereign, before she were heard for herself; and really did so. But as the particulars of that accusation were kept a profound secret from Queen Mary and her Commissioners, there was no remedy left them but simply to deny. This indeed was done: both the Queen herself, and her Commissioners in her name, did absolutely deny that ever she wrote to any creature for such purposes; and affirmed, that if there were any such writings, they were false, feigned, forged, and invented by Murray, Morton, and their accomplices themselves: and this they undertook to prove, providing they might be permitted to take a view of the pretended originals, and get copies of them; but neither the one nor the other could ever be obtained; without which nothing could be done.

It appears indeed, by a letter from the Bishop of Ross to Queen Elizabeth, dated the 17th of December, 1568, that he had got some general account of the letters, and the contents, by word of mouth, either from some of the English Commissioners, or, which is rather more probable, from Secretary Maitland; by which account, imperfect as it was, he points out several strong presumptions of the forgery, and several marks of the insufficiency of the letters, but at the same time fell into some small mistakes concerning them, as might be well expected in one who argued from his memory, concerning writings of which he had only heard: so his observations went for no-thing.

Queen Mary and her Commissioners perceiving this double dealing, that these conferences, to which Elizabeth had urged her to consent, for pardoning her rebels, and being reconciled to them, so that they might live in security, and she enjoy her kingdom in peace for the future, were so un-accountably carried on to no other purpose, but purely to her dishonour; and the very means of clearing herself thus denied her, they resolved to go to work another way, by which they might prove the forgery by inference, seeing they were debarred of the means whereby it could have been done in the direct manner. They accused Murray, Morton and their associates, as the authors, inventers, and some of them, the executers of that murder, and engaged to prove that accusation also against them, and actually began to collect some additional proof; for though they knew the matter from the beginning, and wanted not proof, the Queen had declined to take this method hitherto; be-cause, as she truly said herself, " It could not seem fit nor convenient to stand before foreign judges to accuse them, and much less to be accused by them, they being offenders, &c.," though at last by those wicked and shameless pro-ceedings, she found herself obliged to accuse them.

Things had hitherto been carried on altogether accord-ing to the intention and desire both of Murray's faction, and of Queen Elizabeth and her court: but this method of pro-ceeding cast a heavy damp on all their spirits, and thrust their noses quite out of joint. Great was the affront, that a woman, in their own prison, even though she was a Queen, assisted by two servants only, should, at such a cri-tical juncture, have fallen upon the only proper method to disclose their secrets, and disturb the schemes that had been formed and pursued for several years, by people who thought themselves the very prime politicians in the world; and it cannot be denied but they had acquired some qualifications, that are reckoned chiefly necessary to form adepts in the science, by drinking deeply of the potion that secured them against all shame and qualms of conscience.

Various were the expedients thought of to ward this deadly blow. They were all of them conscious that the accusation was just; and therefore the matter must not be brought to a trial: Something however must be attempted to raise their fallen countenances.

Murray and Morton knew themselves to be principally levelled at; for which reason, before the accusation should be formally presented, they bravely resolved that the question should be determined, not by a full and fair hearing, but by a duel, to be fought, not by either of them in person, but by proxy. For this purpose they engaged Patrick Lord Lindsay, a very inconsiderate man, whom they used as a meer tool, to send a challenge to Lord Herries, for accusing Lord Regent Murray's Grace and his company, of the King's murder; which he did upon the 22d of December.

Lord Herries would fight with none of their proxies on that occasion, but only with the principals; because, he said, " It was meetest that traitors should pay for their own treason." But Murray and Morton were too tender of their own dear skins, to endanger them in the like manner as they did Lord Lindsay's. They therefore most meanly applied to the Earl of Leicester, Queen Elizabeth's minion, for his assistance to mollify Lord Herries; who thereupon sent word to that nobleman to come to court that very day, upon some importunate suit of the Earl of Murray. Lord Herries absolutely refused to see Murray upon any terms, unless it should be either to avow the accusation, or the cartels exchanged that day betwixt him and Lindsay, of which he sent back copies to Leicester, assuring him, that if his presence was wanted on that account, he should not fail to come, if God spared his life, at the hour that his Lordship should appoint.

This answer made the case still worse. Cowardice permitted not the good Regent, or his companion Morton, to fight, though they had begun the quarrel; and guilt hindered them from standing the trial of the cause.

To rid them of this perplexity, they had recourse to Queen Elizabeth, who never had deserted them in a dishonourable cause, or wicked action, and they never had occasion to apply to her on any other account: with her therefore they bemoaned their present hard situation; and she did as much as she could to relieve them. But this served only to fix guilt more closely upon them: For upon the 24th of December, in the Council-chamber at Hampton-court, the Duke of Norfolk having, in presence of others of the English Commissioners, declared to the Bishop of Ross and Lord Herries, how " the Earl of Murray had bemoaned him to Queen Elizabeth and her council, that it was come to his knowledge, how it was murmured and bruited, that he and his company were guilty of the murder which they had laid to the Queen's charge; and he understood the same had proceeded from the Queen of Scotland's Commissioners:" therefore required whether either of these two would so accuse the other party? as if that had not been avowedly done before!

The answer was in greater readiness than they were aware, namely, " That they had that very day received the Queen their mistress's special command to accuse them of that crime; and would publicly do so, in presence of the Queen of England and her council, desiring that they might have her presence for that effect." And the next day being assigned, they accordingly did accuse them of the King's murder, and shewed their Sovereign's instructions for their warrant; at the same time they produced her answers to Murray's accusation, which he calls " the eik," and their own answer to his solemn protestation. They likewise required to have copies given them of the writings produced against their Sovereign, to the end that they might convict

Murray and his party, both of murdering the King, and of forging papers, and then swearing them upon her, to palliate their own horrid actions.

Elizabeth acknowledged that this desire was very reasonable, but never could be prevailed upon to grant it; and yet, which is altogether unaccountable, they still gave out that Queen Mary would not answer as to the crime of murdering her husband, even when they had in their hands her answers to all that they would allow either herself or her commissioners to see. Neither would they ever permit that any enquiry should be made into Murray's guilt, in the murder of the King; for upon a second application made by the Bishop of Ross and Lord Herries for these purposes, by their mistress's express command, Elizabeth answered, " That it was best some appointment should be made betwixt the Queen of Scotland, her good sister, and her subjects:" although upon the 16th of December, she had told them, " That she could not think them good or trusty servants, or counsellors, to her good sister, who would labour her to appoint with her subjects, at this present, seeing their unnatural behaviour shown by them, in accusing their own native Sovereign:" yet this was now become her own counsel, and had been, ever since the rumour, that Murray was to be accused of the king's murder, had disconcerted them all, Cecil excepted, who was never at a loss; " For, says he, though the Regent, or any of his company, shall be by her charged to be parties to the murder, and to her unlawful marriage, yet is that no discharge of her guiltiness:" as if the Queen had been to accuse them as parties or participants with herself in that fact. She never charged them as having any participants but amongst themselves. Her Commissioners indeed, upon the first of December, in their memorial, drawn up in some haste, after they were made acquainted with Murray's accusation of their mistress, had mentioned the Earl of Bothwell as one who had received a bond written by Murray's party, for that murder:

But no such bond hath hitherto appeared; and as there have
been several ill founded tales told about it, of which afterwards, they seem also to have somewhat rashly taken up
with the vulgar reports.   Certain it is, that no mention is
made either of the Earl of Bothwell, or of such a writing,
in any of their following accusations of Murray's party
before the Queen of England.

The appointment which Queen Elizabeth so lovingly and
modestly proposed, was no other than that Queen Mary
should resign her crown in favour of her son, and live privately in England.   But that resignation being absolutely
refused upon the 9th of January, the Earl of Murray and
his accomplices got their public answer from the privy
council of England the very next day, not so much to their
mind, as they themselves then, and others since have pretended, whether private encouragement or rewards they
received.   Thus were they screened, at that time, from
having the horrid crimes proved against them, of which they
had been accused by their sovereign.

The Bishop of Ross and Lord Herries complained loudly
of this bare-faced, partial, and wicked behaviour; and yet
they knew only the one half.   What would they have said
if they had known the whole, and that all was carried on
by concert by Elizabeth and Murray, which they had entered upon before-hand?   I cannot indeed tell what they
might have said; but these matters were concerted as follows:

Queen Mary arrived in England upon the xvi. day of
May, 1568; and by the beginning of June, the good Regent Murray had made a voluntary offer to accuse her of the
murder of her second husband, before Queen Elizabeth: of
which offer Elizabeth was most graciously pleased to accept,
as appears by her letter to Murray, dated viii. day of June.

Murray, perceiving how agreeable his offer was, wisely
took the opportunity of providing for his own security and
settlement, " because (says he) we would be most loth to

enter in accusation of the Queen, mother of the King our
Sovereign, and then to enter in qualification with her; for,
all men may judge how dangerous and prejudicial that would
be.   Always, in case the Queen's Majesty [of England]
will have the accusation directly to proceed, it were most
reasonable that we understood what we should look to
follow thereupon, in case we prove all that we alledge;
otherwise we shall be as uncertain after the cause is concluded, as we are presently, &c."

He had also a considerable scruple in a material point,
yea, the very chief point, which he wanted to have removed
before-hand, because he perceived, as he says, that the
trial which the Queen's majesty was minded to have taken
was to be used with great ceremony and solemnity:" and this
was even a modest diffidence that he had in his very letters
to Bothwell, whether they would be sustained as genuine,
or containing sufficient proof. ' It may be (says he), that
such letters as we have of the Queen, our sovereign lord's
mother, that sufficiently, in our opinion, prove her consenting to the murder of the King, her lawful husband, shall
be called in doubt by the judges to be constitute for examination and trial of the cause, whether they may stand or
fall: prove, or not.   Therefore, since our servant, Mr.
John Wood, has the copies of these letters, translated in
our language, we would earnestly desire that these copies
may be considered by the judges, who shall have the examination of the matter, that they may resolve us this far,
in case the principal agree with the copy, that then we
prove the cause indeed.   For when we have manifested and
shewed all, and yet have no assurance that what we send
shall satisfy for probation, for what purpose shall we either
accuse, or take care how to prove, when we are not assured
what to prove, or, when we have proved, what shall
succeed ?"

I never yet could find the counter-tally of this transaction
on Queen Elizabeth's part.   There is, in the appendix, a

paper by Cecil, consisting of answers to every one of those questions and doubts; but it cannot be reckoned to have closed the bargain, which must have been concluded entirely in the terms and manner proposed by Murray, as may well appear from this, that the English commissioners took the trouble to compare the pretended French originals, with Murray's pretended translation. It surely was nothing to the purpose, whether Murray's translation was found to be correct, or not: nor can any shadow of a reason be easily assigned, why they should have taken this trouble, unless, for compleating the bargain in Murray's terms, they had first resolved that, in case the originals should agree with his translation, they would sustain them as full proof of the accusation.

Thus was that abominable confederacy concluded in the month of June, betwixt Queen Elizabeth and Murray; so that there remained nothing to be done on his part, but to produce his letters, and to swear home that they were Queen Mary's hand-writing. The only remaining difficulty was, how to induce the Queen to consent to any hearing or conference with her rebels. Much chicane, and no small time was employed in bringing this about, as is to be seen by a paper of Cecil's, published by James Anderson, in which, though it is stuffed with disingenuity, like all others from that hand, this is visible enough. At last, Elizabeth declaring, that she thought it meetest that the differences betwixt Queen Mary and her subjects should be made up by a good appointment, to which she would contribute by her good offices; that nothing was intended, but to restore her to her kingdom in the most easy and peaceable way, to reduce her rebellious subjects to their due obedience, and to provide such terms for their security, as all might continue in a state of tranquility ever afterwards; Mary consented.

But when Murray came to York, ready to give in his accusation, he began to have further scruples about the

sufficiency of all the security he had obtained, either for his
continuing in the regency, or being even assured of his life.
He therefore laid his doubts before the English commissioners, craving to be resolved as to them, before he would accuse his sovereign and sister; and the more to incite and encourage them to answer his demands, he employed four of
his retinue to shew to these commissioners, in a private
manner, his whole proof and evidences. But their answers did not prove satisfactory.

In the mean time the court of England perceiving that
Murray's wheels moved heavily at York, all parties were
called up to London, for the further prosecution of the
matter: and Queen Elizabeth wrote to her commissioners,
" That the more willingly to induce them of the Queen's
part to come to London, who (says she) we think will most
suspect the same, we would have you to use all good means,
whereby the Queen may understand, that this our conference is intended to take away the delay of time: for we
cannot see any likelihood, but by these means, how to end
this cause in honourable sort, and meet for all parties."

" In the dealing herein, ye shall do well to have good
regard that none of the Queen of Scot's commissioners
may gather any doubt of any evil success of her cause; but
that they may imagine this conference of ours principally
to be meant, how her restitution may be devised with surety
of the Prince her son, and the nobility that have adhered
to him, &c." Thus she wrote upon the xvi. day of October,
and upon the xxx. of that month, her privy council met,
for settling the form of their procedure at this conference;
where it was agreed, that two questions should be put to
Murray's party, " 1. How they could answer such matters as
were contained in the reply on the Queen's part? II. Why
they did forbear in their answer to charge the Queen with
guiltiness in the murder, considering that their party had
always given out to the world that she was guilty? Then, if
they should be content to shew sufficient matter to prove her

guilty, it was thought good, for many respects, that they
should be assured that Queen Elizabeth would never restore her to the crown of Scotland, nor permit her to be
restored, without such assurances as their party should
allow to be good for themselves." Which was accordingly
done.

The commissioners met first upon the xxv. of November,
and that day being spent in entering protestations, shewing
their commissions, administering oaths, and the like preliminaries, upon the very next day Murray received from the
English commissioners a full and satisfactory answer in
writing, to all his doubts and demands; and they received
from him in exchange his accusation of the Queen, which
he had in readiness, but would not exhibit, until it was
ushered in by a solemn protestation, in name of himself and
company, " That their former proceedings might serve for
a sufficient testimony to the world, how unwilling they had
ever been to touch their sovereign lord's mother in honour,
or to publish, unto strangers, matters tending to her perpetual infamy.   That (such was their devotion towards her!)
rather than they would spot her honesty with the society of
that detestable murder, they had been content to suffer
their doings to be misrepresented, and themselves blazoned
as traitors and rebels to their native Prince, in whose person
they had put hands undeservedly.   That easy had it been
for them to have wiped off these, and the like objections,
with a few words, if they would have uttered matters,
which they kept in store for the last cast.   [Pray, dash out
those last nine monosyllables, good reader!] For so desirous were they to cover her shame, that they were content
to bear a part of the burden, to their no small danger. They
well remembered what person she was, whom this matter
chiefly touched, even the mother of the King their sovereign, and one to whom, in particular, the most part of
them were bound for benefits received at her hands, and
therefore could not but privately bear her good will; yea,

so far, that if with the perpetual exile of any one, or even a number of them forth of their native country, they could redeem her honour, without danger of the king's person and whole estate, they affirm, (and it must be remembered they are still upon oath) they would willingly banish themselves to that end: but then Scotland could no longer continue to be a kingdom, and the profession of true religion would go to pot, &c." Therefore Queen Elizabeth was bound to put her to death: and yet nothing of all this was to be charged to their account, but wholly to be imputed to their adversaries, her own Commissioners, who, whatever they pretended, sufficiently declared how little they cared what became of her, by pressing them to come to that answer, which, it was known, they had just cause to make, and would make in the end, [Let six monosyllables more be dashed out,] to her perpetual infamy! For they had no delight all this while to see her dishonoured; nor came they willingly to her accusation for a crime so odious, &c.

Now to one who considers, that they had first produced their letters before their Privy Council in December, the year 1567, and having converted the Act of their Council then made into an Act of their Parliament, which they had printed in April 1568, had sent up their letters to London to be considered, and made a bargain about them, as we have seen, in June, and lastly shewed them at York in October, it will appear to have required no small resolution to enter into this protestation before these very men to whom they had communicated all before, even although they were friends. Whether the height of assurance, or depth of hypocrisy, doth predominate in the composition of this paper, is a problem too hard for me; so I leave the solution to their greatest admirers, whose serious attention it claims in a more special manner.

From this narrative of the matter, it is manifest that Queen Elizabeth, seeing she would have the accusation of

Queen Mary directly to proceed, could employ none other
than those who had usurped her crown, and seized all
her riches, however unfit they were on that accouut; be-
·cause they only had proof, while few others believed it;
and was forced to admit the same men as witnesses to
prove their own accusation, for the same reason. Which
being done, how could she, in honour, either have exposed their chief evidences to open view, or given opportunity to have fixed the King's murder on these accusers
and witnesses? The latter would evidently have annulled
her bargain, and spoiled all the contrivance: and the danger from exposing their proofs was not much less; for had
they been detected to be forgeries, which she certainly
dreaded, Ross and Herries, who were thought to be too
clamourous before, would, upon that emergency, have
been ready to rend the very earth with their terrible ex-
clamations. And it might have been suspected, not without some shew of reason, that Herries's sword would no
longer have lurked quietly in his scabbard, whether Murray or Morton would accept his challenge or not; seeing
no other reasonable redress could be obtained.

But this dire catastrophe was prevented, by keeping the
letters out of the view of every one, besides Murray's·
party and the Court of England: and thus they continued a profound secret, till in the year 1571, after Morton had been a second time at London, with the Queen's
silver box, and their letters in it, for a new conference, it
pleased Queen Elizabeth and her Ministers to have them
printed at London, along with George Buchanan's detection, both in the Latin and Scottish languages, and next
year in French. Along with them there was published a
paper drawn up by Cecil to support their credit, but most
falsely pretending that they had been printed in Scotland.

For what purpose they happened to be then printed,
we are informed by Elizabeth herself and her Ministers,

in their instructions, in the year 1571, to one of her Ambassadors or residents in France, for I have not at present the beginning of that paper: But after many insignificant arguments to be made use for convincing the King of France, that he ought not to interpose on Queen Mary's behalf, we have this remarkable prescription,—" And here were it not amiss to have divers of Buchanan's little Latin books, to present, if need were, to the King, as from yourself, and likewise to some of the other Noblemen of his Council; for they will serve to good effect to disgrace her; which must be done, before other purposes can be attained."

In this manner, and for these ends the letters were made known and spread abroad in the world by good Queen Elizabeth, but little to Queen Mary's advantage; for she herself had been long shut up in one prison, and now the Bishop of Ross, her Ambassador, was confined in another; so that they could know little concerning the practices that were carried on in the world.—And had they even been at greater liberty, it is possible they might not have happened on an absolute proof of the forgery from a printed copy. Every one knows that divers indications of forgery may be discovered in a pretended original writing, which must be quite lost in a copy, whether written or printed: indeed had they been at full liberty, as they ought to have been, it is not to be doubted but that and many other crimes, no less heinous and execrable, would have been brought to light, as the Queen herself expressly says.

But however improper accusers and evidences these men were, and however preposterous and absurd their method of proceeding was in reality, yet as in some points it resembled the ordinary form of probation by writ, and a great deal of ceremony having been used as a cloak for concealing the want of sincerity and honesty, it past with

weak understandings as a proof, and has still been pleaded
as such by persons of deep prejudices, and with such it
will continue to be so esteemed, until it shall be quite
disproved by clear evidence; and even then, some who
have their understandings in absolute subjection to their
wills, and their wills of a perverse disposition, will never
change their opinion, or, at least, not acknowledge it,
unless they could perceive their interest in doing so.

All others of tolerable penetration, considering the close
connexion that had always been betwixt Queen Elizabeth
and Murray's party, suspected this whole story as meer
juggle and imposture; but the stronger evidences for the
truth of their conjectures having been kept secret to this day,
they could not shew clearly that it was actually so. They
made their exception against the stile of the letters, which
in fact differs extremely from the Queen's manner of writing;
and this, joined with other presumptions, forms a strong
argument against them; but few are capable of perceiving
the full force of it: and although a man be, for his own
part, well persuaded of a thing of that nature, he will find
it no easy matter to persuade others.

These and the like difficulties have made some of our own
countrymen look upon this matter as a kind of mysterious
abyss, which, although they were persuaded it had once a
bottom, yet did they doubt whether it could ever hereafter
be fathomed. It is therefore not much to be wondered, if
foreigners, like Monsieur Bayle, or others of the like taste
and complexion, do treat this affair as a remarkable foundation for historical Pyrrhonism. Nevertheless it may be said,
that more might have been expected from so high a pre-
tender to reason as Monsieur Pierre Bayle, than to conclude
the question to be undeterminable, after he had run a parallel betwixt the credit that is due to George Buchanan's
satire, or history, call it as you will, and William Camden's
annals of Queen Elizabeth. Was it not possible that both

of them were in the wrong? Yea, for ought that he knew, Camden's errors, though few in comparison, and inconsiderable, were all on the same side of the question with Buchanan's vile fictions: which for the most part is really the fact.

But perhaps this is all that foreigners, like Bayle, can do, who probably do not imagine that there are better evidences to be had for determining these points: or, if they have any such notion, know not to whom they should apply, or where to search for them. But it would ill become natives of this country, who have fairer opportunities for inquiry, as having more ready access to indubitable documents of the transactions of those times, to put off their readers, or consume their own time with prattle about the veracity or credit of this or that historian; a method not to be borne with, except in matters of high antiquity, in which perhaps nothing better is to be had.

It is therefore purposed in this small treatise, to go to the fountain-head, and strictly to examine whatever evidence the Queen's enemies brought, either to convict her, or to vindicate themselves; and as for the method, to proceed on the same plan which the Queen and her Commissioners appear to have chalked out for themselves, viz. first to demonstrate the forgery of the pretended letters to Bothwell; and then to shew that Murray, Morton, and their accomplices, were the first contrivers, and some of them the real executers of the murder of the King.

The first mention that I have met with of any writing under the Queen's hand, from which her guilt in the murder of her husband was said to appear, is in a letter from Sir Nicholas Throckmorton to Queen Elizabeth, dated from Edinburgh the 25th day of July 1567, by which he acquaints her, that Morton and his associates designed to charge their Queen, among other things, " with the murder of her husband, of which they said they had as apparent proof against her, as might be, as well by the testimony of her own hand-writing, which they had recovered, as also by sufficient witnesses." Now some will be apt to think that the letters to Bothwell are meant by this word, " hand-writing:" and, I confess, I would also have been of that opinion, if they had not affirmed with the same breath, that they had sufficient witnesses too. Had the Queen herself murdered him, or been present when the deed was done, it was possible to have had witnesses; but as that was not the case, it surpasseth an ordinary capacity to imagine how they could possibly have had them. It is to be further observed, that however sufficient these witnesses may be supposed, yet they must needs have been guilty themselves, as well as the Queen; and thence another very hard question arises, What becomes of these witnesses? Certainly they could not be extant upon the 4th day of December that same year; for then the matter having been reasoned upon at great length, and with good deliberation, in their council and convention, for sundry days, no other way, or means, could be found, for vindicating themselves, or accusing the Queen, but the letters to Bothwell only. Now had there been such witnesses, there would have been one other way by them, which could not have been forgot, when the men were reduced to so great straits. And of what service they might have been to the cause the next year in England, every one must see, who considers that when Queen Elizabeth had bent her whole mind to blacken Queen Mary's character, under the pretence of friendship, and of giving her assistance, she was of necessity obliged to receive both for accusers and witnesses, those most open and notorious rebels and traitors, who had imprisoned their Sovereign's person, usurped her royal authority, and seized her whole riches and revenues; in the possession of all which Elizabeth was by compact to maintain them for their pains, as hath been shewn. The transaction indeed must have been infamous at any rate, but not to so evident a degree, if there had been other sufficient witnesses than these accusers, who were thereby both to have their lives and estates secured, which they confess they had forfeited, and to enjoy those rewards of the highest nature besides.

By the same letter we learn, that they then accused the Queen of two other crimes; the first whereof was " tyranny, for violating both their common and statute laws, and, namely, for the breach of those statutes which were enacted in her absence, and confirmed by Monsieur de Randan, and Monsieur D'Oisel, in the French King her husband's name and hers." They mean the acts of their pretended parliament 1560. But in the first place, Messrs. de Randan and D'Oisel had no such commission, either from the King of France, or from her. Secondly, they had both left the kingdom before these pretended laws were framed. And in the third place, not one of these pretended statutes was ever ratified or held as law, till Murray got two of them confirmed in his parliament in December 1567, after the Queen was in prison.   .

A third crime, which they said they were to lay to her charge, was " incontinency, as well with the Earl of Bothwell, as with others, having sufficient proof against her for that crime." As they never wanted sufficient proof, it is much they did not run over the decalogue, and ascribe to her every species of crime. Their proof is to be seen in G. Buchanan's detection, that extraordinary performance, which Queen Elizabeth was so good as to disperse through France. In it we have such a senseless inconsistent story about the Queen, and Dame Reres, Margaret Carwood and Bothwell, and a window and a belt, and every thing, either within doors or without, clearly seen in a dark night, by those who were not present, as has scarcely any parallel in other romances, even the most absurd. Yet he proves all by the confession of a dead man, to wit, George Dalgleish, which, says he, yet remains on record; although in that confession there is not one single word of the story. But if the dead

man's confession will not do, the Queen's own will certainly
be sufficient, for, we have Buchanan's word for it, she confessed it herself. A reader who is not acquainted with Mr.
Buchanan or his books, will be apt to think, that as she
was a Roman Catholic, this confession had been made to
some knavish little priest, who had thus revealed it again.
But that was not the case ; the confession was made to the
most ghostly of all ghostly fathers and mothers, even to the
good Regent the Earl of Murray, and his dear mother the
Lady Lochlevin. Mr. Buchanan's word will be sufficient to
make this story pass with some well disposed people ; but,
for the conviction of others, it were to be wished that
Murray had sworn to the truth of it, or else had put it into
Dalgleish's confession : for to affirm that it was to be found
there, when it is not, has an extreme ugly aspect.

Was it not somewhat unlucky, that the Queen's hand-
writing should have been first mentioned amongst so many
absurdities and falsehoods? And doth not that give a handle
for suspecting this proof to have been as ill founded as the
rest? It will perhaps be asked, Why all this ado about
mentioning her writings in July 1567: doth it not appear
from the act of Murray's privy-council in September 1568,
that they had got them in June the preceding year? It is
so said there indeed : but how are we to know whether that
tale has more truth in it than their former stories? In any
event this letter of Throckmorton's is so far useful, as it directly confronts their holy protestation, that they always declined to publish this matter to strangers, and thus shews
how much credit is due to their assertions, even when upon
oath.

The letters seem to have made their first public appearance in Murray's privy-council, in time of a convention upon
the 4th day of December 1567.

They were next produced in Murray's parliament that
same month.

Thirdly, there was a translation of them, (as Murray calls it) sent to London, to be considered by the council there, in the beginning of June 1568.

The fourth time of their appearance was when Morton delivered them, box and all, to Murray in his privy-council, 16th September 1568.

They were shewed privately to the English commissioners at York, by four of Murray's retinue, amongst whom was Mr. George Buchanan, upon the 10th day of October 1568.

They were produced before the English commissioners at London, upon the 8th day of December 1568, and by them examined, compared and recorded.

Their last public appearance was in Lenox's privy-council, when they were re-delivered to Morton, then going to London, upon the 22d day of January 1571, and there also they were entered upon record.

But neither the pretended originals, nor either of these records, can be found at present, though no small enquiry hath been made after them.

Morton had got the originals again into his hands, and with him they remained, until he was accused of the King's murder, upon the 17th of January 1581. After which the Earl of Angus, as his heir by tail, having taken the inspection and charge of his effects, till the issue of his trial should be seen, the box and letters fell into his hands, and still was kept by him and his successors; for I find an anonymous historian who wrote about the restoration of King Charles II. affirming that the box and letters were at that time to be seen with the Marquis of Douglas; and it is thought by some, that they are still in that family, though others say they have since been seen at Hamilton. What pity it is that they are not sought out and engraven on brass!

Hence it is not easy to account for what we read in the Naudæana, that Gabriel Naudé saw these letters at Rome. If a printed copy is meant, it was no strange sight, nor was

it necessary to go to Rome for it: and the pretended originals were not seen to be there, in his days, wherever they
may be now.   He adds, " That, for his part, he is willing
to believe all that Monsieur de Thou and Buchanan have
said of the Queen to be true."   A rash declaration to come
so abruptly from a man of sense; it savours much of an in-
terpolater's polluting hand; and these Ana's are known to be
of little or no authority.   But however it came there,.it re-
flects little honour on Mr. Naudé.   Every one knows that
there were such letters, whether he saw them or not: but,
unless he could have shewn that they were the Queen's
own, this declaration is foolish.   Yet as if it were to the
purpose, we see it taken hold of in a hodge-podge of im-
pertinence and blunders of divers people amassed together,
and lately printed at Aberdeen, on account chiefly, as it
would seem, of an obscene word, which in the Naudæana
stands in a dead language; but they have translated it, and·
insist on it, thereby displaying the impurity, as well as the
malice, of their hearts.   Who can but pity that poor weak
man, who is used as a vehicle for transmitting such rotten-
wares, and thereby exposed to be so miserably pelted, instead of the proprietors!

The records that were made of these letters would be of
little more use than the printed copies, for the discovery of
the forgery; so that we need not be very anxious about
them.   The extracts from them of such paragraphs as were
thought most to the purpose, by the English commissioners,
are still to be seen.   The letters were printed at London in
the year 1571, at the end of Buchanan's detection, three in
Latin, and all in the Scottish language, where they studied
to preserve the Scottish dialect, that they might seem to
have been published in Scotland, as Cecil gave out; but their
anxiety in that matter, made them sometimes mistake the
older English syllabication for Scottish, putting nat for
not, and the like, and thus betrayed themselves.

The first edition of the detection and letters in French,

was also published at London, though it bears in the title-page that it was printed at Edinburgh by Thomas Waltem, as appears from its giving an account, (folio 82) of the execution of Mather and Barney, which it says happened in the beginning of that year 1572. Now these men were hanged, drawn and quartered, according to the English fashion, upon the 11th day of February that year, for treason against Cecil, and the printing of that book was finished upon the thirteenth day of the same month, as it testifies itself; and therefore must have been done at London, and not at Edinburgh.

It was a common custom in those days, that when the English court thought proper to publish any scandalous books, or pamphlets, they made the title-pages bear that they were printed in Scotland; such as these editions of the detection: the books De furoribus Gallicis: Le Revielle matin, both in French and in Latin, Junius Brutus, &c.

In the same year 1572, the detection and letters were published at St. Andrews, in Scotland, by Robert Leckprevik, which James Anderson would impose upon us as the first edition, as also that it had been translated from the Latin by Mr. Buchanan himself: Neither of which is true. That they have been printed in England before that time, as was said already, we learn from Alexander Hay's letter to Knox, dated the 14th day of December 1571: and that the translation was made by some other person, who hath not always rightly apprehended the true meaning of the Latin, could be made appear at great length, if the matter were of any moment: but, whoever wants to see the truth, may find some examples in Mr. Thomas Ruddiman's notes upon that work. All these editions were consulted in printing the letters in this book.

It is to be observed, that the editions in the Scottish language have eight letters, and the French only seven. Murray actually presented eight before the English commissioners, but they did quietly reject one of that number, and

accepted of the other seven only. Hence that one is wanting in the edition in French, which was certainly published
at London, by Cecil, notwithstanding all his dissimulation
and assertions to the contrary, either in the book itself, or
elsewhere. He it was who drew up the supplement at the end
of it against the Queen and Duke of Norfolk, and had all
in readiness to be published, how soon the Duke should be
beheaded, which, as he expected, should have been upon
the 11th day of February, 1572. But that matter being
put off for some time, to his great grief, he had a few alter-
ations to make, and thus the book was finished at the print-
ing-house only upon the 13th of that month.

Of all the evidences that were found out for proving the
letters to be the Queen's own writing, the first in the proper natural order, though not in time, is a sort of stipulation betwixt Murray and Morton, in their privy-council,
the xvi. day of September, 1568, before they set out for
England; by which Morton delivers up to Murray the box
and letters in it: and Murray, in return, gives him an act of
council, for his exoneration, containing an ample testimo-
nial and declaration, "that Morton had all along truly and
honestly kept the said box, and whole writings and pieces
within the same, without any alteration, augmentation, or
diminution thereof, in any part or portion;" then obliges
himself to make them all forthcoming for the benefit of all
concerned. I call this the first evidence in the natural
order, because, although they had been the year before
produced both in their council and parliament, there had
never been any mention made how or when they got them.
This deficiency is now made up; for in this act we are told,
"that they were found with the late George Dalgleish,
servant to the Earl of Bothwell, upon the xx. day of June,
1567." And thus all is well, had we been told who found
them.

But here it comes naturally to be questioned, how Murray or his council, and especially he himself, who was in

France at the time, could so readily and roundly attest,
either that this box and letters were found with Dalgleish,
or that Morton had so honestly preserved them all that time,
without any manner of change or alteration? This seems
repugnant to common sense, and is so far from answering their purpose, that it affords the most vehement presumption of fraud.

Their acts of council and parliament in December, 1567,
may be reckoned another of their evidences, for they cannot well be counted separately, because their act of parliament is nothing but the fag-end of their act of council;
which council was held for devising before-hand, "how
and by what means a full and perfect law and security
might be obtained, and made, for all those who either by
deed, counsel, or subscription, had entered in their cause
since the beginning. And, the matter being largely, and
with good deliberation, reasoned at great length, and upon
sundry days, at last the whole lords, barons, and others,
could find no other way or means to find or make the said
security, but by producing these letters; which, they declared, they were most loth to do, for the love they bore
to the Queen's person, who was once their sovereign, and
for the reverence of his majesty, whose mother she was,
and also on account of the many good and excellent gifts
wherewith God sometime endued her, if otherwise the
sincerity of their intentions and proceedings from the beginning might have been known to foreign nations, and
the inhabitants of this isle (of whom many as yet remained
in suspense of judgment) satisfied and resolved of the righ-
teousness of their quarrel; and the security of themselves
and their posterity, by any other means, could have been
provided and established."

Behold how lucky a hit this, that it should have chanced
Dalgleish to be apprehended with the letters, at a time of
so great distress. These they produced in parliament, and
obtained security in their own very terms, with the altera-

tion of only one single word, but a most cruel and unlucky word it was, and might have undone all.

In their act of privy-council, which they presented by way of petition to their parliament, they had affirmed that the letters were written and subscribed by the Queen's own hand: but when they came to be produced before the parliament, O, miserable neglect! the subscription had even been forgotten to be added; and when they had once appeared thus publicly without it, could never afterwards be supplied: and both the seal, it seems, and indorsation, had been forgotten also. No very inconsiderable defects!

The parliament therefore could not find them to have been subscribed by her; but they found them to be holograph; for instead of saying they were written and subscribed with her own hand, as the act of council has it, they say the letters were written wholly with her own hand; and all the rest of the act is in Murray's own or his council's words.

It may be said that it was proof enough, if the parliament found them to be written by her, although the subscription was wanting. But whoever will object to this, ought first to satisfy us how papers, which upon the iv. of December, are affirmed by an assembly of twenty-eight persons, to have been subscribed, came to appear thereafter not to have been subscribed, nor ever after pretended to have been so by those very persons themselves, when so often mentioned. For though this circumstance may at first view appear small and trifling, any thinking person who maturely considers it, will perceive that they had designed to have presented their letters to the parliament formally subscribed by the Queen, by whatever mishap it fell out that it was not done; and then it will become extreamly hard to believe that any of these letters had been written by her, any more than subscribed, even although the parliament had sworn to it.

If any body shall express their amazement how the parliament could have allowed an act to pass in their name, in which it was said, that these letters were wholly written by the Queen's own hand; I refer them to the reasons given for their conduct in that matter by a numerous assembly of the greatest personages in the kingdom, of whom many were there present, viz. " There was nothing done in their parliament that might prejudge the Queen's honour in any, sort, her grace never having been called nor accused thereof: for what was done was not to declare her grace guilty of any crime, which of reason no ways could be done against her majesty uncalled; but only an act made for safety of themselves from forfeiture, who treasonably had put hands on her majesty's most noble person, and imprisoned her grace, only founding their proceedings upon just meaning, as they alledged; which sundry noblemen who were her grace's favourers, then present; bore withal, most principally for safety of her grace's life, which, before their coming to parliament, was concluded and subscribed by a great part of those who had seized her person, to be taken from her in a most cruel manner, as is notoriously known; suppose sundry of the noblemen, partakers with themselves, refused to subscribe the same, or consent to her death in any ways.

"And in case any such act had been made, the same cannot prejudge her majesty in any sort, in respect they had no lawful power to hold a parliament. And also it is against all laws and reason to condemn any creature on life, until they be first called to use their lawful defences, or, at least, presented in judgment and heard.

" And likewise it is against all laws and reason, and also it was never seen in practice, that ever the subjects were judges of the Prince, but should always obey them, yea, albeit they be wicked, as the scripture declares."

This is the true state of the matter. We see by their own petition, drawn up in their council, that they desired to have it enacted thus and thus, only as a full and perfect law and security for themselves and their posterity; which they affirm they could not devise by any other means. Murray, with twenty-seven of his satellites or partisans, who were all petitioners for it, and so ought not to have been present, sat and voted for having it past; and all who favoured the Queen were obliged to consent to let them have that security, in their own terms, lest they should murder her; which some of them had concluded to have been done, and had subscribed a covenant for that end; and George Buchanan, who that very year had been moderator of the general assembly of the kirk, had by this time prepared his dialogue *de jure regni*, for justifying all these purposes, from which one may well learn what was in agitation.

If it shall seem strange that any of these men, who so amply testified the great love and good will that they bore to her person, on account of her high rank, and many good and excellent gifts and virtues, should have been at the very same time consulting and covenanting to cut her off; there is nothing in this more than the same persons did over again the next year, while they declare their devotion, private affection, and good wishes towards her, both for private and public respects, and acknowledge the most part of them were bound to her for benefits received at her hands; and yet in the same paper will have Queen Elizabeth to crave her husband's blood at her hands, as being bound so to do by God's ordinance, and at the next meeting, Elizabeth and they together prevailed with that weak man, the Earl of Lenox, to give in a petition to the same purpose. And this may suffice to shew that there are no great things to be built upon these acts of their council and parliament: not to insist that men of as great judgment as were among them, affirmed that the letters were none of her writing,

It is still to be kept in remembrance, that these letters had past both in their Privy Council and Parliament, with-

out any account given how, or when they should have
come to their hands. Dalgleish was then alive, and possibly might have denied that ever he had them. But he
being put to a cruel death amongst others, in January
following, 1568, the box was said, at its next appearance, to have been found with him, upon the xx. day of
June, 1567: but by whom is not said, in either of the
two receipts that are granted for it. It would seem Dalgleish had not been apprehended by Morton himself; and
thence would arise a chasm in the progress of the letters,
which, as is commonly received, was from the Queen to
Nicholas Hubert, or French Paris, who gave them to
Bothwell, who gave them to Sir James Balfour, who
gave them to Dalgleish, from whom they were taken
by Morton, who gave them to Murray, after he kept
them truly and honestly for near xv. months, as Murray
beareth witness. But that ever Sir James Balfour had
them, or that Morton had them from Dalgleish, no man
is warranted to say, by any original accounts of them that
appear at present. They must have passed through as
many hands at least, and probably more: but here we are
as yet in the dark. Morton's declaration of the manner
how he came by them, which he exhibited before the
English Commissioners upon the ix. day of December,
1568, ought surely to have cleared up this matter, which
perhaps it may do afterwards, for at present it cannot be
found.

Were people at liberty to form their judgment concerning the matter from such short hints as occur, it behoved them to conceive of it as not a little mysterious.
Thus the English Commissioners, after Murray's deputies
had instructed them privately in these matters, upon the
x. day of October, use the following words, in relation
to the manner how the box, &c. was found: "The manner
how these men came by them is such as, it seemeth, that

God, in whose sight murder and bloodshed of the innocent is abominable, would not permit the same to be hid,
or concealed." Something very uncommon is always
hinted at, whenever this affair is mentioned.

· As the whole stress, in a manner, of the cause depends
fundamentally upon this declaration (for without it, what
would all the rest signify?) we must allow that there has
been something in it. There is indeed an obvious and
weighty objection : Morton had always been in a confederacy with the enemies of his country, and partaker in
its spoils, both before, at and after the reformation; and
was one of the principal assassins when David Rizio was
murdered, and the Queen so horribly abused, and made
prisoner; that he was also one of the contrivers and executers of the King's murder; and, lastly, the ringleader
in imprisoning the Queen in Lochlevin; therefore his
oaths and declarations could hardly have been regarded,
or accepted, in any cause, far less in this, could his single
testimony be received for the basis of the whole fabrick.
On the other hand, it is to be considered, that if these, or
the like objections, should have been allowed of, they
would have debarred all the rest, as well as him, from
bearing testimony in this cause, as they had been all more
or less concerned in the same transactions; by which
means our famous letters would have been rendered quite
insignificant, and we should also have been deprived of the
declaration by Murray and all the rest of his Commissioners
the next day, which may be esteemed as the capital of all.
It is in these words:

" We, by the tenor hereof, testify, avow and affirm,
upon our honours and consciences, that the whole missive
writings, sonnets, obligations, and contracts, are undoubtedly the said Queen's proper hand-writ; except the
contract in Scots, dated at Seton, the v. day of April,
1567, written by the Earl of Huntly, which also we un-

derstand and perfectly know to be subscribed by her, and will take the same upon our honours and con- sciences," &c.

But no man ought to overload his conscience; and whoever swears 'more than he can know, doth no service to the cause, but hurt. Other people use to swear that they truly believe, or are persuaded, that this or that paper is of such a person's writing : but here is all point blank, undoubted knowledge and perfect certainty in this declaration, which was given for corroboration of their oath made before, as if that had not been sufficient.

And their swearing so positively to the Queen's bare subscription, consisting only of six letters, of which one might easily forge a hundred in a day, so as neither she herself, nor any of them could be able to discern the difference, discovers such a keenness and resolution to go through stitch with their matters, as in men who must have been acquainted with the nature of writings and of oaths, can be called by no other proper appellation, than that of deliberate perjury. All men, it is likely, will not sufficiently comprehend the ground of this observa- tion, but the most part of fine writers and engravers know that the matter is so, and they are the most compe- tent judges, which is enough to me. They swear at the same time that the Earl of Huntly wrote the paper at which this subscription was: ought they not also to have proved his hand-writing, or to have got him to acknowledge the fact some way or other?

Hitherto we have spoke only of what may be strictly called home-proofs, as depending wholly upon their own knowledge and consciences. Now as to their auxi- liaries :—

1 They introduced one Thomas Crawford, whom they call a Gentleman of the Earl of Lenox's, as the person of whose conference with the Queen, on her way to Glasgow, some mention is made in the first letter; and he

swore to some words that then past betwixt the Queen
and him.   But what trifling, what penury of evidence was
this! the Queen surely was not alone with Crawford upon
the road to Glasgow; and thus other persons of her retinue might have known what words past, as well as
either of them, and from them these words might have
come into the letters; or, what hindered but Crawford
might have divulged them himself? so whether he swore
true or not as to that matter, it is the same thing.   Yet
though this part of her testimony was idle, that which
follows was not so.   He fell upon a way to swear to
most of the contents of that letter, without seeing it, and
it is as long as all the rest put together: and a very certain
way it was:

For he swore, " That as soon as the Queen of Scots had
spoken with the King his master at Glasgow, from time to
time, he, Crawford, was secretly informed by the King of
all things which had passed betwixt the Queen and the
King, to the intent that he should report the same to
the Earl of Lenox, his master; because the said Earl durst
not then, for displeasure of the Queen, come abroad! and
that he did immediately at the very time, write the same,
word by word, as near as he possibly could carry the same
away: and, sure he was, that the words now reported in his
writing, concerning the communication between the Queen
of Scots and him, upon the way near Glasgow, are the
very same words, in his conscience, that were spoken: and
that the others, reported to him by the King, were the
same in effect and substance, as they were delivered by the
King to him, though not perhaps the very words themselves.
[One would think they might have been in the very same
words.]   *Causa scientiæ patet.*

The Earl of Lenox indeed was never much worth; and if
he did not see the Queen on that occasion, it may be thought
he has not been on the mending hand.   But what then? let
the gentleman's evidence be considered.   Give ear, ye po-

liticians, and state judges: we have read and heard of screwing up an evidence to the just tone; of twisting and torturing a letter, or the like, till it would bear the proper intended meaning; of straining and stretching a paragraph of statute, till a man, perhaps not much beloved by the great or godly, might, by a select jury, be believed to be within the verge: but say, can it be made appear from all your journals, that such a matchless masterly testimony, so clear and convincing, was ever given, or received by any of you, as that the evidence should have had a copy of a Queen's billet-doux in his pocket, wherewith to convict her, without ever having seen the original; nay even before she could have had time to write it? 'Tis thought it cannot be done. But what did I say? a copy! that it could not be: they were both originals; and the one might well have passed for the other, had not Crawford's been subscribed, while the other wanted the subscription.

This matter then seems to be near at a point. There is no room left for answering. Crawford, who knew best, has sworn clear and full: and let any man swear the contrary, who can. So it is hoped every one is by this time fully and entirely satisfied of the capacity and integrity as well of Crawford the evidence, as of Murray and Morton, plaintiffs, and of the most honourable the judges; as also with regard to the letters, whether they are not to be reckoned genuine; for there can be no doubt from the very beginning as to Crawford's copy, because he acknowledged the writing, and swore to it in open court: but if any reader doth not as yet find himself convinced, he will do best to stop short here; for all that is to follow will have no effect upon him.

There still remains another testimony of the subsidiary kind, which appeared not till nearly eight months after their proof at London had been concluded; and that arose from two confessions of Nicholas Hubert, otherwise called

French Paris, who is said to have carried almost all the letters betwixt the Queen and the Earl of Bothwell. The last confession is here printed, it being the most material, and clear in all points. It contains not only a particular account upon what occasions the letters were written and sent, but also expresses his knowledge of some remarkable points contained in them, which had been communicated to him, with plain tokens and circumstances, as that he himself delivered to the Earl, not only the first letter, but also the bracelets therein-mentioned: that letter likewise, which is here printed in the last place, past through his hands, together with the ring that is said to be sent along with it. In like manner he was the bearer of one of the letters for the rape, which he delivered to the Earl out of his own hand; and got from him an answer making for that purpose. He gives particular and plain indications of the Queen's privity to the contrivance and execution of the murder, which none of the rest, who had formerly been put to death as guilty of that crime, had ever touched upon; for not one of them had said a word against the Queen at all. In short, he is as clear with relation to the Queen's guilt, both in the murder and rape, as he is to the Earl's, with whom he was present at both. So that had he been at London to bear testimony along with Thomas Crawford, their joint evidence would surely have appeared so clear and ample, as they must needs have borne down all opposition, doubt or contradiction; especially when it is considered, that Paris made this confession against his own life, and was put to a cruel death on that very account: so that it is hardly to be imagined, that he would have uttered any thing that was not strictly true.

Yet not the less, however clear and particular these testimonies may appear, if the letters themselves shall after all happen to be disproved, what will become of the testimonies? And how will any one be able to account for them?

'Tis manifest they must stand or fall together; for which reason I shall defer the consideration of the testimonies, till the letters are first discussed.

. But though these letters do by no means prove the facts for which they were produced; they contain several things mean and base, highly unbecoming any woman; but absolutely impossible to have dropt from the pen of this accomplished Princess; one possest of a soul so noble, born in a station and character so highly exalted; tenacious of her dignity and honour, even amidst the utmost malevolence of fortune; and never resigning but with her last breath, the conscious sense of virtue and decorum. Therefore, in the next place, let us see whether it may be made appear manifestly and unanswerably, that they were none of the Queen's writing, but the real manufacture of Murray's own party, whose character every thing in them exactly suits.

NICHOLAS HUBERT'S, OR FRENCH PARIS'S FIRST CONFESSION, 9TH AUGUST, 1569.

"I confess here before God and the world, That upon Wednesday or Thursday before the Sunday of the King's murder, I being in the Queen's chamber, at the Kirk of Field, in company of divers others, abiding her coming from the King's chamber, my Lord Bothwell came where I was, and rounded unto me, saying, Paris, I find me not well of my sickness, the Dysentery that thou knowest. Canst thou not find me out some quiet place, where I may * * * * * *? On my faith, said I, my Lord, I was never in this chamber till now; notwithstanding, my Lord, I shall seek out some place: which I did: and having found a quiet nook, betwixt two doors, I said unto him, Come on, my Lord, if you be so hasty. And we being therein entered, I closed the door upon us, taking his gown from him, and began to loose his points. He looks to me, and asks how I did. Well, my Lord, said I, I thank God, and you that hath caused me to be made chamber-child of the Queen's chamber. He an-

swered me, that that was not enough, and that he would do
more for me.   I said I was content, and that I desired no
more in the Queen's house, conform unto my quality, and
that I was content with the same.   He answered me, that
I should want nothing whereof I should shew him: for, says
he, thou hast done me good and lawful service, since thou
hast served me, and I know thou hast hid my shame and
dishonour, where thou hadst occasion to declare the same,
when thou went from my service forth of England.   My
Lord, said I, I have done nothing but the duty of a servant.   Now, well Paris, said he, for as much as I have
found thee a true and faithful servant, I will tell thee one
thing, but keep it under the pain of thy life, that no
creature know thereof.   My Lord, said I, it pertaineth not
to a servant to reveal his master's secrets, when he for-
biddeth him: but if ye think it be any thing that ye think
I cannot keep closs, tell it not me.   Wots thou what the
matter is, saith he?   If that this King here above get on
his feet over us Lords of this realm, he would both be
masterful and cruel; but as for us, we will not thole such
things; and also it is not the fashion of this country; and
therefore among us we have concluded to blow him up
with powder within this house.   In hearing this I said
nothing, but looked down to the ground.   My heart and
senses turned suddenly, to hear him say such things.
Then looks he to me, and says, What thinkest thou man?
My Lord, I am thinking upon that which ye have said to
me, which is a great and no small thing.   And what
thinks thou thereof, said he?   What think I, my Lord,
quoth I, it mot please you, appardon me, if I shall tell,
according to my poor spirit, what I think.   What wouldst
thou say, quoth he? wouldst thou preach?   Said I, ye shall
hear.   Well, said he, say on, say on.

    " My Lord, said I, since these five or six years that I
have been in your service, I have seen you in great troubles, and never saw any friends that did for you.   And

now, my Lord, ye are furth of all your troubles, thanked
be God, and further in court, as all the world says, than
ever ye was: and, for my part, I see every one, great
and small, make their court to you. But, I know not
who laughs upon you, that would see you otherwise. I
know not, my Lord, ye are of this country; moreover it
is said, that ye are the greatest Lands-lord of this country;
and also, seeing ye are married, at which time a man
should be sitten down, then or never, therefore, my Lord,
if ye take such an enterprise in hand, which is great, it
shall be the greatest trouble that ever ye had above all
others; for every one will cry, Have at you: And ye will
see it. And well, said he, hast thou done? It mot please
you, my Lord, appardon me that I have said, according to
my poor understanding. And, beast that thou art, says he,
thinkest thou that I do it my alone, or of myself? My
Lord, said I, I know not how ye do it, but I know it shall
be the greatest trouble ever ye had. How-can that be,
quoth he? for I have Lethington, who is esteemed one of
the best ingines, or spirits of his country, who is the en-
terpriser of all this thing: and then I have my Lord Argile, my Lord Huntly, my brother, my Lord of Morton,
Ruthven, and Lindesay. As for these three ones, they
will never fail me, for I spake for their grace; and I have
the hand-writs of all those that I have told thee of; and
also we were willing to have done it the last time that we
were at Craigmillar: but thou art but a beast, and a silly
poor spirit, and not worthy to understand or know any
thing of consequence. Faith, my Lord, said I, it is true;
for my spirit serveth me not for such things, but rather to
do you service in all that I may. Now, well, well, my
Lord, they may well make you master and principal of the
deed, but, when it is done, they may happen to lay all
the whole upon you, and then shall be the first that shall
cry, Ha, ha, at you; yea and them that shall put you first
to death, if they may.

" But, my Lord, said I, pray you have mind of one, whom ye have not mentioned. I know well that he is beloved of all the commons of this country, and of us Frenchmen: that when he governed the space of two or three years, there were no troubles in the country: all went well: money had the course. But now, no man is seen that hath any money, and nought else is there now since but troubles. He that I spoke of is wise, and hath good friends and allies. What is he that, said he? My Lord, said I, it is my Lord of Murray: I pray you, what part taketh he? He will not, said he, meddle with the matter. My Lord, said I, he is the more wise. Then he turned about his face to me: My Lord of Murray! my Lord of Murray! my Lord of Murray! he will neither hinder us, nor help us; but all is one. Well, well, my Lord, said I, he doth it not without cause, and ye will see it. Hereupon he commanded me to take the key of the Queen's chamber-door in the Kirk of Field. I refusing; wherefore then, said he, have I placed you in the Queen's chamber, but to draw service out of thee? Alas, my Lord, said I, it is to do you service in all things, so far as I may: but I thought with myself, and said nothing, (because I feared him) if I had known this thing, the chamber should never have chambered me. And thereupon he went from me forth of that hole, where he had ****.

" In this mean time, viz. on Sunday at night, long after supper, come John Hepburn and John Hay, and knock at the door, and entered where I was, and brought powder with them in pocks, and laid it down in the midst of the chamber: in doing of which my Lord of Bothwell came down to them, and said, Lord God! what a din ye make! They may hear above all that ye do. And so he looks, and sees me, and asks me what I was doing there, and bad me follow him up to the King's chamber; which I did, and came and stood beside my Lord of Argile; with whom my Lord Bothwell was speaking. The Queen went toward the Abbay, and went up where Bastian's bridel was, and I was up in a nook, where my Lord of Bothwell came to me, and asked, what ailed me to gloom so, and to be so sad, and that I made such a gloomy countenance before the Queen? he should graith me in such a sort, as I never was in my life. I care not, my Lord, said I, what ye do to me now, beseeching you to give me leave to go to bed, for I am sick. Nay, said he, I will that ye come with me. Thereupon he went into his chamber, and after changing clothes, he went forth, taking with him the tailor and me; and so went and entered within the garden of the King's lodging: the tailor stood still by the wall-side, and I beside him. My Lord Bothwell came to the garden door, and then came again to us, where also John Hay and John Hepburn came; and incontinent, by they had spoken with him, behold! like a tempest and a great thunder-clap rose up. For fright I fell to the ground, and my hair stood prick-up like elsons. Alas, my Lord, said I, what is this? I said I had been at many great interprises, but never interprise feared me so much as this hath done. By my faith, said I, such a thing as this will never have a good end, and ye will see it. O beast! said he to me, and boasted to strike at me with his whinger; but he drew it not out.

" Thereupon he began to make speedily away, and we after him. He thought to have past over the wall at Leith-wynd, but he could not. Then sent he John Hepburn to the porter, and caused the port to be opened. Then went he down the backside of the Canongate; and John Hay and we went down the high-gate: then said I, John Hay, of such as this will never come good. It is true, says he, we have greatly offended God: but what remedy? we must shew our selves vertuous, and pray to God.

" Bothwell, in his high chamber in the Abbay, sent the tailor for me, where were the laird of Ormeston, Hob

Ormeston, John Hepburn, Dalgleish, Powrie, and I. My
Lord asked if I had promised any thing to the King. Nay,
my Lord, quoth I. Seest thou not these Gentlemen, quoth
he, &c. who have abandoned all for my service? And if
thou thinkest that thou hast offended God, the same lieth
not to thy charge, but to mine, who caused thee to do it:
for it is the Lords of this country it self, who, with me,
have committed this crime ; and, for all the pains that
can be put to you, ye must never tell this again. If ye
have will to go your way, ye shall depart right soon, and
be recompensed." *

I have now given the substance of Mr. Goodall's vindication ; and I take my leave of that writer, by citing the
concluding observations of his Preface, by which it will
appear the compiler and advocate was not without his
prejudices.

" But whatever has been said, to the disparagement of
that Princess, or whoever said it, signifies nothing: for
Mary Queen of Scots so far excelled all other Sovereign
Princes who ever yet appeared on the face of the earth,
that, as if she had not been of mortal nature, all the arts
and contrivances of her numerous and malicious enemies
have not availed to fix upon her one crime, shall I say,
nay, not one single foible, either while on the throne, or
in the jail, from her cradle to her grave, unless the want
of omniscience or omnipotence shall be reckoned in her a
defect. This is the very truth: and this can and shall be
made manifest, to the admiration and satisfaction of all
good men, and to the shame and confusion of all others,
who shall ever, in time coming, dare to gainsay."

I shall not enter upon the critical examination of the
Letters with Goodall. I leave my readers to form their
own conclusion.

* Vide Cotton. Lib. Caligula, B. 9. folio 370.

A CRITICAL DISSERTATION CONCERNING THE MURDER OF
KING HENRY, AND THE GENUINENESS OF THE QUEEN'S
LETTERS TO BOTHWELL. BY WILLIAM ROBERTSON, D.D.

IT is not my intention to engage in all the controversies,
to which the murder of King Henry, or the letters from
Mary to Bothwell, have given rise; far less to appear as an
adversary to any particular author, who hath treated of
them. To repeat, and to expose all the ill-founded assertions with regard to these points, which have flowed from
inattention, from prejudice, from partiality, from malevolence, and from dishonesty, would be no less irksome to
myself, than unacceptable to most of my readers. All I
propose is, to assist others in forming some judgment concerning the facts in dispute, by stating the proofs produced
on each side, with as much brevity as the case will admit,
and with the same attention and impartiality, which I have
endeavoured to exercise in examining other controverted
points in the Scottish history.

In order to account for the King's murder, two different
systems have been formed. The one supposes Bothwell to
have contrived and executed this crime. The other imputes
it to the Earls of Murray, Morton, and their party.

The decision of many controverted facts in history, is a
matter rather of curiosity than of use. They stand de-
tached; and whatever we determine with regard to them,
the fabric of the story remains untouched. But the fact
under dispute in this place is a fundamental and essential
one, and according to the opinion which an Historian
adopts with regard to it, he must vary and dispose the whole
of his subsequent narration. An historical system may be
tried in two different ways, whether it be consistent with
probability, and whether it be supported by proper evidence.

Those who charge the King's murder upon Bothwell
argue in the following manner; and though their reasonings.
have been mentioned already in different places of the narrative, it is necessary to repeat them here. Mary's love for
Darnley, say they, was a sudden and youthful passion.
The beauty of his person was his chief merit. His capri-
cious temper soon raised in the Queen a disgust, which
broke out on different occasions. His engaging in the conspiracy against Rizio, converted this disgust into an indignation, which she was at no pains to conceal. This breach
was perhaps, in its own nature, irreparable; the King certainly wanted that art and condescension which alone could
have repaired it. It widened every day, and a deep and
settled hatred effaced all remains of affection. Bothwell
observed this, and was prompted by ambition, and perhaps
by love, to found on it a scheme, which proved fatal both to
the Queen, and to himself. He had served Mary at different
times with fidelity and success. He insinuated himself into
her favour, by address and by flattery. By degrees he
gained her heart. In order to gratify his love, at least his
ambition, it was necessary to get rid of the King. Mary
had rejected the proposal made to her for obtaining a
divorce. The King was equally hated by the partizans of
the house of Hamilton, a considerable party in the
kingdom; by Murray, one of the most powerful and
popular persons in his country; by Morton and his associates, whom he had deceived; and whom Bothwell
had bound to his interest by a recent favour. Among
the people Darnley was fallen under extreme contempt.
He expected, for all these reasons, that the murder of the
king would pass without any enquiry. And to Mary's
love, and to his own address and good fortune, he trusted
for the accomplishment of the rest of his wishes. What
Bothwell expected really came to pass. Mary, if not privy
herself to the design, connived at an action which rid her

of a man whom she had such good reason to detest. A few months after, she married the person who was both suspected and accused of committing the murder.

Those who charge the guilt upon Murray and his party, reason in this manner. Murray, say they, was a man of boundless ambition. Notwithstanding the illegitimacy of his birth, he had early formed a design of usurping the Crown. On the Queen's return into Scotland, he insinuated himself into her favour, and engrossed the whole power into his own hands. He set himself against every proposal of marriage that was made to her, lest his own chance of succeeding to the crown should be destroyed. He hated Darnley, and was no less hated by him. In order to be revenged on him, he entered into a sudden friendship with Bothwell, his ancient and mortal enemy. He encouraged him to perpetrate the crime, by giving him hopes of marrying the Queen. All this was done with a design to throw upon the Queen herself the imputation of being accessary to the murder, and under that pretext, to destroy Bothwell, to depose and imprison her, and to seize the sceptre, which he had wrested out of her hands.

The former of these systems has an air of probability, is consistent with itself, and solves appearances. In the latter, some assertions are false, some links are wanting in the chain, and effects appear, of which no sufficient cause is produced. Murray, on the Queen's return into Scotland, served her with great fidelity, and by his prudent administration rendered her so popular, and so powerful, as enabled her with ease to quash a formidable insurrection raised by himself in the year 1565. What motive could induce Murray to murder a Prince without capacity, without followers, without influence over the nobles, whom the Queen, by her neglect, had reduced to the lowest state of contempt, and who, after a long disgrace, had regained (according to the most favourable supposition) the precarious possession of her favour only a few days before his death? It is difficult to conceive what Murray had to fear from the King's life. It is no easy matter to guess what he could gain by his death. If we suppose that the Queen had no previous attachment to Bothwell, nothing can appear more chimerical than a scheme to persuade her to marry a man, whose wife was still alive, and who was not only suspected, but accused, of murdering her former husband. But that such a scheme should really succeed, is still more extraordinary. If Murray had instigated Bothwell to commit the crime, or had himself been accessary to the commission of it, what hopes were there that Bothwell would silently bear from a fellow criminal all the persecutions which he suffered, without ever retorting upon him the accusation, or revealing the whole scene of iniquity? An antient and deadly feud had subsisted between Murray and Bothwell; the Queen with difficulty had brought them to some terms of agreement. But is it probable that Murray would chuse an enemy, to whom he had been so lately reconciled, for his confidant in the commission of such an atrocious crime? Or, on the other hand, would it ever enter into the imagination of a wise man, first to raise his rival to supreme power, in hopes that afterwards he should find some opportunity of depriving him of that power? The most adventurous politician never hazarded such a dangerous experiment. The most credulous folly never trusted such an uncertain chance.

But however strong these general reasonings may be, we must decide according to the particular evidence produced. This we now proceed to examine.

That Bothwell was guilty of the King's murder appears, 1. From the concurring testimony of all the cotemporary historians. 2. From the confession of those persons who suffered for assisting at the commission of the crime, and who enter into a minute detail of all its circumstances. Anders. v. 2. 165. 3. From the acknowledgment of Mary's own Commissioners, who allow Bothwell to have been one of those who were guilty of this crime. Good. v. 2. 213. 4. From the express testimony of Lesley Bishop of Ross, to the same effect with the former. Def. of Q. Mary's Hon. An. 2. 76. Id. v. 3. p. 31. 5. Morton, at his death, declared that Bothwell had solicited him, at different times, to concur in the conspiracy formed against the life of the King; and that he was informed by Archibald Douglas, one of the conspirators, that Bothwell was present at the murder. Crawf. Mem. App. 4. The letter from Douglas to the Queen, published in the Appendix to Vol. II. No. 12. confirms Morton's testimony. 6. Lord Herreis' promises, in his own name, and in the name of the nobles who adhered to the Queen, that they would concur in punishing Bothwell as the murderer of the King. Append. Vol. I. No. 23.

The most direct charge ever brought against Murray is in these words of Bishop Lesley: " Is it unknown," addressing himself to the Earl of Murray, " what the Lord Herreis said to your face openly, even at your own table, a few days after the murder was committed? Did he not charge you with the foreknowledge of the same murder? Did not he, *nulla circuitione usus*, flatly and plainly burden you, that riding in Fife, and coming with one of your most assured and trusty servants the same day whereon you departed from Edinburgh, said to him, among other talk, This night ere morning Lord Darnley shall lose his life?" Defence of Queen Mary, Anders. v. 2. 75. But the assertion of a man so heated with faction as Lesley, unless it were supported by proper evidence, is of little weight. The servant to whom Murray is said to have spoken these words, is not named; nor the manner in which this secret conversation was brought to light mentioned. Lord Herreis was one of the most zealous advocates for Mary, and it is remarkable that in all his negociation at the Court of England, he never once repeated this accusation of Murray. In answering the chal-

lengergiven him by Lord Lindsay, Herreis had a fair opportunity of mentioning Murray's knowledge of the murder;
but though he openly accuses of that crime some of those
who adhered to him, he industriously avoids any insinua-
tion against Murray himself. Keith Pref. XII. Mary
herself, in a conversation with Sir Francis Knolles, accused Morton and Maitland of being privy to the murder,
but does not mention Murray. And. 4, 55. When the
Bishop of Ross and Lord Herreis themselves appeared before the English Council, January 11, 1569, they declared
themselves ready, in obedience to the Queen's command,
to accuse Murray and his associates of being accessary to
the murder, but " they being also required, whether they
or any of them, as of themselves, would accuse the said
Earl in special, or any of his adherents, or thought them
guilty thereof;" they answered, " that they took God to
witness that none of them did ever know any thing of the
conspiracy of that murder, or were in Council and foreknowledge thereof; neither who were devisers, inventors,
and executors of the same, till it was publicly discovered
long thereafter by some of the assassins who suffered death
on that account." Good. v. 2. 308. These words are
taken out of a register kept by Ross and Herreis themselves, and seem to be a direct confutation of the Bishop's
assertion. The Bishop himself repeats the same thing in
still stronger terms. And. 3. 31.

The Earls of Huntly and Argyll, in their Protestation
touching the murder of the King of Scots, after mentioning the conference at Craigmillar concerning a divorce,
of which we have given an account, Vol. I. 330. add " So
after these premises, the murder of the King following,
we judge in our consciences, and hold for certain and truth,
that the Earl of Murray and Secretary Lethington were
authors, inventors, counsellors, and causers of the same
murder, in what manner, or by whatsomever persons the
same was executed." Anders. v. 4. 188. But, 1. This is

nothing more than the private opinion or personal affirmation of these two noblemen. 2. The conclusion which they make has no connection with the premisses on which they found it. Because Murray proposed to obtain for the Queen a divorce from her husband with her own consent, it does not follow that therefore he committed the murder without her knowledge. 3. Huntly and Argyll were at that time the leaders of that party opposite to Murray, and animated with all the rage of faction. 4. Both of them were Murray's personal enemies. Huntly, on account of the treatment which his family and clan had received from that nobleman. Argyll was desirous of being divorced from his wife, with whom he lived on no good terms. Knox, 328. and by whom he had no children. Crawf. Peer. 19. She was Murray's sister, and by his interest he had obstructed that design. Keith, 551. These circumstances would go far towards invalidating a positive testimony; they more than counterbalance an indeterminate suspicion. 5. It is altogether uncertain whether Huntly and Argyll ever subscribed this protestation. A copy of such a protestation as the Queen thought would be of advantage to her cause, was transmitted to them by her. Anders. v. 4. 186. The protestation itself, published by Anderson, is taken from an unsubscribed copy, with blanks for the date and place of subscribing. On the back of this copy is pasted a paper, which Cecil has marked "Answer of the Earl of Murray to a writing of the Earls of Huntly and Argyll." Anders. 194, 195. But it can scarce be esteemed a reply to the above-mentioned protestation. Murray's answer bears date at London, January 19, 1568. The Queen's letter, in which she inclosed the copy of the protestation, bears date at Bowton, Jan. 5, 1568. Now it is scarce to be supposed that the copy could be sent into Scotland, be subscribed by the two Earls, and be seen and answered by Murray within so short a time. Murray's reply seems intended only to prevent the impression which vague and uncertain accusations of his enemies might make in his absence. Cecil had got the original of the Queen's letter into his custody. Anders. vol. 4. 186. This naturally leads us to conjecture that the letter itself, together with the inclosed protestation, were intercepted before they came to the hands of Huntly and Argyll. Nor is this mere conjecture alone. The letter to Huntly, in which the protestation was inclosed, is to be found, Cott. Lib. Cal. C. 1. fol. 280, and is an original subscribed by Mary, though not written with her own hand, because she seldom chose to write in the English language. The protestation is in the same volume, fol. 282, and is manifestly written by the same person who wrote the Queen's letter. This is a clear proof that both were intercepted. So that much has been founded on a paper not subscribed by the two Earls, and probably never seen by them. Besides, this method which the Queen took of sending a copy, to the two Earls, of what was proper for them to declare with regard to a conference held in their own presence, appears somewhat suspicious. It would have been more natural, and not so liable to any misinterpretation, to have desired them to write the most exact account, which they could recollect of what had passed in the conversation at Craigmillar.

The Queen's Commissioners at the Conferences in England accused Murray and his associates of having murdered the King. Good. 2. 281. But these accusations are nothing more than loose and general affirmations, without descending to such particular circumstances, as either ascertain their truth, or discover their falsehood. The same accusation is repeated by the nobles assembled at Dumbarton, Sept. 1568. Good. 2. 359. And the same observation may be made concerning it.

All the Queen's advocates have endeavoured to account for Murray's murdering of the King, by supposing that it was done on purpose, that he might have a pre-

tence of disturbing the Queen's Administration, and thereby
rendering ineffectual her general Revocation of Crown
lands, which would have deprived him and his associates
of the best part of their estates. Lesley Def. of Mary's
Hon. p. 73. But whoever considers the limited powers
of a Scottish Monarch, will see that such a revocation
could not be very formidable to the nobles. Every King
of Scotland began his reign with such a revocation; and
as often as it was renewed, the power of the nobles rendered it ineffectual. The best vindication of Murray and
his party from this accusation, is that which they presented to the Queen of England, and which hath never
hitherto been published.

Answers to the objections and alledgance of the Queen,
    alledging the Earl of Murray Lord Regent, the Earls of
    Morton, Marr, Glencairn, Hume, Ruthven, &c. to have
    been moved to armour, for that they abhorred and
    might not abide her revocation of the alienation made
    of her property.

PAPER OFFICE.

It is answered, that is alledged but all appearance, and
it appears God has bereft the alledgance of all wit and
good remembrance, for thir reasons following:

Imprimis, as to my Lord Regent, he never had occasion to grudge thereat, in respect the Queen made him
privy to the same, and took resolution with him for the
execution thereof, letting his Lordship know she would
assuredly in the samine except all things she had given to
him, and ratefy them in the next Parliament, as she did
indeed; and for that cause wished my Lord to leave behind him Master John Wood, to attend upon the same, to
whom she declared, that als well in that as in all others
her grants it should be provided, yea of free will did
promise and offer before ever he demanded, as it came to
pass without any let or impediment, for all was ratified

F f

by her command, and hand-write, at the parliament, but any difficulty.

Item as to my Lord of Morton, he could not grudge thereat quha never had of her property worth twenty dollars that ever I knew of.

Item the same, may I say of my Lord Glencairn.

Item the same, I may say of my Lord Hume.

Item the same, I may say of my Lord Ruthven.

Item the same, I may say of my Lord Lindsay.

Only my Lord of Marr, had ane little thing of the property quilk alsua was gladly and liberally confirmed to him, in the said parliament preceeding a year; was never ane had any cause of miscontent of that revocation, far less to have put their lives ane heritage to so open and manifest ane danger as they did for sic ane frivole cause.

Gyf ever any did make evill countenance, and show any miscontentment of the said revocation, it was my Lord of Argyll in speciall, quha spak largely in the time of parliament theiranents to the Queen herself, and did complain of the manifest corruption of ane act of parliament past upon her majesty's return, and sa did lett any revocation at that time; but the armor for revenge of the King's deid was not till twa months after, att quhat time there was no occasion given thereof, nor never a man had mind thereof.

Having thus examined the evidence which has been produced against the Earls of Murray and Bothwell, we shall next proceed to enquire whether the Queen herself was accessory to the murder of her husband.

No sooner was the violent death of Darnly known, than strong suspicions arose, among some of her subjects, that Mary had given her consent to the commission of that crime. And. 2. 156.   We are informed, by her own ambassador in France, the Archbishop of Glasgow, that the sentiments of foreigners, on this head, were no less unfavourable to her. Keith, Pref. ix.   Many of her nobles loudly accused her of that crime, and a great part of the nation, by supporting them, seem to have allowed the accusation to be well founded.

Some crimes, however, are of such a nature, that they scarce admit of a positive or direct proof. Deeds of darkness can seldom be brought perfectly to light. Where persons are accused not of being principals, but only of being accessaries to a crime; not of having committed it themselves, but only of giving consent to the commission of it by others; the proof becomes still more difficult: and unless when some accomplice betrays the secret, a proof by circumstances, or presumptive evidence, is all that can be attained. Even in judicial trials, such evidence is sometimes held to be sufficient for condemning criminals. The degree of conviction which such evidence carries along with it, is often not inferior to that which arises from positive testimony; and a concurring series of circumstances satisfies the understanding no less than the express declaration of witnesses.

Evidence of both these kinds has been produced against Mary. We shall first consider that which is founded upon circumstances alone.

Some of these suspicious circumstances preceded the King's death; others were subsequent to it. With regard to the former, we may observe that the Queen's violent love of Darnley was soon converted into an aversion to him no less violent; and that his own ill conduct, and excesses of every kind, were such, that if they did not justify, at least they account for this sudden change of her disposition towards him. The rise and progress of this domestic rupture, I have traced with great care in the history, and to the proofs of it which may be found in papers published by other authors, I have added those contained in App. No. XVI. and XVII. The Earls of Murray, Morton, Bothwell, Argyll, and Huntly, considered the scheme of procuring for the Queen a divorce from her husband, as one of the most flattering proposals they could make to her, and employed

it as the most powerful inducement to prevail on her to
consent to a measure, which they had much at heart,
but from which they knew her to be extremely averse.
And. 4. p. 2. 188. Du Croc the French ambassador, who
was an eye-witness of what he describes, not only represents her disgust to Darnley to be extreme, but declares
that there could be no hopes of a reconcilement between
them. " The Queen is in the hands of physicians, and I
do assure you is not at all well; and do believe the principal part of her disease to consist in deep grief and sorrow :
nor does it seem possible to make her forget the same.
Still she repeats these words, "I could wish to be dead."
You know very well that the injury she has received is ex-
ceeding great, and her majesty will never forget it. To
speak my mind freely to you, I do not expect, upon several accounts, any good understanding between them [i. e.
the King and Queen] unless God effectually put to his
hand. His bad deportment is incurable, nor can there ever
be any good expected from him for several reasons, which
I might tell you was I present with you. I cannot pretend to foretell how all may turn, but I will say, that matters cannot subsist long as they are, without being accompanied with sundry bad consequences." Keith, Pref. vii.
Had Henry died a natural death, at this juncture, it must
have been considered as a very fortunate event to the Queen,
and as a seasonable deliverance from a husband who had
become altogether odious to her. Now as Henry was
murdered a few weeks afterwards, and as nothing had happened to render the Queen's aversion to him less violent;
the opinion of those who consider Mary as the author of an
event, which was manifestly so agreeable to her, will appear, perhaps, to some of our readers to be neither unnatural
nor over refined. If we add to this, what has been observed in
the history, that in proportion to the increase of Mary's
hatred of her husband, Bothwell made progress in her favour ; and that he became the object not only of her confi-

dence but her attachment, that opinion acquires new strength. It is easy to observe many advantages which might redound to Mary as well as to Bothwell from the King's death; but excepting them, no person and no party in the kingdom could derive the least benefit from that event. Bothwell, accordingly, murdered the King, and it was, in that age, thought no violent imputation on Mary's character, to suppose that she had consented to the deed.

The steps which the Queen took after her husband's death, add strength to that supposition. 1. Melvil, who was in Edinburgh at the time of the King's death, asserts that " every body suspected the Earl of Bothwell; and those who durst speak freely to others, said plainly that it was He." P. 155. 2. Mary having issued a proclamation, on the 12th of February, offering a reward to any person, who should discover those who had murdered her husband; And. 1. 36. a paper in answer to this was affixed to the gates of the Tolbooth, February 16, in which Bothwell was named as the chief person guilty of that crime, and the Queen herself was accused of having given her consent to it. And. 2. 156. 3. Soon after, February 20, the Earl of Lennox, the King's father, wrote to Mary, conjuring her, by every motive, to prosecute the murderers with the utmost rigour. He plainly declared his own suspicions of Bothwell, and pointed out a method of proceeding against him, and for discovering the other authors of the crime, no less obvious than equitable. He advised her to seize; and to commit to sure custody, Bothwell himself, and those who were already named as his accomplices: to call an assembly of the noble; to issue a proclamation, inviting Bothwell's accusers to appear; and if, on that encouragement, no person appeared to accuse them, to hold them as innocent, and to dismiss them without farther trial. And. 1. 40. 4. Archbishop Beatoun, her ambassador in France, in a letter to Mary, March 9th, employs arguments of the ut-

most weight to persuade her to prosecute the murderers
with the greatest severity. "I can conclude nathing, (says
he) by quhat zour majesty writes to me zourself, that sen
it has plesit God to conserve zow to make a rigorous vengeance thereof, that rather than it be not actually taine, it
appears to me better in this warld that ze had lost life and
all. I ask your majestie pardon that I writ sa far, for I
can heir nathing to zour prejudise, but I man constraindly
writ the samin, that all may come to zour knawledge; for
the better remede may be put therto. Heir it is needfull
that ze forth shaw now rather than ever of before, the
greite vertue, magnanimitie, and constance that God has
grantit zow, be quhais grace, I hope ze sall overcome this
most heavy envie and displesir of the committing thereof,
and conserve that reputation in all godliness, ze have con-
quist of lang, quhich can appear na wayis mair clearlie,
than that zow do sick justice that the haill world may declare zowr innocence, and give testimony forever of thair
treason that has committed (but fear of God or man) so
cruel and ungodlie a murther, quhairof there is sa meikle
ill spoken, that I am constrainit to ask zow mercy, that neither can I or will I make the rehearsal therof, which is owr
odious. But alas! madame, all over Europe this day there
is na purpose in head sa frequent as of zour majestie, and of
the present state of your realm, quhilk is in the most part
interpretit sinisterly." Keith, Pref. ix. 5. Elizabeth, as
appears from Append. Vol. I. No. XIX. urged the same
thing in strong terms. 6. The circumstances of the
case itself, no less than these solicitations and remonstrances, called for the utmost vigour in her proceedings.
Her husband had been murdered in a cruel manner, almost
in her own presence. Her subjects were filled with the
utmost horror at that crime. Bothwell, one of her principal favourites, had been publicly accused as the author of
it. Reflections, extremely dishonourable to herself, had
been thrown out. If indignation, and the love of justice,

did not prompt her to pursue the murderers with ardour, decency, at least, and concern for vindicating her own character, should have induced her to avoid any appearance of remissness or want of zeal.

But instead of this, Mary continued to discover, in all her actions, the utmost partiality towards Bothwell. 1. On the 15th of February, five days after the murder, she bestowed on him the reversion of the superiority of the town of Leith, which in the year 1565 she had mortgaged to the citizens of Edinburgh. This grant was of much importance, as it gave him not only the command of the principal port in the kingdom, but a great ascendant over the citizens of Edinburgh, who were extremely desirous of keeping possession of it. 2. Bothwell being extremely desirous to obtain the command of the castle of Edinburgh, the Queen, in order to prevail on the Earl of Mar to surrender the government of it, offered to commit the young prince to his custody. Mar consented; and she instantly appointed Bothwell governor of the castle. And. 1. Pref. 64. Keith, 379. 3. The inquiry into the murder, previous to Bothwell's trial, seems to have been conducted with the utmost remissness. Buchanan exclaims loudly against this. And. 2. 24. Nor was it without reason that he did so, as is evident from a circumstance in the affidavit of Thomas Nelson, one of the King's servants, who was in the house when his master was murdered, and was dug up alive out of the rubbish. Being examined on the Monday after the King's death, " This deponar schew that Bonkle had the key of the sellare, and the Queenis servandis the keyis of her shalmir. Quhilk the Laird of Tillibardin hearing, said, Hald thair, here is ane ground. Efter quhilk words spokin, thai left of, and procedit na farther in the inquisition.' And. 4. p. 2. 167. Had there been any intention to search into the bottom of the matter, a circumstance of so much importance merited the most careful enquiry. 4. Notwithstanding Lennox's repeated sollicitations, notwithstanding the reasonableness of his demands, and the necessity of complying with them, in order to encourage any accuser to appear against Bothwell, she not only refused to commit him to custody, or even to remove him from her presence and councils; And. 1. 42, 48. but by the grants which we have mentioned, and by other circumstances, discovered an increase of attachment to him. 5. She could not avoid bringing Bothwell to a public trial ; but she permitted him to sit as a member in that meeting of the Privy Council, which directed his own trial; and the trial itself was carried on with such unnecessary precipitancy, and with so many other suspicious circumstances, as to render his acquittal rather an argument of his guilt than a proof of his innocence. These circumstances have all been mentioned at length, vol. I. p. 403, &c. and therefore are not repeated in this place. 6. Two days after the trial, Mary gave a public proof of her regard for Bothwell, by appointing him to carry the sceptre before her at the meeting of Parliament. Keith, 378. 7. In that parliament, she granted him a ratification of all the vast possessions and honours which she had conferred upon him, in which was contained an ample enumeration of all the services he had performed. And. 1. 117. 8. Though Melvil, who foresaw that her attachment to Bothwell would at length induce her to marry him, warned her of the infamy and danger which would attend that action, she not only disregarded this salutary admonition, but discovered what had passed between them to Bothwell, which exposed Melvil to his indignation. Melv. 156. 9. Bothwell seized Mary as she returned from Stirling, April 24. If he had done this without her knowledge and consent, such an insult could not have failed to have filled her with the most violent indignation. But according to the account of an old MS. " The friendly love was so highly contracted between this great princess and her enormous subject, that there was no end thereof (for it was constantly esteemed by all men that either of them loved other

carnally), so that she suffered patiently to be led where the
lover list, and all the way neither made obstacle, impediment, clamour or resistance, as in such accidents use to be,
or that she might have done by her princely authority, being accompanied with the noble Earl of Huntly, and Secretary Maitland of Lethington." Keith, 383. Melvil,
who was present, confirms this account, and tells us that
the officer, by whom he was seized, informed him that nothing was done without the Queen's consent. Melv. 158.
10. On the 12th of May, a few days before her marriage,
Mary declared that she was then at full liberty, and that
though Bothwell had offended her by seizing her person,
she was so much satisfied with his dutiful behaviour since
that time, and so indebted to him for past services, that she
not only forgave that offence, but resolved to promote him
to higher honours. And. 1. 187. 11. Even after the confederate nobles had driven Bothwell from the Queen's presence, and though she saw that he was considered as the
murderer of her former husband by so great a part of her
subjects, her affection did not in the least abate, and she
continued to express the most unalterable attachment to
him. "I can perceive (says Sir N. Throgmorton) that the
rigour with which the Queen is kept, proceedeth by order
from these men, because that the Queen will not by any
means be induced to lend her authority to prosecute the
murder; nor will not consent by any persuasion to abandon the Lord Bothwell for her husband, but avoweth constantly that she will live and die with him; and saith that
if it were put to her choice to relinquish her crown and
kingdom, or the Lord Bothwell, she would leave her kingdom and dignity to go a simple damsel with him, and that
she will never consent that he shall fare worse, or have
more harm than herself." App. p. 42. See also p. 44.
From this long enumeration of circumstances, we may,
without violence, draw the following conclusion. Had
Mary really been accessary to the murder of her husband;

G g

had Bothwell perpetrated the crime with her consent, or
at her command; and had she intended to stifle the evidence against him, and to prevent the discovery of his guilt,
she could scarce have taken any other steps than those she
took, nor could her conduct have been more repugnant to
all the maxims of prudence and of decency.

The positive evidence produced against Mary may be
classed under two heads.

1. The depositions of some persons who were employed
in committing the murder, particularly of Nicholas Hubert, who in the writings of that age is called French Paris.
This person, who was Bothwell's servant, and much trusted
by him, was twice examined, and the original of one of his
depositions, and a copy of the other, are still extant. It
is pretended that both these are notorious forgeries. But
they are remarkable for a simplicity and naïveté which it is
almost impossible to imitate; they abound with a number
of minute facts and particularities, which the most dexter-
ous forger could not have easily assembled, and connected
together with any appearance of probability; and they are
filled with circumstances, which can scarce be supposed to
have entered the imagination of any man, but one of Paris's
profession and character. But, at the same time, it must
be acknowledged that his depositions contain some improbable circumstances. He seems to have been a foolish talka-
tive fellow; the fear of death; the violence of torture; and
the desire of pleasing those in whose power he was, tempted
him, perhaps, to feign some circumstances, and to exaggerate others. To say that some circumstances in an affidavit
are improbable or false, is very different from saying that
the whole is forged. I suspect the former to be the case
here; but I see no appearance of the latter. Be that as it
will, some of the most material facts in Paris's affidavits rest
upon his single testimony; and for that reason, I have not
in the history, nor shall I in this place, lay any stress upon
them.

2. The letters said to be written by Mary to Bothwell. These have been frequently published. The accident, by which the Queen's enemies got them into their possession, is related Vol. I. 435. When the authenticity of any ancient paper is dubious or contested, it may be ascertained either by external or internal evidence. Both these have been produced in the present case.

I. External proofs of the genuineness of Mary's letters. 1. Murray and the nobles who adhered to him affirm, upon their word and honour, that the letters were written with the Queen's own hand, with which they were well acquainted. Good. 2. 64, 92. 2. The letters were publicly produced in the parliament of Scotland, December, 1567, Good. 2. 360; and were so far considered as genuine, that they are mentioned, in the act against Mary, as one chief argument of her guilt. Good. 2. 66. 3. They were shewn privately to the Duke of Norfolk, the Earl of Sussex, and Sir Ralph Sadler, Elizabeth's commissioners at York. In the account which they give of this matter to their mistress, they seem to consider the letters as genuine, and express no suspicion of any forgery; they particularly observe, "that the matter contained in them is such that it could hardly be invented and devised by any other than herself; for that they discourse of some things, which were unknown to any other than to herself and Bothwell; and as it is hard to counterfeit so many, so the matter of them, and the manner how these men came by them is such, as it seemeth that God, in whose sight murder and bloodshed of the innocent is abominable, would not permit the same to be hid or concealed." Good. 2. 142. They seem to have made such an impression on the Duke of Norfolk, that in a subsequent letter to Pembroke, Leicester and Cecil, he has these words, " If the matter shall be thought as detestable and manifest to you, as, for aught we can perceive, it seemeth here to us." Good. 2. 154. 4. After the conferences at York and Westminster were finished, Elizabeth resolved to

call together the Earls who were then at court, and to lay
before them the whole proceedings against the Scottish
Queen, particularly that " the letters and writing exhibited
by the Regent, as the Queen of Scots' letters and writings,
should also be shewed, and conference [i. e. comparison]
thereof made in their sight, with the letters of the said
Queen's being extant, and heretofore written with her
own hand, and sent to the Queen's majesty: whereby may
be searched and examined what difference is betwixt them."
Good. 2. 252. They assembled accordingly, at Hampton
Court, December 14 and 15 1568; and " The originals
of the letters supposed to be written with the Queen of
Scots own hand, were then also presently produced and perused; and being read, were duly conferred and compared,
for the manner of writing, and fashion of orthography, with
sundry other letters long since heretofore written, and
sent by the said Queen of Scots to the Queen's Majesty
——In collation whereof no difference was found." Good. 2.
256. 5. Mary having written an apologetical letter for her
conduct to the Countess of Lennox, July 10, 1570*, she

---

* Mary's letter has never been published, and ought to have a place
here, where evidence on all sides is fairly produced. " Madam, if
the wrang and false reportis of rebellis, enemeis weill kwawin for
traitouris to zow, and alace to muche trusted of me by zoure advice,
had not so far sturred you aganis my innocency, (and I must say
aganis all kyndness, that zow have not onelie as it were condempnit
me wrangfullie, bot so hated me, as some wordis and opene deideis
hes testifeit to all the warlde, a manyfest mislyking in zow aganis
zour awn blude) I wold not have omittit thus lang my dewtie in
wryting to zow excusing me of those untrew reporties made of me.
But hoping with Godis grace and tyme to have my innocency knawin
to zow, as I trust it is already to the maist pairt of all indifferent
personis, I thocht it best not to trouble zow for a tyme till that such
a matter is moved that tuichis us bayth, quhilk is the transporting
zoure littil son, and my onelie child in this countrey. To the quhilk
albeit I be never sa willing, I wald be glaid to have zoure advyse
therein, as in all uther thingis tuiching him. I have born him, and
God knawis with quhat danger to him and me boith; and of zow he
is descendit. So I meane not to forzet my dewtie to zow, in schewin
herein any unkyndness to zow, how unkyndlie that ever ze have delt

transmitted it to her husband then in Scotland; and he returned to the Countess the following answer: " Seeing you have remittit to me, to answer the Queen the King's mother's letters sent to you, what can I say but that l do not marvell to see hir writ the best she can for hirself, to seame to purge hir of that, quhairof many besyde me are certainly persuadit of the contrary, and I not only assurit by my awin knawledge, but by her handwrit, the confessionis of men gone to the death, and uther infallibil experience. It wull be lang tyme that is hable to put a mattir so notorious in oblivioun, to mak black quhyte, or innocency to appear quhair the contrary is sa weill knawin. The maist indifferent, I trust, doubtis not of the equitie of zoure and my cause, and of the just occasioun of our mislyking. Hir richt dewtie to zow and me, being the parteis interest, were hir trew confessioun and unfeyned repentance of that lamentable fact, odious for hir to be reportit, and sorrowfull for us to think of. God is just, and will not in the end be abused; but as he has manifested the trewth, so will he puneise the iniquity." Lennox's Orig. Regist. of Letters. In their public papers, the Queen's enemies may be suspected of advancing what would be most subservient to their cause; not what was agreeable to truth, or what flowed from their own inward conviction. But in a private letter to his own wife, Lennox had no occasion to dissemble; and it is plain, that he not only thought the Queen guilty, but believed the authenticity of her letters to Bothwell.

with me, bot will love zow as my awnt, and respect zow as my moder in law. And gif ye ples to knaw farther of my mynd in that and all uther thingis betwixt us, my ambassador the bishop of Ross sall be ready to confer with zow. And so after my hairtlie commendationis, remitting me to my saide ambassador, and zour better consideratioun, I commit zow to the protectioun of Almyghty God, quhom I pray to preserve zow and my brother Charles, and caus zow to knaw my pairt better nor ze do. From Chatisworth this x of July 1570.

To my Ladie Lennox   Youre natural gude Nice
my moder in law.   and lovynge dochter. M. R.

II. With regard to the internal proofs of the genuineness of the Queen's letters to Bothwell, we may observe,
1. That whenever a paper is forged with a particular intention, the eagerness of the forger to establish the point
in view, his solicitude to cut off all doubts and cavils, and
to avoid any appearance of uncertainty, always prompt
him to use expressions the most explicit and full to his
purpose. The passages foisted into ancient authors by
Heretics in different ages ; the legendary miracles of the
Romish saints; the supposititious deeds in their own favour produced by monasteries ; the false charters of homage
mentioned Vol. I. p. 13. are so many proofs of this assertion. No maxim seems to be more certain than this,
that a forger is often apt to prove too much, but seldom
falls into the error of proving too little. The point which
the Queen's enemies had to establish, was " that as the
Earl of Bothwell was chief executor of the horrible and
unworthy murder perpetrated, &c. so was she of the foreknowledge, counsel, device, persuader, and commander
of the said murder to be done." Good. 2. 207. But of
this there are only imperfect hints, obscure intimations,
and dark expressions in the letters, which however convincing evidence they might furnish if found in real letters,
bear no resemblance to that glare and superfluity of evidence which forgeries commonly contain. All the advocates for Mary's innocence in her own age, contend that
there is nothing in the letters which can serve as a proof
of her guilt. Lesley, Blackwood, Turner, &c. abound
with passages to this purpose; nor are the sentiments of.
those in the present age different. " Yet still it might
have been expected (says her latest defender) that some
one or other of the points or articles of the accusation
should be made out clearly by the proof. But nothing of
that is to be seen in the present case. There is nothing
in the letters, that could plainly shew the writer to have
been in the foreknowledge, counsel, or device of any.

murder, far less to have persuaded or commanded it; and as little is there about maintaining or justifying any murderers." Good. 1. 76. How ill advised were Mary's adversaries to contract so much guilt, and to practise so many artifices in order to forge letters, which are so ill contrived for establishing the conclusion they had in view? Had they been so base as to have recourse to forgery, is it not natural to think that they would have produced something more explicit and decisive? 2. As it is almost impossible to invent a long narration consisting of many circumstances, and to connect it in such a manner with real facts, that no mark of fraud shall appear; for this reason skilful forgers avoid any long detail of circumstances, especially of foreign and superfluous ones, well knowing that the more these are multiplied, the more are the chances of detection increased. Now Mary's letters, especially the first, are filled with a multiplicity of circumstances, extremely natural in a real correspondence, but altogether foreign to the purpose of the Queen's enemies, and which it would have been extreme folly to have inserted if they had been altogether imaginary, and without foundation. 3. The truth and reality of several circumstances in the letters, and these, too, of no very public nature, are confirmed by undoubted collateral evidence. Lett. 1. Good. 2. p. 1. The Queen is said to have met one of Lennox's gentlemen, and to have some conversation with him. Thomas Crawford, who was the person, appeared before Elizabeth's Commissioners, and confirmed, upon oath, the truth of this circumstance. He likewise declared, that during the Queen's stay at Glasgow, the King repeated to him, every night, whatever had passed, through the day, between her Majesty and him, and that the account given of these conversations in the first letter, is nearly the same with what the King communicated to him. Good. 2. 245. According to the same letter there was much discourse between the King and

Queen concerning Mynto, Hiegait, and Walcar.   Good. 2.
8, 10, 11.   What this might be, was altogether unknown,
till a letter of Mary's preserved in the Scottish college at
Paris, and published, Keith, Pref. vii. discovered it to be
an affair of so much importance as merited all the attention she paid to it at that time.   It appears by a letter
from the French Ambassador, that Mary was subject to a
violent pain in her side.   Keith, ibid.   This circumstance
is mentioned, Lett. 1. p. 30. in a manner so natural as can
scarce belong to any but a genuine production.   4. If we
shall still think it probable to suppose that so many real
circumstances were artfully introduced into the letters by
the forgers, in order to give an air of authenticity to their
production; it will scarce be possible to hold the same
opinion concerning the following particular.   Before the
Queen began her first letter to Bothwell, she, as is usual
among those who write long letters containing a variety
of subjects, made notes or memorandums of the particulars she wished to remember; but as she sat up writing
during a great part of the night, and after her attendants
were asleep, her paper failed her, and she continued her
letter upon the same sheet, on which she had formerly
made her memorandums.   This she herself takes notice of,
and makes an apology for it: " It is late; I desire never to
cease from writing unto you, yet now after the kissing of
your hands, I will end my letter.   Excuse my evil writing,
and read it twice over.   Excuse that thing that is scriblit,
for I had na paper zesterday, quhen I wrait that of the
memorial." Good 2. 28.   These memorandums still appear
in the middle of the letter; and what we have said seems
naturally to account for the manner how they might find
their way into a real letter.   It is scarce to be supposed,
however, that any forger would think of placing memorandums in the middle of a letter, where, at first sight,
they make so absurd and so unnatural an appearance.
But if any shall still carry their refinement so far, as to

suppose that the forgers were so artful to throw in this circumstance, in order to preserve the appearance of genuineness, they must at least allow that the Queen's enemies, who employed these forgers, could not be ignorant of the design and meaning of these short notes and memorandums; but we find them mistaking them so far as to imagine that they were the credit of the bearer, i. e. points concerning which the Queen had given him verbal instructions. Good. 2. 152. This they cannot possibly be; for the Queen herself writes with so much exactness concerning the different points in the memorandums, that there was no need of giving any credit or instructions to the bearer concerning them. The memorandums are indeed the contents of the letter. 5ˉ Mary, mentioning her conversation with the King about the affair of Mynto, Hiegait, &c. says, " The morne [i.e. to morrow] I will speik to him upon that point ;" and then adds, " As to the rest of Willie Hiegait's, he confessit it; but it was the morne [i. e. morning] after my cumming or he did it." Good. 2. 9. This addition, which could not have been made till after the conversation happened, seems either to have been inserted by the Queen into the body of the letter, or, perhaps, she having written it on the margin, it was taken thence into the text. If we suppose the letter to be a real one, and written at different times, as it plainly bears, this circumstance appears to be very natural; but no reason could have induced a forger to have ventured upon such an anachronism, for which there was no necessity. An addition, perfectly similar to this, made to a genuine paper, may be found, Good. 2. 282.

But, on the other hand, Mary herself and the advocates for her innocence have contended that these letters were forged by her enemies, on purpose to blast her reputation, and to justify their own rebellion. It is not necessary to take notice of the arguments which were produced, in her own age, in support of this opinion; the observations

which we have already made, contain a full reply to them.
An author, who has enquired into the affairs of that period with great industry, and who has acquired much
knowledge of them, has lately published (as he affirms)
a demonstration of the forgery of Mary's letters. This
demonstration he founds upon evidence both internal and
external. With regard to the former he observes, that
the French copy of the Queen's letters is plainly a translation of Buchanan's Latin copy; which Latin copy is only
a translation of the Scottish copy; and by consequence,
the assertion of the Queen's enemies, that she wrote them
originally in French, is altogether groundless, and the
whole letters are gross forgeries. He accounts for this
strange succession of translations, by supposing that when
the forgery was projected, no person could be found capable of writing originally in the French language letters
which would pass for the Queen's; for that reason they
were first composed in Scottish; but unluckily the French
interpreter, it would seem, did not understand that language; and therefore Buchanan translated them into
Latin, and from his Latin they were rendered into French.
Good. 1. 79. 80.

It is scarce necessary to observe, that no proof whatever
is produced of any of these suppositions. The manners of
the Scots, in that age, when almost every man of rank
spent a part of his youth in France, and the intercourse
between the two nations was great, render it altogether
improbable that so many complicated operations should
be necessary, in order to procure a few letters to be
written in the French language.

But without insisting farther on this, we may observe,
that all this author's premisses may be granted, and yet his
conclusion will not follow, unless he likewise prove that
the French letters, as we now have them, are a true copy
of those which were produced by Murray and his party in
the Scottish Parliament, and at York and Westminster.

But this he has not attempted; and if we attend to the history of the letters, such an attempt, it is obvious, must have been unsuccessful. The letters were first published at the end of Buchanan's Detection. The first edition of this treatise was in Latin, in which language three of the Queen's letters were subjoined to it; this Latin edition was printed A. D. 1571. Soon after a Scottish translation of it was published, and at the end of it were printed, likewise in Scottish, the three letters which had formerly appeared in Latin, and five other letters in Scottish, which were not in the Latin edition. Next appeared a French translation of the Detection, and of seven of the letters; this bears to have been printed at Edinburgh by Thomas Waltem, 1572. The name of the place, as well as of the printer, is allowed by all parties to be a manifest imposture. Our author, from observing the day of the month, on which the printing is said to have been finished, has asserted that this edition was printed at London; but no stress can be laid upon a date found in a book, where every other circumstance with regard to the printing is allowed to be false. Blackwood, who (next to Lesley) was the best informed of all Mary's advocates in that age, affirms that the French edition of the Detection was published in France: "Il [Buchanan] a depuis adjousté a ceste declamation un petit libelle du pretendu mariage du Duc de Norfolk, et de la façon de son proces, et la tout envoyé aux freres a la Rochelle, lesquiels voyants qu'il pouvoit servir a la cause, l'ont traduit en François, et iceluy fut imprimeé a Edinbourg, c'est a dire a la Rochelle, par Thomas Waltem, nom aposté et fait a plaisir. Martyre de Marie. Jebb. 2. 256." The author of the Innocence de Marie goes farther, and names the French translator of the Detection. " Et iceluy premierement composé (comme il semble) par George Buchanan Escossoys, et depuis traduit en langue Françoise par un Hugonot, Poitevin (advocat de vocation) Camuz, soy disant gentilhomme, et un de plus remarquez sediteux de France. Jebb. I. 425, 443." The concurring testimony of two cotemporary authors, whose residence in France afforded them sufficient means of information, must · outweigh a slight conjecture. This French translator does not pretend to publish the original French letters as written by the Queen herself; he expressly declares that he translated them from the Latin. Good. 1. 103. Had our author attended to all these circumstances, he might have saved himself the labour of so many criticisms to prove that the present French copy of the letters is a translation from the Latin. The French editor himself acknowledges it, and so far as I know no person ever denied it.

We may observe that the French translator was so ignorant, as to affirm that Mary had written these letters, partly in French, partly in Scottish. Good. 1. 103. Had this translation been published at London by Cecil, or had it been made by his direction, so gross an error would not have been admitted into it. This error, however, was owing to an odd circumstance. In the Scottish translation of the Detection, two or three sentences of the original French were prefixed to each letter, which breaking off with an &c. the Scottish translation of the whole followed. This method of printing translations was not uncommon in that age. The French editor observing this, foolishly concluded that the letters had been written partly in French, partly in Scottish.

If we carefully consider these few French sentences of each letter which still remain, and apply to them that species of criticism, by which our author has examined the whole, a clear proof will arise, that there was a French copy not translated from the Latin, but which was itself the original from which both the Latin and Scottish have been translated. This minute criticism must necessarily be disagreeable to many readers; but luckily a few sentences only are to be examined, which will render it extremely short.

In the first letter, the French sentence prefixed to it ends with these words, *y faisoit bon*. It is plain this expression, *veu ce que peut un corps san cœur*, is by no means a translation of *cum plane perinde essem atque corpus sine corde*. The whole sentence has a spirit and elegance in the French, which neither the Latin nor Scottish have retained. *Jusques a la dinée* is not a translation of *toto prandii tempore;* the Scottish translation *quhile denner-time*, expresses the sense of the French more properly; for anciently *quhile* signified *until* as well as *during*. *Je n'ay pas tenu grand propos* is not justly rendered *neque contulerim sermonem cum quoquam*; the phrase used in the French copy, is one peculiar to that language, and gives a more probable account of her behaviour than the other. *Jugeant bien qu'il n'y faisoit bon*, is not a translation, or *ut qui judicarent id non esse ex usu*. The French sentence prefixed to Lett. 2. ends with *apprendre*. It is evident that both the Latin and Scottish translations have omitted altogether these words, *et toutefois je ne puis apprendre*. The French sentence prefixed to Lett. 3. ends with *presenter*. *J'aye veillè plus tard la haut* is plainly no translation of *diutius illic morata sum;* the sense of the French is better expressed by the Scottish *I have walkit later there-up*. Again, *Pour excuser vostre affaire* is very different from *ad excusandum nostra negotia*. The five remaining letters never appeared in Latin; nor is there any proof of their being ever translated into that language. Four of them, however, are published in French. This intirely overturns our author's hypothesis concerning the necessity of a translation into Latin.

In the Scottish edition of the Detection the whole sonnet is printed in French as well as in Scottish. It is not possible to believe that this Scottish copy could be the original from

which the French was translated. The French consists of
verses which have both measure and rhyme, and which, in
many places, are far from being inelegant. The Scottish
consists of an equal number of lines, but without measure or
rhyme. Now no man could ever think of a thing so absurd
and impracticable, as to require one to translate a certain
given number of lines in prose into an equal number of
verses, where both measure and rhyme were to be observed.
The Scottish, on the contrary, appears manifestly to be a
translation of the French; the phrases, the idioms, and
many of the words are French, and not Scottish. Besides,
the Scottish translator has, in several instances, mistaken
the sense of the French, and in many more expresses the
sense imperfectly.. Had the sonnet been forged, this could
not have happened. The directors of the fraud would
have understood their own work. I shall satisfy myself
with one example, in which there is a proof of both my assertions. Stanza viii. ver. 9.

> Pour luy j'attendz toute bonne fortune,
> Pour luy je veux garder santè et vie
> Pour luy tout vertu de suivre j'ay envie.

> For him I attend all gude fortune,
> For him I will conserve helthe and lyfe,
> For him I desire to ensue courage.

Attend, in the first line, is not a Scottish but a French
phrase; the two other lines do not express the sense of the
French, and the last is absolute nonsense.

The eighth letter was never translated into French. It
contains much refined mysticism about devices, a folly of
that age, of which Mary was very fond, as appears from several other circumstances, particularly from a letter concerning impresas by Drummond of Hawthornden. If Mary's
adversaries forged her letters, they were certainly employed
very idly when they produced this.

' From these observations it seems to be evident that there was a French copy of Mary's letters, of which the Latin and Scottish were only translations.   Nothing now remains of this copy but those few sentences which are prefixed to the Scottish translation.   The French editor laid hold of these sentences, and tacked his own translation to them, which, so far as it is his work, is a servile and a very wretched translation of Buchanan's Latin; whereas in those introductory sentences, we have discovered strong marks of their being originals, and certain proofs that they are not translated from the Latin.

It is apparent, too, from comparing the Latin and Scottish translations with these sentences, that the Scottish translator has more perfectly attained the sense and spirit of the French than the Latin.   And as it appears that the letters were very early translated into Scottish, Good. 2. 76; it is probable that Buchanan made his translation not from the French but from the Scottish copy.   Were it necessary, several critical proofs of this might be produced. One that has been already mentioned seems decisive.   *Diutius illic morata sum* bears not the least resemblance to *j'ay veillè plus tard la haut;* but if, instead of *I walkit* [i. e. watched] *laiter there-up,* we suppose that Buchanan read *I waitit,* &c. this mistake, into which he might so easily have fallen, accounts for the error in his translation.

These criticisms, however minute, appear to be well founded.   But whatever opinion may be formed concerning them, the other arguments with regard to the internal evidence remain in full force.

The external proof of the forgery of the Queen's letters, which our author has produced, is extremely specious, but not more solid than that which we have already examined. According to Murray's diary, Mary set out from Edinburgh to Glasgow January 21, 1567; she arrived there on the 23d; left that place on the 27th; she, together with the King, reached Linlithgow on the 28th, stayed in that town only one night, and returned to Edinburgh before the end of the month. But according to our author, the Queen did not leave Edinburgh till Friday, January 24; as she stayed a night at Callendar, she could not reach Glasgow sooner than the evening of Saturday the 25th, and she returned to Linlithgow on Tuesday the 28th. By consequence, the first letter which supposes the Queen to have been at least four days in Glasgow, as well as the second letter, which bears date at Glasgow, Saturday morning, whereas she did not arrive there till the evening, must be forgeries. That the Queen did not set out from Edinburgh sooner than the 24th of January, is evident (as he contends) from the public records, which contain a Precept of confirmation of a life-rent by James Boyd to Margaret Chalmers, granted by the Queen on the 24th of January at Edinburgh; and likewise a letter of the Queen's dated at Edinburgh on the same day, appointing James Inglis taylor to the Prince her son. That the King and Queen had returned to Linlithgow on the 28th, appears from a deed in which they appoint Andrew Ferrier keeper of their palace there, dated at Linlithgow, January 28. Good. 1. 118.

This has been represented to be not only a convincing, but a legal proof of the forgery of the letters said to be written by Mary; but how far it falls short of this, will appear from the following considerations.

I. It is evident from a declaration or confession made by the Bishop of Ross, that before the conferences at York, which were opened in the beginning of October 1568, Mary had, by an artifice of Maitland's, got into her hands a copy of those letters which her subjects accused her of having written to Bothwell. Brown's trial of the Duke of Norfolk, 31, 36. It is highly probable that the Bishop of Ross had seen the letters before he wrote the defence of Queen Mary's honour in the year 1570. They were published to all the world, together with Buchanan's Detection, A. D. 1571. Now if they had contained any error so gross,

and so obvious, at that time, to discovery, as the supposing the
Queen to have passed several days at Glasgow, while she was
really at Edinburgh; had they contained a letter dated at
Glasgow Saturday morning, though she did not arrive there
till the evening; is it possible that she herself, who knew her
own motions, or the able and zealous advocates who appeared
for her in that age, should not have published and exposed
this contradiction, and, by so doing, have blasted, at once,
the credit of such an imposture? In disquisitions which are
naturally abstruse and intricate, the ingenuity of the latest
author may discover many things, which have escaped
the attention, or baffled the sagacity of those who have
formerly considered the same subject. But when a matter of fact lay so obvious to view, this circumstance of
its being unobserved by the Queen herself, or by any of her
adherents, is almost a demonstration that there is some mistake or fallacy in our author's arguments. And so far are
any either of our historians, or of Mary's defenders, from
calling in question the common account concerning the
time of the Queen's setting out to Glasgow and her returning from it, that there is not the least appearance of any
difference among them with regard to this point. But
farther,

2. Those papers in the public records, on which our author rests the proof of his assertions, concerning the Queen's
motions, are not the originals subscribed by the Queen, but
copies only, or translations of copies of those originals. It
is not necessary, nor would it be easy to render this intelli-
gible to persons unacquainted with the forms of law in
Scotland; but every Scotsman conversant in business will
understand me, when I say that the precept of confirmation
of the life-rent to Boyd is only a Latin copy or note of a
precept, which was sealed with the Privy-seal, on a warrant from the signet-office, proceeding on a signature which
bore date at Edinburgh the 24th of January; and that the
deed in favour of James Inglis is the copy of a letter, sealed
with the Privy-seal, proceeding on a signature which bore

date at Edinburgh January 24.   From all this we may argue
with some degree of reason, that a proof founded on papers,
which are so many removes distant from the originals, cannot be but very lame and uncertain.

3. At that time all public papers were issued in the name
both of the King and Queen; by law, the King's subscription was no less requisite to any paper than the Queen's;
and therefore unless the original signatures be produced in
order to ascertain the particular day when each of them
signed, or to prove that it was signed only by one of them,
the legal proof arising from these papers would be, that
both the King and Queen signed them at Edinburgh, on
the 24th of January.

4. The dates of the warrants or precepts issued by the
sovereign, in that age, seem to have been in a great measure arbitrary, and affixed at the pleasure of the writer; and
of consequence, these dates were seldom accurate, are often
false, and can never be relied upon.   This abuse became so
frequent, and was found to be so pernicious, that an act of
parliament, A. D. 1592, declared the affixing a false date to
a signature to be High Treason.

5. There still remain, in the public records, a great number of papers, which prove the necessity of this law, as well
as the weakness and fallacy of our author's arguments. And
though it be no easy matter, at the distance of two centuries, to prove any particular date to be false, yet surprising
instances of this kind shall be produced.   Nothing is more
certain from history, than that the King was at Glasgow
24th January 1567; and yet the record of signatures from
1565 to 1582, fol. 16th, contains the copy of a signature
to Archibald Edmonston said to have been subscribed by
our Sovereigns, i. e. the King and Queen at Edinburgh, January 24, 1567; so that if we were to trust implicitly the
dates in the records of that age, or to hold our author's argument to be good, it would prove that not only the Queen,
but the King too, was at Edinburgh on the 24th of January.

It appears from an original letter of the Bishop of Ross,

that on the 25th of October 1566, Mary lay at the point of death; Keith, App. 134; and yet a deed is to be found in the public records, which bears that it was signed by the Queen that day. Privy-seal, Lib. 35. fol. 89. Ouchter-lony*.

Bothwell seized the Queen as she returned from Stir-ling, April 24th, 1567, and (according to her own account) carried her to Dunbar with all diligence.   And. 1. 95. But our author, relying on the dates of some papers which he found in the records, supposes that Bothwell allowed her to stop at Edinburgh, and transact business there.   No-thing can be more improbable than this supposition.   We may therefore rank the date of the deed to Wright, Privy-seal, Lib. 36. fol. 43. and which is mentioned by our author, Vol. 1. 124. among the instances of the false dates of papers which were issued in the ordinary course of business in that age.   Our author has mistaken the date of the other paper to Forbes, ibid. it is signed April 14th, not April 24th.

If there be any point agreed upon in Mary's history, it is, that she remained at Dunbar from the time that Bothwell carried her thither, till she returned to Edinburgh along with him in the beginning of May.   Our author himself allows that she resided twelve days there, Vol. 1. 367. Now though there are deeds in the records which bear that they were signed by the Queen at Dunbar during that time, yet there are others which bear that they were signed at Edinburgh; e. g. there is one at Edinburgh, April 27th, Privy-seal, Lib. 36. fol. 97.   There are others said to be signed at Dunbar on that day.   Lib. 31. Chart. No. 524, 526. Ib. lib. 32. No. 154, 157.   There are some signed at

*N.B. In the former editions, another instance of the same nature with those which go before and follow was mentioned; but that, as has since been discovered, was founded on a mistake of the person em-ployed to search the records, and is therefore omitted in this edition. The reasoning, however, in the Dissertation stands still in full force, notwithstanding this omission.

Dunbar April 28th.   Others at Edinburgh April 30th, Lib.
32. Chart. No. 492.   Others at Dunbar May 1st.   Id. ibid.
No. 158.   These different charters suppose the Queen to
have made so many unknown, improbable, and inconsistent journeys, that they afford the clearest demonstration
that the dates in these records ought not to be depended
on.

This becomes more evident from the date of the charter
said to be signed April 27th, which happened that year to
be a Sunday, which was not, at that time, a day of business in Scotland, as appears from the books of *sederunt,*
then kept by the Lords of the session.

From this short review of our author's proof of the forgery
of the letters to Bothwell, it is evident that his arguments
are far from amounting to demonstration.

Another argument against the genuineness of these letters is founded on the stile and composition, which are said
to be altogether unworthy of the Queen, and unlike her
real productions.   It is plain, both from the great accuracy
of composition in most of Mary's letters, and even from her
solicitude to write them in a fair hand, that she valued herself on those accomplishments, and was desirous of being
esteemed an elegant writer.   But when she wrote at any
time in a hurry, then many marks of inaccuracy appear.   A
remarkable instance of this may be found in a paper published, Good. 2. 301.   Mary's letters to Bothwell were
written in the utmost hurry; and yet under all the disad-
vantages of a translation, they are not destitute either of
spirit or of energy.   The manner in which she expresses her
love to Bothwell hath been pronounced indecent and even
shocking.   But Mary's temper led her to warm expressions
of her regard; those refinements of delicacy, which now
appear in all the commerce between the sexes, were, in
that age, but little known, even among persons of the
highest rank.   Among Lord Royston's papers there is a series of letters, from Mary to the Duke of Norfolk, copied

from the Harleian Library, P. 37, B. 9. fol. 88, in which
Mary declares her love to that nobleman in language,
which would now be reckoned extremely indelicate.

The sonnets and some of Mary's letters to Bothwell
were written before the murder of her husband ; some of
them after that event, and before her marriage to Bothwell.
Those which are prior to the death of her husband abound
with the fondest expressions of her love to Bothwell, and
plainly discover that their familiarity had been extremely
criminal. We find in them, too, some dark expressions,
which her enemies employed to prove that she was no
stranger to the schemes which were forming against her
husband's life. Of this kind are the following passages:
" Alace! I nevir dissavit any body; bot I remit me altogidder to zour will. Send me advertisement quhat I sall
do, and quhatsaever thing come therof, I sall obey zow.
Advise too with zourself, gif ze can find out ony mair
secret inventioun by medicine, for he suld tak medecine
and the bath at Craigmillar." Good. 2. 22. " See not hir
quhais fenzeit teiris suld not be sa meikle praisit and
estemit, as the trew and faithfull travellis quhilk I sustene
for to merite hir place. For obtaining of the quhilk,
aganis my natural, I betrayis thame that may impesche
me. God forgive me," &c. ibid. 27. " I have walkit laiter
thairup, than I wald have done, gif it had not been to
draw something out of him, quhilk this berer will schaw
zow, quhilk is the fairest commodity that can be offerit to
excuse zour affairis." Ibid 32. From the letters posterior
to the death of her husband, it is evident that the scheme
of Bothwell's seizing Mary by force, and carrying her
along with him, was contrived in concert with herself, and
with her approbation.

Having thus stated the proof on both sides ; having examined at so great length the different systems with regard
to the facts in controversy; it may be expected that I
should now pronounce sentence. In my opinion, there are

only two conclusions, which can be drawn from the facts which have been enumerated.

One, that Bothwell, prompted by his ambition or love, encouraged by the Queen's known aversion to her husband, and presuming on her attachment to himself, struck the blow without having concerted with her the manner or circumstances of perpetrating that crime. That Mary, instead of testifying much indignation at the deed, or discovering any resentment against Bothwell, who was accused of having committed it, continued to load him with marks of her regard, conducted his trial in such a manner as rendered it impossible to discover his guilt, and soon after, in opposition to all the maxims of decency or of prudence, voluntarily agreed to a marriage with him, which every consideration should have induced her to detest. By this verdict, Mary is not pronounced guilty of having contrived the murder of her husband, or even of having previously given her consent to his death; but she is not acquitted of having discovered her approbation of the deed, by her behaviour towards him who was the author of it.

The other conclusion is that which Murray and his adherents laboured to establish, "That as James, sumtyme Erle of Bothwile, was the chiefe executor of the horribill and unworthy murder, perpetrat in the person of umquhile King Henry of gude memory, fader to our Soveraigne Lord, and the Queenis lauchfull husband; sa was she of the foreknowledge, counsall, devise, perswadar and commandar of the said murder to be done." Good. 2. 207.

Which of these conclusions is most agreeable to the evidence, that has been produced, I leave my readers to determine.

Nothing need be added to this impartial statement of the case: let us now see what will be urged by Tytler.

EXTRACTS FROM TYTLER'S ENQUIRY.

The sudden death of King Francis effected a melancholy change in the affairs of the young Queen of Scots in France. Queen Mary, to the finest parts, a graceful carriage, and easy and dignified manners, joined the most beautiful figure of any woman of the age. Her wit and affability had gained the hearts of the French. By her interest and influence, her uncles the Princes of Lorraine swayed the Councils of King Francis. The Queen-mother, the famous Katherine of Medicis, who during the short period of the reign of Francis had, with reluctance, given place to her daughter-in-law, now resumed her former sway, and studied to give every mortifying proof of neglect to the Queen of Scots. Mary, conscious of her dignity, had too much spirit to brook degradation. She determined to comply with the solicitation of her own subjects, and returned to Scotland, where she was received with the greatest demonstrations of joy.

Behold now this young Queen, at the age of nineteen, alone, a stranger, and almost without a friend, in her own dominions! in the midst of a people fierce and rude! the nobles, proud and almost independent, whom her father, the high-spirited James, found himself unable to control! the major part of the nation, of the new religion, were led by the clergy, a rigid, morose, and illiberal set of men; conscious of their power over the people, and jealous of the Queen as the protector of the Catholic religion. In this situation it would have been no easy matter for a Prince endued with the greatest wisdom and fortitude to have sat easy on so tottering a throne : what then was to expected from the unexperienced years and

sex of so young a Princess, thus beset with dangers on
every side? Yet such was the prudent conduct of this
young Queen, her affable and winning carriage, and her
native dignity, tempered with easy politeness of manners,
that she not only commanded respect, but gained the
hearts of her subjects: so that had Mary had no other
difficulties to have encountered, these, by her good conduct and government, she would have conquered. But
she had still a more dangerous and formidable enemy to
struggle with—Elizabeth Queen of England.

Let us look at a Summary and Trial of the Evidence.

The learned and judicious Bayle has made a very just
observation on the case of Queen Mary and her adversaries: " One of two things (says that author) must have
been the case; either that they who forced that Princess
out of her kingdom, were the greatest villains in nature;
or that she was the most infamous of women. These are
two scales of a balance, equally poised; you cannot load
the one without lightening the other precisely to the same
degree. In the same manner, whatever serves to acquit
the Queen, aggravates the guilt of her enemies in the
same proportion; and whatever serves to load the Queen,
extenuates their crime in a like degree."

Here then we have a just balance, in which the case of
Mary and her accusers may with certainty be weighed,
and by this standard judged and determined with great
exactness.

The weights to be put in the scales are, the proofs which
were exhibited by the Earls of Murray and Morton, of the
crimes with which they charged their Queen; which are
likewise to be considered as the proofs of their own justification, for rising in arms against their Sovereign, for imprisoning her, and, finally, for the long train of her calamities, and death, all consequent to their rebellion.

The scales being now fairly loaded, and the balance

exactly poised, let us carefully examine the weights, before we pretend to abstract one grain from the scales. One
scruple taken from either of them, must alter the poise.
If then we take out the heaviest weight, and put it in the
opposite scale, that directly preponderates, the other
flies up.

We shall, therefore, begin with examining the heaviest
weight in the scale against the Queen, that is, her letters
to Bothwell: and, to avoid all imputation of partiality,
let us try them according to the rules of equity, as in a
court of justice, by hearing both sides. We begin with
the accusers.

1. The Earl of Morton at first produced those letters,
and affirmed, on his word of honour, that his servants
seized them in the custody of George Dalgleish, one of
Bothwell's servants, who had brought them out of the
Castle of Edinburgh.

2. The Earls of Murray and Morton affirm, on their honour, that they are the hand-writing of the Queen, both
in their own Secret Council, and in the Regent's Parliament in Scotland, and before Queen Elizabeth and her
Council in England.

3. They are produced at York and Westminster to the
English Council, and compared with other letters of
Mary's hand-writing, and appear to be similar to them.

4. And lastly, several of the incidents mentioned in the
letters themselves, such as the conversations between the
King and Queen at Glasgow, are, by Crawford, one of the
Earl of Lennox's vassals, affirmed, upon oath, to be true.

Such are the proofs brought in support of the letters.
Let us now turn to the other side, and hear what are the
answers, and the objections made to them on the part of
Queen Mary.

1. Queen Mary denies the letters to be her hand-
writing, and asserts them to be forged by her accusers,
Murray, Morton, and Lethington ; and offers to prove this.

K k

2. Morton's bare affirmation of the way in which the letters came into his hands, as he is a party, can never in equity be regarded. Nay, the letters appearing first in his hands, was of itself suspicious. Besides, his stifling the evidence of Dalgleish, or forbearing to interrogate him judicially, how he came by these letters, which would have put this affair in a true light; and his neglecting to examine his own servants publicly, who seized Dalgleish with the box, as to what they knew of that affair; and, in place of the legal declaration of those who were the only proper witnesses to prove this fact, obtruding his own affirmation only: these omissions, I say, double the suspicion, that he himself, and his faction, were the contrivers of the letters.

3. The affirmation of Murray and Morton on the authenticity of the letters, both in Scotland and England, can bear no greater degree of credit, than Queen Mary's denial, and the affirmation of herself, and most of the nobility of Scotland, that those letters were forged.

4. The similarity of one hand-writing to another, is such a proof as no man can be certain of: far less in the case of these letters, appearing in so clandestine a way, in the hands of Morton, the Queen's inveterate enemy and accuser. Add to this, what is affirmed by Mary, that her enemies had often counterfeited letters in her name; which is corroborated by a contemporary author, who relates it as a well-known fact, that Lethington, her Secretary, had often practised this vile fraud.

5. That several of the incidents mentioned in the letters might be very true, is not denied. The plan of the forgers was surely to intersperse truth with falsehood. Crawford's testimony on the truth of several of the incidents mentioned in the letters might therefore be true, and yet the letters themselves might be forged.

But the objections to the letters on the part of the Queen, are of a different nature.

1. The letters, as exhibited by Murray and Morton, wanted the dates, place from which they were written, the subscriptions, seals, and addresses. Could any judge or jury, then, have admitted these letters as authentic, and as written by Queen Mary to the Earl of Bothwell, upon the bare word of her accuser?

2. The only proof they could have brought to support their affirmation, was by the oath of Hubert, that he got the letters from the Queen's own hand, and delivered them to Bothwell; and by Dalgleish, that he got them from Sir James Balfour, in the Castle of Edinburgh, and was carrying them to Bothwell; and lastly, by Morton's servants, who seized Dalgleish with the box and letters. It is impossible, therefore, to frame any plausible reason, why these several persons were not called upon to prove these facts, but this only, that there was not a word of truth in the story.

3. The letters are produced in public, under different dresses. Before the Secret Council, they bear to be subscribed by the Queen's hand; in their second appearance, before Regent Murray's Parliament, they want the subscription altogether. This is proved by the acts of Council, and of Parliament, in the registers.

4. While the conferences were going on at York, the letters were privately, and in secret conference, shown by Lethington and Buchanan, to the English Commissioners, but carefully concealed from Queen Mary and her Commissioners.

5. The Queen, on the first hearing of those letters, earnestly supplicates to have inspection of the originals, and to be allowed copies: from which she offers to prove them to be forged and spurious. Both requests are refused to her, the letters are delivered back to her accusers, and to her dying day she never could get a sight of these originals, or attested copies of them.

6. The letters, of which copies only are now extant,

are, to demonstration, proved, and forced to be acknowledged, even by the writers against the Queen, to be palpable translations from the Scotch and Latin of George
Buchanan.

And, lastly, Murray and Morton, the Queen's accusers,
in order to make good their charge or accusation against
the Queen, have produced false and forged evidence, viz.
Hubert's confession, which we have proved to be a forgery:
from whence the same presumption, had we no other
proof against the letters, must arise, that they are forged
likewise.

Such are the proofs on both sides for and against the
authenticity of the letters. Let us now put the question
to any impartial person who understands the nature of
evidence, would those letters, found in the custody of
Morton, destitute of subscription, seal, and address, and in
the face of so many other unsurmountable objections,
have been sustained as genuine authentic writings, in any
court of law or justice, upon the bare appearance or similarity of the Queen's hand-writing, and the naked word
of Murray and Morton the accusers? I am not afraid of
the imputation of rashness, when I venture to say, that at
this day, I am convinced that no impartial jury, or judge,
could, upon conscience, have given judgment for these
letters as genuine, and returned a verdict and sentence in
their favour as such.

If this is the case, I think, with Monsieur Bayle's approbation, he himself holding the balance, I may venture
to take this weight from Murray and Morton's scale, and
put it into Queen's. The case then is determined at once,
the scale is turned in favour of the Queen. But still there
remains another weight against her, that is, Hubert's
confession: this we have so recently proved to be a
forgery, that it is needless here to recapitulate the objections to a piece of manufacture abounding with so many
absurdities and improbabilities (as Dr. Robertson acknow-

ledges), and altogether destitute of every essential requisite to a judicial paper. If this weight is taken from
Murray and Morton's scale, and put to the Queen's, what
then remains in the opposite? Nothing but conjectures,
arguments *à priori,* and inferences drawn from false premises, all as light as air! The Queen's scale, then, preponderates; that of her adversaries flies up, and kicks the
beam.

I shall give more of the Reverend Gentleman's opinions than I give of any other author, because he is at once the most zealous and prejudiced advocate of Mary. I wish my enemies no greater toil than the perusal of his thousands of misrepresentations, quibblings, cavillings, and repetitions —echoed by his follower, Mr. Chalmers.

One great infelicity of Mary's life was this, that she had a brother. He was indeed a bastard. He was, therefore, precluded from all possibility of mounting the throne. But he was precluded only by laws. These alone created the impossibility. And laws might be reversed by power. He appears to have been a man of strong and vigorous parts. They were of that kind, however, which are most common in the world, and which shew themselves more in the weakness of others, than in their own strength. His vigour was art, not intellect. His parts were a sagacity of genius, which pointed out all the artifice of insidiousness to him; a dexterity of mind, which enabled him to use that artifice with great success; and a versatility of spirit, which qualified him for disguising both to the eyes of the world. With only the title to distinction, which his bastard alliance to the crown lent him; with only the slender possessions of a bastard, to communicate power; and with only the slight connections of a bastard to furnish influence; he raised himself superior to his sovereign, and he seated himself on her throne. He had the address, likewise, to make the most cunning and the most ambitious of his cotemporaries, to be subservient to his cunning, and ministerial to his ambition; to commit the enormities themselves, which were necessary to his purposes; and even to dip their hands in murder, that he might enjoy the sovereignty. But he displayed an address, still greater than this. Though he had not one principle of religion within him; though he had not even oné grain of honour in his soul; and though he was guilty of those more monstrous crimes, against which God has peculiarly denounced damnation; yet he was denominated a good man by the Reformers at the time, and he has been considered as an honest man by numbers to our days.

He felt the solicitations of ambition stirring within him, so early and so strongly, that, before he was seventeen, he entered into a correspondence with the court of England, and engaged in a traitorous conspiracy with it, against his country, his sovereign, and his family. Such a youth was sure to be a man uncommonly busy and factious. He was then a mere ecclesiastic, however, with the title of the Prior of St. Andrew's. The laws of the church bending too readily before the pressure of the state, admitted such young ecclesiastics then, and still admit them, within the regions of popery He was settled in the church by his royal father, to keep him out of all secular employments, and to prevent all disturbances from his ambition and birth. He afterward obtained another priory, that of Pittenween, in his own country; and a third, that of Mascon, in France. He had a dispensation from the Pope for his bastardy, which unqualified him, as it now unqualifies, for possessing any of the endowments of the Church. He had also a bull from the Pope, for holding his French priory together with his Scotch preferments. And he took the usual oath of obedience to the Pope.

But the peaceful duties of a divine could never have satisfied the keen and restless temper of his spirits. Whatever the sagacity of James the Fifth foresaw, and whatever his prudence endeavoured to avert, by shrouding him in a cassock, and fixing him in a stall, all was realized. The turbulent activity of his son's soul, broke through every restraint; the churchman became secularized; the Prior was transformed into an Earl; and the bastard proved eventually the curse of his father's family. His genius called him out to those scenes principally, where he might have a play for his activity in cunning, and might give a scope to his turbulence in intrigue. He took his station on the forbidden ground near the throne. His talents for business recommended him to the service of it; and his ambition kept a steady eye upon it. The distracted state of the nation was congenial to a spirit like his. He loved the mazes of political life. He loved to thicken the shades, and to entangle the walks, more and more. He loved to stand himself upon an eminence, in the centre of his own labyrinths; to view all about him, embarrassed by the difficulties which he himself had made; and to enjoy the distress which he himself was occasioning at the moment. He loved still more, and with a more sanguinary cunning, to raise a tempest around him; to direct it at the heads of those, who stood in the way of his aspiring thoughts; and to sit all the while, seemingly unconcerned in the work. And when the reformation broke out in all its wildness and strength, he closed in with it; put on the sanctified air of a reformer, wrapped himself up in a long cloak of puritanism, attached all the popular leaders among the clergy to him, and prepared to make them his useful steps to the throne.

But even all this united, could not have been effectual to the ruin of Mary. She met with the additional misfortune of having a cousin and a female upon a neighbouring throne. England was then governed by Elizabeth. Her character was very different from Mary's. In all the stronger and deeper lineaments of the mind, it was much superior. But it was much inferior also, in all the amiable, the elegant, and the dignified graces of the heart and understanding. With a turn of religion, which gave her a predilection for protestantism, she could have induced herself, I fear, either to continue the idolatrous devotions of popery, to adopt the manly service of the church of England, or to take up the wild worship of the puritans, just as the scale of her interest had strongly inclined. The voice of her subjects was for the second. She, therefore, became a mother to religion and the church. Yet her regard for either was not sufficient to keep her from acts of oppression to the one, and from deeds of outrage to the other. She was busy through her whole reign, in robbing the church of its possessions, by every petty trick of sacrilegious imposition which she could play upon it, and by every bolder exertion of sacrilegious authority which she could make against it. Her private life, too, was stained with gross licentiousness. The maiden Queen had many gallants. And her politicks were one vast system of chicane and wrong, to all the nations about her.

She was particularly fond of embarrassing them with dissensions among themselves, that she might be secure from their attempts upon her. This low and ungenerous kind of management, indeed, shelters itself with the many, who have virtue enough to startle at an open knavery, under the dignified appellation of necessity. But let us not injure our hearts, by imposing upon our understandings. Dishonesty is never necessary. God never did, God never will create a necessity for knavery. Man alone does this, and then has the impudence to charge his own forgery upon God. But Elizabeth and her ministers, I doubt not, whatever they might pretend to the virtuous body of the nation, triumphed in the happy inventiveness of their souls for mischief; exulted over their long and laboured trains of misery; and considered themselves as the wise and intelligent spirits of the creation, who sat in their orbs, presided over their elements, and regulated the movements of all with their fingers. They knew not that they were thus making themselves the very dæmons of vengeance, to all within the sphere of their activity. They reflected not, that history would in time break through the clouds, in which they had wrapped themselves up for their mischievous purposes; and expose them in their fiend-like operations, to the gaze of men. And while the subjects of Elizabeth were applauding the stratagems of policy, which she was practising upon the states around them ; and were enjoying their success, in the tranquillity of their own country, and in the distractions of others: they were little aware, that the hour was soon to come, when by the just retributions of an indignant Providence, those states should play back upon us the stratagems, which had been practised upon them; should foment disturbances among us, by the same arts of unhallowed wisdom ; should triumph over us with an equal success from them; and should help to work us up, into all the frenzy of fanaticks, and into all the insanity of regicides. May the strong and awful retaliation be a lesson of national wisdom for ages.

Elizabeth, however, had some special grounds of animosity against Mary. The latter had a title, such as it was, to the throne of the former. This was naturally preferred by the prejudices of the papist, to the right of Elizabeth herself. Mary had even assumed the arms and appellation of Queen of England, when she was Queen of France. And though she had forborne to take them, ever since she became her own mistress ; Elizabeth had none of that generosity about her, which could forgive. She had been alarmed. She was still alarmed. The papists continued the claim, though Mary resigned it. She might one day see a formidable competitor for the crown in her, supported by all the popish faction in the island, and seconded by all the popish powers on the continent. Elizabeth's life was a life of mischief and of misery ; of mischief to others, in the plots which she was always forming against them ; and of misery to herself, in the fears and apprehensions which she was always entertaining of them. She was continually forging schemes of malignity against them, from some visionary fears of her own concerning them. She then changed her visionary into real fears, from the jealousies which she conceived of their retaliating upon her ; and she was finally obliged to fabricate new schemes of

mischief against them, in order to prevent or to counteract
the designs, which she was sure they would form against
her, because she was sensible they had every right to form
them. Thus does Providence punish the insidious with airy
suspicions at first, torment them with well-grounded jealousies afterwards, and curse them at last with the success
of their own machinations.

But this was not all. In the eyes of both papists and
protestants, Mary had a right of eventual succession to the
crown. If Elizabeth should die without legitimate issue,
by all the principles of the constitution, Mary was to fill
her place. The expectation of this, made Mary to resign
the other. And, by the hope of this, Elizabeth might
have managed her completely. But that Queen had a
weakness, often incident to strong passions and little religion. She viewed her successor as such, with an eye of
malignity. She could not bear to see another ready, even
after her death, to step into the vacant throne. She,
therefore, kept the succession undetermined to the last.
She thus endangered all the happiness of her kingdom,
merely for the gratification of her humour. She suffered
the law of Henry her father, which in a gust of ill-will,
and in a freak of tyranny, had broke through the natural
course of descent, and cut off the race of Scotland from
the succession, still to remain unrepealed against them;
though she had once had the same sort of law, and from
the same kind of principle, made against herself. She was
the genuine daughter of Henry! She carried the impression of his mind, strongly stamped upon her. She particularly did so on this occasion. She had her gusts of ill
will and her freaks of tyranny. She equally sacrificed the
grand lines of the constitution to them. She even proceeded
farther in both, than ever Henry did. She had it once
enacted indirectly, but plainly, by a law, that the crown
should be worn after her death by her natural issue; a de-
signation of her offspring, that, in its ordinary import,

comprehends equally the spurious and the legitimate, and,
in its legal acceptation, peculiarly means the spurious.
She even prohibited any of her subjects, by the terror of
severe penalties in the law, from intimating, in any manner
or form, who was the next heir to the crown after her
death, except it was her natural issue. She even died
at last, though she had no issue at all, without settling
who was to succeed her; leaving the constitutional heirs of
the throne under the ban of a prohibitory law, suffering no
others to be appointed, and resigning up the nation to all
the horrors of a civil war. These, indeed, the good
sense of the nation happily prevented. With one concur-
rent voice, they broke through the prohibitory law. They
did what Elizabeth should have done. They called the
constitutional heirs to the throne. But Elizabeth must have
meant the reverse of all this. She meant to leave " her
good people," that worst of all political calamities to a
nation, an unsettled succession. She must have foreseen all
the rising evils of it; yet she still left it. She left it, as a
legacy of mischief after her death. Though counselled by
her parliaments, and entreated by her people, she still persisted in her obstinacy of not ascertaining the succession.
She even did worse. She prepared the way for additional
pretenders to the crown, from any real or asserted bastards
of her own. She thus did all she could do in her life, to
make England

A stage,
To feed contention in a lingering act.

And it is therefore the less to be wondered at, that she persecuted a woman, who was her cousin by blood and her
heir by right, because she was her cousin and her heir.

But there was still another motive, and of as hostile a
nature as any before, and perhaps more powerful than any,
in the conduct of Elizabeth to Mary. The former could
not be content with the great superiority which she had
over the latter; in a hardy vigour of understanding, in a

WHITAKER.] MARY QUEEN OF SCOTS. 261

deep knowledge of the world, and in the mysterious refinements of policy, in the strength of her nation, and in
the splendour of her government. She must arrogate a
superiority too, in the very orb in which Mary shone so
transcendently. She must triumph over her in beauty, and
in dress; in those very accomplishments, which give the
sex such an influence upon us, but in which we never think
of rivalling them. Elizabeth was a man in most other respects. She should have been peculiarly one in this. But
the womanly part of her predominated here, over the
manly. And she who could box her generals upon occasion, could not bear to be surpassed in accomplishments
purely feminine, by the most handsome, the most graceful,
and the most improved princess of her age.

All united to make Elizabeth an enemy to Mary. As a
Queen, and as a woman; as actuated by political jealousies,
as stimulated by personal humours, and as impelled by female vanities; she became at first a pretended friend to betray her, and she appeared at last an open-enemy to
destroy her. She lavished all her arts of deception
upon her. She then found herself so entangled in the
strings of her own nets, that she could not either retreat or
advance. And she thought herself obliged in the end, for
the sake of her own security, to terminate in desperation,
what she had commenced in jealousy. She arraigned a
Queen of Scotland, before a tribunal of English nobles.
She thus set an example, infamous in itself, pernicious to
society, and peculiarly pernicious and infamous to her own
country; of having a sovereign condemned to the block,
by subjects. She urged her meaner dependents upon assas-
sinating Mary, that she might not behead her; but she
found even their consciences revolting at the villainous inti-
mation. She then signed the bloody warrant, with her
own hand. She could be wantonly jocular, at doing it.
She could pretend to recall it, when it had been sent away.
She could pretend to lay the guilt of it upon her secretary's
head. She could yet deny to Mary for ever, what was

never denied to the meanest criminal before—the favour of
having a clergyman of her own communion to attend her.
She could point her persecution against the soul, as well as
the body, of Mary.   And at length she stained her conscience with one of the foulest murders that the annals of
earth can produce; then felt herself almost petrified with
horror, at the related execution of what she had commanded;
felt herself peculiarly haunted at the close of life, with the
frightful image of the deed which she had committed; and
killed herself at last with a sullen bravery of melancholy,
the most extraordinary that is to be met with in history.
Hear this, all ye who are tempted by the solicitations of
artifice, to leave the line of rectitude, and to violate the
laws of conscience.   Ye will be dreadfully breaking in
upon your bosom-peace, by the deed.   One enormity
is sure to lead you to another.   Ye will feel yourselves at
the end of all, surrounded with your own stratagems, encir-
cled with your own snares; and bound fast in the very cen-
ter of your own designs.   And ye will then, like the
wretched Elizabeth, fancy yourselves compelled to cut your
way through them, with crimes, with horror, and with
damnation attending upon you.

On these flagitious principles, and with this horrible
issue to them, Elizabeth engaged in intrigues against
Mary.   She banded with her ambitious brother, and her
seditious clergy.   She furnished them with assistance secretly.   She lent them her countenance openly.   And,
from both, they at length drove their Sovereign out of the
country.   She took refuge in Elizabeth's dominions.   She
thus gave her one of the finest opportunities, that time
had ever presented to an heroical mind, of acting with a
dignified spirit of honour at the last.   Mary was surely reduced
duced below her envy at present.   She had been ravished
by one of her brutal barons.   She had been exposed as a
captive, to all the scorn of her rabble.   She had been
locked up in a dungeon within a lake.   She had been
there committed to the care of that very woman, who was

the mother of her bastard brother; who insulted over her with the natural insolence of a whore's meanness, in asserting the legitimacy of her own child, and in maintaining the illegitimacy of Mary; and actually carried the natural vulgarity of a whore's impudence so far, as to strip her of all her royal ornaments, and to dress her up like a mere child of fortune, in a " course broune cassoke." She had even been accused of adultery to her late husband. She had even been charged with the murder of him. And she had been thus charged and accused, not in the private discourses, or the private publications, of the rebels; but in full form, in open Parliament, and in the hearing of all the world. In such a situation, all the little jealousies of the rival will surely melt away in the compassions of the woman. Nor can she any longer be afraid of Mary. The dreaded competitor for the crown of England, has now lost her own ; and now lies (as it were) at her feet, soliciting her kindness, and imploring her assistance. Every generous sentiment, that ever harboured in the mind of Elizabeth, will therefore be called into life again. Every tender sensibility, that ever was felt at the heart of Elizabeth, will again be roused into activity. Both will unite their powers. And Elizabeth will eagerly catch, at the happy opportunity for glory; will seal it down to her honour, in all the future ages of our annals ; and will descend to posterity with these illustrious titles, the Friend of Order, the Assertor of Justice, and the Vindicator of an Injured Queen.

But Elizabeth had no sensibilities of tenderness, and no sentiments of generosity. She looked not forward to the awful verdict of history. She shuddered not at the infinitely more awful doom of God. Regardless of her own invitation, of her own promises, and of every sanction human or divine ; she flew upon the unhappy Queen, seized her as a prey, and imprisoned her as a felon. I blush as an Englishman to think, that it was an English

Queen who could do this; that it was one of the most
enlightened princess, that ever sat upon the throne of
England; and that it was one, whose name I was taught
to lisp in my infancy, as the honour of her sex, and the
glory of our isle.

Yet she did even more than this. She obliged the unwilling rebels to come forward with their asserted evidences against her. She forced them upon pretending
to substantiate their accusation of adultery, and to au-
thenticate their charge of murder. And, at last, she entered into a diabolical compact with them, to receive
their spurious evidences as genuine; to receive them in
such a manner, as should preclude all possibility of detecting their spuriousness; and to vouch them for genuine,
by their own authority: so to blast the character of Mary
with all the world, for the gratification of her own paltry
revenge; and then to keep her in prison for life, or to deliver her up to her rebels, for the support of their scandalous usurpation.

Nor let it be suspected, that I exaggerate in saying this.
The records of it all are still in being. They are indelible
monuments of the infamy of Elizabeth, and of the innocence of Mary. And I shall lay them at full length before my readers.

Mary was one of those characters which we meet with
very seldom in the world; and which, whenever they appear, are applauded for their generosity by a few, and
condemned for their simplicity by the many. They have
an easy affiance of soul, that loves to repose confidence,
even when confidence is weakness. They thus go on, still
confiding, and still confounded; unable to check the cur-
rent of affiance which runs strong in their bosoms, and
suffering themselves to be driven before it in their actions.
And all the first half of their lives forms one continued
tissue, of confidences improperly placed, and of perfidies
natural to be expected. Such a person was Mary! She

once had her bastard brother, and his adherents, under her feet; but too easily forgave them. She once had all her other rebels, under the harrows of the law; but too readily released them. The former rose in rebellion, and were defeated. The latter murdered her foreign secretary in her presence, and even imprisoned her own person in her palace; and yet were overpowered by the management of the Queen, and the fidelity of her Peers. And she not only allowed them to return home from their banishment, but restored them to their estates, to their honours, and even to their posts about her court. She thus enabled them to repeat their rebellions, with equal power and with improved experience. In so doing, she was certainly guilty of great folly. Yet she did more than this. She afterwards took the verbal assurances of the very same men in rebellion, who, to be rebels at first, must have previously broken through the strongest assurances that man can give, even their very oaths; and who, to be rebels again, must have violated every additional obligation of gratitude and honour.

But she took their words, notwithstanding. She relied upon them so implicitly, as to put her person into their hands. Then they behaved just as such ungrateful, dishonourable, and perjured wretches were sure to behave. They thrust her into a prison. They forced her to resign her crown. They nominally placed her son on the throne, and really fixed themselves upon it. By her affability, dignity, and prudence, she won upon the hearts of those about her. By their aid she escaped out of prison. She escaped too at a critical period, when the villains that detained her in prison, were resolving to execute the menaces which they had been for some time throwing out, and were meditating their grand stroke of murder against her. Yet she was still the same in this point. Her late experience, very severe as it was, had not cured this original milkiness of her mind. She was still credulous in the honesty of mankind, and still con-

fident of the sincerity of others. She raised an army in an
instant. She was defeated, however. And she again repeated the nearly fatal stroke of confidence before. She
flew from the perfidies of her rebels, and threw herself upon
the perfidies of Elizabeth. She found Elizabeth even more
perfidious than they. And from this exertion of abused
confidence, she could never recover herself afterwards.

Nor let her be too freely censured for all. In the present constitution of things, where the original dignity of
man is in a perpetual conflict with the introduced spirit of
meanness; that affection of the heart, which does it most
credit in reality, becomes its greatest reproach in the eyes
of the many. A generous confidence in the virtue of others,
is the mark of a soul, conscious of the energy of virtue in
itself, buoyed up by its own vigour within, and not yet
drawn down by the attraction of earth below. Mary's was
one of this kind. Time, if time had been allowed her, would
have forced her to learn the necessary wisdom of the world.
The great multitude of mankind learn it, without the aid of
time. They look into their own hearts, and read it there.
They have no stubbornness of virtue to subdue, and no for-
wardness of honour to restrain. Mary had. She was cast
in a much superiour mould. And she died at last a martyr,
to the sincerity of virtue in herself, and to a reliance upon
it in others.

She took refuge in England on the 16th of May, 1568;
being little more than twenty-five years old. On the 22d
of June following, the bastard brother, now Earl of Murray
and regent of Scotland, addressed himself to Elizabeth's
agent at Edinburgh in these terms: " Because we persave
the trial," he said, " *quhilk the Quenis Majestie*" of England " *is myndit to have taken,* is to be usit with grit ceremonye and solemnites; we wald be maist laith [most loth]
to enter in accusation of the Quene, moder of the King our
Soverane, and syne [afterwards] to enter into qualification
with hir: for all men may judge, how dangerous and prejudicial that suld be. Alwayis, in cais the Quenis Majestie

will **have** the accusation directlie to proceid: it were maist ressonabill we understude quhat we suld luke to follow thairupon, in cais we preive all that we alledge; utherwayis we sal be als [as] incertane efter the caus concludit, as we are presentlie [at present]. And thairfoir we pray zow [you] require hir Hienes, in this point to resolve us." Murray wanted not to bring forward the accusation of Mary. He was already in possession of the regency. He could not be in possession of more, even if he succeeded in the accusation. He might not succeed. He knew well the defectiveness of his proofs. He was, therefore, very naturally full of apprehensions concerning the event. But Elizabeth would have the accusation to proceed. And he was scheming plainly to make a formal agreement with her, before he ventured to produce his evidences. He saw the eagerness of the Queen, to have them produced. He durst not refuse her. The slightest assistance lent to Mary against him, would have overset him at once from his seat of usurpation. Yet he prudently refused to gratify her, before he had entered into some stipulations to his own advantage. He would be left in the regency by Elizabeth, if he proved his charges; and Mary should never be assisted by Elizabeth, in disturbing him.

·' Thus plainly did Elizabeth urge the unwilling Murray, to come forward with a charge of adultery, and with a charge of murder, against Mary. Yet, at this very time, she was pretending to Murray himself, not to intend to invite any charges against her; not to mean to allow of any faults in her; and merely to design a settlement of all differences between her and him, upon reasonable terms. So hypocritical was she, at the very outset of the business! Yet she was still more so. At this very time, when she was stimulating Murray to accuse Mary, and yet telling him she did not want him to accuse her; she was then pressing Mary to agree to a conference with Murray, in order to give opportunity for introducing the accusation, and yet under an ex-

press stipulation of making Murray by it to restore the
crown to Mary. These two facts together, unite to form
such an extreme of hypocrisy, and such a comprehensive-
ness of dissimulation; as is scarcely to be credited. I therefore proceed to prove them.

We have already seen, that " the Quenis Majestie was
myndit to have a trial taken" concerning Mary, and that she
" would have the accusation directlie to proceid" against
her. Yet in a set of objections and answers, written by her
Prime-minister Cecil himself, and relating to this message
of Murray's, " the Quene's Majesty," it is said, " never
meaneth so to deale in the cause as to proceed to any condemnation of the Queen of Scots; but hath a desyre, to com-
pound all differences betwixt hir and hir subjects; and
therein not to allow any faults, that shall appear to be in
the Quene; but by reasonable and honourable conditions to
make some good end, with sufficient suerty for all partyes."
And at the same time, as Mary herself informs us, " hir
Grace of hir guidness did promise to support me, and to re-
pone me in my awin realme be hir grace's forces onlie;
quhair throw I misterit not [I should not trouble myself] to
require any uther prince, for assistance in my causis; and,
in hoip theirof, desyrit me ernestlie to desist and ceis fra all
suit, at the King of Spain and uther princes handis for support; quhilk desyre I obeyit, putting my haill confidence,
nixt God, in hir Grace's promises." With such a variation
of hypocrisy, was Elizabeth acting at this moment! But
having thus induced Mary to drop all applications to foreign
princes for aid, by a solemn promise of restoring her to her
crown, with her own soldiery; she then began to falter a
little in her promise. " Then," says Mary, " hir Grace
thinking it to be mair meit, that all my causis sould be set
forward be sum gude dress, rather than be force; hir
Hienes desyrit me alswa very ernestlie, to suffer hir a short
space to travel with the Erle of Murray and his adherents
(quha had submittit thair haill causis in hir handis), to

cause thame repair the wrangis and attemptatis committit
aganis me their soverane, and contrair thair alledgeance
and dewtie; and to desist and ceis in times cuming; quhair
throw I micht be reponit in my realme, auctoritie and government thairof, but [without] ony impediment, and be
her Hienes's labouris and moyen, rather than be force of
armis; desyring alswa, that I wald use hir counsal toward
the wrang and offences committit be thame, how the samin
sould be repairit to my honour, and my clemencie be usit
towardis thame be hir Grace's sicht." So explicit was she
still, in her promise of restoring Mary to her throne; even
when she was forming her plan for keeping her out of it.

Nor let any doubt arise upon the mind of my reader, as to
the validity of Mary's evidence against Elizabeth. She must
be the only evidence of what she only can know, the contents of Elizabeth's letters to her. All indeed is confirmed
by a memorial, which her Commissioner, the Bishop of
Ross, presented to Elizabeth herself. At Mary's coming
into England, he says to Elizabeth, " Zour Majestie causit
hir to be. thankfullie ressavit, and tuik in hand to dress hir
causis to her honour and weill; sobeit scho wald leive the
seiking of ayd and support of all uther princes, and stay hirself onlie upon zour Hienes; quhilk, upon the trust foirsaid, scho willinglie obeyit." But, what doubly confirms
all, Elizabeth at this very time, says the same Bishop in a
treatise afterwards, " did assure the moste Christian Kinge
of Fraunce,". of success in this treaty; " promisinge to doe
her exact diligence, to procure the restitution of the Quene
our Sovereigne to her crowne and realmes, and a goode
agreement to be made amongest her subjects, for the com-
moun quietnes of the realme." And, to preclude all possibility of doubt, Sir Francis Knollys informs Cecil by a
letter of July 28th, 1568, that my Lord Herris, just returned from Elizabeth to Mary, assured the latter in his and
Lord Scroop's requested presence: he was authorized by
Elizabeth to say, " yf she wold commyt hyr cause to be

heard by hyr Hyghnes order,—as—hyr deare cousine and
frende—hyr Hyghnes wold surely sett hyr agayne in hyr
seate of regiment and dignitye regall ;" if her rebels should
bring any satisfactory reasons for their behaviour, " condi-
tionnally," that her rebels should be pardoned ; and, if
they did not, " then her Hyghnes wold absolutely " sett
hyr in hyr seat regall." So seemingly mounted up to the
very apex of hypocrisy at once, does Elizabeth here appear !
So seemingly does the first stroke of the pencil, complete
the picture of dissimulation in her ! But we shall see her picture heightened, with a thousand touches of dissimulation
besides ; and herself mounting infinitely higher on the pin-
nacle of hypocrisy, hereafter.

Murray's overture to Elizabeth, is the fundamental
evidence of all. To that overture Elizabeth undoubtedly
acceded. We have not, indeed, her immediate answer to
it ; though we know that she actually returned one.
" When their letters, contayning the doubt before by
them moved," say the commissioners of Elizabeth to
Murray and Murray's associates, a little afterwards at
York, " were delivered to the Quene's Majestie's handes ;
they knew that immediately hir Highnes did forthwith
depeche [dispatch] her answer thereunto." This answer
has been lost. We have what is called an answer, in the
objections and replies which I have just mentioned, as
drawn up by Cecil with a view to this letter of Murray's.
But, as those could be only the rudiments of an answer,
so could they not be of the real and actual one. They
carry with them the appearance of a paper merely ostensible. Let the reader judge, from one of the objections
and replies.—" Obj. They would be loth to enter fyrst
into an accusation of the Quene, and then after that to
enter into a qualification.—Ans. The Quene's Majesty never
ment to have any to come, to make any accusation of the
Queen : but meaning to have some good end to grow betwixt the Quene and hir subjectis, was content to hear

any thing which they had to say for themselves; and, if they will. come into hir Majesty's realme, they shall be heard."

This evidently bears such an air of hypocrisy upon the face of it, as could never be hoped to be successfully imposed upon a Murray. It could be calculated only, for his exhibition of it to [some of his honester. adherents. Such a hypocrite as Murray is never to be taken in by dissimulation; nor will such a hypocrite as Elizabeth ever attempt to do it.. And that it was not. the real answer given to Murray, is plain from what are equally satisfactory to us, with the real one itself; but which are very different from this ostensible one of Cecil's; the instructions of Elizabeth to her Commissioners afterwards, and a letter of Elizabeth's to. Murray, dated the same day with the instructions.

" Where we hear say," says Elizabeth, on September the 20th to Murray, " that certain reports. are made in sundry parts of Scotland; that whatsoever should fall out now upon. the hearing of the Queen of Scot's cause, in any proof to convince [convict] or to acquit the said Queen, concerning the horrible murder of her late husband our cousin; we have determined to restore her to her kingdom and government; we do so much mislike hereof,.as we cannot indure the same to receive any credit; and. therefore we have thought good to assure you, that the same.is untruly devised by the authors to our dishonour. For as we have been always certified from our said sister, both by her letters and messages, that she is by no means guilty or participant of that murder, which we wish to be true; so surely, if she should be found justly to be guilty thereof, as hath been reported of her, whereof we would be very sorry;.then, indeed, it should behove us to consider otherwise of her cause, than to satisfy her desire, in restitution of her to the government of that kingdom. And. so we would have you and all others think, that

should be disposed to conceive honourably of us and our
actions." This is sufficiently explicit. But let us turn to
the instructions, which are equally dated on the 20th of
September, in the grand commission for the whole.
These do, what Elizabeth's letter does not. These plainly
refer to Murray's message before. These directly reply to
it. And they run thus. "If the Earle of Murray and
his partie shall alledge," she says, " that although they
can justly convince [convict] the Quene of the great
crimes wherewith she hath been burdened; yet they find
it not expedient so to do, upon the doubt they have, that
the Quene's Majesty will, notwithstanding any crime
proved upon her, restore her to her kingdom and rule,
whereupon they should never be free from her indignation; and so they will stay and not proceed, without they
may know her Majestie's purpose, in case the said Quene
should be proved guilty of her husband's murder: it may
be answered by the Quene's Majestie's Commissioners,
that, if her Majestie shall find it to be plainly and manifestly proved, surely her Majestie would think hir unworthy of a kingdom: and would not stayne her own
conscience, by restoring her to a kingdom." All therefore shews us very plainly, the answer of Elizabeth to the
overture of Murray; that answer which she returned, as
the Commissioners have told us already, " immediately"
and " forthwith" upon the receipt of Murray's doubts. If
he could convict Mary of the crimes with which he
charged her, he would have no need to enter into any
accommodation with her. Mary was never to be restored
by Elizabeth. Yet all the while, let me again remark,
Elizabeth was writing ostensibly to Murray, that she
wanted no one to accuse Mary; that she never meant to
condemn her on any accusation; that she should allow of
no faults in her; and that she would endeavour to settle all differences betwixt her and her subjects, upon
grounds reasonable and honourable to both. And all the

while, too, Elizabeth was promising Mary herself to restore her, to make her subjects submit to her, force them
to repair her wrongs, and oblige them to accept her clemency. In so much stronger light still does the hypocrisy
of Elizabeth appear, at the very commencement of this
business.

Her Commissioners afterwards applied these very words
in their commission, to the resolution of the very same
doubt; when it was alleged again by the rebels. They
even applied them, as resolving the doubt in the very same
manner. Murray declared to them at York, they tell us,
that he and his associates " were desirous to understand, if
in this action they shall prove all things directly, wherewith they maye and do burden the Quene, their sovereigne's
mother ; how they maye be assured to be free and without
daunger of the said Quene's displeasure, if she should be restored to her former estate : to whome it was saide by the
Quene's Majestie's Commissioners, that as in few wordes
her Highnes had delivered them her pleasure therein, so
wolde they in few wordes deliver the same unto them ;
which was, that indede her Majestie's desire hath always
bene from the begynning, that the said Quene might be
founde free, specially from the crime of her husband's
murder; nevertheless, if her Majestie shall fynde to be
playnelye and manifestly proved (whereof she wolde be
verie sorie), that the said Quene of Scottes was the devisor
and procurer of that murder, or otherwise was giltie thereof ;
surely her Majestie wolde thinke her unworthy of a kingdome, and wolde not staine her owne conscience in mayntenance of such a detestable wickedness, by restoring her
to a kingdome. Then the regent [Murray] opened the
cause, why he moved this question : declaring, that it was
not only put out and published in Scotland, but even now
in this citie ; that either she should be amplie restored, or
otherwise by some degrees restored and sent home amongs
them ; and do not let to saye, that they have the Quene's

Majestie's promes to shew in writinge, to confirm the same. It was answered thereunto by the Quene's Majestie's Commissioners, that it weare by them to be considered, from whence those wordes came; if from their adverse partie, who can let them speak what themselves will devise? But, surely, either from her Majestie, or any by [of] her Commissioners, they could not affirm the same; for when their Lettres, conteyninge the doubt before by them moved, weare delivered to the Quene's Majestie's handes; they knew that immediately her Highnes did forthwith depeche her answer thereunto, in sorte as (if nothinge had byn now spoken by us, her Grace's Commyssioners) it might have satisfied that doubt and question." Elizabeth therefore answered their doubt before, exactly as her instructions to her Commissioners spoke, and exactly as her Commissioners spoke from those instructions to the rebels;/that she would not restore Mary to her crown, if the rebels could prove her guilty of murder: though she had been assuring those rebels, that she would allow no faults in Mary; and though she had been promising Mary herself, that she would restore her. And as the Commissioners informed Elizabeth herself, of the written promise that was ready to be shewn from Elizabeth, for the restoration of Mary; of their denial of it; and of their assurance in the language of her letter to the rebels, and of her instructions to them her Commissioners, that Mary would not be restored if proved guilty; the Commissioners unwittingly exhibit the hypocrisy of Elizabeth, in a still stronger light than ever.

Murray must have seen the hypocrisy plainly himself, from the ostensible and the real answer of Elizabeth compared together. He must have seen it much more plainly, from the writing which was ready to be produced, with Elizabeth's promise to Mary in it. But he was too much an hypocrite himself to be offended with the duplicity of a sister in hypocrisy. He was only acting hitherto, in order to please some of his honester adherents. He had a much deeper game to [play for himself, as I shall soon shew. This proves the message by Middlemore, and the application to the Commissioners, to have been calculated merely for others. And these others were now called upon by no less a bribe, than the promise of Murray's continuance in the royalty under the name of regent, and consequently of their own continuance in places of power and profit under him; to charge the Queen boldly with the murder of her husband, to screw up their invention for evidences to the highest pitch, and to produce them confidently before the court.

But, as I have intimated already, neither Murray nor Elizabeth would rest the cause merely upon this. They must, both of them, go much farther to answer their respective purposes. Accordingly Murray in the address before, which was to be reported to Elizabeth, and which, as we have already seen, was actually reported to her, spoke additionally thus; " Further," he says, " it may be, that sic [such] letteris as we heif of the Quene, our Soverane Lordis moder, that sufficientlie in our opinion preivis hir consenting to the murthure of the King hir lauchfull husband; sall be callit in doubt be the juges, to be constitute for examinatioun and trial of the caus, whether they may stand or fall, pruif or not: thairfoir, sen our servand Mr. Jhone Wode hes the copies of the samin letteris translatit in our language, we wald earnestly desyre, that the saidis copies may be considerit be the juges;—that they may resolve us this far, in cais the principal agrie with the copie, that then we pruif the caus indeed: for when we have manifested and schawin all, and zet [yet] sall haif na assurance that it we send sall satisfie for probatioun, for quhat purpois sal we ather accuse or take care how to pruif." Thus had Murray the effrontery to propose to Elizabeth, that her Commissioners, which were to be appointed, should receive as evidence of the highest crimes in Mary, a set of letters pretended to be written by her; should peruse them over, before they were produced as evidence ; peruse only copies, and even only translations of them ; and then assure him, whether they would admit them as full evidence of guilt, not if the originals appeared to be written in her own hand, but if the originals agreed with the copies.

This was such a proposal, as required no refinements of religion, and asked no delicacies of honour, to spurn at it with contempt.   A common share of religion or of honour must have rejected it with scorn.   Only the lowest strain of probity, which works in the breast of the vulgar ; only the modesty that adheres to a young sinner ; and only the shame, that silently pulls the heartstrings of all but abandoned vice ; would have considered the proposal as an insult, and dismissed it with disdain.   But did Elizabeth do so ? In that ostensible paper which I have mentioned before, she pretended to do so.   There we find the following question and answer.   *Quest.* " Whyther, if the originals shall accord with the copys of the wrytings produced to charge the Quene of Scots, the proof shall be thought sufficient ?"   *Ans.* " No proves can be taken for sufficient, without hearyng of both partyes."   This was speaking honestly.   But I have so clearly convicted this paper of falsehood already, and it shews us so plainly its own hypocrisy, that we cannot be imposed upon by it.   Whether Elizabeth did reject this proposal of Murray's, let facts tell. They cannot lie.   They cannot deceive us.   Let, particularly, the conduct of her Commissioners speak at large, hereafter.   And let her own conduct speak briefly at present.   Murray had plainly intimated, that unless this proposal was agreed to, he would not come forward with his evidence.   " When we haif manifestit and schawin all," he says, " and zet sall haif na assurance, that it we send sall satisfie for probatioun ; for quhat purpois sall we ather accuse, or take care how to pruif !"   Elizabeth, therefore, must have now seen the writings to be spurious, if she ever believed them to be genuine ; and have now known the man to be a villain of the first magnitude, if she ever thought any better of him. Yet she still proceeded in the business; she still encouraged the man to come forward with his accusations; and still persisted in calling for the writings.

Murray, indeed, must have long trafficked in villainy, as he had long maintained a connection with her; before he could have risen to such a pitch of familiarity with the evil spirit within her, as to think of making her such an overture. But he knew her too well, to be afraid of any virtuous resentment from her. Associates in enormity always pay that compliment to goodness, to have the strongest contempt for one another. He saw her eagerness to blast the character of Mary. She would comply with any proposals, however flagitious, that ministered to her purposes. And her Commissioners acted nearly, as Murray had required they should act.

The Commissioners met Murray and some of his party at York, in the month of October following. They then give this account of Murray's proceedings and their own, there. "The said Erle," they say, "hath been content privatlie to shew us such matter, as they have to condempne the Queen of Scottes, of the murder of her husband: and so they sent unto us the Lord of Lethingtoun, James Makgill, and Mr. George Boqwhannan, and another, being a Lord of the Session; which in private and secret conference with us, not as Commissioners, as they protested, but for our better instruction, shewed unto us some letters." That the Commissioners should have suffered any papers, and papers of such a criminating nature, and especially such as went to the very heart and soul of their commission, to be brought before them in a clandestine manner; was a most astonishing act of absurdity and injustice. But Murray had required it before. Elizabeth must therefore have privately commanded it now. She accordingly, in her immediate reply to this account of their conduct, passes not the slightest censure upon such a gross and palpable violation of decency. She even intimates her approbation of it. " We have of late," she says, " receaved your several letters, with all such other matters contained in sundry writings, as by your said letters hath been mentioned," meaning some extracts and accounts of Murray's letters, sent by them to Elizabeth; " upon consideration whereof, we have found such difficulties how to make a certen resolute answer unto yow, as we are rather moved to have furder advice of others of our counsell, now absent, and likewise of you ther; wherefore we are desirous to have some understanding of your opinions." And the requisition of Murray, the conduct of the Commissioners, and the reply of Elizabeth, are all so many rays uniting in one point.

But the Commissioners go on thus: " We have noted to your Majestie the chiefe and—speciall points of the said letters, written, as they say, with her own hand; to the intent it may please your Majestie to consider of them, and so to judge whether the same be sufficient to convince [convict] her of the detestable crime of the murder of her husband; which in our opinions and consciences, if the said letters be written with her own hand, is very hard to be avoided." This extra-judicial judgment of the Commissioners, so contrary to reason and common sense, was another particular in Murray's requisitions. He required it to be done. And it was actually done. By this means, evidences were produced clandestinely to the Commissioners. These were received by them, just as if they had been regularly presented in open court. Large accounts are drawn up of them. Larger extracts are made from them. Both are transmitted to Elizabeth and her council. The Commissioners declare openly to both, that they have already prejudged her cause. And, all the while, Mary and her Commissioners are totally ignorant of the whole transaction; and are preparing to enter upon a trial, that is in a great measure determined against them already.

The only doubt expressed by the Commissioners, is this, Whether the letters were her own hand-writing. But how did they act upon this, the capital point of the whole? They shall tell us themselves. " These men heare," they say, " do constantly affirm the said letters, which they produce of her own hand; to be her own hand indede ; and do offer to swear and take their oaths thereupon." They never compared the produced writings, that pretended to be of her hand, with any other writings, that were acknowledged to be so. They much less called in the Commissioners of Mary, to assist them in the collation. They rested all upon the affirmation of the producers, and upon the credit of their offered oaths. And they were precluded from communicating even the contents of them to Mary's Commissioners ; by the artful mode in which they had been exhibited to them, not as Commissioners, but as private gentlemen.

In such a manner, was the first part of the trial conducted; with a very near conformity to the original requisitions of Murray, and to the great disgrace of Elizabeth and her Commissioners. These acted in all, no doubt, under the private directions of her. And Murray was only doing in all, what he and she had already concerted should be done. Hence Murray proposed to put them clandestinely in possession of his papers ; and they agreed to peruse them clandestinely. Hence they thought themselves at liberty as Commissioners, though they were exhibited to them as private gentlemen, to communicate a long account of them to Elizabeth, but not to give any to Mary ; and to make large extracts from them, with their own opinions occasionally intimated as they went along. And hence they spoke out their opinion pretty plainly at last, upon the whole. " These men," they say, " do offer to swear and take their oaths thereupon, the matteir conteyned in them being such, as could hardly be invented or devised by any other than by herselfe ; for that they dis-

course of some things, which were unknowen to anie
other than to herself and Bothwell : and as it is hard to
counterfeit so manie, so the matter of them, and the manner how these men came by them, is such, as it seemeth
that God, in whose sight murder and bludshed of the innocent is abhommable [abominable], would not permit
the same to be hid or concealed." They thus condemn the
Queen of the murder charged upon her, in a formal dispatch to Elizabeth ; and upon letters, unuathenticated by the
producers, uncollated by themselves, uncommunicated to
her and her Commissioners. They condemn her, upon the
offer of oaths to their genuineness, from the very producers themselves ; and upon certain particulars in them,
which they say were unknown to all except her and
Bothwell ; but which they could only have heard to have
been so, from the very producers themselves. And they
condemn her upon the manner in which the letters came
into the hands of the producers; which they affirm to
have been a signal mark of God's interposal to punish
murder and bloodshed in her; but which they must equally
have heard, from the very producers themselves. · Such
was the astonishing dishonesty with which the Commissioners acted towards her in this outset of the business!
Yet Elizabeth approved of all. She liked their proceedings. · She liked them so well, that she wanted to have
their further advice upon the subject; and that she continued them as Commissioners, when she adjourned the
trial to London.

The Commissioners, however, were not entrusted with
all the schemes of Elizabeth in this matter. They consisted of the Duke of Norfolk, the Earl of Sussex, and
Sir Ralph Sadler. Some of these were too honourable for
such a confidence. But one of them, no doubt, and Sir
Ralph Sadler assuredly, had his private instructions for
managing the business, just as it was managed. And when
Murray exhibited his papers clandestinely to them, he

did it, as I have already hinted, merely in a private concert with her and this Commissioner. He did it, as they
tell us themselves, " to the intent, they [Murray, &c.]
wolde know of us, how your Majestie understanding the
same, wolde judge of the sufficiencie of the matter; and
whether, in your Majestie's opinion, the same will extend to condempne the Queen of Scottes, of the said murder." They accordingly ask her opinion. " We are,"
they say to her, " most humblie beseaching your Majestie,
that it may please the same to advertise us, of your opinion and judgement therein." But had Elizabeth never
seen the letters before? She certainly had. Copies of
them had been sent to London by Murray, as I have
shewn already, above four months before. These Murray
had even offered by his address of the 22d of June, to
communicate to Elizabeth, for the consideration of the
Commissioners that she was to appoint. She did not appoint them, till the 20th of September following. But
could Elizabeth refrain all this time from looking into the
letters, from feeding her love of scandal against Mary,
and from inspecting the ground-work of all her future
operations against her? Certainly she could not. She saw
the letters. She knew them, as well before the Commissioners imparted their contents to her, as she did afterwards. And she even contrived a method of communicating the letters to them unperceived. Murray had desired of
Elizabeth to have them laid before her Commissioners, previously to their sitting in judgment upon them; and to
have their private opinion before-hand, concerning their
competency or incompetency to prove his allegations.
This was now done. The papers were offered to be laid
before them, by Murray. The secret emissary of Elizabeth among them, probably, influenced them to admit the
offer. The papers were produced. The Commissioners
perused, abstracted, and extracted from them. And they

then communicated their opinions on the whole to Elizabeth; and through her, no doubt, to Murray.

In this artful manner, does Elizabeth appear to have
acted towards her own commissioners. Her whole life was
nothing but one scene of artifice and dishonesty. Her duplicity upon the present occasion is evidenced, by the requisitions of Murray at first, and by the conduct of her commissioners afterwards. These are the two parts of a tally.
Who can doubt their relation?

Yet though the commissioners, from the plain influence
of some emissary of Elizabeth's among them, and from
the violent force of their own credulity, had acted with a
gross dishonesty to Mary; Elizabeth saw, even from this
very dispatch, that they would not do all which she wanted
them to do. Murray had required in addition to all the
rest, and indeed as the grand support of all, that the papers
should be admitted for evidences, without any enquiry into
their hand-writing. But Elizabeth now found from the
complexion of their despatches, marked as they strongly
were with all the features of a hasty faith, a rash judgment, and a practising insidiousness; that they would come
at last to the point, which should have been the first in the
process of their inquiry. They had begun their accounts of
the writings produced, with those proper guards of doubt,
" as they say," and " as it is said." These they had sometimes dropt, in the intemperate rising of their spirits upon
Mary's presumed guilt. But they had again recurred to
them. And they had at last concluded their dispatch, with
mentioning the letters to be " written, as they say, with
her own hand;" and with intimating their opinion of her
guilt, " if the said letters be written with her own hand."
The next step therefore must have been, to have had the letters produced formally before the commissioners; and then to
have had their authenticity examined. This was what
Elizabeth never meant to be done. Yet it must immediately

be done, if the present commissioners went on. And Elizabeth, therefore, put an instant end to their commission.

This commission had been issued at first, in order " to pronounce in the cause of the murder." The commissioners themselves say as much, in a formal answer to some questions asked by Murray, concerning their authority. " They take their commission to be so ample," they say, "as by the same they may well enter and proceade to that controversie." And any one who knows the character of Elizabeth, and considers the end of all her proceedings, must know that this was the great and ruling object of the whole. Yet into this the commissioners never entered. They sat only seven days, before their grand dispatch above. The first four of these were spent in the necessary preliminaries of the work. On the fifth, being the 8th day of October, the commissioners of Mary presented their complaint against her rebels. Murray, instead of replying, wanted previously to be assured, exactly in the style of his former requisitions to Elizabeth : " if in this action they shall prove all things directly, wherewith they may and do burthen the Quene, their sovereigne's moder; how they may be assured to be free, and without daunger of the said Quene's displeasure." The next day, being the 9th of October, they put in some questions in writing to the same purport. These were answered instantly by the commis-sioners. But Murray was not satisfied with their answer. He would have one from Elizabeth herself. And the writing to Elizabeth, and the waiting for her answer, necessarily produced a suspension of business for some days· In this state of suspension it was, that Murray offered and proceeded to present his papers clandestinely to the commissioners. The delay, therefore, was created artfully for the purpose. On the 9th of October, Murray put in his written questions. On the 9th of October, the commissioners sent up to Elizabeth for her answers to them. On the 10th,

Murray put in that reply to Mary's complaint, which he had deferred before. And, in the afternoon of that very day, he communicated his evidences of the murder privately to the commissioners. These evidences he had utterly refused to produce before. Only the very day before, in his paper of questions to the commissioners, he had said thus: " The resolutioun of these articlis is sa necessary for us, and of sa great importance, that we can na ways enter to the accusation or tryal of the murther, before we be fully answerit thairin." Yet the very next day, and when all accusation was formally superseded for a time, he could privately enter into that accusation, and even lay his evidences for it privately before them.

This is such a manœuvre in management, as shews plainly the public accusation to have been superseded, in order to give room for preferring the private one : for the perusal of the papers by the commissioners ; for transmitting an account of them to Elizabeth ; and for Elizabeth to see their opinions concerning them, to view the impressions which these had made upon them, and to observe whether they would go all the lengths, which it was requisite for her purposes they should go. She found upon the trial, they would not. She therefore made no reply to Murray's doubts. These wanted no resolution at present. The dispatch concerning them must have reached her two days before the others concerning the letters. Yet she wrote no answer to it. This appeared strange at the very time. " Because I am advertised from York," says Sir Francis Knollys, " that hyr majestie doth hetherto stay the answering of the artycles of my Lord of Murraye and his partie ; therefore," &c. These pressed for an immediate answer. The whole business of the accusation was prevented from beginning to move. And had she not been in the secret of Murray's management, she must have answered them immediately. But, by being in the secret, she knew no answer was required. She expected another dispatch, with an account of the letters. It arrived. It was very much what she wished But it was not all that she wanted. "She was," says, in express terms, the sagacious author of the memoirs published by Crawford, "but indifferently pleased with what had past." And for this reason, though the commissioners were yet only at the very entrance of the business, had yet received only one paper from each side, and these could necessarily be only formal and general, the mere ground-work of their future proceedings; she dissolved their commission at once.

She could not have received their dispatch concerning the letters, before the 14th or 15th of October; and on the 16th she sent word of her intention to break up the Commission directly. She broke it up accordingly. She issued out a new Commission. To the former three she added five others, Sir Nicholas Bacon, the Earls of Arundel and Leicester, Lord Clinton, and Sir William Cecil. She did this, say the cotemporary memoirs of Crawford, "because she had suspected Norfolk, and would balance his interest;" because she would balance his own voice, and his influence over his relation, the Earl of Sussex, in his. And she ordered them to sit, not at York, but at Westminster: that they might be more immediately under her own inspection and influence.

Thus did Elizabeth still continue to found her denial of justice, upon the ground of a known falsehood. But she must have been particularly averse to the proposition of hearing Mary in her own defence before all the nobility of England, and before all the ambassadours of foreign powers. Their presence would be an insurmountable bar to her designs. Nor did she even choose to hear Mary at all. She rather chose to keep her at a distance, while her more honourable rebels were allowed a free access to the court; to break down her spirits by confinement; to tarnish her reputation by invited charges; and to be at once her betrayer, accuser, and judge. Nothing less than this, could have suited the

purposes of Elizabeth. Yet even she could not positively
refuse such a request. She owned it to be " a verie ressonabill" one. She promised to grant it hereafter. But she
must first hear the evidences of the accusation against her.
Why must she? She chose it. " *Stat pro ratione voluntas.*"
Yet had she not heard them before ? She certainly had.
She had even seen them.

Did Elizabeth, however, hear Mary afterwards in her
own defence, before the nobility and ambassadours? No !
Did she afterwards hear her, before any selected number of
her own obedient ministers in Privy-council ? No ! Did she
afterwards hear her before any other persons ? No ! She
never heard her at all. When she was accused, she would
not admit her to her presence, till she had seen the evidences of the accusation, which indeed she had already seen
before. And when she had seen them again, then, then
Mary was unworthy to be admitted into her presence.
This is such a strain of shuffling and deceit, as must amaze
a man of honour to hear. of. Yet it is very true. " As for
her coming to hir presence," Elizabeth then said, " considering at the first when she came into this realme, hir Majesty could not fynd it than agreeable to her honor—being
defamed only by common report ; much less could she now
think it either mete or honourable for hir to come to hir
presence, considering the multitude of matters and presumptions now lately produced against hir, such as indede
greved hir Majesty to think of." Elizabeth, on the 4th of
December, thought it very reasonable she should be heard
in her own defence. Elizabeth, on the 16th of the same
month, thought it very unreasonable. She had considered,
that she would not admit her into her presence when she
first came to England, and when she was accused only by
common report. But she had forgotten, that even then
Mary had been accused by much more than common report, even in form before Murray's Privy-council and Murray's parliament. She had also forgotten, that since her

coming into England, even since she had been accused in form again before the Commissioners, she had thought it very reasonable she should be admitted. And she now pretended to grieve over the evidences produced: when she had said after she had seen them, that she did not believe the accusation grounded upon them; and when she had peculiarly caused them to be produced at present.

This is such a frightful picture of hypocrisy, that it hurts my honest feelings, even to hold it up to the public. It is so dreadfully finished in every part; that we can see nothing but one uniform view of hypocrisy on every side. Every turn of countenance in the figures, every movement of the body in them, the whole of their drapery and disposition, all bespeak the foulest hypocrisy. Yet this is only the fore-ground of the piece. We have still more behind.

On Mary's Commissioners requiring permission for Mary to come up and defend herself; Elizabeth thought it expedient to present another scene of equivocation to the world. " As for the Quene coming in person to her Majestie," she said—" she concluded it to be best for the said Quene, that the said accusers should be roundly charged and reproved herein." She meant, she added, " to charge the Earl of Murray, as reason was, and to reprehend and impugn the accusation by all good means, in the favour of the said Quene of Scottes." So she promised. But how did she act? Did she " roundly charge and reprove" Murray and his accomplices? Did she " reprehend and impugn the accusation," which they had thus produced? And did she exert " all good means in favour of the said Quene of Scottes?" Let the sequel tell, so truly characteristick of her general duplicity.

Three days after her promise, on the 7th of December, the Commissioners of Elizabeth called Murray and his colleagues before them, and addressed them in these words: " My Lords, the Quene's Majestie hath commanded us to

say unto you, that her Highness thinketh [it] very much
and very strange, that you should accuse her [Mary] of so
horrble a cryme." This was the substantial part of their
chiding address. It was what Elizabeth pretended to call
" a round charging and reproof," and " a reprehending and
impugning the accusation by all good means." The promise
and the performance are just as much alike, we see, as a
storm in nature and a storm in the playhouse are.

But the Commissioners did not end here. Her Majesty,
they add, "therefore hath called us to say unto you; that
although you, in this doing, have forgot your duties of allegiance toward your Soveraine, yet her Majestie meaneth
not to forget the love of a good sister, and of a good neighbour and friend." Elizabeth, then, is determined at last to
discharge the duties of a good neighbour, a real friend, and
a loving sister to Mary. She has strangely " paltered" with
her promise indeed, in the reproof before. But she will
now serve her. Yet how does she serve her? The very
next words of the Commissioners will shew the kindness
intended. And the fact immediately subsequent, will shew
the kindness performed.

" What you are to answer to this," say the commissioners, " we are here ready to hear." But why was an
answer expected? According to Elizabeth's promise, the
rebels were to be sharply rebuked for their presumption, in
thinking to accuse Mary of murder. To this no answer was
requisite. They had accused. This was their offence. For
this they were to receive a severe reprimand. And the accusation was thus to be " impugned," by every honest exertion of friendship in Elizabeth. Yet, notwithstanding
all this, the rebels are called upon to answer. They are
called upon, in order to bring forward the concerted reply;
and to conclude the whole in a manner, directly the reverse
of Elizabeth's seeming intentions.

Thus are the commissioners, with principles of honour all
alive and active in the breasts of some of them, made to

become mere gentlemen-ushers to her hypocrisy, and mere
running-footmen to her᛫ revenge. Their souls must have
been shocked with the employ.᛫ But they were obliged to
submit to it. The bold barons, that had so often assaulted
the throne even of our warlike monarchs, all crouched at
the feet of this Henry the Eighth in petticoats. And they
were mean enough to carry on an evident scheme of collusion betwixt her and Murray.᛫ They therefore gave the rebuke in such gentle terms, so contrary to what they themselves had some of them heard her promise. They therefore called also upon the rebels to reply, when all reply was
precluded by the apparent nature of the business. But the
real was very different.

Murray, accordingly, came prepared for the latter. He
knew the farcical operations, in which these mere shifters
of the scenes to him and to her, were now to be engaged.
He heard them calmly. He replied. He expressed his
sorrow; for having offended Elizabeth by his accusation of
Mary. But to " satisfie" her, he would do——what? He
would retract the accusation, to be sure, for which he
" found" Elizabeth, as he says himself, " to be grievously
offended" with him. And thus Elizabeth will at last have
" impugned the accusation by all good means, in favour of
the said Queen of Scots." This undoubtedly was the natural process in the business. But there was nothing natural in the whole. It was merely an acted drama, from the
beginning to the end of it. Murray, therefore, in order to
" satisfy" Elizabeth for the " grievous offence" given, would
repeat it, and aggravate it highly. He would proceed to
prove what he had charged.

This was plainly the point to which Elizabeth and Murray had been mutually tending, by all these side-move-
ments. Murray had actually brought his proofs with him.
The commissioners were actually ready to receive them.
They had indeed called for them, in calling for a reply to
their rebuke. And thus the " round charge and reproof,"

which Elizabeth threatened to give Mary's accusers; the
" reprehending and impugning the accusation by all good
means in her favour," which Elizabeth promised to Mary's
commissioners; and " the love of a good sister, and of a
good neighbour and friend," which Elizabeth the moment
before declared by her own commissioners, she " meaned
not to forget" to Mary ; all terminated—in making the accusation to be maintained against her, and in encouraging
the evidences to be produced for it.

All this was a very proper prelude to the second appearance of the letters. They appeared the next day. But
what could be expected in fairness or in decency, as to the
examination of them ; from a woman so apparently hypocritical and base, as Elizabeth is here shown to be by her
own proceedings; and from men so apparently mean and
servile, as the commissioners are equally shewn to be from
theirs? The conduct of both we must naturally expect to
proceed in the same strain. It cannot well exceed the
other. And yet, I think, it did.

" This daye," say the commissioners, on the 8th of December, " the Earle of Murray, according to the appoyntment yesterday, came to the Quene's Majestie's commissioners, saying: That as they had yesternight produced and
shewed sundry writings," &c. " so for the further satisfaction, both of the Queene's majestie and theyr lordships,
they were ready to produce and show a great number of
letters wrytten by the said Quene, wherin, as they said,
might appear very evidently her inordinate love towards the
said Erle Bothwell, with sundry other arguments of her
guiltyness of the murder of her husband. And so thereupon they produced several wrytings wrytten in the like
Romain hand, as others her letters which were showed
yesternight, and avowed by them to be wrytten by the
said Quene." This is the account, we must remember,
given by the commissioners themselves, concerning their
own proceedings. We cannot desire a better authority for

censuring them. And they cannot ask a better testimony in their own vindication.

Yet what does their account say, for vindication or for censure? It says this. The commissioners at York, on the previous production of the letters, had rested their authenticity on the credit of the offered oaths of the producers. The commissioners at Westminster were more attentive to the rules of common sense and common honesty. They compared them with other writings. They found them, on examination, to be " wrytten in the like Romain hand, as others which were shewed yesternight." And so far they acted with apparent justness. But this was in appearance only. In reality they acted as unjustly and as absurdly as the commissioners at York. Yet they conducted themselves with more address. They were more cunning and more knavish. The addition of five to the former three, had given a strong predominancy to the spirit of Elizabeth and of villainy, among them. The majority of the three were honest in intention, and weak in practice. The majority of the eight were actually knaves in design, actually knaves in practice, but studiously courting the semblance of honesty. They therefore pretended to do, what the others had not done; and to examine the grand point on which the whole accusation rested, the hand-writing of the letters. But how did they examine it? In a manner that must have pronounced them to be idiots, if we had not known them to be otherwise; and in a manner that must pronounce them to be knaves, as we know them to have been men of sense. Like persons totally incompetent to the management of business, but in truth acting ministerially in a work of profligacy; they compared the letters produced, not with letters furnished by Mary's commissioners, not with letters even furnished by any indifferent persons, but with letters presented by the producers themselves. They collated them with " others her letters, which were shewed yesternight" (for " they had yesternight produced and

shewed sundry writings"), " and avowed by them to be
wrytten by the said Quene." And they thus collated one
forgery with another.

We have other letters of Mary's, that equally melted
away. We see a whole set of them appearing in the
silver box with the eight, and even produced with the
eight at Westminster. They were in Scotch, while the
eight were in French. They were witnesses with the
eight, to Mary's hatred of her husband, and to Mary's
love of Bothwell. Yet they were withdrawn, while the
eight remained behind. And, while the eight were allowed to walk the world and enjoy the sun, these were
remanded back into the dungeons of darkness in which
they were born, and there strangled by the murderous
hands of their own parents.

All this lays open a new source of conviction to our
minds. It serves also to show us, that as different parts
of the rebel forgeries were executed by different persons,
and some quite unknown to the others; as Lethington assuredly made the letters, and Buchanan composed the
sonnets, and Lethington transcribed both into a hand-
writing imitative of Mary's; so Morton probably drew up
the first contract for Mary, which was therefore written in
a chancery hand, unlike her's; Morton also drew up probably the second contract, in the pretended hand-writing
of Huntly, his immediate predecessor in the office of
Chancellor; and Murray himself, who was the presiding
genius of the whole villainy, and set all the implements
of iniquity to work, probably fabricated with his own
hand the confessions of Paris, &c.

. Buchanan has long had the supereminent infamy among
the friends of Mary, of having forged the letters from her
to Bothwell. It was not given to him very early *. Yet
it has been continued to him very steadily. But I am

* The forgery was originally attributed to Mary Bethune or
Beaton, one of Mary's Maids of Honour. Jebb, i. 524, and ii. 243.

compelled by the force of evidence, to clear Buchanan of this villainy, and to lay it upon another.

The first time that the idea of a set of forged letters was suggested to the rebels, was on the 24th of July, 1567. It was pretty certainly a spark, struck off from the mind of Lethington, by the friendly collision of the ideas of adultery and murder, then floating among the mob of clergy and gentry in Edinborough, and his own habits of forging the hand-writing of Mary. These habits are sufficiently attested by his own confession; as he acknowledged in secret to the Commissioners at York, that he had frequently forged her writing. His active hand, therefore, caught the spark as it flew; threw in the combustibles, which his active genius could always furnish; and fanned both immediately into a little flame. He is expressly said by the rebels themselves, to have been " esteemed" by them, as " one of the best engines or spirits of his country." He is particularly-reported. to have had " a crafty head and fell [or sharp] tongue." Elizabeth also is declared by her own embassadour to have known him well, " for his wisdom to conceive, and his wit to convey, whatsoever his mind is bent unto to bring it to pass." And he is described by another cotemporary, to have been " naturally enclined to plotting and intriguing; and fond of encountering difficulties, as tools that served to sharpen his wit, of which he had a very great stock." He instantly conceived the plan of a series of letters, fabricated in a writing similar to Mary's, and proving all that the mob asserted; in order to terrify Mary into the wanted resignation. He instantly connected it, with its proper accompaniments. His mind had always a quickness of invention, and a vigour of formation about it. And his tongue, which was as lively as his fancy, instantly reported the whole, for a system already in existence, to Throgmorton; to whose lodgings he frequently repaired, and in whose ear he frequently

whispered, or pretended to whisper, the secret designs of
the party.   He was, no doubt, the principal channel of intelligence to Throgmorton on all occasions.   He was the
only channel upon this.   Had the project of the letters
been known to any, except the relator and the reporter,
it must soon have crept out among the busy partizans in
the city, and appeared in some of Throgmorton's intel-
ligences concerning them.   Such a pretended discovery, if
it had once gone out beyond the two, would not long have
crept.   It would quickly have raised itself upon its feet.
It would have stalked forth in gigantic formidableness
among the amazed crowds.   And it was privately intimated to Throgmorton only, that he might act in conjunc-
tion with Lethington, and his four associates in treachery;
that he might write like them to Mary, upon the dangers
that were pressing upon her from every side; and so might
unite to drive the poor doe, which they could not hunt
down, into the toils prepared for her.

I here rest, and am grateful for the relief.   To wade
through the three volumes of Whitaker, and see his eternal repetitions of Goodall, is no easy matter.   My reader,
of course, would not be obliged by hearing Chalmers ring
the changes on these two writers.

LAING.

I have patiently gone through the pages of this, as well as through those of every other author whom I have cited; and, I should not follow the dictates of my own judgment were I to enlarge my volume by extracts from his work—for such would merely be an affirmance or corroboration of all that has been added by his predecessors against Mary.

Laing is a warm opponent of the advocates for the innocence of the Queen, and he has shown a great many Jacobite fallacies. He has also the credit of having brought to light one of the original letters of the Gilt Casket.

MR. CHALMERS.

This gentleman's Journal, or Diary of Mary, interspersed
as it is with historical and official selections, contains but
little in favour of her innocence.   He praises his partizans,
Goodall, Tytler, and Whitaker; and as the two latter sound
their gongs on the notes of the former, so he, frisky and fortified with their joint knowledge, rings the changes upon
them all; and comes in for the plate in the following brief,
confident, and amusing manner:—" He makes the Regent
Murray the principal in the murder of Darnley!—Bothwell
only Murray's agent—and the lovely Queen not even a *parti-
ceps criminis!*"—Of the Letters he says, whilst speaking of
forgeries—" Of the same nature are the documents which
Murray gave into Elizabeth's Commissioners as proofs of his
charge—the whole may be seen in Goodall." Mr. Chalmers,
who so cavalierly takes leave of his readers, without laying
the documents before them, may, if he pleases, in his next
edition, (should Mʳ·Murray's shelves be lightened of their
Quartos and Octavos, about the Queen of Scots, during
his life) tell the world that my volume contains all
that is necessary to be known about Queen Mary.—But I
cannot leave this subject before I answer the charge of
Chalmers against Murray in the language of Hume—and
tell him who were the murderers of Darnley. By this statement, which he has called forth, I would not have the world
to infer or imagine that *David Chalmers*, one of the murderers in 1587, was of the same race or kin with George
Chalmers the advocate and compiler of the Life of Mary
Queen of Scots in 1822, because he happened to be of the
same party.   Far be such wicked thoughts from myself and
readers.—But the Earl of Lenox, father of the murdered
King Henry, charged the Earl of Bothwell, Sir James
Balfour, Gilbert Balfour, and *David Chalmers*, with the
murder of his son—and all Scotland at the time justly be-

lieved these men, with four others of the Queen's household, the guilty regicides!

But Chalmers only repeats Mary's order to her Commissioners to charge Murray—and Hume says in answer— " Unless we take this angry accusation of Mary to be an argument of Murray's guilt, there remains not the least presumption which should lead us to suspect him to have been anywise an accomplice in the King's murder. That Queen never pretended to give any proof of the charge, and her Commissioners *affirmed at the time* that they *themselves knew of none*, though they were ready to maintain its truth by their mistress's orders, and would produce such proof as *she would send them!* Faithful servants.

" An English Whig who asserts the reality of the Popish Plot—an Irish Catholic who denies the massacre in 1641— and a Scotch Jacobite who maintains the innocence of Queen Mary—must be considered as men beyond the reach of argument or reason."

MISS BENGER.

This Lady has compiled two neat volumes entitled Memoirs of Mary Queen of Scots, at the Court of Henry the Second. And she quotes and praises Chalmers, whose work was published sometime before that of Miss Benger. She writes agreeably, and I hope as advantageously for herself and booksellers, as her work is pleasing and interesting to people who cannot go deeper into the Queen's history than our fair Authoress appears to have travelled. Her work treats of Mary's childhood; and, with this volume and Hume's History of the Reign of Elizabeth, contains all that need be known about the lovely Queen of Scots.

I opened the case with the historical account of Hume, and I conclude with the same admirable and correct author. As I have read, so I could have cited, the same authors whom he quotes; but who could do so with such perspicuity and elegance as Hume?

When I commenced with Buchanan, Hume had brought Mary to England for refuge; and Queen Elizabeth had become arbitress between Mary and the States of Scotland: and the conferences at York, Westminster, and at Hampton Court, are detailed in the following pages.

CONFERENCES AT YORK AND HAMPTON COURT.   OCT. 4.

The Commissioners appointed by the English Court for the examination of this great cause, were the Duke of Norfolk, the Earl of Sussex, and Sir Ralph Sadler; and York was named as the place of conference. Lesley Bishop of Ross, the Lords Herries, Levingstone, and Boyde, with three persons more, appeared as Commissioners from the Queen of Scots. The Earl of Murray, Regent, the Earl of Morton, the Bishop of Orkney, Lord Lindesey, and the Abbot of Dunfermling, were appointed Commissioners from the King and Kingdom of Scotland. Secretary Lidington, George Buchanan, the famous poet and historian, with some others, were named as their assistants.

It was a great circumstance in Elizabeth's glory, that she was thus chosen umpire between the factions of a neighbouring kingdom, which had, during many centuries, entertained the most violent jealousy and animosity against England; and her felicity was equally rare, in having the fortunes and fame of so dangerous a rival, who had long given her the greatest inquietude, now entirely at her disposal. Some circumstances of her late conduct had disco-

vered a bias towards the side of Mary : her prevailing interests led her to favour the enemies of that Princess: the
professions of impartiality, which she had made, were open
and frequent; and she had so far succeeded, that each side
accused her Commissioners of partiality towards their adversaries. She herself appears, by the instructions given
them, to have fixed no plan for their decision; but she
knew the advantages which she should reap, must be great,
whatever issue the cause might take. If Mary's crimes
could be ascertained by undoubted proof, she could for ever
blast the reputation of that Princess, and might justifiably
detain her for ever a prisoner in England: if the evidence
fell short of conviction, it was intended to restore her to the
throne, but with such strict limitations as would leave Elizabeth perpetual arbiter of all differences between the parties in Scotland, and render her in effect absolute mistress
of the kingdom.

Mary's Commissioners, before they gave in their complaints against her enemies in Scotland, entered a protest,
that their appearance in the cause should nowise affect the
independence of her crown, or be construed as a mark of
subordination to England: the English Commissioners received this protest, but with a reserve to the claim of England. The complaint of that Princess was next read, and
contained a detail of the injuries which she had suffered
since her marriage with Bothwell: that her subjects had
taken arms against her, on pretence of freeing her from captivity; and when she put herself into their hands, they
had committed her to custody in Lochlevin; had placed her
son, an infant, on the throne; had taken arms against her
after her deliverance from prison; had rejected all her proposals for accommodation; had given battle to her troops;
and had obliged her, for the safety of her person, to take
shelter in England. The Earl of Murray, in answer to
this complaint, gave a summary and imperfect account of
the late transactions: that the Earl of Bothwell, the known

murderer of the late King, had, a little after committing
that crime, seized the person of the Queen, and led her to
Dunbar; that he acquired such influence over her, as to
gain her consent to marry him, and he had accordingly procured a divorce from his former wife, and had pretended
to celebrate his nuptials with the queen; that the scandal
of this transaction, the dishonour which it brought on the
nation, the danger to which the infant Prince was exposed
from the attempts of that audacious man, had obliged the
nobility to take arms, and expose his criminal enterprises;
that after Mary, in order to save him, had thrown herself
into their hands, she still discovered such a violent attachment to him, that they found it necessary, for their own and
the public safety, to confine her person, during a season,
till Bothwell and the other murderers of her husband could
be tried and punished for their crimes; and that during this
confinement, she had voluntarily, without compulsion or violence, merely from disgust at the inquietude and vexations
attending power, resigned her crown to her only son, and
had appointed the Earl of Murray Regent during the minority. The Queen's answer to this apology was obvious;
that she did not know, and never could suspect, that Bothwell, who had been acquitted by a jury, and recommended
to her by all the nobility for her husband, was the murderer of the king; that she ever was, and still continues,
desirous that if he be guilty he may be brought to condign
punishment; that her resignation of the crown was extorted from her by the well-grounded fears of her life, and
even by direct menaces of violence; and that Throgmorton,
the English ambassador, as well as others of her friends,
had advised her to sign that paper, as the only means of
saving herself from the last extremity, and had assured her
that a consent given under these circumstances, could never
have any validity.

So far had the Queen of Scots seemed plainly to have
the advantage in the contest; and the English commission-

ers might have been surprised that Murray had made so
weak a defence, and had suppressed all the material imputations against that princess, on which his party had ever
so strenuously insisted; had not some private conferences
previously informed them of the secret. Mary's commissioners had boasted that Elizabeth, from regard to her kinswoman, and from her desire of maintaining the rights of
sovereigns, was determined, how criminal soever the conduct of that princess might appear, to restore her to the
throne; and Murray, reflecting on some past measures of
the English court, began to apprehend that there were but
too just grounds for these expectations. He believed that
Mary, if he would agree to conceal the most violent part
of the accusation against her, would submit to any reasonable terms of accommodation; but if he once proceeded so
far as to charge her with the whole of her guilt, no composition could afterward take place; and should she ever be
restored, either by the power of Elizabeth, or the assistance of her other friends, he and his party must be exposed
to her severe and implacable vengeance. He resolved,
therefore, not to venture too rashly on a measure which it
would be impossible for him ever to recall; and he privately
paid a visit to Norfolk and the other English commissioners,
confessed his scruples, laid before them the evidence of
the Queen's guilt, and desired to have some security for
Elizabeth's protection, in case that evidence should, upon
examination, appear entirely satisfactory. Norfolk was
not secretly displeased with these scruples of the Regent;
he had ever been a partizan of the Queen of Scots: secretary Lidington, who began also to incline to the party, and
was a man of singular address and capacity, had engaged
him to embrace farther views in her favour, and even to
think of espousing her: and though that Duke confessed,
that the proofs against Mary seemed to be unquestionable,
he encouraged Murray in his present resolution, not to pro-

duce them publicly in the conferences before the English commissioners.

Norfolk, however, was obliged to transmit to court the queries proposed by the Regent. These queries consisted of four particulars. Whether the English commissioners had authority from their sovereign to pronounce sentence against Mary, in case her guilt should be fully proved before them? Whether they would promise to exercise that authority, and proceed to an actual sentence? Whether the Queen of Scots, if she were found 'guilty, should be delivered into the hands of the Regent, or, at least, be so secured in England, that she never should be able to disturb the tranquillity of Scotland? and, Whether Elizabeth would also, in that case, promise to acknowledge the young king, and protect the Regent in his authority?

Elizabeth, when these queries, with the other transactions, were laid before her, began to think that they pointed towards a conclusion more decisive and more advantageous than she had hitherto expected. She determined, therefore, to bring the matter into full light; and under pretext that the distance from her person retarded the proceedings of her commissioners, she ordered them to come to London, and there continue the conferences. On their appearance, she immediately joined in commission with them some of the most considerable of her council; Sir Nicholas Bacon, lord keeper, the Earls of Arundel and Leicester, Lord Clinton, Admiral and Sir William Cecil, secretary. The Queen of Scots, who knew nothing of these secret motives, and who expected that fear or decency would still restrain Murray from proceeding to any violent accusation against her, expressed an entire satisfaction in this adjournment; and declared that the affair, being under the immediate inspection of Elizabeth, was now in the hands where she most desired to rest it. The conferences were accordingly continued at Hampton Court; and Mary's commissioners, as before, made no scruple to be present at them.

The Queen, meanwhile, gave a satisfactory answer to all Murray's demands, and declared, that though she wished and hoped, from the present inquiry, to be entirely convinced of Mary's innocence, yet, if the event should prove contrary, and that princess should appear guilty of her husband's murder, she should, for her own part, deem her ever after unworthy of a throne. The Regent, encouraged by this declaration, opened more fully his charge against the Queen of Scots, and after expressing his reluctance to proceed to that extremity, and protesting that nothing but the necessity of self-defence, which must not be abandoned for any delicacy, could have engaged him in such a measure, he proceeded to accuse her in plain terms of participation and consent in the assassination of the King. The Earl of Lenox, too, appeared before the English commissioners ; and, imploring vengeance for the murder of his son, accused Mary as an accomplice with Bothwell in that enormity.

When this charge was so unexpectedly given in, and copies of it were transmitted to the Bishop of Ross, Lord Herries, and the other commissioners of Mary, they absolutely refused to return an answer; and they grounded their silence on very extraordinary reasons ; they had orders, they said, from their mistress, if any thing were advanced that might touch her honour, not to make any defence, as she was a sovereign princess, and could not be subject to any tribunal ; and they required that she should previously be admitted to Elizabeth's presence, to whom, and to whom alone, she was determined to justify her innocence. They forgot that the conferences were at first begun, and were still continued, with no other view than to clear her from the accusations of her enemies ; that Elizabeth had ever pretended to enter into them only as her friend, by her own consent and approbation, not as assuming any jurisdiction over her; that this princess had, from the beginning, refused to admit her to her presence, till she should vindicate herself from the crimes imputed to her; that she had therefore discovered no new signs of partiality by her perseverance in that resolution; and that though she had granted an audience to the Earl of Murray and his colleagues, she had previously conferred the same honour on Mary's commissioners; and her conduct was so far entirely equal to both parties *.

As the commissioners of the queen of Scots refused to give in any answer to Murray's charge, the necessary consequence seemed to be, that there could be no farther proceedings in the conference. But though this silence might be interpreted as a presumption against her, it did not fully answer the purpose of those English ministers who were enemies to that princess. They still desired to have in their hands the proofs of her guilt; and in order to draw them with decency from the regent, a judicious artifice was employed by Elizabeth. Murray was called before the English commissioners; and reproved by them, in the queen's name, for the atrocious imputations which he had the temerity to throw upon his sovereign: but though the earl of Murray, they added, and the other commissioners, had so far forgotten the duty of allegiance to their prince, the

* Mary's complaint of the Queen's partiality in admitting Murray to a conference, was a mere pretext in order to break off the conference. She indeed employs that reason in her order for that purpose: (see Goodall, vol. 2. p. 184,) but in her private letter, her commissioners are directed to make use of that order to prevent her honour from being attacked. (Goodall, vol. 2. p. 183.) It was therefore the accusation only she was afraid of. Murray was the least obnoxious of all her enemies. He was abroad when her subjects rebelled, and reduced her to captivity; he had only accepted of the Regency when voluntarily proffered him by the nation. His being admitted to Queen Elizabeth's presence was therefore a very bad foundation for a quarrel, or for breaking off the conference; and was plainly a mere pretence.

queen never would overlook what she owed to her friend, her neighbour, and her kinswoman; and she therefore desired to know what they could say in their own justification. Murray, *thus urged, made no difficulty in producing the proofs of his charge against the Queen of Scots; and among the rest, some love-letters and sonnets of her's to Bothwell, written all in her own hand; and two other papers, one written in her own hand, another subscribed by her,* and written by the Earl of Huntley; each of which contained a promise of marriage with Bothwell, *made before the trial and acquittal* of that nobleman.

  ˙ All these important papers had been kept by Bothwell in a silver box or casket, which had been given him by Mary, and which had belonged to her first husband, Francis; and though the princess had enjoined him to burn the letters as soon as he had read them, he had thought proper carefully to preserve them as pledges of her fidelity, and had committed them to the custody of Sir James Balfour, deputy-governor of the castle of Edinburgh. When that fortress was besieged by the associated lords, Bothwell sent a servant to receive the casket from the hands of the deputy-governor. Balfour delivered it to the messenger; but as he had at that time received some disgust from Bothwell, and was secretly negociating an agreement with the ruling party, he took care, by conveying private intelligence to the Earl of Morton, to make the papers be intercepted by him. *They contained incontestible proofs of Mary's criminal correspondence with Bothwell, of her consent to the King's murder, and of her concurrence in the violence which Bothwell pretended to commit upon her.* Murray fortified this evidence by some testimonies of corresponding facts; and he added, some time after, the dying confession of one Hubert, or French Paris, as he was called, a servant of Bothwell's, who had been executed for the King's murder, and who directly charged the Queen with her being accessory to that criminal enterprise.

Mary's commissioners had used every expedient toward this blow, which they saw coming upon them, and against which, it appears, they were not provided with any proper defence. As soon as Murray opened his charge, they endeavoured to turn the conference from an inquiry into a negociation; and though informed by the English commissioners that nothing could be more dishonourable for their mistress, than to enter into a treaty with such undutiful subjects, before she. had justified herself from those enormous imputations which had been thrown upon her, they still insisted that Elizabeth should settle terms of accommodation between Mary and her enemies in Scotland. They maintained that, till their mistress had given in hei answer to Murray's charge, his proofs could neither be called for nor produced : and finding that the English commissioners were still determined to proceed in the method which had been projected, they finally broke off the conferences, and never would make any reply. *These papers, at least translations of them, have since been published. The objections made to their authenticity are, in general, of small force : but were they ever so specious, they cannot now be hearkened to; since Mary, at the time when the truth could have been fully cleared, did, in effect, ratify the evidence against her, by recoiling from the inquiry at the very critical moment, and refusing to give an answer to the accusation of her enemies *.*

But Elizabeth, though she had seen enough for her own satisfaction, was determined that the most eminent persons of her court should also be acquainted with these transactions, and should be convinced of the equity of her proceedings. She ordered her Privy-council to be assembled, and, that she might render the matter more solemn and authentic, she summoned, along with them, the Earls of Northumberland, Westmoréland, Shrewsbury, Worcester, Huntingdon, and Warwick. All the proceedings of the English

* *Vide* the observations of Hume, before the Appendix.

commissioners were read to them: the evidences produced
by Murray were perused : a great number of letters written
by Mary to Elizabeth were laid before them, and the hand-
writing compared with that of the letters delivered in by
the Regent: the refusal of the Queen of Scots'. commissioners to make any reply, was related: and on the whole
Elizabeth told them, that as she had from the first thought
it improper .that Mary, after such horrid crimes were imputed to her, should be admitted to her presence before
she .had, in some measure, justified herself from the
charge; so now, when her guilt was confirmed by so many
evidences, and all answer refused, she must, for her
part, persevere more. steadily in that resolution. Elizabeth next called in the Queen of Scots' commissioners,
and after observing that she deemed it much more de-
cent for their mistress to continue the conferences, than
to require the liberty of justifying herself in person, she told
them, that Mary might either send her reply by a person
whom she trusted, or deliver it herself to some English
nobleman, whom Elizabeth should appoint to wait upon
her: but as to her resolution of making no reply at all, she
must regard it as the strongest confession of guilt; nor
could they ever be deemed her friends who advised her to
that method of proceeding. These topics she enforced still
more strongly in a letter which she wrote to Mary herself.
   The Queen of Scots had no other subterfuge from these
pressing remonstrances, than still to demand a personal
interview with Elizabeth: a concession which, she was
sensible, would never be granted; because Elizabeth
knew that this expedient could decide nothing ; because it
brought matters to extremity which that Princess desired to
avoid; and because it had been refused from the beginning,
even before the commencement of the conferences. In
order to keep herself better in countenance, Mary thought
of another device. Though the conferences were broken
off, she ordered her Commissioners to accuse the Earl of

Murray and his associates as the murderers of the King:
but this accusation, coming so late, being extorted merely
by a complaint of Murray's, and being unsupported by any
proof, could only be regarded as an angry recrimination
upon her enemy. She also desired to have copies of the
papers given in by the regent; but as she still persisted in
her resolution to make no reply before the English Commissioners, this demand was finally refused her. ·

As Mary had thus put an end to the conferences, the
regent expressed great impatience to return into Scotland;
and he complained, that his enemies had taken advantage
of his absence, and had thrown the whole government
into confusion. ' Elizabeth therefore dismissed him; and
granted him a loan of 5000l. to bear the charges of his
journey. During the conferences at York, the Duke of
Chatelrault arrived at London, in passing from France;
and as the Queen knew that he was engaged in Mary's
party, and had very plausible pretensions to the regency
of the King of Scots, she thought proper to detain him
till after Murray's departure. But notwithstanding these
marks of favour, and some other assistance which she
secretly gave this latter nobleman, she still declined acknowledging the young King, or treating with Murray as
regent of Scotland.

  Orders were given for removing the Queen of Scots
from Bolton, a place surrounded with Catholics, to Tut-
bury, in the county of Stafford, where she was put under
the custody of the Earl of Shrewsbury. Elizabeth entertained hopes that this Princess, discouraged by her misfortunes, and confounded by the late transactions, would
be glad to secure a safe retreat from all the tempests with
·which she had been agitated; and she promised to bury
every thing in oblivion, provided Mary would agree, either
voluntarily to resign her crown, or to associate her son
·with her in the government; and the administration to remain, during his minority, in the hands of the Earl of

Murray.   But that high-spirited Princess refused all treaty
upon such terms, and declared that her last words should
be those of a Queen of Scotland.   Besides many other
reasons, she said, which fixed her in that resolution, she
knew, that if, in the present emergency, she made such
concessions, her submission would be universally deemed
an acknowledgment of guilt, and would ratify all the
calumnies of her enemies.

Mary still insisted upon this alternative; either that
Elizabeth should assist her in recovering her authority, or
should give her liberty to retire into France, and make
trial of the friendship of other Princes; and as she asserted that she had come voluntarily into England, invited by many former professions of amity, she thought
that one or other of these requests could not, without the
most extreme injustice, be refused her.   But Elizabeth,
sensible of the danger which attended both these proposals, was secretly resolved to detain her still a captive;
and as her retreat into England had been little voluntary,
her claim upon the 'Queen's generosity appeared much
less urgent than she was willing to pretend.   Necessity, it
was thought, would, to the prudent, justify her detention:
her past misconduct would apologise for it to the equitable:
and though it was foreseen, that compassion for Mary's
situation, joined to her intrigues and insinuating behaviour,
would, while she remained in England, excite the zeal
of her friends, especially of the Catholics, these incon-
veniences were deemed much inferior to those which
attended any other expedient.   Elizabeth trusted also to
her own address for eluding all these difficulties: she purposed to avoid breaking absolutely with the Queen of
Scots, to keep her always in hopes of an accommodation,
to negociate perpetually with her, and still to throw the
blame of not coming to any conclusion, either on unfore-
seen accidents, or on the obstinacy and perverseness of
others.

The Duke of Norfolk was the only Peer that enjoyed the
highest title of nobility; and as there was at present no
Princes of the Blood, the splendour of his family, the opu-
lence of his fortune, and the extent of his influence, had
rendered him without comparison the first subject in England. The qualities of his mind corresponded to his high
station: beneficent, affable, generous, he had acquired the
affections of the people: prudent, moderate, obsequious, he
possessed, without giving any jealousy, the good graces of
his sovereign. His grandfather and father had long been
regarded as the leaders of the Catholics; and this heredi-
tary attachment, joined to the alliance of blood, had procured him the friendship of the most considerable men of
that party; but as he had been educated among the reformers, he was sincerely devoted to their principles, and
maintained a strict decorum and regularity of life, by which
the Protestants were at that time distinguished; he thereby
enjoyed the rare felicity of being popular even with the most
opposite factions. The height of his prosperity alone
was the source of his misfortunes, and engaged him in attempts from which his virtue and prudence would naturally have for ever kept him at a distance.

Norfolk was at this time a widower; and being of a suitable age, his marriage with the Queen of Scots had appeared so natural, that it had occurred to several of his
friends and those of that Princess ; but the first person who,
after Secretary Lidington, opened the scheme to the Duke,
is said to have been the Earl of Murray, before his departure
for Scotland. That nobleman set before Norfolk both the
advantage of composing the dissensions in Scotland by an
alliance which would be so generally acceptable, and the
prospect of reaping the succession of England ; and in order
to bind Norfolk's interest the faster with Mary's, he proposed that the Duke's daughter should also espouse the
young King of Scotland. The previously obtaining of Eli-

zabeth's consent, was regarded, both by Murray and Norfolk, as a circumstance essential to the success of their project; and all terms being adjusted between them, Murray took care, by means of Sir Robert Melvil, to have the design communicated to the Queen of Scots. This Princess replied, that the vexations which she had met with in her two last marriages, had made her more inclined to lead a single life; but she was determined to sacrifice her own inclinations to the public welfare: and therefore, as soon as she should be legally divorced from Bothwell, she would be determined by the opinion of her nobility and people in the choice of another husband.

It is probable that Murray was not sincere in this proposal. He had two motives to engage him to dissimulation. He knew the danger which he must run in his return through the north of England, from the power of the Earls of Northumberland and Westmoreland, Mary's partisans in that country; and he dreaded an insurrection in Scotland from the Duke of Chatelrault and the Earls of Argyle and Huntley, whom she had appointed her lieutenants during her absence. By these feigned appearances of friendship, he both engaged Norfolk to write in his favour to the northern noblemen; and he persuaded the Queen of Scots to give her lieutenants permission, and even advice, to conclude a cessation of hostilities with the Regent's party.

The Duke of Norfolk, though he had agreed that Elizabeth's consent should be previously obtained before the completion of his marriage, had reason to apprehend that he never should prevail with her voluntarily to make that concession. He knew her perpetual and unrelenting jealousy against her heir and rival; he was acquainted with her former reluctance to all proposals of marriage with the Queen of Scots; he foresaw that this Princess's espousing a person of his power and character and interest, would give the greatest umbrage; and as it would then become necessary to reinstate her in possession of her throne on some tolerable terms, and even to endeavour the re-establishing of her character, he dreaded lest Elizabeth, whose politics had now taken a different turn, would never agree to such indulgent and generous conditions. He therefore attempted previously to gain the consent and approbation of several of the most considerable nobility; and he was successful with the Earls of Pembroke, Arundel, Derby, Bedford, Shrewsbury, Southampton, Northumberland, Westmoreland, Sussex *. Lord Lumley and Sir Nicholas Throgmorton cordially embraced the proposal: even the earl of Leicester, Elizabeth's declared favourite, who had formerly entertained some views of espousing Mary, willingly resigned all his pretensions, and seemed to enter zealously into Norfolk's interests. There were other motives besides affection to the Duke, which produced this general combination of the nobility.

Sir William Cecil, Secretary of State, was the most vigilant, active, and prudent minister ever known in England; and as he was governed by no views but the interests of his Sovereign, which he had inflexibly pursued, his authority over her became every day more predominant. Ever cool himself, and uninfluenced by prejudice or affection, he checked those sallies of passion, and sometimes of caprice, to which she was subject; and if he failed of persuading her in the first movement, his perseverance, and remonstrances, and arguments, were sure at last to recommend themselves to her sound discernment. The more credit he gained with his mistress, the more was he exposed to the envy of her other counsellors; and as he had been supposed to adopt the interests of the House of Suffolk, whose claim seemed to carry with it no danger to the present establishment, his enemies, in opposition to him, were naturally

* Ancestor of the present noble family of Salisbury and Exeter.

led to attach themselves to the Queen of Scots. Elizabeth
saw, without uneasiness, this emulation among her courtiers,
which served to augment her own authority; and though
she supported Cecil, whenever matters came to extremities, and dissipated every conspiracy against him, particularly one laid about this time for having him thrown into
the Tower on some pretence or other, she never gave him
such unlimited confidence as might enable him entirely to
crush his adversaries.

Norfolk, sensible of the difficulty which he must meet
with in controlling Cecil's counsels, especially where they
concurred with the inclination as well as interest of the
Queen, durst not open to her his intentions of marrying the
Queen of Scots; but proceeded still in the same course, of
increasing his interest in the kingdom, and engaging more
of the nobility to take part in his measures. A letter was
written to Mary by Leicester, and signed by several of the
first rank, recommending Norfolk for her husband, and sti-
pulating conditions for the advantage of both kingdoms:
particularly, that she should give sufficient surety to Elizabeth, and the heirs of her body, for the free enjoyment of
the crown of England; that a perpetual league, offensive
and defensive, should be made between their realms and
subjects; that the Protestant religion should be established
by law in Scotland; and that she should grant amnesty to
her rebels in that kingdom. When Mary returned a favourable answer to this application, Norfolk employed himself with new ardour in the execution of his project; and
besides securing the interests of many of the considerable
gentry and nobility who resided at court, he wrote letters
to such as lived at their country seats, and possessed the
greatest authority in the several counties. The Kings of
France and Spain, who interested themselves extremely in
Mary's cause, were secretly consulted, and expressed their
approbation of those measures. And though Elizabeth's
consent was always supposed as a previous condition to the

finishing of this alliance, it was apparently Norfolk's inten-·
tion, when he proceeded such lengths without consulting
her, to render his party so strong, that it should no longer
be in her power to,refuse it.

It was impossible that so extensive a conspiracy could en-·.
tirely escape the Queen's vigilance and that of Cecil. She
dropped several intimations to the Duke, by which he
might learn that she was acquainted with his designs; and
she frequently warned him to beware on what pillow he reposed his head: but he never had the prudence or the courage to open to her his full intentions. Certain intelligence
of this dangerous combination was given her first by Leicester, then by Murray*, who, if ever he was sincere in
promoting Norfolk's marriage, which is much to be doubted,
had at least intended, for his own safety, and that of his
party, that Elizabeth should, in reality, as in appearance,
be entire arbiter of the conditions, and should not have her
consent extorted by any confederacy of her own subjects.
This information gave great alarm to the court of England;
and the more so, as those intrigues were attended with
other circumstances, of which, it is probable, Elizabeth
was not wholly ignorant.

Among the nobility and gentry that seemed to enter into
Norfolk's views, there were many who were zealously attached to the Catholic religion, who had no other design
than that of restoring Mary to her liberty, and who would
gladly, by a combination *with foreign powers, or even at the
expense of a civil war, have placed her on the throne of England.* The Earls of Northumberland and Westmoreland,
who possessed great power in the north, were leaders of
this party; and the former, nobleman made offer to the
Queen of Scots, by Leonard Dacres, brother to Lord Dacres,

* Lesley, p. 7I. It appears by Haynes, p. 1521,˙525, that Elizabeth
had heard rumours of Norfolk's dealing with Murray; and charged
the latter to inform her of the whole truth, which he accordingly
did. See also the Earl of Murray's letter produced on Norfolk's
trial.

that he would free her from confinement, and convey her to
Scotland, or any other place to which she should think proper to retire. Sir Thomas and Sir Edward Stanley, sons of
the Earl of Derby, Sir Thomas Gerrard Rolstone, and other
gentlemen, whose interests lay in the neighbourhood of the
place where Mary resided, concurred in the same views; and
required that, in order to facilitate the execution of the
scheme, a diversion should, in the mean time, be made from
the side of Flanders. Norfolk discouraged, and even in appearance suppressed, these conspiracies; both because his duty
to Elizabeth would not allow him to think of effecting his
purpose by rebellion, and because he foresaw that, if the
Queen of Scots came into the possession of these men, they
would rather choose for her husband the King of Spain, or
some foreign prince, who had power as well as inclination,
to re-establish the Catholic religion.

When men of honour and good principles, like the
Duke of Norfolk, engage in dangerous enterprises,
they are commonly so unfortunate as to be criminal by
halves; and while they balance between the execution of
their designs and their remorses, their fear of punishment
and their hope of pardon, they render themselves an easy prey
to their enemies. The Duke, in order to repress the surmises spread against him, spoke contemptuously to Elizabeth of the Scottish alliance; affirmed that his estate in
England was more valuable than the revenue of a kingdom
wasted by civil wars and factions; and declared that, when
he amused himself in his own tennis-court at Norwich,
amidst his friends and vassals, he deemed himself at least a
petty prince, and was fully satisfied with his condition.
Finding that he did not convince her by these asseverations,
and that he was looked on with a jealous eye by the ministers, he retired to his country-seat without taking leave.
He soon after repented of this measure, and set out on his
return to court, with a view of using every expedient to
regain the Queen's good graces; but he was met at St.

Alban's by Fitz-Garret, lieutenant of the band of pen-
sioners, by whom he was conveyed to Burnham, three
miles from Windsor, where the court then resided. He was
soon after committed to the Tower, under the custody of
Sir Henry Nevil. Lesley, Bishop of Ross, the Queen of
Scots' ambassador, was examined and confronted with Norfolk before the council. The Earl of Pembroke was confined to his own house. Arundel, Lumley, and Throgmorton were taken into custody. The Queen of Scots
herself was removed to Coventry; all access to her was,
during some time, more strictly prohibited; and Viscount
Hereford was joined to the Earls of Shrewsbury and Huntingdon in the office of guarding her.

A rumour had been diffused in the North of an intended
rebellion; and the Earl of Sussex, president of York,
alarmed with the danger, sent for Northumberland and
Westmoreland, in order to examine them ; but not finding
any proof against them, he allowed them to depart. The
report meanwhile gained ground daily; and many appearances of its reality being discovered, orders were dispatched
by Elizabeth to these two noblemen to appear at court, and
answer for their conduct. They had already proceeded so
far in their criminal designs, that they dared not to trust
themselves in her hands ; they had prepared measures for a
rebellion; had communicated their design to Mary and her
ministers; had entered into a correspondence with the
Duke of Alva, governor of the Low Countries; had obtained his promise of a reinforcement of troops, and a supply of arms and ammunition ; and had prevailed on him to
send over to London Chiapino Vitelli, one of his most famous captains, on pretence of adjusting some differences
with the Queen; but in reality with a view of putting him
at the head of the Northern rebels. The summons sent to
the two Earls, precipitated the rising, before they were
fully prepared; and Northumberland remained in suspence
between opposite dangers, when he was informed that some

of his enemies were on the way with a commission to arrest him. He took horse instantly, and hastened to his associate Westmoreland, whom he found surrounded with his
friends and vassals, and deliberating with regard to the measures which he should follow in the present emergency.
They determined to begin the insurrection without delay;
and the great credit of these two noblemen, with that zeal for
the Catholic religion which still prevailed in the neighbourhood, soon drew together multitudes of the common people. They published a manifesto, in which they declared,
that they intended to attempt nothing against the Queen,
to whom they avowed unshaken allegiance; and that their
sole aim was to re-establish the religion of their ancestors,
to remove evil counsellors, and to restore the Duke of Norfolk and other faithful peers to their liberty and to the
Queen's favour. The numbers of the malcontents
amounted to four thousand foot and sixteen hundred horse;
and they expected the concurrence of all the Catholics in
England.

The Queen was not negligent in her own defence,
and she had beforehand, from her prudent and wise
conduct, acquired the general good will of her people;
the best security of a sovereign: insomuch that even
the Catholics in most countries expressed an affection
for her service; and the Duke of Norfolk himself, though
he had lost her favour, and lay in confinement, was not
wanting, as far as his situation permitted, to promote the
levies among his friends and retainers. Sussex, attended
by the earls of Rutland, the lords Hunsdon, Evers, and
Willoughby of Parham, marched against the rebels at the
head of seven thousand men, and found them already advanced to the bishopric of Durham, of which they had
taken possession. They retired before him to Hexham;
and hearing that the earl of Warwick and lord Clinton
were advancing against them with a greater body, they

found no other resource than to disperse themselves without striking a blow. The common people retired to their houses: the leaders fled into Scotland. Northumberland was found skulking in that country, and was confined by Murray in the castle of Lochlevin. Westmoreland received shelter from the chieftains of the Kers and Scots, partisans of Mary; and persuaded them to make an inroad into England, with a view of exciting a quarrel between the two kingdoms. After they had committed great ravages, they retreated to their own country. This sudden and precipitate rebellion was followed soon after by another still more imprudent, raised by Leonard Dacres. Lord Hunsden, at the head of the garrison of Berwick, was able, without any other assistance, to quell these rebels. Great severity was exercised against such as had taken part in these rash enterprises. Sixty-six petty constables were hanged; and no less than eight hundred persons are said, on the whole, to have suffered by the hands of the executioner. But the queen was so well pleased with Norfolk's behaviour, that she released him from the Tower; allowed him to live, though under some shew of confinement, in his own house; and only exacted a promise from him not to proceed any farther in his negociations with the queen of Scots.

Elizabeth now found that the detention of Mary was attended with all the ill consequences which she had foreseen when she first embraced that measure. This latter princess, recovering, by means of her misfortunes and her own natural good sense, from that delirium into which she seems to have been thrown during her attachment to Bothwell, had behaved with such modesty and judgment, and even dignity, that every one who approached her was charmed with her demeanour; and her friends were enabled, on some plausible grounds, to deny the reality of all those crimes which had been imputed to her. Compassion for her situation, and the necessity of procuring her liberty, proved an incitement among all the partisans to be active in promoting her cause: and, as her deliverance from. captivity, it was thought, could nowise be effected but by attempts dangerous to the established government, Elizabeth had reason to expect little tranquillity so long as the Scottish queen remained a prisoner in her hands. But as this inconvenience had been preferred to the danger of allowing that princess to enjoy her liberty, and to seek relief in all the Catholic courts of Europe, it behoved the queen to support the measure which she had adopted, and to guard, by every prudent expedient, against the mischiefs to which it was exposed. She still flattered Mary with hopes of her protection, maintained an ambiguous conduct between that queen and her enemies in Scotland, negociated perpetually concerning the terms of her restoration, made constant professions of friendship to her : and by these artifices endeavoured both to prevent her from making any desperate efforts for her deliverance, and to satisfy the French and Spanish ambassadors, who never intermitted their solicitations, sometimes accompanied with menaces, in her behalf. This deceit was received with the same deceit by the queen of Scots: professions of confidence were returned by professions equally insincere: and while an appearance of friendship was maintained on both sides, the animosity and jealousy, which had long prevailed between them, became every day more inveterate and incurable. These two princesses in address, capacity, activity, and spirit, were nearly a match for each other; but unhappily, Mary, besides her present forlorn condition, was always inferior, in personal conduct and discretion, as well as in power, to her illustrious rival.

Elizabeth and Mary wrote at the same time letters to the regent. The Queen of Scots desired that her marriage with Bothwell might be examined, and a divorce be legally pronounced between them. The Queen of England gave Murray the choice of three conditions; that Mary should be restored to her dignity on certain terms;

that she should be associated with her son, and the administration. remain in the regent's hands, till the young
Prince should come to years of discretion ; or that she
should be allowed to live at liberty as a private person
in Scotland,' and have an honourable settlement made in
her favour. Murray summoned a convention of states, in
order to deliberate on these proposals of the two Queens:
no answer was made by them to Mary's letter, on pretence
that she had there employed the style of a sovereign, addressing herself to her subjects ; but in reality, because
they saw that her request was calculated to prepare the
way for a marriage with Norfolk, or some powerful Prince,
who could support her cause, and restore her to the
throne. They replied to Elizabeth, that the two former
conditions were so derogatory to the royal authority of
their Prince, that they could not so much as deliberate
concerning them : the third alone could be the subject of
treaty. It was evident that Elizabeth, in proposing conditions so unequal in their importance, invited the Scots to
a refusal of those which were the most advantageous to
Mary ; and as it was difficult, if not impossible, to adjust
all the terms of the third, so as to render it secure and
eligible to all parties, it was concluded that she was not
sincere in any of them.

ASSASSINATION OF THE EARL OF MURRAY. 1570.

It is pretended that Murray had entered into a private
negociation with the Queen, to get Mary delivered into
his hands ; and as Elizabeth found the detention of her
in England so dangerous, it is probable that she would
have been pleased, on any honourable or safe terms, to rid
herself of a prisoner who gave her so much inquietude.
But all these projects vanished by the sudden death of the

·Regent,ᶦ who was.assassinated (Jan. 23), in revenge of a
private injury, by a gentleman of, the name of Hamilton.
Murray was a person of considerable vigour, abilities, and
constancy; but, though he was not unsuccessful, during
his regency, in composing the dissensions in Scotland, his
talents shone out more eminently in the beginning than
in the end of his life. His manners were rough and
austere, and he possessed not that perfect integrity, which
frequently accompanies, and can alone atone for, that un-
amiable character.

    By the death of the Regent, Scotland relapsed into
anarchy. Mary's party assembled together, and made
themselves masters of Edinburgh. The Castle, commanded by Kirkaldy of Grange, seemed to favour her
cause ; and, as many of the principal nobility had embraced that party, it became probable, though the people
were in general averse to her, that her authority might
again acquire the ascendant. To check its progress, Elizabeth dispatched Sussex with an army to the north, under colour of chastising the ravages committed by the
borderers. He entered Scotland, and laid waste the
lands of the Kers and Scots, seized the castle of Hume,
and committed hostilities on all Mary's partisans, who, he
said, had offended his mistress by harbouring the English
rebels. Sir William Drury was afterward sent with a
body of troops, and he threw down the houses of the
Hamiltons, who were engaged in the same faction. The
English armies were afterward recalled by agreement with
the Queen of Scots, who promised, in return, that no
French troops should be introduced into Scotland, and
that the English rebels should be delivered up to the
Queen by her partisans.

    But though the Queen, covering herself with the pre-
tence of revenging her own quarrel, so far contributed
to support the party of the young King of Scots, she was
cautious not to declare openly against Mary; and she

even sent a request, which was equivalent to a command; to the enemies of that Princess, not to elect, during some time, a **Regent** in the place of Murray. Lenox, the King's grandfather, was therefore chosen temporary Governor, under the title of Lieutenant. Hearing afterward that Mary's partisans, instead of delivering up Westmoreland, and the other fugitives, as they had promised, had allowed them to escape into Flanders; she permitted the King's party to give Lenox the title of Regent; and she sent Randolph, as her resident, to maintain a correspondence with him. But notwithstanding this step, taken in favour of Mary's enemies, she never laid aside her ambiguous conduct, nor quitted the appearance of amity to that Princess. Being importuned by the Bishop of Ross, and her other agents, as well as by foreign Ambassadors, she twice procured a suspension of arms between the Scottish factions, and by that means stopped the hands of the Regent, who was likely to obtain advantages over the opposite party. By these seeming contrarieties she kept alive the factions in Scotland, increased their mutual animosity, and rendered the whole country a scene of devastation and of misery. She had no intention to conquer the kingdom, and consequently no interest or design to instigate the parties against each other; but this consequence was an accidental effect of her cautious politics, by which she was engaged, as far as possible, to keep on good terms with the Queen of Scots, and never to violate the appearances of friendship with her, at least those of neutrality.

The better to amuse Mary with the prospect of an accommodation, Cecil and Sir Walter Mildmay were sent to her with proposals from Elizabeth. The terms were somewhat rigorous, such as a captive Queen might expect from a jealous rival; and they thereby bore the greater appearances of sincerity on the part of the English Court. It was required that the Queen of Scots, besides re-

nouncing all title to the crown of England during the
lifetime of Elizabeth, should make a perpetual league,
offensive and defensive, between the kingdoms; that she
should marry no Englishman without Elizabeth's consent,
nor any other person without the consent of the states
of Scotland; that compensation should be made for the
late ravages committed in England; that justice should
be executed on the murderers of King Henry ; that the
young Prince should be sent into England, to be educated there; and that six hostages, all of them noblemen, should be delivered to the Queen of England, with
the castle of Hume, and some other fortress, for the security of performance. Such were the conditions upon
which Elizabeth promised to contribute her endeavours towards the restoration of the deposed Queen. The necessity of Mary's affairs obliged her to consent to them; and
the Kings of France and Spain, as well as the Pope, when
consulted by her, approved of her conduct; chiefly on
account of the civil wars, by which all Europe was at
that time agitated, and which incapacitated the Catholic
Princes from giving her any assistance.

Elizabeth's commissioners proposed also to Mary a plan
of accommodation with her subjects in Scotland; and after
some reasoning on that head, it was agreed that the queen
should require Lenox, the regent, to send commissioners,
in order to treat of conditions under her mediation. The
partisans of Mary boasted, that all terms were fully settled
with the court of England, and that the Scottish rebels
would soon be constrained to submit to the authority of
their sovereign: but Elizabeth took care that these rumours
should meet with no credit, and that the king's party should
not be discouraged, nor sink too low in their demands.
Cecil wrote to inform the regent, that all the queen of
England's proposals, so far from being fixed and irrevoca-
ble, were to be discussed anew in the conference; and desired him to send commissioners who should be constant in

the king's cause, and cautious not to make concessions which
might be prejudicial to their party. Sussex also, in his letters, dropped hints to the same purpose; and Elizabeth
herself said to the abbot of Dunfermling, whom Lenox had
sent to the court of England, that she would not insist on
Mary's restoration, provided the Scots could make the jns-
tice of their cause appear to her satisfaction; and that,
even if their reasons should fall short of full conviction,
she would take effectual care to provide for their future
security.

The parliament of Scotland (March 1) appointed the
Earl of Morton and Sir James Macgill, together with the
abbot of Dunfermling; to manage the treaty. These commissioners presented memorials, containing reasons for the
deposition of their Queen; and they seconded their arguments with examples drawn from the Scottish history, with
the authority of laws, and with the sentiments of many famous divines. The lofty ideas which Elizabeth had entertained, of the absolute, indefeasible right of sovereigns,
made her be shocked with these republican topics; and she
told the Scottish commissioners, that she was nowise satisfied with their reasons for justifying the conduct, of their
countrymen; and that they might, therefore, without at-
tempting any apology, proceed to open the conditions
which they required for their security. They replied, that
their commission did not empower them to treat of any
terms which might infringe the title and sovereignty of
their young king, but, they would gladly hear whatever
proposals should be made them by her Majesty. The conditions, recommended by the Queen were not disadvan-
tageous to Mary; but as the commissioners still insisted,
that they were not authorised to treat in any manner concerning the restoration of that princess, the conferences
were necessarily at an end; and Elizabeth dismissed the
Scottish commissioners, with injunctions, that they should
return, after having procured more ample powers from their

parliament. The Bishop of Ross openly complained to the English council, that they had abused his mistress by fair promises and professions; and Mary herself was no longer at a loss to judge of Elizabeth's insincerity. By reason of these disappointments, matters came still nearer to extremities between the two princesses; and the Queen of Scots, finding all her hopes eluded, was more strongly incited to make, at all hazards, every possible attempt for her liberty and security.

An incident also happened about this time, which tended to widen the breach between Mary and Elizabeth, and to increase the vigilance and jealousy of the latter princess. *Pope Pius V. who had succeeded Paul, after having endeavoured in vain to conciliate by gentle means the friendship of Elizabeth, whom his predecessor's violence had irritated, issued at last a bull of excommunication against her, deprived her of all title to the crown, and absolved her subjects from their oaths of allegiance. It seems probable, that this attack on the Queen's authority was made in concert with Mary, who intended by that means to forward the northern rebellion; a measure which was at that time in agitation.* John Felton affixed this bull to the gates of the Bishop of London's palace; and scorning either to fly or to deny the fact, he was seized and condemned, and received the crown of martyrdom, for which he seems to have entertained so violent an ambition.

NEW CONSPIRACY OF THE DUKE OF NORFOLK.

All the enemies of Elizabeth, in order to revenge themselves for her insults, had naturally recourse to one policy, the supporting of the cause and pretensions of the Queen of Scots; and Alva, whose measures were ever violent, soon opened a secret intercourse with that princess. There was one Rodolphi, a Florentine merchant, who had resided about fifteen years in London, and who, while he conducted his commerce in England, had managed all the correspondence of the court of Rome with the Catholic nobility and

gentry. He had been thrown into prison at the time when
the Duke of Norfolk's intrigues with Mary had been discovered; but either no proof was found against him, or the
part which he had acted was not very criminal; and he
soon after recovered his liberty. This man, zealous for the
Catholic faith, had formed a scheme, in concert with the
Spanish Ambassador, for subverting the government, by a
foreign invasion and a domestic insurrection; and when he
communicated his project, by letter, to Mary, he found that,
as she was now fully convinced of Elizabeth's artifices, and
despaired of ever recovering her authority, or even her
liberty, by pacific measures, she willingly gave her concurrence. The great number of discontented Catholics were
the chief source of their hopes on the side of England; and
they also observed, that the kingdom was, at that time,
full of indigent gentry, chiefly younger brothers, who having at present, by the late decay of the church, and the yet
languishing state of commerce, no prospect of a livelihood
suitable to their birth, were ready to throw themselves into
any desperate enterprise. But in order to inspire life and
courage into all these malcontents, it was requisite that
some great nobleman should put himself at their head; and
no one appeared to Rodolphi, and to the Bishop of Ross,
who entered into all these intrigues, so proper, both on
account of his power and his popularity, as the duke of
Norfolk.

This nobleman, when released from confinement in the
Tower, had given his promise, that he would drop all intercourse with the queen of Scots; but finding that he had
lost, and as he feared beyond recovery, the confidence and
favour of Elizabeth, and being still, in some degree, restrained from his liberty, he was tempted, by impatience
and despair, to violate his word, and to open anew his correspondence with the captive princess. A promise of marriage was renewed between them; the duke engaged to
enter into all her interests: and as his remorses gradually

diminished in the . course of these . transactions, he was
pushed to give his consent to enterprises still more criminal:
Rodolphi's plan was, that the duke of Alva should, on some
other pretence, assemble a great, quantity of shipping in
the Low Countries; should transport 'a body of six thousand foot, and four thousand horse, into England ; should
land them at Harwich, where the duke of Norfolk was to
join them with all his friends; should thence march directly to London, and oblige the queen to submit to whatever terms the conspirators should please to impose on her.
Norfolk expressed his assent to this plan ; and three letters,
in consequence of it, were written in his name by Rodolphi,
one to Alva, another to the pope, and a third to the king
of Spain; but the duke, apprehensive of the danger, refused to sign them. He only sent to the Spanish ambassador a servant and a confidant, named Barker, as well to
notify his concurrence in the plan, as to vouch for the authenticity of these letters; and Rodolphi, having obtained
a letter of credence from the ambassador, proceeded on 'his
journey to Brussels and to Rome. . The duke of Alva and
the pope embraced the scheme with alacrity: Rodolphi
informed Norfolk of their intentions; and every thing
seemed to concur in forwarding the undertaking.

Norfolk, notwithstanding these criminal enterprises, had
never entirely forgotten his duty to his sovereign, his country, and his religion ; and though he had laid the plan both
of an invasion and insurrection, he still flattered himself,
that the innocence of his intentions would justify the violence of his measures, and that, as he aimed at nothing but
the liberty of the queen of Scots, and the obtaining of Elizabeth's consent to his 'marriage, he could not justly reproach himself as a rebel and a traitor. It is certain, however, that, considering the queen's vigour and spirit, the
scheme, if successful, must finally have ended in dethroning
her ; and her authority was here exposed to the utmost
danger.

The conspiracy hitherto had entirely escaped the vigilance of Elizabeth, and that of secretary Cecil, who now bore the title of Lord Burleigh. It was from another attempt of Norfolk's, that they first obtained a hint, which, being diligently traced, led at last to a full discovery. Mary had intended to send a sum of money to Lord Herries, and her partisans in Scotland; and Norfolk undertook to have it delivered to Bannister, a servant of his, at that time in the north, who was to find some expedient for conveying it to Lord Herries. He intrusted the money to a servant who was not in the secret, and told him that the bag contained a sum of money in silver, which he was to deliver to Bannister with a letter: but the servant conjecturing, from the weight and size of the bag, that it was full of gold, carried the letter to Burleigh; who immediately ordered Bannister, Barker, and Hickford, the duke's secretary, to be put under arrest, and to undergo a severe examination. Torture made them confess the whole truth; and as Hickford, though ordered to burn all papers, had carefully kept them concealed under the mats of the duke's chamber, and under the tiles of the house, full evidence now appeared against his master. Norfolk himself, who was entirely ignorant of the discoveries made by his servants, was brought before the council; and though exhorted to atone for his guilt, by a full confession, he persisted in denying every crime with which he was charged. The queen always declared, that if he had given her this proof of his sincere repentance, she would have pardoned all his former offences; but finding him obstinate, she committed him to the Tower, and ordered him to be brought to his trial. The Bishop of Ross had, on some suspicion, been committed to custody before the discovery of Norfolk's guilt; and every expedient was employed to make him reveal his share in the conspiracy. He at first insisted on his privilege; but he was told, that as his mistress was no longer a sovereign, he would not be regarded as an ambassador, and that, even if

that character were allowed, it did not warrant him in con-
spiring against the sovereign at whose court he resided. As'
he still refused interrogatories, he was informed of the con-
fession-made by Norfolk's servants, after which he no longer
scrupled to make a full discovery; and his evidence put
the guilt of that nobleman beyond all question. A jury of
twenty-five peers unanimously passed sentence upon him
(Jan. 13.) The trial was quite regular, even according to
the strict rules observed at present in those matters; except
that the witnesses gave not their evidence in court, and
were not confronted with the prisoner; a laudable practice
which was not at that time observed in trials for high
treason.

The queen still hesitated concerning Norfolk's execution,
whether that she was really moved by friendship and compassion towards a peer of that rank and merit, or that, af-
fecting the praise of clemency, she only put on the appearance of these sentiments. Twice she signed a warrant for
his execution, and twice revoked the fatal sentence; and
though her ministers and counsellors pushed her to rigour,
she still appeared irresolute and undetermined. After four
months' hesitation, a parliament was assembled, and the
commons addressing her, in strong terms, for the execution
of the duke (May 8); a sanction which, when added to
the greatness and certainty of his guilt, would, she thought,
justify, in the eyes of all mankind, her severity against that
nobleman. Norfolk died with calmness and constancy
(June 2); and though he cleared himself of any disloyal
intentions against the queen's authority, he acknowledged
the justice of the sentence by which he suffered. That we
may relate together affairs of a similar nature, we shall
mention, that the Earl of Northumberland, being delivered
up to the queen by the regent of Scotland, was also, a few
months after, brought to the scaffold for his rebellion.

The Queen of Scots was either the occasion or the cause
of all these disturbances; but as she was a Sovereign Prin-

cess, and might reasonably, from the harsh treatment which she had met with, think herself entitled to use any expedient for her relief, Elizabeth durst not, as yet, form any resolution of proceeding to extremities against her. She only sent Lord Delawar, Sir Ralph Sadler, Sir Thomas Bromley, and Dr. Wilson, to expostulate with her, and to demand satisfaction for all those parts of her conduct which, from the beginning of her life, had given displeasure to Elizabeth : her assuming the arms of England, refusing to ratify the treaty of Edinburgh, intending to marry Norfolk without the Queen's consent, concurring in the northern rebellion, practising with Rodolphi to engage the King of Spain in an invasion of England, procuring the Pope's bull of excommunication, and allowing her friends abroad to give her the title of Queen of England. Mary justified herself from the several articles of the charge, either by denying the facts imputed to her, or by throwing the blame on others. But the Queen was little satisfied with her apology, and the parliament was so enraged against her, that the commons made a direct application for her immediate trial and execution. They employed some topics derived from practice and reason, and the laws of nations; but the chief stress was laid on passages and examples from the Old Testament, which, if considered as a general rule of conduct (an intention which it is unreasonable to suppose), would lead to consequences destructive of all principles of humanity and morality. Matters were here carried farther than Elizabeth intended; and that Princess, satisfied with shewing Mary the disposition of the nation, sent to the house her express commands not to deal any farther at present in the affair of the Scottish Queen. Nothing could be a stronger proof that the Puritanical interest prevailed in the house, than the intemperate use of authorities derived from Scripture, especially from the Old Testament; and the Queen was so little a lover of that sect, that she was not likely to make any concession merely in deference to their solicitation. She shewed, this session, her disapprobation of their schemes in another remarkable instance. The commons had passed two bills for regulating ecclesiastical ceremonies; but she sent them a like imperious message with her former ones; and by the terror of her prerogative, she stopped all farther proceedings in those matters.

But though Elizabeth would not carry matters to such extremities against Mary, as were recommended by the parliament, she was alarmed at the great interest and the restless spirit of that Princess, as well as her close connections with Spain; and she thought it necessary both to increase the rigour and strictness of her confinement, and to follow maxims different from those which she had hitherto pursued in her management of Scotland. That kingdom remained still in a state of anarchy. The Castle of Edinburgh, commanded by Kirkaldy of Grange, had declared for Mary; and the Lords of that party, encouraged by his countenance, had taken possession of the capital, and carried on a vigorous war against the Regent. By a sudden and unexpected inroad, they seized that nobleman at Stirling; but finding that his friends, sallying from the Castle, were likely to rescue him, they instantly put him to death. The Earl of Marre was chosen Regent in his room; and found the same difficulties in the government of that divided country. He was therefore glad to accept of the mediation offered by the French and English Ambassadors; and to conclude on equal terms a truce with the Queen's party. He was a man of a free and generous spirit, and scorned to submit to any dependance on England; and for this reason, Elizabeth, who had then formed intimate connections with France, yielded with less reluctance to the solicitations of that court, still maintained the appearance of neutrality between the parties, and allowed matters to remain on a balance in Scotland. But affairs soon after took a new turn: Marre died of melancholy, with which the distracted state of the country affected him : Morton was chosen Regent ; and as this nobleman had secretly taken all his measures with Elizabeth, who no longer relied on the friendship of the French court, she resolved to exert herself more effectually for the support of the party which she had always favoured. She sent Sir Henry Killegrew ambassador to Scotland, who found Mary's partisans so discouraged by the discovery and punishment of Norfolk's conspiracy, that they were glad to submit to the King's authority, and accept of an indemnity from all past offences. The Duke of Chatelrault and the Earl of Huntley, with the most considerable of Mary's friends, laid down their arms on these conditions. The garrison alone of the Castle of Edinburgh continued refractory. Kirkaldy's fortunes were desperate ; and he flattered himself with the hopes of receiving assistance from the kings of France and Spain, who encouraged his obstinacy, in the view of being able, from that quarter, to give disturbance to England. Elizabeth was alarmed with the danger ; she no more apprehended making an entire breach with the Queen of Scots, who, she found, would not any longer be amused by her artifices ; she had an implicit reliance on Morton ; and she saw that by the submission of all the considerable nobility, the pacification of Scotland would be an easy, as well as a most important, undertaking. – She ordered, therefore, Sir William Drury, governor of Berwick, to march with some troops and artillery to Edinburgh, and to besiege the castle. The garrison surrendered at discretion : Kirkaldy was delivered into the hands of his countrymen, by whom he was tried, condemned, and executed ; Secretary Lidington, who had taken part with him, died soon after a voluntary death, as is supposed ; and Scotland, submitting entirely to the Regent, gave not, during a long time, any farther inquietude to Elizabeth.

We shall not enter into a long discussion concerning the authenticity of these letters. We shall only remark in general, that the chief objections against them are, that they are supposed to have passed through the Earl of Morton's hands, the least scrupulous of all Mary's enemies; and that they are to the last degree indecent, and even somewhat inelegant, such as it is not likely she would write. But to these presumptions we may oppose the following considerations.

1. Though it be not difficult to counterfeit a subscription, it is very difficult, and almost impossible, to counterfeit several pages, so as to resemble exactly the hand-writing of any person. These letters were examined and compared with Mary's hand-writing, by the English privy-council, and by a great many of the nobility, among whom were several partisans of that princess. They might have been examined by the Bishop of Ross, ·Herries, and others of Mary's commissioners. The Regent must have expected that they would be very critically examined by them; and had they not been able to stand that test, he was only preparing a scene of confusion to himself. Bishop Lesley expressly declines the comparing of the hands, which he calls no legal proof. Goodall, vol. 2. p. 389.

2. The letters are very long, much longer than they needed to have been, in order to serve the purposes of Mary's enemies; a circumstance which increased the difficulty, and exposed any forgery more to the risk of a detection.

3. They are not so gross and palpable as forgeries commonly are, for they still left a pretext for Mary's friends to assert, that their meaning was strained to make them appear criminal. See Goodall, vol. 2. p. 361.

4. There is a long contract of marriage, said to be written by the Earl of Huntley, and signed by the Queen, before Bothwell's acquittal. Would Morton, without any necessity, have thus doubled the difficulties of the forgery and the danger of detection?

5. The letters are indiscreet; but such was apparently Mary's conduct at that time: they are inelegant; but they have a careless, natural air, like letters hastily written between familiar friends.

6. They contain such a variety of particular circumstances as nobody could have thought of inventing, especially as they must necessarily have afforded her many means of detection.

7. We have not the originals of the letters, which were in French: we have only a Scotch and Latin translation from the original, and a French translation professedly done from the Latin. Now it is remarkable the Scotch translation is full of Gallicisms, and is clearly a translation from the French original; such as *make fault, faire des fautes ; make it seem that I believe, faire semblant de la croire ; make brek, faire breche; this is my first journey, c'est ma premiere journée ; have you not desire to laugh, n'avez vous pas envie de rire ?* the place will hold unto the death, la place *tiendra jusqu' à la mort ; he may not come forth of the house this long time, il ne peu pas sortir du logis de long tems ; to make me advertisement, fair m'avertir ; put order to it, mettre ordre a cela ; discharge your heart, decharger votre cœur ; make gud watch, faites bonne garde,* &c.

8. There is a conversation which she mentions between herself and the King one evening: but Murray produced before the English commissioners the testimony of one Crawford, a gentleman of the Earl of Lenox, who swore that the King, on her departure from him, gave him an account of the same conversation.

9. There seems very little reason why Murray and his associates

should run the risk of such a dangerous forgery, which must have rendered them infamous, if detected ; since their cause, from Mary's known conduct, even without these letters, was sufficiently good and justifiable.

10. Murray exposed these letters to the examination of persons qualified to judge of them ; the Scotch council, the Scotch parliament, Queen Elizabeth and her council, who were possessed of a great number of Mary's genuine letters.

11. He gave Mary herself an opportunity of refuting and exposing him, if she had chosen to lay hold of it.

12. The letters tally so well with all the other parts of her conduct, during that transaction, that these proofs throw the strongest light on each other.

13. The Duke of Norfolk, who had examined these papers, and who favoured so much the Queen of Scots that he intended to marry her, and in the end lost his life in her cause, yet believed them authentic, and was fully convinced of her guilt. This appears not only from his letters above-mentioned to Queen Elizabeth and her ministers, but by his secret acknowledgment to Bannister, his most trusty confidant. See State Trials, vol. 1. p. 81. In the conferences between the Duke, Secretary Lidington, and the Bishop of Ross, all of them zealous partisans of that Princess, the same thing is always taken for granted. Ibid. p. 74, 75. See farther MS. in the Advocates' Library, A. 3. 28. p. 314, from Cott. Lib. Callig. c. 9. Indeed the Duke's full persuasion of Mary's guilt, without the least doubt or hesitation, could not have had place, if he had found Lidington or the Bishop of Ross of a different opinion, or if they had ever told him that these letters were forged. It is to be remarked, that Lidington, being one of the accomplices, knew the whole bottom of the conspiracy against King Henry, and was, besides, a man of such penetration, that nothing could escape him in such interesting events.

14. I need not repeat the presumption drawn from Mary's refusal to answer. The only excuse for her silence is, that she suspected Elizabeth to be a partial judge : it was not indeed the interest of that Princess to acquit and justify her rival and competitor ; and we accordingly find that Lidington, from the secret information of the Duke of Norfolk, informed Mary by the Bishop of Ross, that the Queen of England never meant to come to a decision ; but only to get into her hands the proofs of Mary's guilt, in order to blast her character. See State Trials, vol. 1. p. 77. But this was a better reason for declining the conference altogether, than for breaking it off on frivolous pretences, the very moment the chief accusation was unexpectedly opened against her. Though she could not expect Elizabeth's final decision in her favour, it was of importance to give a satisfactory answer, if she had any, to the accusation of the Scotch commissioners. That answer could have been dispersed for the satisfaction of the public, of foreign nations, and of posterity. And surely, after the accusation and proofs were in Queen Elizabeth's hands, it could do no harm to give in the answers. Mary's information, that the Queen never intended to come to a decision, could be no obstacle to her justification.

15. The very disappearance of these letters is a presumption of their authenticity. That event can be accounted for no way but

from the care of King James's friends, who were desirous to destroy every proof of his mother's crimes. The disappearance of Morton's narrative, and of Crawford's evidence, from the Cotton Library, Calig. c. 1, must have proceeded from the like cause. See MS. in the Advocates' Library, A. 3. 29. p. 88.

I find an objection made to the authenticity of the letters, drawn from the vote of the Scotch privy-council, which affirms the letters to be written and subscribed by Queen Mary's own hand; whereas the copies given in to the parliament a few days after, were only written, not subscribed. See Goodall, vol. 2. p. 64. 67. But it is not considered that this circumstance is of no manner of force; there were certainly letters, true or false, laid before the council; and whether the letters were true or false, this mistake proceeds equally from the inaccuracy or blunder of the clerk. The mistake may be accounted for; the letters were only written by her; the second con- tract with Bothwell was only subscribed. A proper accurate distinc- tion was not made; and they are all said to be written and subscribed. A late writer, Mr. Goodall, has endeavoured to prove that these let- ters clash with chronology, and that the Queen was not in the places mentioned in the letters on the days there assigned. To confirm this, he produces charters and other deeds signed by the Queen, where the date and place do not agree with the letters. But it is well known that the date of charters, and such-like grants, is no proof of the real day on which they were signed by the sovereign. Papers of that kind commonly passed through different offices: the date is affixed by the first office, and may precede very long the day of the signature.

The account given by Morton of the manner in which the pa- pers came into his hands, is very natural. When he gave it to the English commissioners, he had reason to think it would be canvassed with all the severity of able adversaries, interested in the highest degree to refute it. It is probable that he could have con- firmed it by many circumstances and testimonies, since they de- clined the contest.

The sonnets are inelegant; insomuch that both Brantome and Ronsard, who knew Queen Mary's style, were assured, when they saw them, that they could not be of her composition. Jebb. vol. 2. p. 478. But no person is equal in his productions, especially one whose style is so little formed as Mary's must be supposed to be. Not to mention that such dangerous and criminal enterprises leave little tranquillity of mind for elegant poetical compositions.

In a word, Queen Mary might easily have conducted the whole conspiracy against her husband, without opening her mind to any one person except Bothwell, and without writing a scrap of paper about it; but it was very difficult to have it conducted so that her conduct should not betray her to men of discernment. In the pre- sent case her conduct was so gross as to betray her to every body; and fortune threw into her enemies' hands papers by which they could convict her. The same infatuation and imprudence, which happily is the usual attendant of great crimes, will account for both. It is proper to observe, that there is not one circumstance of the fore- going narrative, contained in the history, that is taken from Knox, Buchanan, or even Thuanus, or indeed from any suspected authority.

A LETTER

FROM MARY QUEEN OF SCOTS TO ELIZABETH QUEEN OF ENGLAND,
FROM THE HOUSE OF LORD SHREWSBURY, AT SHEFFIELD,
WHERE SHE HAD LONG BEEN A PRISONER.

I. According to what I have promised you and you have desired, I declare to you now, that with regret that such things have
been brought into question, but very sincerely and without any passion, for which I appeal to my God as witness, that the Countess of
Shrewsbury told me what follows concerning you, pretty nearly in
these terms: to the most part of which I protest to have replied,
reprehending the said lady for believing or talking so freely of you;
as matter, that I did not believe, and do not believe at present,
knowing the nature of the Countess, and with what spirit she was
then egged on against you.

II. First, that one, to whom she said you had made a promise
of marriage before a lady of your bed-chamber, had lain down in-
finite times with you, with all the freedom and familiarity that can
be used betwixt a husband and wife; but that undoubtedly you
was not as all other women are, and for this reason it was folly in all
those who favoured your marriage with Monsieur the Duke of Anjou,
because it could never be consummated; and that you would not
ever give up the liberty of bespeaking love, and of having your
pleasure continually with new lovers; regretting this, said she, that
you would not be content with Master Haton, and one other of this
realm; but that, for the honour of the country, she was most
grieved, that you not only had pawned your honour with a stranger
of the name of Simier, going to find him by night in the chamber of
a lady, whom the said Countess blamed greatly for this business,
where you kissed him, and used divers dishonest familiarities with
him, but also revealed the secrets of the realm to him, betraying to
him your own counsellors.

III. That you behaved with the same dissoluteness towards the
Duke his master, who had been to find you one night at the door of
your bed-chamber, where you met him with only your shift and
bed-gown on; and that afterwards you suffered him to enter, and
that he stayed with you nearly three hours.

IV. As to the said Haton, that you ran him down by violence,
making the love which you bore him appear so public, that he himself was constrained to retire from you; and that you gave Kiligreu

a box on the ear, because he had not brought back the said Haton, whom you had sent him to recall, and who had departed from you in wrath, for some reproaches which you had uttered to him, on account of certain buttons of gold which he had upon his clothes.

V. That she had laboured to make a match between the said Haton and the late Countess of Lenox her daughter; but, for fear of you, durst not enterprize it; that even the Earl of Oxford durst not re-accord with his wife, for fear of losing the favour which he hoped to receive by making love to you.

VI. That you was profuse to all such persons, and those who meddled with such practices; as to one Gorge, of your bed-chamber, to whom you had given three hundred pounds in rents, because he had brought you the news of Haton's return; that to all others you was very ungrateful and niggardly; and that there were but three or four persons in the realm to whom you had ever been bountiful.

VII. Counselling me, while she laughed extremely, to enter my son in the lists for making love to you; as a matter that would greatly serve me, and would dislodge Monsieur the Duke from his quarters, who would prove very prejudicial to me if he continued there: and on my replying that this would be taken for an absolute mockery, she answered me, that you was as vain, and had as good an opinion of your beauty, as if you were some goddess of the sky; that she would take it upon her life, she could easily make you believe it, and you would receive my son in this light.

VIII. That you took so great a pleasure in flatteries beyond all reason, that it had been said to 'you expressly, that there was no venturing at times to look full upon you, because your face shone like the sun; that she, and other ladies of the court, were constrained to use this language; and that, in her last journey to you, she and the late Countess of Lenox, while she was speaking to you, durst not look the one towards the other, for fear of bursting out into a laugh, at the flams which she was putting upon you; praying me at her return to rebuke her daughter, whom she could not ever persuade to do the same; and, as to her daughter Talbot, she was sure she could not ever refrain from laughing in your face.

IX. The said lady, Talbot, when she went to perform the reverence, and to take the oath to you, as one of your servants, immediately on her return relating the act to me [Mary], as an act done in mockery, begged me to accept the like, but more felt and full towards me, which I refused a long time; but at last, constrained by her tears, I suffered her to do it; she saying, that she would not, for any thing in the world, be in your service, near your person, because she should be in fear, that when you was in wrath, you would-do to her as you did to her cousin Skedmur, one of whose fingers you broke, and made those of the court believe that it was broken by a chandelier falling down from above; and that you gave another lady, as she was waiting upon you at table, a great blow with a knife upon the hand.

X. And, in a word, because of these last points, and common petty reports, you may believe that you was acted and represented by my women, as in a comedy among themselves; and, finding it out, I swear to you, that I forbad my women from meddling in such work any more.

XI. Further, the said Countess at another time apprized me, that you would fain have appointed Rolson to make love to me, and try to dishonour me, either in fact, or by evil report; for which he had instructions from your own mouth: that Ruxby came here about eight years ago, to make an attempt upon my life: having talked with you yourself, who had told him that it was the business to which Walsingham would recommend and direct him.

XII. When the said Countess prosecuted the marrriage of her son Charles with one of the nieces of my Lord Paget, and when you, on the other hand, wanted to have her, by pure and absolute authority, for one of the Knoles, because he was your relation, she exclaimed against you, and said that it was an actual tyranny, in wanting to carry off at your fancy all the heiresses in the land; and that you had used the said Paget with indignity, by abusive words; but that at last the nobles of this realm would not suffer this from you, if you addressed yourself to some other ladies, whom she knew well.

XIII. About four or five years ago, when you was sick, and I also at the same time, she says to me, that your sickness proceeded from the closing up of an ulcer, which you had in one leg; and that without doubt, as you was coming to lose your menses, you would die soon; pleasing herself upon it, in a vain imagination which she has had a long time, from the prophecies of one called John Lenton, and of an old book, that foretold your death by violence, and the succeeding of another queen, whom she interpreted to be me ; regretting only, that by the said book it was foretold, that the queen who must succeed you should reign only three years, and should die like you by violence, which was represented even in painting, upon the said book, of which there was a concluding leaf, containing something which she never chose to tell me. She knows herself, that I [Mary] always took this for pure folly ; but she did lay her account well, to be the principal lady with me, and also that my son should marry my niece Arbela.

XIV. At the close, I swear again all at once upon my faith and honour, that what is above is very true ; and that such of it as concerns your honour, has never fallen from me with a design to give you·pain by revealing it ; and that it shall never be known from me, who consider it as very false.   If I can have that happiness to speak with you, I will tell you more particularly the names, times, places, and other circumstances to make you understand the truth, both of these things, and of others, which I reserve till I shall be wholly assured of your friendship, which as I desire more than ever so, if I can obtain it this time, you shall not have a relation, friend, or even subject, more faithful and affectionate than I shall be to you.

For God's rest assured of her, who is willing and able to obey you.

From my bed, forcing my arms and·pains to serve you,

MARY·REGINA.

Sheffield, April, 1584.

APPENDIX,

CONTAINING SOME OF

THE PUBLIC DOCUMENTS

RELATING TO

THE LETTERS OF MARY.

◆

THE CURIOUS READER MAY REFER TO THE COTTON LIBRARY,
STATE PAPER OFFICE, MURDIN, SIR RALPH SADLER, AND
GOODALL, FOR THE WHOLE OF THE DOCUMENTS
CONNECTED WITH THE COMMISSION.

The Commissioners of the Queen of England.

Duke of Norfolk.
Earl of Sussex.
Sir Ralph Sadler, Knt.
At Hampton-Court the whole Council were added to the party.—H. C.

The Names of the Commissioners for the Queen of Scots.

The Bishoppe of Ross.
The Lord Boyde.
The Lord Levingston.
The Lord Herys.
The Abbot of Kylwinning.
Sir John Gordon of Lochinvar, Knt.
Sir James Cockburn of Skirling, Knt.—Examinator.

The Names of the Commissioners on the part of the Prince.

The Earle of Murray.
The Earle of Morton.
The Bishoppe of Orknay.
The Lord Lyndesay.
The Abbot of Dumfermeline.

The Names of the Assistants.

The Laird of Lethington.
James Macgill.
Henry Balnavys.
The Laird of Lochlevin.
Mr. George Boqwhannan.
Mr. David Lyndesay.

APPENDIX.— No. I.

A memorial for the order in proceeding of the Duke of Norfolk, the Erle of Sussex, and Sir Ralph Sadler, the Queen's Majestie's commissioners, appointed and authorised by her Majestie's commission to meet at the city of York, with such of the nobility of Scotland, as shall be authorised from the Queen of Scots on the one part, and with such of others of the nobility of the same realme, as shall be appointed for, and in the name of the Prince the said Quene's son, entitled also King of Scots, on the other.

I. The said commissioners shall notify to the Queen of Scots, or to her commissioners, the tenor of their commission, and shall require the sight of the said Queen's commission, and thereupon offer themselves ready to do all good offices for the honor and wealle of the said Quene, according to their commission, and as they are specially charged by the Quene's Majestie in that behalfe.

II. They shall also signify to the Erle of Murray, or to such as shall come in the name of the Prince, the cause of their coming, and require the sight of their commission, and so shall use expedition for their meeting in some convenient place; and shall first devise, by some special order, that neither of the two parties, nor any of their traines, shall move any trouble against other by speche, countenance, or act, directly or indirectly, during the time of this treaty. For which purpose it may be well done to cause a certificate to be made to them of the numbers and special names of the persons of either part, so as by order they may be favourably used in the said city, and that no other disorderly persons of Scotland, or other strangers, under colour of this assembly, shall have resort to the said city.

III. They shall fyrst heare the requests or complaints of the Quene of Scots, commissioners apart by themselves, and require,

them to have them put in writing briefly, and therewith they shall
also apart charge the other party as earnestly, as the cause shall require, and shall demand their answers, not only in speche, but also
in writing.

IV. They shall declare to both the parties, how her Majesty hath
expressly charged them, in conference with them about this charge,
that they should in all their actions regard their duties to Almighty
God, and in no wise to furder any thing, otherwise than their consciences should bear witness in the presence of God, to be honest,
just, reasonable and true: For so hir Majesty expresly said to them
with great earnestness, that her intention in this action was grounded upon a sound conscience in the sight of God; and as she had
conceived the same in the fear of God, so she committed the same
charge to them, hoping that they would discharge the trust reposed
in them, and wished the like to be found in the parties with whom
they should treat at this tyme; and that both they hir commissioners,
and all the rest, wold, before they entred into this action, take a corporal oath to advance and furder nothing, but that which in their
consciences they shall think to be true, honest, reasonable and just.
And to that end the commissioners may move both parties, as they
shall find their dispositions, to receive a solemn oath, and proceed
accordingly upon the foundation of the fear of God, which is the
beginning of all wisdom.

V. As soon as tyme shall serve convenient to treat with both parties together, how to come to some reasonable end, these, and such
like things hereafter following, are to be well considered:

1. If the Erle of Murray and his partie shall alledge, that although
they can justly convince the Quene of the great crimes wherewith
she hath been burdened, yet they find it not expedient so to do,
upon the doubt they have that the Quene's Majestie will, notwithstanding any crime proved upon her, restore her to her kingdom
and rule, whereupon they should never be free from her indignation; and so they will stay and not proceed, without they may know
her Majestie's purpose, in case the said Quene should be proved
guilty of her husband's murder.

It may be answered by the Quene's Majestie's commissioners,
That indeed her Majestie's desire had been alwise from the beginning, that the said Quene might be found free, specially from the
cryme of her husband's murder. Nevertheless, if her Majestie shall
find it to be plainly and manifestly proved, (whereof she would be
very sorry) that the said Quene of Scotts was the deviser and procurer of that murder, or otherwise was guilty thereof, surely her
Majestie would think her unworthy of a kingdom, and wold not
stayne her own conscience in mayntainance of such a detestable

'wickedness, by restoring her to a kingdom. But if it shall not be proved probably and apparently, that she was guilty of her husband's death; yet, because the suspicions and conjectures to be produced against her, may seem nearly to touch her in misgovernment of herself, and that sundry other her apparent actions, as well in the marriage of Bothwell, and maintenance of him in his notorious tyranny, as in other things, may seme to deminish and abase her princely estate and reputation of a 'Quene and governor of a realme; the Quene's Majestie, meaning to have some good end of all these troubles, as thairby peace and tranquillity might be recovered and continue in that realme, and that reasonable consideration might be had of the princely state, whereunto she was born, from the which she never departed, but, for fear of her life, wold have it considered by them, being subjects borne of that realme, in what sort and in what manner she might be restored to her crown, without danger of her relapse into the like defaults, and without any like civil dissentions to follow as of late hath happened.

And the said commissioners having thus answered, and declared her Majestie's plain manner and intention, shall say, they must needs leave it to the choyce of them, being principal parties hereto, what they will do therin. Whereupon if they shall be content, and procede to charge her as guilty of her husband's death, and shall produce matter manifestly probable to convince her thereof, then the commissioners shall spedily advertise her Majestie.

But if they shall, notwithstanding the commissioners foresaid answer, either forbeare to charge her, or shall shew no sufficient matter to convince her of the murder of her husband, then, according to the answer aforemaid, it must be required of them to consider in what sort the said Quene may be restored to her crown, according to her estate, without danger of a relapse to fall into misgovernment, or without the danger of her subjects to fall into her displeasure without their just desert. And though there may be many ways to be thought of not unmete, yet before any devise shall be touched by her Majestie's commissioners, they of the other party shall first be induced to propound their devises, which, because they are likely to be for the advantage and surety of themselves, and prejudicial and very dishonourable for the Quene of Scotts, the Quene's Majestie's commissioners shall, by conference with them, labour to induce them to some indifferent means, and do their uttermost that both the parties may, upon conferences together, accord to have her restored to her kingdom, with such conditions as thereby she may be restrained from misgovernment and disorder of hir realme. And herein good foresight wold be had, that the same may come and procede from the other parties, either of the one side or the other,

and not from her Majestie's commissioners, who may well say, that
it properly belongeth to themselves, to propound and devise the
manner how their own country shall be governed. Whereupon the
Quene's Majestie's commissioners shall offer all indeferency to furder
such means as shall seme reasonable for both parties. And because
her Majestie's commissioners may be also instructed what may seme
to her Majestie reasonable in this case, her Majestie would have
them understand certen things hereafter following, which they shall
take rather for instruction, to judge thereby the reasonableness of
the things propounded, either by the Scottish Quene's commissioners, or by the others, than directly to propound any of them as
things devised or desired by her Majestie. And as things shall be
propounded on the one party, tending for their advantage, so the
same may be notifyed to the other, and by conference so ordered, as
the articles and devises that shall tend to abridge the Quene's authority, may plainly appear to come of themselves, and not of her Majestie's commissioners.

First, It semeth very mete, that this treaty shuld be tripartite;
that is, betwixt the Quene's Majestie of England on the one party,
as principall author and mediator of the same, and the Quene of
Scotts on the second, and the Prince hir son on the third. And that
the whole accord may be also speedily confirmed by act of parliament in Scotland; whereby both the Quene of Scotts and her subjects may be in justice bound to observe the same; and the Quene
of England, by her great seale of England, to mayntene the same.
And that also from the end of the treaty, until some convenient time
to follow the end of the same parliament, there might remaine three
or four good hostages of either part in England, for the more orderly
holding of the parliament, and better observation of the treaty. And
hereunto may well be added to be thought of, that the said parliament might be kept and ended before the Queen of Scotts return to
her contrey.

I. The first article in this accord wold be in this manner or such
like: That all things, (saving only the murder of the King) which
have been attempted by the Quene, or any of her party against
them, which took the part of her son the Prince as their King: And
all things on the said Prince's part, and them which avowed their
actions in his name as King, from the death of the Quene's husband,
shuld be committed, after this treaty ended, to a perpetual oblivion;
and that no action, damage, offence, calumniations or reproach,
shuld, at any time to come, be used or extended any manner of wise,
be one against the other, upon some great paines.

II. It is most necessary to be provided, that by the said Quene
of Scotts own princely motion, upon good perswasion to be made

to her in that behalfe, it may be accorded, That the realme of Scotland may be governed under her as Quene of the realme, by a grand councell of a convenient number, to be now chosen and stablished at the tyme of this treaty, of the noble and wise men of birth of that realme, and the same to be alwise renewed by the more part, or two third parts of the said councell, when any of the persons of the said councell shall depart, or become impotent to serve. For otherwise the quiet of the Quene herself, and the realme also, by private government, shall be easily broken, and the whole fruit of this treaty, and the Quene's Majestie's labours, utterly frustrate. In which matter also is to be remembred, in what sort the principall officers of the realme shall be appointed, being at the Quene's disposition, as ambassadors and messengers to and from forrayn Princes, the Chancellor, the Archbishops, Bishops, the Lord Justice, the Controller, the Treasurer, the Admiral, the Chamberlain, the President and Lords of Session, the Captains of castles, the Sheriffs, the Provosts of burghs, the Wardens of the marches, and all officers of finances, and such like, as may be for the good observation of this treaty.

III. It is to be remembred, that the Quene, in respect of her undescrete marriage with Bothwell, may accord not to marry, nor contract marriage with any person, without the assent of her thré estates, or the more part thereof, upon payne that the person with whom she shall contract, and all others counselling or furdering the same, shall be, *ipso facto*, adjudged as traitors, and shall suffer death and forfit, as in cases of treason.

IV. That all good means be devised and accorded how to procede severely against the said Bothwell, and all other subjects or servants to the crown of Scotland, for the murder of the said King, or for maintainance and comfort of the said murderers, and their lands confiscated to the crown of Scotland, with a clause, never to be granted away from the crown, without assent of parliament.

V. That all laws and orders accorded upon by parliament, as well before the Quene's imprisonment as since, for the helpe and sustentation of the Ministers of the Church, and for the advancement of true religion, and abrogating of idolatry and superstition, may remayne in full force, and continew without repealing of the same, otherwise than by a sufficient parliament.

VI. In particular also, it is meet to be remembred, that no stranger born be entertained in that realme in the room of a captain or of a soldier: nor that any stranger born have any office spiritual or temporal within the realme; nor that any pension be granted to any stranger out of any office spiritual or temporal; nor that any person bear any office within that realme, which openly by any act hereafter shall hereafter avow that the Bishop of Rome ought to take any other preheminence within that realme, than such as the King or Quene of that realme and their successors, with the consent of the thré estates in parliament, shall allow.

VII. It is also very necessary to provide for the safety of the life of the young Prince, considering all such as shall live in Scotland having been indeed privy to the murder of his father, though not thereof convinced, shall and may be suspected, that they will desire the death of the Prince, fearing his avenge when he shall come to age. And in this behalfe it is to be well considered, in what place, and with what person he shall remayne, and with what allowance of the revenue of the crowne he shall be maintained ; and if it may be indirectly procured to come of the Quene of Scotts herself, it seemeth good and safe for all parties, that the Prince might be brought and nourished in England, in the charge and custody of persons of the birth of Scotland.

VIII. It were also meet, that the titles and challenges of the crown heretofore made, as well by one party as another, were made perfectly clear and certainly established, thereby to take away factions amongst the subjects.

IX. It may be reasonably required of the Erle of Murray and others, that, considering the many difficulties that may arise upon the understanding of this treaty, and specially in choice of the great officers of the realme, by reason of many competitors amongst the nobility, that it may be at the request of the whole nobility of Scotland, and with the good consent of the Quene of Scotts accorded, that the Quene's Majesty of England may have power to be as umpire and principal arbiter, to determine upon all contraversies arysing upon this treaty, and specially in choice of any such officer, so as her Majestie make no other interpretation, nor name none to any office, but such as shall be adjudged or named by the Quene herself, or by one-third part of the grand counsell of the realme for the tyme being: and that whosoever shall intromit himself to do any thing therein contrary, and without the judgment of the Quene's Majestie of England, as above is limited, shall be judged as a perturbator of the common tranquilitie of that realme, and shall be incapable of any manner of office for ever, or otherwise punished with some sharp paine ; and that it shall be leefull for any of the nobility or subjects of Scotland, being grieved or injured with any thing committed against this treaty, to resort to the Quene's Majestie of England, to make reasonable complaint, without any impechment of the Quene of Scotts, or any other ; and that for so doing they shall incur no forfeiture of life, lands, or goods, nor be any wise damaged in their body.

X. It is also necessary, for the more assurance of the observation of this treaty in the behalf of the subjects of Scotland, to be accorded, that if the Quene of Scotts shall willingly break, or permit to be broken, any part of this treaty concerning the surety of any of hir subjects, which have, since the death of hir husband, and before the present treaty, holden part against her, and that such her breaking, or permission of the breaking, be fyrst notifyed to the Quene of Scotts, and adjudged by the Quene of England against the Quene of Scotts, having thereto the assent of the third part of the grand councell aforementioned, or of six Lords of parliament of Scotland, being not parties against the said Quene at the time of this treaty, or their heyres succeeding them in their estates, being above the age of twenty-one. In those cases, without such reformation made by the Quene of Scotts, as to the said Quene of England, and the said third part of the said councell, or the said number of six Lords of Scotland aforesaid, shall seem meet, and be assigned and notified to the said Quene.

It shall be leefull, immediately upon publique knowledge gyven by the Quene of England, by open proclamation in the towns of Berwick and Carlisle, conteyning the particular brech of the treaty, and the manifest refusal of the reformation, for the Prince of Scotland, her son, or any of the nobility of Scotland for him, whilst he shall be under the age of fourteen, (if he, the Prince, be then living) ; and if he shall be dead, then for the next heyre to that crown, to enter into the real possession of the said crown and kingdom, and every part thereof, in like manner as the said Quene were departed from this life ; and the said Quene shall, by virtue of this treaty, forbear to hold the said state or title, as Quene of that realme, and shall not enjoy any thing of the said realme, otherwise than such provision of the yerely revenue of the said crown, as heretofore hath been allowed at any time to any wife of a King of Scotts for a dowry, if she so will accept and obey the foresaid judgment of the Quene of England, being made with the assent of the said third part of the said counsell, or of the said six Lords of Scotland, or their heyres being of the age of twenty-one. And whosoever shall attempt any thing contrary to the said Prince, or the next heyre to the crown, fayling the Prince, after his or their entry or clayme of the said crown, shall be ipso facto taken and used to all intents, as a traytor adjudged and condemned.

CERTEN OTHER THINGS NECESSARY TO BE REMEMBRED IN THIS
TREATY, FOR THE BEHALFE OF THE QUENE'S MAJESTIE AND
HER REALME.

Inprimis, that the treaty made at Edinburgh in July, Anno Dom.
1560, may be ratifyed and confirmed. In the treating whereof, if
objection be made, that there are certain clauses in the said treaty,
as namely in the fifth article, which do bring great prejudice to the
Quene of Scotts, in that it is accorded, that she shuld, from the
time of that treaty, forbear to use the stile, title, or armories of
England, whereby it may be indirectly gathered, that she shall be
excluded, not only during the life of the Quene's Majestie, and of
the lifes of the heyres of her Majestie's body, (which indeed was
expressely ment on both parts at the time of the treaty) but also
after the determination of the lifes of the Quene's Majestie (which
God long preserve), and also of the heyres of her body, of which
cause at the time of the treaty no mention was made; therefore now
at this treaty, after the said confirmation to be made of the said
treaty made at Edenburgh, there may be a proviso thereto now of
new devised, that no part of the said treaty made at Edenburgh
shall bind the said Quene of Scotts, or her children, after the determination of the life of the Quene's Majestie (which God long
preserve), and the heyres of her body.

II. It wold be also required, if it may be reasonably obteyned,
that a league shuld be made at this tyme betwixt the Quenes of England and Scotland for themselves, their realmes and subjects; that
either of the realmes shuld ayd the other, in case that any other
prince should fyrst invade them, or any parcel of them, without
notorious cause gyven by open wars to the invador; wherein if any
difficulty be made, because of the old league of France and Scotland, first, there may be much said, and cannot be denied, of the
commissioners of Scotland, to prove that Scotland hath these many
hundred years taken more harm than good by that treaty.

And secondly, Tho' the treaty with France shall be thought percase not meet to be utterly dissolved, yet in this particular sort to
contract, as is expressed in this article, may be said, is not against
the true intent of the league of France; for by that treaty the Kings
of Scotland are bound to ayde France, if England shuld move war
against France, but not if France shall fyrst move war against
England.

III. As it is well covenanted by ancient leagues betwixt England

and Scotland, that neither of them shuld receave or ayde any rebell as fugitive of the other; so the like accord would be made at this tyme for Ireland and Scotland.

IV. It wold be also accorded, that if the Quene of Scotts, during her life, shall ayde, or willingly permit any of hers to ayde any prince or potentate, to invade, by hostility, the realmes of England or Ireland, or any isles, or members of any of the said kingdoms, that thereupon immediately the said Quene shall forfeit and loose all manner of title or challenge that she hath, or any wise can pretend, to be inheritable to the crown of England or Ireland.

V. It were necessary that the contraversy yerely arising, by occasion of certen grounds upon the frontiers in the east marches, commonly called the threap-land, or debatable, were determined by judgment, that such of that which is to be proved not litigious, may be so established in the quiet possession of them that have right; and the rest that is litigious and doubtful, to be equally divided by metts and bounds, as the debatable was in the west borders in the time of King Edward the VIth.

VI. If the Quene of Scotts shall send any message or letter to the commissioners, they shall hear it; and if the same shall require any answer, they shall gyve or write such answer as to their discretions shall seem meet, being not repugnant to these instructions, and of their doings shall advertise her Majestie.

A LETTER FROM THE DUKE OF NORFOLK TO SIR WILLIAM CECILL, FROM YORK, THE 15TH OF OCTOBER, 1568.

Paper-Office.—An original in the Duke's hand.

We have lytle of news to wrytte unto you, but remayne expectyng letters from her Majestie, tyll the recepte wheroff we knowe not wyche waye to prosede. Thys cawse ys the huirtfullyst and dangeroust that ever I lette in. Yf you sawe and harde the constante affyrmyng of bothe sydis, not withowte great stowtnes, you wolde wonder. 1 fynd by sume speches cast owte by thys Quenis com. myssioners, that yf in the ende sche be dryvene to her tryall, sche wyll desyer that sche maye be present in person, a thyng that in my opynyon hathe neade of good consyderacyon. You schall fynde in the ende, that as there be sume fewe in thys companye that mynde playnlye and trulye, so ther be others that seke hollye to sarve ther owne partycular turnes, the wyche beyng done, they care not what becumes nether of Quene nor Kynge. And this good Mr. Secretarye, beyng more weryyd with the inconstancys of thes mene's doyngs, than with enye other travel, I bede you most hartelye farewell. From Yorke, this 15th of October, 1568.

Yours most beholdyng,

T. NORFOLKE.

P. S.   The Quene of Scottes, in respect of herselfe, I thynke, hath better frynds of the Regent's side than of here owne.

———

A LETTER TO QUEEN ELIZABETH, FROM HER COMMISSIONERS AT YORKE, THE 11TH OF OCTOBER, 1568.

An Original.—Cotton. Lib. cal. c. i. fol. 198.

Please it your most excellent Majestie to understand, that sithens our last despeches, the Erle of Murray and his colleagues, to occupie the time, have put in their answeare to the complaynts exhibited by their adverse partie, the copie of which answeare we send herewith to your Majestie. And albeit they have in the same touched nothing plainlie in the cause of the murder, whereupon they staye and suspend thair proceadings, untill they may be resolved in their articles proponed unto us, which we sent in our last letters to your Majestie, yet the said Erle hath been content privatlie to shew us such matteir as they have to condempne the Quene of Scottes of the murder of her husband, to the intent they wolde know of us, how your Majestie, understanding the same, wolde judge of the sufficiencie of the matter; and whether, in your Majestie's opinion, the same will extend to condempne the Quene of Scottes of the said murder.

And so they sent unto us the Lord of Lethingtoun, James Makgill, and Mr. George Boqwannan, and an other being a Lord of the Session, which in private and secret conference with us, not as commyssioners, as they protested, but for our better instruction, after declaration of such circumstances as led and induced to vehement presumptions to judge her giltie of the said murder, shewed unto us the copie of a bond, bearing date the 19th of Aprill 1567, to the which the most part of the lords and counsaillors of Scotland have put to their hands; and, as they saye, more for feare than any lyking they had of the same. Which band conteyned two special points, the one a declaration of Bothwell's purgation of the murder of the Lord Darnley, and the other a generall consent to his marriage with the Quene, so far forthe as the lawe and her owne likinge shoulde allowe. And yet, in proufe that they did it not willinglie, they procured a warrant, which was now shewed unto us, bearing date the 19th of Aprill, signed with the Quene's hand, whereby she gave them licence to agree to the same, affirming that before they had such warrant, there was none of them that did, or wolde set to their hands, saving onlie the Earl of Huntley.

There was also in the copie of the bande, a copie of a warrant followinge much to that effect, savinge that the one did licence to doe, and the other seemed to discharge and pardone that was done, which bears date the 14th of Maye. It appeared also, that the selfe-same daye of the date of this band, being the 19th of Aprill, the Earl of Huntley was restored by parliament; which parliament was the occasion that so many lords were there assembled, which being all invited to a supper by Bothwell, were induced after supper, more for fear than otherwayes, to subscribe to the said bond, two hundred harkebusiers being in the court, and about the chamber-door wheare they supped, which weare all at Bothwell's devotione; which the said lords so muche misliked, that the next morning, by four of the clocke, fewe or none of them weare left in the towne, but departed without taking their leave. . -

Thear was also a contract shewed unto us, signed with the Quene's hand, and also with Bothwell's, bearing date the 5th of Aprill, written, as it is said, with the Earl of Huntley's own hand, who, with one Thomas Hebourne, weare the only witnesses to the same. Which contract beareth date before Bothwell's purgation of the murder, whereof he was not tried nor pourged before the 12th of Aprill followinge, and also before the processe of divorce began between Bothwell and his wief, which was not begunne before the 1st of May, and yet with speede ended within eight dayes, and the ungodlie marriage betweene the Quene and him solempnized the 15th of May after; and also the 15th of June following, the Quene herselfe was taken by her nobilitie. The counterfiete and colourable taking of the Quene by Bothwell, when he carried her to Dunbar, was the 24th of Aprill after the death of her husband, who was murdered the 10th of February 1567.

There was also a contract shewed unto us, of the Quene's own hand, of the marriage to be had betweene her and Bothwell, bearing no date; which had not *verba de præsenti*, as the other had, bearing date the 5th of Aprill. It appeared also unto us by two letters of her owne hand, that it was by hir own practice and consent, that Bothwell should take her and carry her to Dunbar, of pollicie, as the Lord of Lethington told us, because else theare could be no de-

vyse in lawe to pardon his foul fact of the murder, affirming that,
by the lawes of that realme, a pardon for great offences includeth all
lesser factes and offences, but extendeth to none greater than that
which is pardoned ; and therefore, except he should commit the
highest offence, which is treason, as he did in laying violent hands
upon his soveraigne, no pardon culd serve to excuse him of the
murder; and having his pardon for the treason, it sufficeth also for
the murder.   A fit pollicie for a detestable fact.

After the devise of the murder was determined, as it seemed by
the sequell, they inferred upon a letter of her own hand, that there
was another meane of a more cleanly conveyance devised to kill the
King ; for there was a quarrell made betwixt him and the Lord
Robert of Holie-roode-house, by carrying of false tales betwixte
theme, the Quene being the instrument, as they sayde, to bring it to
pass ; which purpose, if it had taken effect, as it was very likelie,
(for the one geving the lye to the other, they were at daggers draw-
inge) it had eased them of the prosecution of the develish fact,
which, this taking none effect, was afterwards most tirannously
executed.

Aftewards, they shewed unto us one horrible and long letter of
her own hand, as they saye, conteyning foule matteir, and abominable to be either thought of, or to be written by a prince, with diverse
fond ballades of her own hand ; which letters, ballades, and other
writings before specified, weare closed in a little coffer of silver and
gilte, heretofore geaven by her to Bothwell.   The said letters and
ballades do discover such inordinate love betweene her and Bothwell, her loothsomeness and abhorringe of her husband that was murdered, in such sorte as everie good and godlie man can not but detest and abhorre the same.

And these men heare do constantlie affirme the said letters, and
other writings, which they produce of her own hand, to be her own
hand indede ; and do offer to swear and take their oaths thereupon,
the matteir conteyned in them being such, as could hardlie be invented or devised by any other than by her selfe; for that they discourse of some things, which weare unknowen to anie other than to
herself and Bothwell : and as it is hard to counterfiete so manie, so
the matter of them, and the manner how these men came by them is
such as, it seemeth, that God, in whose sight murder and bludshed
of the innocent is abhommable, wolde not permit the same to be hid
or concealed.

In a paper here inclosed we have noted to your Majestie the chiefe
and speciall points of the said letters, written, as they say, with her
own hand, to the intent it may please your Majestie to consider of
them, and so to judge whether the same be sufficient to convince her

of the detestable crime of the murder of her husband, which, in our opinions and consciences, if the said letters be written with her own hand, is verie hard to be avoided. Most humblie beseaching your Majestie, that it may please the same to advertise us of your opinion and judgment therein, and to direct us with such spead as to your Highness shall be thought convenient, how we shall proceade further in this great mattier. And so for the more expedition, sending this blotted letter to your Majestie, (whereof we crave pardon) we beseche Almightie God to preserve your most excellent Majestie in good healthe and long lief, most prosperously to reigne over us. From your Majestie's citie of York, the xi. of October 1568.

Your Majestie's most humble,
faithful, and obedient subjects,
T. NORFOLKE,
T. SUSSEX,
R. SADLER.

THE ANSWER OF THE EARL OF MURRAY.

The Answer of us James Erle of Murray, Regent of the realme of Scotland, and remanent Commissionaris appointit for the King's Majestie of Scotland, our Soverain Lord, in his Hienes behalf, and for our selfis, and remanent States and pepill, his Majestie's faithful and obedient subjectis, to the lettre presentit to your Grace and my Lords Commissionaris for the Quene's Majestie of England, on the behalf of the Quene moder to our Soverane Lord.

An Original.—Cott. Lib. cal. c. l. fol. 202.

It is notour to all men, how umquhile King Henry, father to our Soverane Lord, was horribly murderit in his bed. James, sumetime Erle Bothwell, being well knawn for chief author thairof, enterit in so great credit and authoritie with the Quene, then our soverane, that, within thré monethis efter the murther of hir husband, the said Erle plainlie enterprisit to ravish hir persoun, and leid hir to Dunbar castell, haldand hir there as captive a certane space, during quhilk he causit divorce be led betwixt him and his lauchfull wyfe, and suddanlie, at the end thairof, accomplisit a pretendit marriage betwix him and the Quene. Quhilk strange and hastie proceding of that godles and ambicious man, efter murthering of the Quenis

husband, in sic sort, to atteyne to hir awin marriage, the governament of the realme, and powar over hir sone our Soverane Lordis
persoun, with the ignominy spokin amangis all nations of that murther, as though all the nobilitie had bene alike culpabill thairof,
sua movit the hartis of a gude nomber of thame, that thay thocht na
thing mair godlie, nor mair honorabill in the sicht of the warld,
than, be punishing of the said Erle, chief author of the murther, to
releive otheris saikleslie calumpniat thairof, to put the Quene to
fredome furth of the bondage of that tyran, that presumptouslie had
enterprisit to revysh and marie hir, quhais lauchfull husband he
could not be, nather she his lauchfull wyfe: and to preserve the
innocent persoun of our native Prince furth of the handis of him
that murtherit his fader. For quhilk purpos taking armis, the said
Erle cume againis us, leading the Quene, then our soverane, in his
company, as a defence and cloik to all his wicketnes, accumpanyit
with a greit force that he had brocht to the feild, with greit ordinance, and wagit men of weir: quhair, to decide the querrel, quhilk
was onlie intentit aganis him and the remanent knawin murtheraris,
without bluidsched of ony innocent man, it wes offerit, at twa severall times, be the noblemen seiking the punishment of the murther,
to try the matter with him in singular battell, according to the law
of armis, as he be his cartell of befoir had proclamit. Quhilk being
schiftit, delayit, and in the end uterlie refusit be him, he escapit be
flicht; and the Quene, preferrand his impunity to hir awin honour,
wald sé him conveyit away: and to the end he suld not be followit
nor persewit, she come hir self to the noblemen assemblit aganis him,
quhilk convoyit hir to Edinburgh; and, being thair, informit her
of the verie causis that had drevin thame to that forme of dealing,
humblie requiring that sho wald be content to sé the said Erle, and
uthers the King hir husbandis murthereris, punishit, and that pretendit and unlauchfull marriage, quhairin scho was improvisitlie
enterit, to be dissolvit for hir awin honour, the saulgard of hir sone,
and the quietnes of hir realme and subjectis. To quhilk na uther
answere culd be obtenit, bot rigorus minassing, on the ane part
avowand to be revengit on all thame that had schawin thameselfis
in that cause, and on the uther part offerand to leif, and gif over, the
realme and all, sua scho might be sufferit to posses the murtherar of
hir husband. Quhilk hir inflexible mynd, and extremitie of necessitie compellit thame to sequestrate hir persoun, for a season, fra
the company, and having intelligence with the said Erle Bothwell,
and uthers his fautouris, quhill further tryal mycht be takin, and
executioun maid for the murther. During the quhilk tyme, sho
finding hir self, be lang irksum and tedious travail takin be hir in
the government of the realme and lieges thairof, sa vexit and weryit,

that hir body, sprite, and senses were altogidder unable langer to
occúpy that realme; and persaving, be thingis that had past before
that tyme betwixte hir and hir pepill, that nowther sho culd wele
allowe of thair doingis, nor thay like of hir fashiounis; and for uther
considerationis móving hir for the tyme, thairfoir dimittit and renuncit the office of governament of the realme and lieges' thairof, in
favouris of hir onlie and maist deir sone the Prince of the samin.
And, becaus of his tender youth and inability to use the said governament in his awin persoun, during his minoritie, constituted me
the said Erle of Murray (being then absent furth off the realme,
and without my knowledge) Regent to his Grace, the realme, and
lieges; and quhill my returning, or in caise of my deceise, or not
acceptatioun, maid and constitute divers otheris noblemen, Regentis,
as her several commissiounis to that effect, subscrivit with hir hand,
and under the Privie Seill, beris; and that voluntarlie, na compulsion, violence, nor force usit or practisit to move hir thairto. According to the quhilk hir dimissioun and resignatioun, the King, now
our Soverane Lord, was dewlie, richtly, and orderlie crownit, in-
vestit and possessit in the kingdome: and I the said Erle of Murray
lauchfullie placeit, enterit, and admittit to the said office of regentrie.
Quhilkis coronation of our said Soverane Lord, and acceptatioun of
the said office of regentrie, wer not onlie ressavit, and universallie
obeyit over all the haill realme, as lauchfull and sufficient, evin be
the maist part of thame that, in thir six monethis last bypast, hes
withdrawin thair debtfull obedience fra his Grace's authoritie, and
interprisit to establische and set up ane uther; but als in a lauchfull, fré, and plane parliament, quhairat they were present, the same
coronatioun and acceptatioun of the office of Regentrie, wer be
perpetual lawes maid, and publict actis sett fúrth, decernit to be
lauchfully, sufficiently, and richtuouslie done; as alswa all uther
thingis intentit, spokin, writtin, or done be thame, or any of thame,
to that effect, sen the tenth day of Februar 1566, upon the quhilk
day the said umquhile King Henry, then the Quenis lauchfull husband, was murtherit, unto the dait of the said act, and in all tyme
to cum, tuiching the said Quene, and deteyning of hir persoun, that
cause, and all thingis depending thairon; the intromissioun or dis-
ponyng upoun hir propertie, casualities, or quhatsumever thing per-
tening, or that ony wayis micht pertene to hir; likas at mair lenth is
contenit in the actis, lawis, and constitutionis concludit, maid, and
sett furth in the said parliament. Quhilkis actis and lawis with
our Soverane Lordis authoritie, and the regiment of me the said
Erle of Murray, wer universallie obeyit over all the realme, but
contradictioun; quhill sum of the nobilitie and utheris, that in the
said parliament be fré votes, and utherwayis be thair hand-writtis,

had acknawlegit and avancit the Kingis authority, and regiment established in his name, impatient to sé the puir pepill of the realme enjoy quietnes and gud dayis, and disdainand to sé justice proceid as it was begun, and liklie to have continewit, to the punisment of mony offendaris over the haill cuntrie, according to the lawes ; first practizit to bring the said Quene out of Lochlevin, contrary to the actis maid in the parliament, and then be open force to destroy and subvert the publict governament and authoritie of our Soverane Lord establishit be the Estatis, against thair promissit obedience and hand-writtis ; and for that purpos procedit in all kynd of hostilitie, quhill on the 13th day of May last bypast, that God respectand the equitie of the cause, confoundit thair interprise, and grantit the victorie to the King and sic as constantlie continewit in his obedience ; zit sensyne they have perseverit in thair rebellioun, abstractand their debtfull obedience fra our Soverane Lord and his auctoritie, practizing all thingis that mycht subvert and overthraw the samin, in halding of housis, proclayming of uther auctoritie, cuming to the feildis in weirlike manner with displayit banneris, taking and impresoning of officiaris of armis and utheris fré personis, raising of impositiouns of burrowis, and, under pretence of law, summoning housis, banishing and rigorously persewing divers the Kingis gude subjectis, for na uther cause but onlie the serving of the King thair native Soverane Lord.

It is thairfore requirit in his Hienes behalf, that he, and his Regent in his Hienes behalf, may peciabillie injoy and governe his realme, according to God's calling ; and that his Majestie's disobedient subjectis may be causit recognosce thair debtfull obedience, and quhat the ordour of Justice hes ordainit may ressave full executioun. Protesting alwayis, that notwithstanding this our answer, we may eik to the same, as the occasioun sall serve, and as the neid may require.

JAMES, Regent.   MORTOUN.
PATRICK.   AD. ORCHAD.
LINDSAY.   DUMFERMLING.

A BRIEF NOTE OF THE CHIEF AND PRINCIPALL POINCTS OF THE QUENE OF SCOTTES LETTRES WRITTEN TO BOTHAILL, WHICH MAY TEND TO HER CONDEMPNATION, FOR HER CONSENT AND PROCUREMENT OF THE MURDER OF HER HUSBAND, AS FARRE FORTHE AS WE COULDE BY THE READINGE GATHER.

First, the plaine and manifest wordes conteyned in the said lettres, declaringe the inordinat and filthie love betwene her and Bothaill.

Next, the like wordes plainlie declaringe how she hated and abhorred her said husband.

Then for the declaration of the conspiracie, and her procurement and consent to the murder of her said husband, how she toke her journey from Edenburghe to Glasco, to visite him beinge theare sicke, and purposely of intent to bringe him with her to Edenburghe.

She wrote to Bothaill from Glasco, how she flattered her said husband, to obtaine her purpose; and that the Earle of Lenox his father, that daye that she was devisinge to bringe his sonne to Edenburghe, did blede at the noose and mowthe, willing the said Bothaill to ghesse what presage it was.

She wrote also, that she was about a worke that she hated greatly, and that she lied and dissembled to get creadite with her husband, and to bringe her faschious purpose to passe, confessing herselfe therein to do the office of a traiteresse, which, were it not to obey Bothaill, she had lever be dead then do it, for her harte did blede at it.

Also she wrote that she had wonne her husband to goo with her to Edenburghe, and to do whatsoever she wolde have him to do, saying, Alas! she never deceaved anie before, remittinge herselfe altogether to the will and pleasure of Bothaill, wherein she wold obey him, whatsoever come thereof; requyring him to advise with himself, if he coulde fynde owt anie other secreat invention by medicine, for her husband was to take medicine, and the Bath also at Cragmiller.

She biddethe Bothaill to burn the lettre, for it was over dangerous to them, and nothinge well said in it, for that she was thinkinge upon nothinge but fascherie, requyringe him that, sithens to obey him, her dear love, she spared neither honour, conscience, hazard, nor greatnes whatsoever, he woulde take it in good parte; and that he wold not see her, whose fained tears shoulde not be so muche praised, as the faithefull travailles which she susteyned to merite her place, for the obteyninge whereof against her nature, she betraied him that might impeche it, prayinge God to forgeave her, and to geave unto Bothaill, her only love, the happe and prousperitie which she his humble and faithfull love wishithe unto him; hoopinge shortely to be another thinge unto him, for the rewarde of her yrkesome troubles.

Finally, she wrote to Bothaill, that accordinge to her commission, she wolde bringe the man with her; prayinge him to worke wisely, or els the whole burden wolde lye on her shoulders; and specially to make good watche, that the bird escaped not owt of the cage.

EXAMINATUR.

NOTES DRAWIN FURTH OF THE QUENIS LETTERS SENT TO THE ERLE BOTHWELL.

From the Paper-Office.

Imprimis, after lang discourse of hir conference with the King hir husband in Glascow, sche wreitis to the said Erle in thir termes: "This is my first jurnay, I sall end the same the morne: I wreite in all thingis, howbeit they be of littill weycht, to the end that ye may tak the best of all to judge upoun. I am doing ane work heir that I haitte gretlie: Haif ye not desyr to lauche, to sie me lie sa weill, at the leist to dissemble so weill, and to tell hym the treuth betwix handis."

Item, Schortlie after : "We are coupled with twae fals racis. The devill syndere us, and God mot knit us togidder for ever for the maist faithful cupple that ever he unitit. This is my faith, I will die in it."

Item, Thairefter, "I am not weill at ease, and zeit verray glaid to wreit unto you quhen the rest are slepand, sen that I can not sleip as they do, and as I wald desyir, that is in your armis my deir luife."

Item, A littill thairefter: "Adverteis me quhat ze haif deliberat to do in the matter ye knaw upoun this point, to the end we may understand utheris wele, that nathing thair throw be spilt."

Item, Thus sche concludis the lettre : "Wareit mocht this pokishe man be, that causes haif sa meikill pane, for without hym I wald haif ane far mair plesant subject to discourse upoun. He is not oer meikle spilt, bot he has gottin verray mekill; he has almaist -slane me with his braith; it is war nor your unclis, and zeit I cum na neirar bot sat in ane cheir at the bed-fute, and he beand at the uther end thairof."

. Item, Thairefter, " Ye gar me dissemble sa far, that I haif horring thairat, and ze caus me almaist do the office of an trahatores. Remember yow, yf it wer not to obey yow, I had raither be deid or I did it, my heart blidis at it. Summa, He will not cum with me, except upoun conditioun that I shall be at bed and bourd with hym as of befoir, and that I sall leif him na efter."

Item, Schortlie thairefter : " Summa, he will gae upoun my word to all places. Alace, I never dissavit any bodie, bot I remit me altogidder to your will. Send me advertisement quhat I sall do, and, quhatsumever sall cum thairof, I sall obey you; advys to with yourself, yf ye can fynd out any mair secreit inventioun be medecein and the baith at Craigmillar."

· Item, " Thairefter, I sall draw out all thingis out of hym, gif ye will that I advow all thingis unto hym; bot I will never rejois to dissave any bodie that trustis in me; zet notwithstanding ye may command me in all thingis. Haif no evill opinioun of me for that cause, be reason ye ar the occasioun of it your self, because for my awn particular revenge I wold not do it to hym.

. . Item, After, " For certaintie he suspectis that thing ye know, and of his lyif; bot as to the last, how sone I speak twae or thrie guid wordis unto hym, he rejois and is out of doubt."

Item, Schortlie thairefter, " all the Hamiltounis are heir with me, and accompanies me verry honorably."

Item, Thairefter, " Be not offendit, for I gif not our mekill credyt now, sence, to obey you, my deir luife, I spare nouther honor, conscience nor gretnes quhatsumever, I pray you tak it in guid part, and not after the interpretation of your fals guid-brother, to quhom, I pray you, gif nae credyns agains the maist faythfull luifer that ever ye had, or ever sall haif. Sie not hir quhais fenzeit tearis suld not be sa mekill praysit, nor estemyt, as the trew and faythfull travaillis, quhilk I sustene to merit hir place, for obtening of quhilk, againis my naturall, I betraye thame that may impesche me. God forgive me, and God gif yow, my onlie luif, the hape and prosperitie that your humble and faythfull luif desyris unto yow, quha hoipis schortlie to be ane uther thing unto yow."

· Item, In the credit gifin to the berar, quhome we understand was Pareis, " Remember yow of the purpois of the Ladie Reires—— of the ludgene in Edinburt."

Item, In ane. uther lettre sent be Betoun : " As to me, howbeit I heir noe farther newes from yow, according to my commission, I bring the man with me to Craigmillar upon Munday, quhair he will

d

be all Wednisday. And I will 'gang to Edinburt 'to draw bluid of me, gif in the mene tyme I get no newes in the contrair from yow."

Item, Verray schortlie after : " Summa, ye will say he makis the court to me, of the quhilk I tak so gret pleseur, that I enter never quhair he is, bot incontinent I tak the seiknes of my syde, I ame soe faschit with it. Yf Pareis bring me that quhilk I send hym for, I treast it sall amend me. I pray yow adverteis me of your newes at length, and quhat I sall do in caice ye be not returnit quhen I cum thair, for, in cais ye work not wyselie, I sie that the haill burthin of this will fall upon my schulderis. Provyde for all thingis, and discourse upon it first your self."

Item, In ane uther lettre: " I pray you, according to your promeis, to discharge your hart to me, utherwayis I will think that my malheure, and the guid composing of thame, that hes not the third part of the faythfull and willing obedience unto yow that I beyre, has wyne, againis my will, that advantage over me quhilk the secund luif of Jason wan ; not that I wolde compair you to ane sa unhappie as he was, nor yit myself to ane soe unpetifull a woman as sche ; howbeit ye cause ma be sumquhat lyck unto hir in ony thing that twichis yow, or that may preserve and keip yow to hir, to quhome ye onlie appertein, yf it may be suer that I may appropriat that quhilk is wonne throuche faythfull, yea only luiffing yow, quhilk I do and sall do all the dayis of my lyif, for pane and evil that can cum thereof. In recompense of the quhilk, and of all the evills quhilk ye haif bein cause of to me, remember you upon the place heir besyd, &c."

A LETTER FROM THE DUKE OF NORFOLK DIRECTED TO THE EARL OF PEMBROKE, LORD STEWARD OF THE QUENE'S MOST HONOURABLE HOUSE, AND TO THE EARL OF LEYCESTRE, AND WILLIAM CECILL, KNIGHT, PRINCIPAL SECRETARY TO THE QUENE'S MAJESTIE, FROM YORK, 12TH OF OCTOBER, 1568.

Paper-office.—An original in the Duke's hand.

AFTER my most hartye commendatyons to your good Lordship, I have forborne all thys whyle to writte ennye thyng unto you, becawse the Quene's Majestye's letters dide ever conteyne as muche as we cowld wrytte off ower procedynges heare; and at thys tyme also we have wrytten in her Hyenes letters what is chancyd off newe. Marrye, the occasyon of thys my wrytyng unto you at thys tyme,

ys to putte you in remembrance off your promysys made unto me,
wyche was that you taryyng behynd wold furder us in thys her
Majestie's sarvys, as we in enye reasonable request cowld desyer.
By thes ower too last letters wrytten unto her Majestie, you maye
see we are gone as far as we cane, tyll we receave answere from her
Highnes ageyne; and for my none parte, I thynke I may assurydlye
saye, that the Regent and ther syde (as by ther warie delyng you
maye perceave) mynde to proceede no furder tyll they maye assure
them selfis, what her Majestye thynkes of thes cawsys, that they have
schewyd us to charge ther Quene withall, what her jugement schall
fall owte therupon, as also after jugement in what leage her Hyenes
(the matter fallyng owte manifestlye) myndes to joyne with ther
Kynge, and them that nowe by ther parlement have the governe-
ment of that realme. Thynk them not my Lords to be to presyse:
Juge them as we wold juge of ower selfis yf we wer in ther cace.
They playe at no small game; they stand for ther lyves, lands and
goods; and they are not ygnorant yf they wolde, for yt ys everye
daye told them, that as longe as they absteyne from towching ther
Quene's honor, sche wyll make with them what reasonable ende they
can devyse. Yt were pytye that they, for so muche trustyng to us,
schuld hender ther owne cawse. Ther ys but too wayes to be taken:
the one, yf the facte schall be thowght as destestable and manefeste
to you, as for owght we can perceave yt semethe here to us, that con-
dygne jugement, with open demonstratyon to the hoпe world, with
the holle cyrcumstancys, and playne, true, and indyfferent pro-
cedying therin, maye directlye appeare; of the wyche for ower owen
dyscharge we doe not omytte to kepe good and suffycyent memo-
ryalls, not forgettyng with what manner of person we have to deale,
nor yeat howe the upryght handlyng of thys cawse schall importe
us bothe in honor and honestye to the holle worlde. The other ys,
yf her Majestie schall not allowe of thys, then to make such a com-
posycion as in so broken a cawse may be; of ether of wyche, for
her Hyenes better sarvys, we desyer to be advertysyd with spede,
havyng nothyng to doe tyll we have full resolutyon from her Majestie, but to dryve on the tyme by dylatorye plees, as by my Lord
Regent's answere sent unto her Hyenes you maye perceave. Whether you take the fyrst waye or the last, one thyng wold be present-
lye well wayed and consyderyd amongst you, and theruppon we to
receave your resolutyon: What meanes and wayes you wyll have
usyd for the reconcylyatyon, and compondyng of the dyfferencys
betwyne the Regent and hys partye of the one syde, and the Duke
with the Hameltons of the other, whoes partye I thynk as good as
ther Quene's. And, for myn oune parte, what ende soever you
take, I thynke you schall make but boched work, yf you doe not
sowndlie and perfectlye conclude thowes dyfferencys: He beying

ther amongst you, you can better tell what humor for reconcylyatyon
he ys in, than we heare; and yeat I feare me, whan you have wrowgt
hyme ther, he must cume hether before enye full conclusyon wyll
be made: As long as he dremes of a maryage to be hade betwyne
hys sone the Lord of Arbrothe and thys Quene, I thynke you schall
fynde that he wyll harkne to no ende, I fynd so muche by sume
secrete intellygense that I have heare. And thus you may see howe
farre, in friendchype to you as to my assuryit frynds, I wade in thys
most brykle cace; for hear is no bodye of enye syde, but that for
feare or mystrust, makes courtesye to utter playnlye ther mynds in
that cace, wherein they knowe not the ende. And so for thys tyme,
wyschyng to your Lordships more quyetnes than we yeat can find
heare, assuryng you that ther ys no hope of farder procedyng heare,
withowt her Majestie's resolute determynatyon, I bede you most
hartelye farewell. From Yorke, this 2d of October, 1568.

Your good Lordship's most assuredly,

T. NORFOLKE.

THE TWELFTH DAYE OF OCTOBER, 1568.

From the Duke of Norfolk's Book of Entries.

THIS daye the Lord Herries, and the Lord Boyde came to the
Quene's Majestie's commyssioners, only to conferre in talk with
them touching the answere of the Regent and his colleagues, to the
complaint before geaven in by the commyssioners and others for the
Quene of Scottes; and required respite of their replication, till such
tyme they heard from the Quene their mistress by their next depeche,
for the which cause the next morninge they dispatched the Byshoppe
of Ross, and the Lord Boyde unto her.

This daye beinge the 13th of October, we received lettres from
the Quene's Majestie, beringe date the 10th.

In the afternoone of the same daye the Quene's Majestie's commyssioners sent to the commyssioners of the Quene of Scottes, wishing that they wolde, according to the Quene's Majestie's pleasure
in her late letters, procure their commyssion to be enlarged: Whereunto in the end, after some debaitinge thereupon, the Lord Herries
promysed, that he wolde send to the Quene his mistress for that purpose, the alteration of which commyssion appeareth by their wordes
hereafter following, which weare delivered in writinge to the Lord
Herries.

" And theare not only to treete, conclude, and indent, upon all
suche heades and articles, as shall be founde, to our said dearest
sister's commyssioners and them, best for the furtheringe of the
glorie of God, the reduction of our said disobedient subjects to their
detfull obedience to us, for good amitie, as well for bygonnes as to
come, betwixt them, and all our obedient subjects : But also to
treat, conclude and determine, of all other mattiers and causes whatsoever in controversie betwene her and her subjects. And further,
&c."

━━━━━━

From a copy indorsed by Secretary Cecil.

As to the estait of my effairis, I doubt not but ye have understand, that at the convention in Zork my rebellis wer confoundit in
all that thay could alledge for cullouring thair insurrectioun, and
my imprisounment. Persaving the quhilk, thay did sa mekill be
moving of sum of the Quene of Ingland's Ministeris, that, aganis
hir promise, scho has lettin thame have hir presence ; and to cullour
thair cuming towardis hir, said, scho wald hirself understand the
continuatioun of this conference, to the effect the samin sould be
the mair promptlie endit with sum happy outgait to my honour and
contentment; and thairfoir desirit, that sum of my commissionaris
sould pass towardis hir incontinent. Bot the proceidingis sensyne
hes schawin it was not the butt scho schot at; for my matter hes
bene prolongit in delayis, in the mene time that my rebellis practisit secreitlie with hir and hir Ministeris. Swa thay have convenit
and accordit, that my sone sould be deliverit in hir handis, to be
nurischit in this countrey as scho sall think guid. Item, declaring
him to be als abill to succeid efter hir deith, in cais scho have na
successioun of hir bodie. For hir suretie the castellis of Edyn-
burgh, Striveling sall be in Inglishmen's keiping on the said Quene
of Ingland's moyens. Item, with hir moyens, and the concurrence of the Erle of Murray, the castel of Dumbarton sall be as-
seigit, and tane out of the handis, gif thay may, and be lykwise

renderit to the said Quene of Ingland's behuif and keiping. Pro-
vyding thir promisis be keippit, scho has promisit to support and
mantene the Erle of Murray in the usurpatioun of my authoritie,
and cause him to be declarit legitime to. succeid unto the crowne of
Scotland efter the deceis of my sone, in cais he die but bairnis gottin of his bodie : and in this cais the Erle of Murray sall acknaw-
ledge to hald the realme of Scotland in few of the Quene of Ingland. Thus all the equitie of my caus, the connoissance of the
quhilk I traistit in the said Quene of Ingland, hes bene renuncit,
and miserabillie sauld for the ruine of my realme, except that God,
and guid Scottis hart of my faithful subjectis, remeid not the samin.
Zit this is not all, thair is ane uther ligge and intelligence betwix
the Erle of Murray and the Erle of Hartford, quha sould marie ane
of Secretarie Cecil's dochteris, quha dois all thair drauchtis. Be
the quhilk lippining, the said Erle of Murray and Hartfurd sould
meit and fortefie ilk ane uther in the successioun that ilk ane of
thame pretends on his awin side ; that is to say, the Erle of Murray on the side of my realme, be ressoun of the said legitimatioun ;
and the Erle of Hartfurd on the side of Ingland, because of umquhill Dame Katheryn, on quhom he begat twa bairnis, swa thay
will be baith bent to my sone's deith ; quha being out of my subjectis handis, quhat can I hoip for but lamentabill tragedie ? Thir
thingis ar concludit amangis the chief of my rebellis, and the ancient and natural enemies of my realme ; and thair restis nathing
now bot the moyens to establish and assuir the said Erle of Murray in his usurpatioun. To begin the samin, thay would have persuadit me, be craft, to have liberallie dimittit my crown, and con-
sentit to the regentrie of the said Erle of Murray ; and to have
causit me condiscend to sik ane unhappy thing, thair has bene usit
all craft and boisting that has bene possibill, with fair promisis. But
séing I was resolvit to do nathing thairin to thair proffit, the Quene
of Ingland namit new Commissionaris with thame that wer alreddie
depute, in nombre of the quhilk the said tratour, and utheris of his
factioun ; and not permitting me to pass thair to declair my awin
ressounis, that thay wald have pretermittit in the said conference.
Quhilk being brokin, for inlaik that the Quene of Ingland has maid
of hir promise, quhilk was, not to permit the Erle of Murray to cum
in hir presence afoir the said conference wer endit ; and mairover,
thair sould be nathing done to the prejudice of my honour, estait
and rycht, that I may have in this countrey efter hir ; my saidis
Commissionaris left the said conference the sixt of this moneth, with
solempnit protestatiounis, that all quhilk wer done thairin to the prejudice of me in ony sort, sall be null and of nane effect noi valor,
and thairon ar deliberat to cum away as soon as is possibill : quhair
of I thocht guid to adverteis zou, to the effect ze may understand

the veritie of the samin matter, and inform our freindis of the samin. I pray zou to assembill our freindis my subjectis, lyk as I have writtin to my Lord of Argyle and Huntlie to haiste to zour releif; doing all the hinder and evill that ze may to the said rebellis, and stop thair returning hame, gif it be possibill; for thay will be reddie befoir zou, gif ze mak not haist. Swa ze being altogidder assemblit in conventioun, not feiring that I sall stop or discharge zour proceidingis, as I did the last time, ze sall declair and schaw publictlie, be oppin proclamatioun, the afoirsaid conspiracie and tressoun, quhilk the said rebellis hes conspirit aganis the weill of the realme of Scotland, intending to put the samin in executioun, to the destructioun thairof, gif thay be not stoppit in dew time; and thairfore ze, with my haill faithful subjectis, and all trew Scottis hartis, will do diligence to stop the performance of thair intentiounis. This undertendit, I am maist asseurit, that at the spring of the zeir ze *** sufficient releif of uther freindis.

Proclame and hald ane parliament, gif ze may.

LETTER FROM QUEEN ELIZABETH TO THE EARL OF MURRAY,
JUNE 8, 1568.

A Copy attested by Secretary Cecil.

BY THE QUENE.

Right trusty and right welle beloved cousin, we greete you welle. For as much as the Queen of Scotts our good sister is lately come into our realme, as we are well assured you knowe, with the causes of her arrivall in the partes where she now is, and that she hath sent to us the Lord Herrys with credit to report unto us her estate, and to discover her whole late trowbles and great injuries done to her by her subjects, begynning at theire notorious ungratefulness upon her pardoning of their former great offences, and receiving them into her favour at our request, and consequently by raysing first force against her, and notwithstanding the yeilding of herself into their hands for avoiding of blodde, and being desirous to reforme any thing that was amiss; yet she was taken and committed to prison, where she was most hardly kept, and could be never heard to answer for herself, but was for fear of her life, compelled to make a dimission of her crown, and in parliament proceeded against her, without hereing of herself or any advocate, and so deprived her of her royal estate. And now finally, she being escaped and accompanyed by her nobilitie, was by force and arms pursued by you and some other particular persons in battle, and so she was compelled to flye into this our realme.

All which things cannot but sound very strange in the ears of us, being a prince sovereign, having dominions and subjects committed to our power, as she had. For remedy whereof she requireth our ayde, as her next cousine and neighbour: and for justification of her whole cause, is content to commit the hearing and ordering of the same simply to us. We have thought good and necessary, not only to impart thus much unto you, wherewith she chargeth you, and others joined with you, considering the government of that realme is in your power at this present, and that by your servant Mr. John Woodd, we have understood your offer, to make declaration unto us of your whole doings; but also to require and advise you, utterly to forbear from all manner of hostility and persecution against all such as have lately taken part with the said Queen, and to suspend all manner of actions and proceedings against them, both by law and arms, as the like is ment by us to be observed on the Queen's part, and others adjoined to her ; and to impart unto us plainly and sufficiently, all that which shall be mete to inform us of the truth for your defences in such waighty crimes and causes, as the said Quene hath allready, or shall hereafter object against you, contrary to the duety of naturall borne subjects : so as we being duely informed on all parts, may, by the assistance of God's grace, direct our actions and orders principally to his glory, and next to the conservation of our owne honour in the sight of all other princes ; and finally, to the maintainance and increase of peace and concord between both these two realmes. And as you shall meane to have us favourable to all your just causes, so we earnestly require you to observe the request of these our lettres.

These words follow in Secretary Cecil's hand.

The trew copy of the Queen's Majesty's lettre to the Earle of Murray, by me,

W. Cecill.

PART OF A NOTE OF WHAT THE EARL OF MURRAY AND HIS COUN-
SELLORS DELIVERED TO MR. MIDDLEMORE, TO BE REPORTED
TO THE ENGLISH QUEEN, IN ANSWER TO THE PRECEDING, 22D
JUNII 1568.

**** And for our offer, to mak her Majestie declaratioun of our
haill doingis, anent that quhairwith the Quene, our Soverane Lordis
mother, chargis us, and otheris, joinit with us ; we have alreddy
sent unto our servand Mr. Jhone Wode, that quhilk we traist sall
sufficientlie resolve hir Majestie of ony thing scho standis doubtful
unto : and zit gif hir hienes will that we send other for mair special
informatioun of the cais, we sall glaidlie follow hir plesoure, with
àls grite haist as possible we can.

Bot because we persave the trial, quhilk the Quenis Majestie is
myndit to have taken, is to be usit wit grit ceremonye and solemni-
teis, we wald be maist laith to enter into accusatioun of the Quene,
moder of the King our Soverane, and syne to enter in qualificatioun
with hir ; for all men may judge how dangerous and prejudicial
that suld be. Alwayis, in cais the Quenis Majestie will have the accusatioun directlie to proceid, it wer maist ressonabill we understude
quhat we suld luke to follow thairupon, in cais we preive all that
we allege : utherwayis we sal be als incertane efter the caus concludit, as we ar presentlie. And thairfoir, we pray zow requyre hir
hienes, in this point to resolve us ; at leist that my Lordis of the
counsal will assure us quhat we sall lippin unto.

Farther, it may be, that sic letteris as we haif of the Quene, our
Soverane Lordis moder, that sufficientlie, in our opinioun, preivis
hir consenting to the murthure of the King hir lauchful husband,
sal be callit in doubt be the juges to be constitute for examinatioun
and trial of the caus, quhether thay may stand, or fall ; pruif, or not.
Thairfoir sen our servand Mr. Jhone Wode hes the copies of the
samin letteris translatit in our language, we wald ernestlie desyre
that the saidis copies may be considerit be the juges that sall haif the
examinatioun and commissioun of the matter, that thay may resolve
us this far, in cais the principal agrie with the copie, that then we
pruif the caus indeed : for quhen we haif manifestit and schawin all,
and zit sall haif na assurance, that it we send sall satisfie for probatioun, for quhat purpois sall we ather accuse, or tak care how to
pruif, quhen we ar not assurit quhat to pruif, or, quhen we have
preivit, quhat sall succeid?

JOURNAL OF THE COMMISSIONERS, INTITULED, THE SESSION AT WESTMINSTER, DEC. 6, 1568, WHEREIN THE ERLE OF MURRAY AND HIS COMMISSIONERS WERE REPROVED FOR ACCUSING OF THE QUENE OF SCOTTS.

At twa of the clock in the afternoon, when all the Quene's Majestie's Commissioners weare assembled in the accustomed chamber to have declared to the Erle of Murray and his collegues, the Quene's Majestie's mislikeing of their late accusation of the Quene, their Soverain, for which purpose the said. Erle and his collegues ought for to be theare present, the Bishop of Ross and his collegues sente one Mr. Borthick to require that they might com to the said Commissioners to declare certen matter. Whereupon the said Commissioners preferringe the said motion to be considered before they proceded with the said Erle of Murray, sent to the said Bishop, to understand whether the matter which they had to declare, was of suche importance as weare meete to be understoode before they should speake with the Erle of Murray, who was presently with them all, ready to speake with them. Whereunto the Bishop answered, that their desire was to speake first with them. And so her Majestie's Commissioners moveinge the Erle and his partie to withdrawe themselves aparte, sent for the said Bishop, who with his collegues being com, said, that they had considered with themselves, since their beinge upon Sattirday last with her Majestie ; that whear they did then perceave that her Majestie mente to procede with the Erle of Murray and his partie, to require proofes upon the allegations produced against the Quene their Soverain, they came to declare that they could no furder procede in this conference, but for their partes would protest, that except the Quene their Mistress might appere in person before the Quene's Majestie, to answere for her selfe, this conference might be dissolved : and to that end they had conceaved their meaninge in writing, which they produced and read. Wherin because they did otherwise repeate the Quene's Majesty's answere made unto them on Sattirday, then was bothe plainly and manifestly knowen unto her Majestie's Commissioners, which were at Hampton-court, in presence of her Majestie, at the giveinge of the answere to them, the same was by them all with one consent ymproved, and thereupon answered, that they could not receave the same writinge of her Majestie's answeare without prejudising of the truth it selfe, and manyfeste offence in their own consciences. And for those respects they required the said Bishop and his collegues to retaine their writing with themselves, offeringe ne-

verthelesse, that if they would at any time offer any writeinge unto
them to this purpose, or any other conteyning the Quene's Majestie's answeare according to the truth therof, they would willingly
receave the same. And so the said Bishop reiteratinge in wordes
their request by way of protestinge, that they meant neither to treat
nor compeare any more in this conference, they went their waie.

After this done, the Erle of Murray and his collegues cumminge
to the Quene's Majesty's Commissioners, weare charged in the
Quene's Majesty's name, by the Lord Keeper in this manner following : .

My Lords, the Quene's Majestie, upon the consideration had of
that you call your eike, being an addition to your former answeare
hath commanded us to say unto you, that her highness thinketh
very much and very strange that, being native subjects to the Quene
of Scotts, you should accuse her of so horrible a cryme, odible both
to God and man, a cryme against law and nature, wherby if you
should prove it true, she should be infamous to all Princes in the
world. And therfore hath willed us to say unto you, that although
you in this doing have forgot your duties of allegiance toward your
Soveraine, yet her Majestie meaneth not to forget the love of a good
sister, and of a good neighbour and friend. What you are to answer to this, we are heare ready to hear. Whereunto the said Erle
and the rest with him answered, that they trusted it had appeared
by their former proceedings both at Yorke and heare, how loath
they weare to enter so farre as they have done to make any accusation of the said Quene. For their coming at the first was by the
Quene's Majestie's commandement, upon the motion of the said
Quene of Scotts, to answere to such thinges as wherewith they
should be charged, which they had done at Yorke: and therin they
thought they had shewed good matter for the mayntenance of their
doings, without entering into any accusation of the said Quene.
And if their adversaries could have been contented to have staid
therupon, they would not have entred farther ; but seing they could
not be allowed to make their defence as they had done, but that
their adversaries, by way of replication, would continue the charge-
ing of them so many wayis with disobedience, where indeed, by
their former answere, they used no other speech for their defence,
but such as were lawfull for them by the last acts of parliament ;
wherein was as great a presence of the three estates of that realme,
as had been at any time these hundred years before : they must require the Quene's Commissioners to consider, that this their entring
further into the matter wherewith the Quene is meant to be charged,
proceedeth not of them, nor of any pleasure they can take to hear
her any ways touched in honour ; but of their adversaries, who here-
by may appear to have less regard of the Quene, though they pre-

tend to be her commissioners themselves. And so with sundry speeches tending all to this effect, and remembring their former protestation, they said, for more satisfaction of the Quene's Majestie, whom they found by the speech lately used unto them to be grievously offended for the manner of their accusation of the Quene, they would shew unto her Majesty's commissioners a collection made in writing of the presumptions and circumstances, by the which it should evidently appear, that as the Erle Bothwel was the chief murtherer of the King, so was the Quene a deviser and maynteyner thereof; the which writing followeth thus, Articles conteyning certaine conjectures, &c

After the reading hereof they also said, that according to the truth conteyned in the same, the three estates of parliament, called by the King now present, their whole actions and proceedings from the murther of the late King weare ratified and approved to be lawfull. In which parliament they said, amongst the three estates, some of them which be now their adversaries were present, and gave their voyces to the same without contradiction. And besides that a greater number of all the estates had not bene known in any parliament these hundred years before.

Wherefore they trusted that the Quene's Majesty being duly thereof informed, would not be so grievously offended with them, as it appeared to them she was, nor think them culpable in these their doings. And therewith they did also present to her Majestie's commissioners the copie of the said act of parliament, and also the names of all the three estates there assembled, subscribed by the register of the parliament; the tenor of both which writings hereafter follow: In the parliament holden and begun at Edenborough, &c.

―――――――――

JOURNAL OF THE COMMISSIONERS.

Die Mercurii, 8. Decembris 1568. at Westminster.

Altered and interlined with Secretary Cecil's hand.

This daye the Erle of Murray, according to the appoyntment yesterday, came to the Quene's Majestie's commissioners, saying, that as they had yesternight produced and shewed sundry wrytings, tending to prove the hatred which the Quene of Scotts bare toward her husband to the tyme of his murder; wherein also they said might appear speciall arguments of her inordinate love towards the Erle Bothwell; so, for the further satisfaction both of the Quene's Majestie, and theyr lordships, they were ready to produce and shew a *great number of other letters wrytten* by the said *Quene*, wherin, as they said, might appear very evidently her inordinate love towards the said Erle Bothwell, with sundry other arguments of her guiltynes of the murder of her husband. And so therupon they produced several wrytings wrytten in French in the lyke Romain hand, as others her letters which were showed yesternight, and avowed by them to be wrytten by the said Quene. Which seven wrytings being copied, were read in French, and a due collation made therof as neere as could be by reading and inspection, and made to accord with the originals, which the said Erle of Murray required to be redelivered, and did thereupon deliver the copies being collationed. The tenors of all which seven wrytings hereafter follow in order, the first being in manner of a sonnet.

O Dieux, ayez de moy, &c.

After this, they did produce and shew three several wrytings in Englishe, subscribed and signed by Sir John Bellendyn, Knight, Justice-clerk in Scotland, wherof the first conteyned two several examinations, the first of John Haye the younger of Tallow, the 13th of September, Anno 1567, the second of John Heyburn, called John of Bowton, being examined upon the murder of the King the 8th of December 1567.

The second writing conteyned the examination of one William Powray, xxiii. Junii 1567, and in the same paper a second examination of the said William Powray the 3d of July then next following.

The third writing conteyneth the examination of one George Dalglych the 26th of June in the same year 1567. All which writings were also produced, being signed by the hand of the foresaid Sir John Bellenden the justice-clerk, and being read, were delivered to the said commissioners, the true tenor wherof hereafter followeth, Apud Edinburgh, 13. die mensis Septembris, &c.

After this they produced and shewed furth in writing, subscribed likewise by the said justice-clerk, a copie of the proces, verdict, and judgment against the foresaid John Hayeburn, John Haye, William Powray, and George Dalglech, as culpable of the murder of the said King, which being read was also delivered, and the tenor therof hereafter followeth, Curia justiciariæ, S. D. N. regis, &c.

After this they produced and shewed forth a wryting in a long paper, being, as they said, the judgement and condemnation by parliament, of the Erle Bothwell, James Ormeston, Robert Ormeston, Patrick Wilson, and Paris a Frenchman, Sym. Armstong, and William Murray, as guilty sundry wayes of treason for the murder of the King. The tenor whereof thus followeth : In the parliament holden at Edinburgh, the 20th daye of Dec. &c.

After this they produced and shewed a wryting signed by Mr.
James Macgill clerk of the register, conteyning a request, by way
of protestation, by the Erles of Huntly and Argile, and the Lord
Herrys, by the which they require to have no faulte imputed unto
them for not doing their duty since the 10th of June 1567, until the
29th of December then following, for the which, by order of parliament, they were acquitted. Which wryting was produced by them
to shew in what sorte the said Erles and the Lord Harrys had acknowledged in parliament their obedience unto the King. The tenor
of which wryting followeth, in the parliament holden at Edinburgh
the 29th Dec! 1567.

JOURNAL OF THE COMMISSIONERS.

ʹApud Westminster, die Jovis, 9. die Decembris, 1568.

Cott. lib. Cal. C. 1. fol. 252.

The Quene's Majestie's Commissioners being occupied in perusing
and reading certain lettres and sonnets wrytten in French, being
duly translated into English, and other wrytings also exhibited yesterday to them by the Erle of Murray and his collegues, the Bishop
of Rosse and Lord Boyd sent Lord Borthick to require accesse
for them to be heard, which was granted to be at one of the clock
after dinner; and the like mòtion being made from the Erle of Murray for accesse also, the same was appoynted to be at two of the
clock. And so the Commissioners proceded untill dinner tyme in
the hearing and perusing of the foresaid writings.

At one of the clock, the Bishop of Rosse and the Lord Boyd
came alone without the Lord Herris and Kilwenning or any other
person, and required the commissioners to receive a wryting in a
long paper, which was subscribed by the said bishop and Lord
Boyd, and also by the Lords Herris and Kilwenning, in forme
of a protestation. Which wryting being considered by the said
commissioners, and found therein underwrytten, presented and
gevin in to the Quene's Majesty's commissioners, &c. by the Quene's
commissioners of Scotland at Westminster the 6th day of Dec. &c.
by the said Bishop, Lord Boyd, Lord Herris and Kilwenning, being commissioners of the Quene of Scots, and so also subscribed by
them four; where indeed the same wryting was not presented either
the said 6th or, at any other time before this present 9th day, nor
was now exhibited, but by the said Bishop and the Lord Boyd only.

The said commissioners shewed unto the said Bishop and Lord Boyd the same matter, who for answear said, that because they and the other two had presented one writing the 6th of this month, wherin was conteyned a lyke protestation as this was, which was not receaved by theyr lordships, for that in the same the Quene's Majestie's answear was not expressed, as theyr lordships affirmed it to have bene given by hir Majestie, they had now in this wryting exhibited this 9th day altered and refourmed the same, and that was the cause why they had so wrytten under this wryting now ex-' hibited. And hereupon being required to shew the other wryting, which they offered upon the 6th of this month, to conferre the difference of them both, the same was produced, and therupon it was found, that these two wrytings did differ concerning the report of the Quene's Majestie's answeare, and in the end also in some other small sentences; and so both the wrytings weare receaved this present day. And for the truth of the circumstances hereunto belonging, to be hereafter better understanded, special clauses were by consent of both partyes added under every of the said wrytings by the publick notary there present, and weare read in the presence of the Quene's Majestie's commissioners, and of the said Bishop and Lord Boyd. The tenor wherof, with the subscriptions, hereafter followeth, My Lords Commissioners, &c.

And in like manner the second.

After this the Erle of Murray and his collegues cam in lyk manner; and first the Erle Morton said, that wher heretofore he had declared by speache, the manner how he cam to the lyttle guilt coffer with the lettres, sonnets, and contracts of marriage therin found, and heretofore exhibited; he had caused the same to be put in wryting, which also he produced subscribed with his hand, and desired to have it read: which being done, he avowed upon his honour, and the oath which he already took, the same to be true, the tenor wherof followeth, The true declaration and reporte, &c.

After this the Erle of Murray required, that one Thomas Nelson, late servitor to the King that was murdered, who did lye in the King's lodging the same night that he was murdered, and scaped by reason of a gret ston wall betwixt the King's chamber and that place wherin he did lye, might be hard upon his oath to report his knowledge therein, who being produced did present a wryting in form of an answeare, of himself to an examination, which being red unto him, he did by a corporal oath affirm the same to be true, the tenor wherof followeth thus, Thomas Nelson sometime servant, &c.

From the records of the court of session commonlie called, The Acts
of Sederunt, lib. 2, fol. 156.

Apud Edinburgum, xii. Maii 1567.

The quhilk day our Soverane Lady comperand personalie in jugement, in presence of the Lordis Chancellar, President, and haill
Lordis of sessioun underwrittin; that is to say, George Erle of
Huntlie, Lord Gordoun and Badzenoch, Chancellar, &c. reverend
faderis in God, Jhone Bishop of Ross, Alexander Bishop of Gallo-
way, Adam Bishop of Orknay, Master William Baillie Lord Pro-
vand, President, Mr. Alexander Dumbar Dene of Murray, Mr. Ro-
bert Maitland Dene of Aberdene, Mr. David Chalmer Chancellar
of Ross, Mr. Archibald Craufurd Persoun of Eglishame, Gawyne
Commendatar of Kilwinning, Sir James Balfour of Pittendreich,
Knyght, Clerk of Register, Richart Maitland of Lethingtoun,
Jhone Bellenden of Auchnoul, Justice-clerk, Knyghtis, William
Maitland zounger of Lethingtoun, Secretar to our Soverane Lady,
Mr. Henry Balnaves of Halhill, Mr. Jhone Gladstanes, and Mr.
Edward Henrysoun, licentiat in the laws: and als in presence of
Jhone Archbishop of Sanctandrois, William Bishop of Dumblane,
David Erle of Craufurd, Lord Lyndesay, George Erle of Caitnes,
Jhone Commendatar of the Abbay of Abirbrothok, Alexander
Commendatar of Culross, Robert Commendatar of Sanct Mary-Isle,
Thesaurer, George Lord Seytoun, Robert Lord Boyd, and Symon
Prestoun of Craigmillar, Knyght, Provest of Edinburgh: being in-
formed of befoir, that the Lordis of sessioun maid sum doubt and
stop to sit for administratioun of justice to the liegis of this realme,
in respect that hir hienes was tane and halden in Dunbar, be James
Erle Boithvile, Lord Halis and Creychtoun, and certane otheris his
complices, contrair hir Majestie's will and mynd: and now the
Quenis Majestie, for declaratioun of hir mynd thairintil, hes allowed the foirsaidis lordis of sessioun, for doing of justice to hir
hienes liegis, sen the tyme foirsaid. And further, hes declared and
declaris, that albeit her hienes was commoved, for the present tyme
of hir taking, at the said Erle Boithvile, and * sensyne be his

---

- * There are written in the same hand with the record, upon the margin, the following words, " Memorandum. This act was put in the
" bukis, efter that the Lord Regent and haill Lordis being in the
" town, upon the xviii. day of October, had seen the samyne, and I
" extractit thairupon."

gude behaving towart hir Hienes, and having sure knawledge of his
thankful service done be him in tyme bigane, and for mair thankful service in tyme coming, that hir hienes stands content with the
said Erle, and hes forgevin, and forgevis him, and all utheris his
complices being with him in company at the tyme foirsaid', all ha-
trent consaved by hir Majestie for taking and impresouning hir at
the tyme foirsaid. And als declaris hir Majestie to be at hir fredome and libertie ; and is mynded to promove the said Erle to fur-
thir honouris, for his service foirsaid. And Mr. David Borthick,
procurator for the said Erle, asketh instrumentis heirof.

THE EVIDENCE OF THOMAS NELSON, CONCERNING THE MURDER
OF KING HENRY DARNLEY.

Cot. lib. Cal. C. 1. fol. 165.

Thomas Nelson sumtyme servand in the chambir to umquhill
King Henry of guide memory of Scotland, examined upon his conscience, declaris, that he wes actual servand to the King the tyme of
his murder, and lang of befoir, and came with him from Glasgow
the time the Quene convoyed him to Edinburgh.

Item, The deponar remembris it wes dewysed in Glasgow, that
the King suld haif lyne first at Craigmillar; bot becaus he had na
will thairof, the purpois was altered, and conclusioun takin, that he
suld ly besyde the Kirk-of-field, at quhilk tyme this deponer be-
leived ever that he suld haif had the Dukis hous, and knew na other
hous, quhill the King lychted, at quhilk tyme he past directlie to
the said Dukis hous, thinking it to be the lugeing prepared for
him : but the contrare wes then schawin to him be the Quene, quha
convoyed him to the other hous, and at his cuming thairto, the
schalmer wes hung, and ane new bed of black figured velvet standing thairin. The keyis of the lugeing wes partlie standing in the
duris, and partlie delivered to this deponer be Robert Balfour
awner, all except the key of that door quhilk passeth through the
sellar and the town-wall, quhilk could not be had ; and thairfoir
Bonkle in the sellar said, he suld clois it weill aneuch within :
quhilkis keyis wes keppit and used be this deponer, and uthers the
Kingis servandis, quhill the Quenis cuming to the lugeing, at the
quhilk tyme the key of the laich chalmer under the king, quhair
sche lay tua nychtis, viz. the Wednisday and Friday befoir his mur-

der, with the key of the passage that past toward the garden, were delivered into the handis of Archibald Betoun, as the deponer remembris, quhilk Archibald wes yscheare of the Quenis chalmer door: befoir quhilk tyme of the Quenis lying in the Kingis lugeing the tua nychts above named, sche caused tak down the utter door that closed the passage toward baith the chalmers, and caused use the samyn door as a cover to the bath-fatt, quherin he wes baithed: and sua ther wes nathing left to stop the passage into the saidis chalmers, but only the portell duris: as alsua sche caused tak down the said new blak bed, sayand, it wald be sulzeit with the bath, and in the place thairof set up an auld purple bed that wes accustomed to be carit. And the saidis keyis that wer delivered in the handis of Archibald Betoun, remaned still in the handis of him and utheris that awaited upon the Quene, and never wer delivered agane to the Kingis servandis: for sche set up ane grein bed for hir self in the said laich chalmer, quherin sche lay the saids twa nychts, and promist alsua to haif bidden thair upon the Sounday at nycht. Bot efter sche had taryd lang, and intertened the King very familiarlie, sche tuk purpois, (as it had bene on the suddan) and departed, as sche spak, to gif the mask to Bastyane, quha that nycht wes mareit; hir servand, namelie, the said Archibald Betoun, and ane Paris Frenchman, havand the keyis of hir chalmer, quherin hir bed stuid in, as alsua of the passage that past toward the gairding: for quhen the Quene wes their, hir servandis had the keyis of the haill house, and duris at hir commandement, for upon the nycht sche used with the Lady Rereis to ga furth to the garding, and ther to sing and use pastyme. Bot fra the first tyme that sche lay in that lugeing, the Kingis servandis had never the key of hir said chalmer agane. The Quene being departed toward Halyrud-hous, the King, within the space of ane hour, past to bed, and in the chalmer with him lay umquhill William Taylour. This deponer and Edward Symonis lay in the litill gallery, that went direct to south out of the Kingis chalmer, havand ane window in the gavel throw the town-wall, and besyde thame lay William Taylour's boy, quhilks never knew of ony thing quhill the hous quherin thay lay wes fallen about thame: out of the quhilk how sone this deponer could be red, he stuid upon the ruynous wall quhill the pepill convened, and that he gat claiths and sua departed, quhill on the Monounday at efternone he wes called and examined, and, amangis utheris thingis, was inquired about the keyis of the lugeing, this deponer schew that Bonkle had the key of the sellar, and the Quenis servandis the keyis of hir chalmer: quhilk the Laird of Tulybardin hearing, said, Hald thair; heir is ane grund. Efter quhilk wordis spoken, thay left off, and proceded na farth er in the inquisition.

The lyke request was made, that one Thomas Crawford, a gentleman of the Earl of Lenox, might be also heard upon his oath, who
was, as they said, the same party of whom mention is made in a
long lettre wrytten in French, and exhibited the 7th of this month,
where it is said, about the beginning of the said lettre, that a gentleman of the Earl of Lenox met the party that wrote the lettre
about four miles from the place where the lettre was wrytten, as in
the copie of the same lettre may appere. Wherupon the said Thomas
Crawford coming before the commissioners, he did present a wryting, which he said he had caused to be made according to the truth
of his knowledge, which being read, he affirmed upon his corporal
oath there taken to be true, the tenor wherof herafter followeth, The
words betwixt the Queen, &c.

And after this was read, the said Crawford said, that as soon as
the Quene of Scotts had spoken with the King his master at Glas
gow from tyme to tyme, he the said Crawford was secretly informed
by the King of all things which had passed betwixt the said
Quene and the King, to the intent he shuld report the same to
the Erle of Lenox his master, because the said Erle durst not then,
for displeasure of the Quene, come abroad, and that he did, immediately at the same tyme, write the same word by word, as near as
he possibly could carry the same away: and sure he was, that the
words now reported in his writing, concerning the communication
betwixt the Quene of Scotts and him, upon the way near Glasgow,
are the very same words, in his conscience, that were spoken: and
that others being reported to him by the King, are the same in effect and substance, as they were delivered by the King to him, tho'
not percase in all parts the very words themselves. The confession
of the said Thomas Crawford, in wryting hereafter followeth thus,
The words betwixt the Queen and me, &c.

After this the said Erle of Murray and his collegues produced
another long writing in royall paper, subscribed by Mr. James Makgill, being, as they said, an act of parliament, conteyning the whole
form of the dimission of the crowne by the Quene, and of the coronation of the king. The which wryting or act, in this manner followeth, In the parliament holden and begun at Edinborough the
15th day of December, the year of God 1567, &c. To be seen in
the beginning of the first edition of the acts of that parliament.

THE JOURNALS OF THE PROCEEDINGS OF THE LORDS OF THE
PRIVY COUNCIL OF ENGLAND, WITH SOME OF THE CHIEF OF
THE NOBILITY, CALLED TO MEET WITH THEM AT HAMPTON-
COURT, THE 14TH AND 15TH DAYS OF DECEMBER, 1568.

Apud Hampton-court, die Martis xiv. Decembris, 1568.

The Quene's Majesty commanded the Lords of her privy counsell
to call unto them the Erles of Northumberland, Westmurland,
Shrewsbery, Worcester, Huntington and Warwyk, to whom being
assembled with the said counsell, was declared, That hir Majesty,
according to hir declaration heretofore made unto them, of the cause
of their calling to hir presence, which was as she should find cause
so to participat unto them (as being principall persons of the nobility of hir realme) the state of the cause of the Quene of Scotts : so
now also finding much tyme to be spent in the hearing of the same
since their coming, and yet nevertheless as much done as possible
was to be don with in this time, and the matter at some staye, by
meanes that the Quene of Scotts commissioners have refused any
more conference; her Majesty thought good, not knowing how by
common report they might be therof ashamed, to let them understand truly and playnly the state of the same, as herein making
them her counsellors, specially to keep the same secret to themselves,
without prejudicing of the one part or the other, by any final opinion or determination to be conceived with themselves : which as hir
Majesty meant to observe for hir self, so would she gladly have it
observed by them.   Which intention of hir Majestie being declared
unto the said lords, they all thanked her Majesty for this hir favourable goodnes so to esteme of them, and promised to observe hir
Majesty's direction, both in the secresy, and in the suspension of
their judgments.

This being done, the whole proceedings of the commissioners,
first at York, and next at Westminster, untill the last session ended
at Westminster about the 10th of this month, was to them sommarely declared and repeated : wherein, besides many circumstances
tending to make demonstration of the sincerity of the Quene's Majesty and hir commissioners, there was briefly shewed unto them, how
the Quene of Scotts commissioners first accused the Erle of Murray
and his collegues, being now in commission for, and in the name of
James King of Scotts: and how they did thereto make answer, by
justification of themselves by the lawes of the realme, without any

special depraving or calumniating the honour of the Quene; and next that of the replication of the other party. And furder was de. clared, how herupon the same treaty and conference, upon reasonable causes, was removed to Westminster; and in what sort the same conference was there revived; and how the Erle of Murray and his collegues, being charged to answer the replication, after protestation made, were unwilling to procede any furder to touche the name and honour of the Quene, if their adversaries had not pressed them with lack of loyalty. For remedy wherof they produced by way of addition to their first answear, wherin they avowed, That as the Erle Bothwell was the executor of the murder, so was the Quene of Scotts a procurer and devisor of the said murder. And after, this was likewise declared unto the said Erles, acording to the several memorials therof already made and put in writing, the which wrytting or act, in this manner followeth : In the parliament holden and begun at Edinborough the 15th day of December, the year of God 1567, &c. [To be seen in the beginning of the first edition of the acts of that parliament.]

PART OF A JOURNAL OF QUEEN MARY'S PROCEEDINGS, EXHIBITED BY MURRAY AND HIS ASSOCIATES, SO FAR AS IT RELATES TO THEIR ACCOUNT OF THE LETTERS TO BOTHVILLE, &c.

From a Copy marked by Cecil, Cot. Libr. Cal. B. ix. fol. 247.

January 21, 1566. The Quene tuik hir journay towards Glascow, and was accompanyit with the Erlis of Huntly and Bothwell to the Kalendar, my Lord Levistoun's Place.

23. The Quene came to Glascow, and on the rode met hir Thomas Crauford from the Erle of Lennux, and Sir James Hamilton, with the rest mentionit in hir letter. Erle Huntly and Bothwell returnit that same nyght to Edynbrough, and Bothwell lay in the town.

24. The Quene remaynit at Glascow, lyck as she did the 25th and the 26th, and hayd the conference with the King whereof she wryttis; and in this tyme wrayt hir bylle and uther letteris to Bothwell. And Bothwell this 24th day was found verray tymus weséing the Kyng's ludging that wes in preparing for him, and the same nycht tuik journay towards Lyddisdaill.

27. The Quene (conforme to hir commission, as she wryttis)

broucht the King from Glascow to the Kalendar towards Edynbrough.

Jan. 28. The Quene broucht the King to Linlythquow, and there
remained all morn, quhill she gat word of my Lord Bothwell his
returning towards Edynbrough, be Hob Ormistoun, ane of the murtheraris. The same day the Erle Bothwell came back from Lyddisdaill towards Edinbrough.

29. She remained all day in Linlythquow with the King, and
wraytt from thence to Bothwell.

30. The Quene broucht the King to Edynbrough, and patt him
in his ludging quhair he endit; and Bothwell keiping tryist met hir
upon the way.

February 5. She ludged all nycht under the King, in the chalmer
quhairin the poulder was layd thairefter, and quhairof Paris her
chalmer-child ressavit the key.

7. She ludged and lay all nycht agane in the foresaid chalmer,
and from thence wrayt that same nycht the letter concerning the
purpose of the Abbot of Halyruidhouse.

8. She confronted the Kyng, and my Lord of Halyruidhouse,
conform to hir letter wrytten the nycht befoir.

9. She and Bothwell soupped at the bankett with the Bishop of
the Yllis, and eftir past up accompanyit with Argyle, Huntly, and
Bothwell, to the King's chalmer, and thair thay remaynit cherissing
him, quhill Bothwell and his complices hayd putt all thingis to ordour, and Paris hir chalmer-child hayd ressavit in hir chalmer the
pulder, and came up agane and gef the sign. And thay departit
to Bastien's banquet and masque, about eleven houris; and their-
efter thay baith returnit to the abbay, and talkit quhill twelve houris
and eftir.

20. Betwixt twa and thré of the clock the King was blawin in
the ayr be the pulder.

11. The Quene wrayt to my Lord of Lennux, promising to tak
tryall.

12. The Kyng's body was broucht down, and layd in the chapell,
and she remaynit at Edinbrough with Bothwell to the 21st heirof.
In this meyn tyme wer mony placardis set up. And Hary Killi-
grew arryvit from the Quene's Majestie [of England.]

21. They past togidder to Seytoun, and thàir past thair tyme
meryly to the 10th of Marche, quhill Le Crok the French ambassa-
dour persuadit hir to return to Edinbrough.

Marche 10. Thay returnit to Edinbrough be persuasion of Le
Crok, quhair thay remaynit quhill the 24th of the same, earnestly
trying the upsetting of the placardis, but never word of the Kyng's
murther. At this tyme my Lord Regent purchaist leif to depart.

Marche 24. Thay returnit agane to Seytoun, and thair past thair tyme meryly in all solace, quill the 10th of Apryll 1567.

April 5. The secund contract of mariage, *per verba de præsenti*, wes maid and wrytten be my Lord of Huntly, quha for his restoring agane the forfaltour, had purchasit ane procuratory subscryvit with his sister's hand, then, wyif to Bothwell: and thair wes the counsale haldin for the cleansing of Bothwell.

9. My Lord Regent departit furth of Scotland.

10. They returnit to Edinbrough, to Bothwell's cleansing.

12. Quhilk wes Setterday, Bothwell wes cleansit werray strangely, as the process beiris.

14. Quhilk wes Mounday, the first day of the parliament, set onlie for reduction of my Lord Huntly's forfaltour.

18. Quhilk wes Friday the day of the summonds of reduction of the Erle of Huntly's forfaltour.

10. Quhilk was Setterday, the decreyt of reduction wes gevin for the Erle of Huntly, and all his freindis. The same nycht the Lordis past the band efter supper to the Erle Bothwell, being drawin secretlie be him to the supper.

21. Viz. Mounday, the Quene raid to Stirling, as it was devysit, and from thence wreyt the letteris concerning the purpose devysit of hir ravishing; quhair Huntly cam to hir, and began to repent him. In the mene tyme Bothwell remainit at Edinbrough, assembling his forces.

23. She came to Linlythquow, and Bothwell came to Haltoun hard by.

24. She sent the Erle of Huntly to Bothwell in the morning, quha met hir upon the way, seamit to ravish hir, and tuik Huntly and the secretarie prisoneris, and led them all to Dumbar, and thair remainit to the 3d of May.

26. The first precept for the partising of the Erle of Bothwell and his wyif, was direct furth from the commissarys of Edinburgh.

27. The second precept of partising, befoir Maister John Manderstoun, commissair to the Bishop of Sanctandrois, wes direct furth.

May 3. She wes conweyit be Bothwell, and all his freindis, with sperris, to Edinbrough castell, and for fear of accusation kast thair sperris from thame by the way; and the nixt Sunday hir bannis wer proclamit to be hir awin precept, subscryvit with hir hand.

12. She cam with Bothwell out of the castell to the tolbuyth befoir the Lordis of session, and tuik hir protestatioun and act thair of hir libertie; and so past togidder, to the abbay.

15. Thay wer publicklie mareit efter baith the sortis of the kirkis, reformit and unreformit, and remaynit to the 7th of June.

June 7. He proposit and rayd against the Lord Howme and Ferneherst, and so past to Melros, and she to Brothwick.

11. The Lordis cam suddanlie to Borthwick: Bothwell fled to Dumbar, and the Lordis retyrit to Edinburgh. She followit Bothwell to Dumbar disguysit.

15. Thay cam from Dumbar to Carbarryehill, quhair the Lordis met thame. The Erle Bothwell fled, and she cam to Edinbrough with the Lordis.

16. She past to Lochlevin, and thair remaynit to the 2d of May, 1568.

20. Dalgleishe, chalmer-child to my Lord Bothwell, wes takin, and the box and letteris quhilk he brought out of the castell. About this tyme my Lord Buthwell fled be sea to the north.

July 24. The Quene maid resignation of hir crowne in favour of hir sone, now our soverane, and past commissiounis of government. At this tyme Sir Nycholas Throgmorton was in Scotland.

29. The King was crownit at Striviling. Middilmoir was present.

August 14. My Lord of Murray, now Regent, returnit furth of France, and cam to Edinbrough.

17. My Lord past to Lochlevin, and spake with the Quene.

22. My Lord now Regent wes movit to accept upon him the commission of regentry, and gef his solemnit ayth for dew ministration.

December 15. The parliament was halden, and all thingis confirmit thairin.

May 2. The Quene escapit furth of Lochlevin, and cam to Hamiltoun, my Lord being in Glascow.

13. The field was strykin at Langsyid, besydis Glascow.

15. Maister Middlemoir, sent from the Quene's Majestie [of England] causit my Lord from thencefurth absteyn from armour and violence.

PROCEEDINGS AT HAMPTON-COURT, MONDAY THE 13TH OF
DECEMBER, 1568.

From a minute of Secretary Cecill.

The Lord Keeper,	Duke of Norfolk,
Lord Marquis Northampton,	Erle of Arundell, ⟩
Erle of Darby,	Erle of Sussex,
Erle of Bedford,	Erle of Lecester,
Lord Admyrall,	Lord Chamberlayn, ˘
William Cecill,	Sir R. Sadler.
Sir Walter Mildmay,	

It was thought mete to advise the Quene's Majesty, that, accord-
yng to hir Majesty's declaration of late made to the rest of the Erles
at ther first comyng thyther, they shuld be duly informed by hir
Majesty's commissioners, of the whole proceedings in the conference at Westminster betwixt them and the commissioners for the
Quene of Scotts, and the Regent and his colleagues; and that also
the original lettres and wrytyngs exhibited by the Regent, as the
Quene of Scotts lettres and wrytyngs shuld also be shewed, and
conference thereof made in their sight, with the lettres of the said
Quene's being extant, and hertofore wrytten with her own hand,
and sent to the Quene's Majesty; wherby may be serched and exa-
myned what difference is betwixt the same.

Item, That the sayd Erles shuld be first charged not to notify
any thing to them shewed to the prejudice of the Quene of Scotts,
untill hir furder answer may be had.

Item, It was thought mete that hir Majesty shuld answer the Bishop of Ross and his company, as servitors to the Scottish Quene, not
as commissioners: "That according to hir last answer made to
them upon the 4th of this month, that she had caused the Erle of
Murray and his company to be streightly and sharply reproved and
rebuked, for ther audacious and unloyall accusation of the Quene,
to whom they were natyve subjects, in such large sort, as a more
ernest and sharper reproof culd not be devised in convenient words:
wherupon they being at the same astonished, answered, That they
did not thynk hir Majesty had any just cause so to reprove and
condemn them, except their adversaries wold deny their former accusation. And therfor to avoyde the hard judgment of hir Majesty, and to deliver themselves of the slander and infamy of un-

g

loyall subjects, they offered to exhibit and shew furth to the commissioners sundry particular proves of great evidency to mayntain
their former answers; which they also meant no wise to produce
but upon such urgent necessitie, as in their former protestation is
contained. And so they have exhibited diverse particular matters
which cannot be but of great presumption to mayntain their former
answer, untill the same may be by some good answer refuted and
avoyded.

" And therfor if the sayd Bishop and his colleagues had not (as it
is supposed) dissolved their commission by Scottish protestations,
wherby they have not, as it is thought, now any authoritie to make
answer thereto, they shuld be made privie to the sayd evidences
and proofs, wherby hir Majesty might have of them some good answer, to the acquitall of the Quene of Scotts hir good sister, which
hir Majesty wold be glad might be accomplished.

" And therfore wisheth that they wold advertise the Quene their
mistress of thus much; and for whose purgation and acquittal hir
Majesty will be both content and glad to receave from hir some good
answer: for hir Majesty meaneth not to prejudice hir, how evident
soever the allegations against hir seme to be, untill she shall answer
the same, if so she will. But as for the demand lately made by
them, to have hir come in person into the presence of hir Majesty,
she cannot agree thereto, without open prejudice to her own honour,
untill by some good answer the great and manifest presumptions
that are now produced against hir, may be either clearly avoyded, or some wise qualefyed. And in the mean tyme, if it shall
please hir to gyve authoritie to any hir commissionars to answer the
same, or otherwise to answer the same hirself, before any to be appointed by the Quene's Majesty, or by any other mean, hir Majesty
will be right glad thereof, and will for that purpose cause expedition to be made of any thyng therto requisit: and untill she may
hear from hir, she will suspend hir judgment, and cause also all
others hir counsellors and ministers, being privie hereunto, to do the
lyke, and to kepe the same in silence."

Apud Hampton-court, die Martis xiv. Decembris 1568.

The Quene's Majesty commanded the Lords of her privy counsell
to call unto them th' Erles of Northumberland, Westmorland,
Shrewsbery, Worcester, Huntington, and Warwyk, to whom being
assembled with the said councell, was declared, That hir Majesty,
according to hir declaration heretofore made unto them of the cause
of their calling to hir presence, which was, as she should find cause,
so to participat unto them, as being principall persons of the nobility of hir realme, the state of the cause of the Quene of Scotts: so

now also finding much tyme to be spent in the hearing of the same
since their coming, and yet nevertheless as much done as possible
was to be done within this time, and the matter at some staye, by
meanes that the Quene of Scotts commissioners have refused any
more conference: hir Majesty thought good, not knowing how by
common report they might be therof informed, to let them understand truly and playnly the state of the same, as herein making them
her counsellors, specially to keep the same secret to themselves,
without prejudicing of the one part or the other, by any final opinion or determination to be conceived with themselves : which as hir
Majesty ment to observe for hir self, so would she gladly have it
observed by them.   Which intention of hir Majestie being declared
unto the said Lords, they all thanked hir Majesty for this hir favourable goodnes so to esteme of them, and promised to observe
hir Majesty's direction, both in the secrecy, and in the suspension of
their judgments.

This being done, the whole procedings of the commissioners, first
at York, and next at Westminster, untill the last session ended at
Westminster about the 10th of this month, was to them sommarely
declared and repeated : wherin, besides many circumstances tending
to make demonstration of the sincerity of the Quene's Majesty and
hir commissioners, there was briefly shewed unto them, how the
Quene of Scotts commissioners first accused the Erle of Murray and
his colleagues, being now in commission for, and in the name of
James King of Scotts: and how they did therto make answer, by
justification of themselves by the lawes of the realme, without any
special depraving or calumniating the honour of the Quene ; and
next thereto, the replication of the other party. And furder was declared, how herupon the same treaty and conference, upon reasonable causes, was removed to Westminster; and in what sort the
same conference was there revived ; and how the Erle of Murray and
his colleagues, being charged to answer the replication, after protestation made, were unwilling to procede any furder to touch the
name and honor of the Quene, if their adversaries had not pressed
them with lack of loyalty. For remedy wherof they produced by
way of addition to their first answear, wherin they avowed, That as
the Erle Bothwell was the executor of the murder, so was the Quene
of Scotts a procurer and deviser of the said murder. And after
this was likewise declared unto the said Erles, acording to the several memorials therof already made and put in writing, the acts
passed in all the former sessions at Westminster : for the more perfect declaration of all which said acts, there was first produced a
writing in manner of articles, which was exhibited to the commissioners the 6th of December, as appears in the memorial of that
session.

And before those articles were read, there were produced sundry lettres written in French, supposed to be written by the Quene of Scotts own hand, to the Erle Bothwell; and therwith also one long sonnet, and a promise of marriage in the name of the said Quene with the said Erle Bothwell. Of which lettres the originals, supposed to be written with the Quene of Scotts own hand, were then also presently produced and perused; and being read, were duly conferred and compared, for the manner of writing and fashion of orthography, with sundry other lettres long since heretofore written, and sent by the said Quene of Scotts to the Quene's Majesty. ˙And next after these was produced and read a declaration of the Erle Morton, of the manner of the finding of the said lettres, as the same was exhibited upon his oath the 9th of December: in collation ˙wherof no difference was found. Of all which lettres and writings the true copies are contained in the memorial of the acts of the sessions of the 7th and 8th of December.

And after this were also produced and read the examination of John Haye the younger of Tallowe, and of John Hepborne, and George Dalglys, who were executed at Edinburgh for the said murder, which be conteyned amongst the acts of the sessions of the 8th of December. And next after that was read the confession and deposition of Thomas Crawfurd, conteyned amongst the writings of the 9th of December.

And forasmuch as the night approached, it was thought good to differ the furder declaration of the rest untill the nixt day following.

Die Mercurii, xv. Decembris, 1568.

The Lords of the privy counsell having the Erles before mentioned with them, declared, That where yesterday mention and report was made of a book of articles being divided into five parts, they shuld also see and heare the same book, and so the same was throughly and distinctly read unto them. And after the same was produced and read, the deposition of one William Powry, one of the four that was executed at Edinburgh, as the same deposition was exhibited the 8th of December. Next wherunto was produced, read and viewed, the original writing, supposed to be written by the Erle of Huntley, being a contract of mariage betwixt the Quene and the Erle Bothwell, dated at Seaton the 5th of Aprill, and subscribed by the Quene and the Erle Bothwell with their own proper handes, as was alledged: the true copy wherof is amongst the things exhibited the 7th of December. After this was also produced and read the extract of the arraynment and deliverance of the Erle Bothwell, by an assise, at Edinburgh, the 12th of April, 1567, according to the copy thereof, being amongst the writings exhibited the 7th of

December. Nixt after this was also produced, read and viewed, a writing subscribed, dated the 10th of this month of December, subscribed by the Erle of Murray and his colleagues, to testify the former writings produced, as written by the said Quene of Scotts, to be hir own hand-writing. Which also is to be seen amongst the writings exhibited to the commissioners the 12th of December.

There was also produced and read a writing of another deposition of Thomas Crawfurd, upon his oath exhibited to the commissioners the 13th of December, concerning certen answers made to him by the foresaid John Hepborne and John Haye, upon the scaffold in Edinburgh, instantly before their execution.

There was also produced, read and shewed to them, the form and manner of the holding of the parliament at Edinburgh the 15th of December 1567, wherin the numbers of the three estates were there expressed, and alledged to be as great an assembly of the said estates, as had been any time by the space of one hundred years before : which writing also is conteyned amongst the rest exhibited the 9th of December.

There was also report made unto them of an act of parliament made at the same time, conteyning the confirmation of the dimission of the crown by the Quene of Scotts, and of the coronation of hir sonne, and of the regency in the person of the Erle of Murray. At which parliament hath bene alledged, that the Erles of Huntley and Argile, and the Lord Herrys, did acknowledge the same authorities: and for that purpose, as a writing was produced before the Commissioners the 8th of December, to prove the same, so was the same writing read this present day; which writing is amongst others exhibited the said 8th day.

Besides the production, reading and shewing of these sundry kinds of writings here before-mentioned, considering the length of time that was spent in reading the foresaid writings, many of them being of great length, there was a short and just report made of sundry other matters which were exhibited to the said commissioners, as the same may plainly appear amongst the acts of the severall sessions of the said commissioners at Westminster; as, the acts of the two severall divorces, which are of great length in writing, and the acts of parliament for the attaynder of all the persons charged with the murder. And it is to be noted, that at the time of the producing, shewing and reading of all these foresaid writings, there was no special choyse nor regard had to the order of the producing therof, but the whole writings lying altogether upon the counsel table, the same were one after an other shewed rather by hap, as the same did ly upon the table, than with any choyse made, as by the natures therof, if time had so served, might have been. And in

the end it was said unto the said Erles, that in this sort they were
now made participant of the whole state of the cause, even as largely
as the rest of hir Majestie's Privy Counsel were: And therfore they
were newly again required to have in remembrance hir Majestie's
first charge to have the same kept in secret by them as hir counsellors in this cause. And that where the Quene of Scotts commissioners being made privy of this the accusation of the said Quene,
have forborn to answer to the same, and refused also to have any
furder conference in this matter, pressing only to have the Quene
their Mistris permitted to come to the presence of the Quene's Majestie to make her answer, and otherwise to make no answer at all;
it hath been considered by her Majestie, and not thought unmeet,
in this sort following, to answer the said commissioners, if they
shall persist in the said request: That hir Majestie will be very
willing and desirous, that some good answer may be made by the
said Quene, either by her commissioners and delegates, or by her
own self, before such sufficient persons as her Majestie would send
to her: But considering her Majestie had at her first coming into
the realm, found it not mete for her own honour to have her, being
so commonly defamed of so horrible crimes, to come to her presence, before she might be therof some wise purged, so also now
the crimes, wherewith she hath been by common fame burdened,
being by many vehement allegations and presumptions, upon things
now produced, made more apparent, she can not, without manifest
blemish of hir own honour, in the sicht of the world, agree to have
the same Q. to cum into hir presence, untill the said horrible crimes
may be by sum just and reasonable answer avoidit and removit
from hir, which hir Majestie would wish might also be.

And in this sort hir Majesty's intention being opened to the said
Erlis, in presence of the said privy council, the said Erlis severally
made answer; First, acknowledging themselves much bound unto
hir Majestie, that it had pleased hir to impart to them the stait
of this great cause, in so plain manner, as they did perceive it;
'wherin they had sene such foul matteris, as they thought truly, in
their consciences, That hir Majestie had just cause herein given to
make to the said commissioners such ane answer, being as reasonable as the case might bear; and the rather for that they could not
allow it as meet for hir Majestie's honour to admit the said Q. to hir
Majestie's presence, as the case now did stand.

From the Paper-office.

MADAME, whilest your cause hath bene herein treated upon, we thought it not needful to write any thing thereof unto you, supposing always that your commissioners wolde thereof advertise, as they saw cause. And now sithen, they have broken this conference, by refusing to mak answer, as they say, by your commandement, and for that purpose they *also have required licence to* * return to you. Although we thinke, yow shall by them perceive the whole procedyngs, yet we cannot but let yow understand by these our letters, That as we have bene very sory of long tyme for your mishappe and greate trouble, so fynd we our sorrows now doubled, in beholding such thyngs as ar produced to prove your self cause of all the same. And our greif herin is also increased, in that we did not thynk at any tyme to have seen or heard such matters of so great apparence and moment to charge and loden yow: nevertheless, both in friendship, nature, [and justice, we ar moved to cover these matters, and stay our judgment, and not to gather any sense hereof to your prejudice, before we may hear of your direct answer therunto, according as your commissioneris understand our meaning to be; which, at their request, is delivered to them in wryting. And as we trust they will advise yow for your honor, to agree to make answer, as we have motioned them, so surely we cannot but, as one Prince and near cousin regarding an other, most ernestly as we may, in termes of freindship, require and charge you, not to forbear from answering. And for our part, as we ar hartely sorry and dismayed to find such matter of your charge, so shall we be as hartely glad and well content to hear of sufficient matter for your discharge. And although we doubt not but you are well certifyed of the diligence and care of your ministers having your commission, yet can we not, beside an allowance generallie of them, specially note to you, your good choice of this bearer, the Bishoppe of Rosse, who hath not only faithfully and wisely, but also so carefully and dutifully, for your honour and weale, behaved himself, and that both privatly and publickly, as

* These words have been dash'd through with a pen, and are accordingly wanting in this letter as published by James Anderson, from Cot. Lib. Cal. c. 1. fol. 272, in the end of the 4th vol. of his Collections, p. 183.

we cannot but in this sort commend him unto yow, as we wish yow had many such devoted discrete servants; for in our judgment we think ye have not any in loyaltie and faithfulnes can overmatch him. And this we are the bolder to wryte, considering we take it the best trial of a good servant to be in adversitie, out of which we hartely wish you to be delivered by the justification of your innocency. xxi. Decemb. 1568.

CHALLENGES BETWIXT THE ERLE OF MURRAY'S PARTY AND LORD HERYS.

From State Papers in Biblioth. Pepysian, Magdalene College, Cambridge, fol. 148.

I. CHALLENGE TO LORD HERYS BY LORD LINDSAY.

Lord Hereis—I am informit, that ze have spokin and affirmit, that my Lord Regentis Grace, and his cumpanie here present, wer giltie of the abhominabill murthour of umquhile the King, our soverane Lordis fader. Gif ze have swa spokin, ze have said untrewlie, and thairin have leyit in zour throte, quhilk I will mantene, God-willing, aganis zou, as becomis me of honour and dewtie : and heirupon I desire zour answer. Subscrivit with my hand, at Kingston, the 22d day of December, 1568.

PATRICK LINDSAY.

II. LORD HERYS'S RETURN TO THE PRECEDING CHALLENGE ; CARRIED BY JOHN HAMILTOUN OF BROOMHILL.

Lord Lyndsay—I have sene ane writing of zours, the xxij of December, and thairby understands, " Ze ar informit, that I have said, and affirmit, that the Erle of Murray, quhom ze call zour Regent, and his cumpanie, ar gyltie of the Quenis husbandis slauchter, father to our Prince, and gif I said it, I have leyit in my throte; quhilk ze will mantene aganis me, as becumis zou of honour and dewtie."

In respect thay have accusit the Quenis Majestie, mine and your native Soverane, of that foul crime, far by the dewtie that guid sub-

jectis aucht, or ever has bene sene to have done to their native Soverane; I have said, "Thair is of that companie, present with the
Erle of Murray, giltie of that abhominabill tressoun, in the foir-
knawledge and consent thairto." That ze wer privie to it, Lord
Lyndsay, I know nocht: and gif ze will say that I have speciallie
spokin of zow, ze lied in your throte; and that I will defend, as of
my honour and dewtie becumis me: bot let aucht of the principallis
that is of thame subscryve the like writing ze have send to me, and
I shall point thame furth, and fight with sum of the tratouris thairin: for metest it is, that tratouris sould pay for thair awin tressoun.
Off London this xxij. December, 1568·

HERYS.

LORD HERYS'S LETTER TO THE ERLE LECESTRE, 22D DECEMBER,
1568.

An original.

Pleis it zour richt honorabill lordship, be adverteisit, ane servant
of the Bishop of Ross has shawin me, zour Lordship desyrit me to
cum to the court thys day; and the occasioun thairof was, upon
sum inoportune suit of the Erle of Murray's.

My Lord—I am reddy, at the Quenis Majestie of this realme's
commandement, or upon zour Lordship's desyre, to cum quhair ze
will command me, and that with my hartlie gude will. For the
Erle of Murray, swa lang as he misknawis his dewtie to his native
Soverane, I will nether for his inoportunes nor plesour travell. Bot,
for my awin trewth and dewtie, gif it be to answer to sic writingis
as first I red befoir zour honouris at Westminster, the Quenis Majestie's commissionaris, and efter presentit unto hir Hienes, I advow
thame, and, with the grace of Almightie God, shall leif na part
unprowin, that trewth and honour requiris; quhairof I haif sent
zour Lordship heirwith ane copie; as alswa ane letter I ressavit this
day of the Lord Lyndsay, with my answer to it. Gif neid sall require my awin presence to advow the samin, it will pleis zour Lordship to adverteis this my servand, and I sall nocht faill to be thair
at the hour appointit be zour Lordship, gif God sall spair my lyif:
to quhais protectioun I hartelie commit zour honorabill Lordship.

Off London the 22d day of December, 1568, be your Lordship's
to command at my power lefullie, with my humbill service,

HERYS.

h

**** At York. The commissioneris for the said Quene, our Soverane
Lordis mother, seikand meanis to hald back the knawledge of the
truth indirectly, made a protestatioun, as that scho was not subject to ony judge on earth, having an imperial crown gevin hir of
God : Quhilk hir protestatioun was nathing agreeing with that
quhilk we lookit for by hir Hienes letter of the viii. of Junii, repor-
tand of the said Quenis contentatioun, to commit the heiring and
ordouring of hir caus simplie to the Quenis Majestie of England.
Quhilk impertinent exceptioun was a likelie presumptioun, that
scho wald nevir be content that the grund of hir actioun sould be
knawin or deliberat upon.

Notwithstanding the commissioneris on hir part presentit hir
clame or accusatioun aganis us, quhairunto we maid answer ; and,
at the occasioun of sum thingis specifeit in the said accusatioun, we
proponit certane articlis, of the quhilk we requirit resolutioun of
the Quenis Majestie of Ingland's commissioneris ; quha, finding the
samin mair weighty nor thay, upon thair commissioun, might weill
resolve ; thay sent for resolutioun of the samin to the Quenis Majestie
and hir counsal. Quhairupon first, the Laird of Lethington, Secretary of our Soverane Lord, and the Clerk-Register, wer callit to
cum up to London ; and, eftir thame, we ourselfis, with the remanent
nobilmen and utheris of the King our Soverane Lordis counsal that
wer with us, past likewayis to the court : quhair the said Quene our
Soverane Lordis moderis commissioneris, preissand the trial of the said
Quenis interes in the murder of the King our Soverane Lordis father,
hir husband ; at last, be thair ernist and incessant provocatioun, it
behuifit us to mak an additioun to our answeris gevin in at York,
quhairin we wer constranit to nominate the said Quene, our Soverane
Lordis mother, as gilty of the foirknawlege, counsal and device of
the horribill murder of the King, our Soverane Lordis fader, perswader and commandar of the said murder to be done, maintenar and
fortifiar of the executouris thairof ; having, before the ingeving of the
said additioun, and befoir we enterit farder in the grund of the matter, maid our solempn protestatioun, that we had na delyte to sé the
said Quene, our Soverane Lordis moder, dishonourit, and that we
came not willinglie to hir accusatioun of so odious a crime ; bot
that we wer thairto enforcit be hir awn preissing, and our adversaris,
hir commissioneris, in quhais default hir schame sould be disclosit,

quhairby thay sould preiss us to cum to that answer, quhilk thay knew we had just caus to mak in the end, and sua to produce sik. evidences as they knew we had; quhilk was indirectly to preiss earnistlie hir perpetual infamie; quhairof, as of befoir, we protestit that thay, and not we, sould be the chief procuraris estemit.

Thay séing us to cum to the plain probatioun of the truth, left off all farder debaiting of the matter as revokt be the Quene, of quhom thay had commissioun, thairby flying the tryal, quhilk of befoir thay constranit us to enter into, for the probatioun of that we had allegit. And then being scharplie rebukit be hir Majesties commissioneris, how we durst be sa bald, to utter ony sik thing contenit in the said additioun for our defence? we were constranit outher to underly the ignominy, or then, be manifestatioun of the very truth, to declair the just grounds of our proceidings: and for that effect we producit certane conjecturis, presumptiounis, likly-heids and circumstancis, quhairby we maid it to appeir, that, as James, sumtime Erle of Bothvile, was the chief executour of the horrible and unworthy murder perpetrat in the persoun of umquhile the King, our Soverane Lordis fader, sa was scho of the foirknaw-lege, counsal, devise, perswader and commandar of the said murder to be done, and maintenar and fortifyar of the executouris thairof. And for verificatioun of the saidis articlis, we producit to the Quenis Majestie of Ingland's commissioneris,

I.—The namis of the Estatis of this realme convenit at Edin-burgh in the month of December MDLXVII. quhair our Soverane Lordis coronatioun and inauguratioun in his kingdom was ratyfeit and found gude.

Item, We producit eight letteris in French, written be the Quenis awin hand, and sent to the said James sumtime Erle of Bothville.

Item, A little contract, or obligatioun, written by the said Quenis awin hand, promising to marry the said Bothville.

Item, An uther contract, written by the Erle of Huntlie's hand, of the date the v. of April 1567.

Item, The depositiounis of the persounis who wer airt and part of the murder, and wer executed for the samin.

Item, The process led aganis thame befoir the Justice and his deputies, quhairupon followit thair executioun to deith.

Item, The process of Bothville's pretendit cleansing befoir the Justice.

Item, A process of divorce, led betwixt the said James sumtime Erle of Bothville, and Dame Jean Gordon his spouse, before the commissaries of Edinburgh, for pretended causis of adultery on the said Erle's part.

Item, Another process of divorce led befoir Mr. John Manderston, as Judge-delegate under the Archbishop of St. Andrews, allegit Primate and Legate.

Item, An instrument of compulsion, proving the said Mr. John to have bene constranit to leid the said process of divorce.

Item, The process of forfeiture led aganis the said James sumtime Erle Bothville.

Item, An act befoir the Lordis of Sessioun, quhairby the Quene, after counterfeited ravishing, declarit herself to be at libertie.

. Item, The said Quenis consent gevin to the Lordis to subscribe the band for the promotioun of the said James Erle Bothville to hir marriage.

Item, The protestatioun maid by the Lord Herris and utheris the time of the parliament.

. Item, The act of the confirmatioun of the Kingis authoritie, and establishing the regency, during his Hienes's minority.

Item, The declaration of Thomas Nelson, spokin be his awin mouth, and writtin with his awin hand.

. Item, The declaratioun of Thomas Crawfurd, alsua spoken by his awin mouth, and writtin with his hand. .

. Item, The declaratioun of the Erle of Mortoun, how the letteris came to his handis.

Item, The affirmatioun of the commissioneris, that the letteris wer the Quenis awin hand-writing.

The copies of all quhilk letteris, conferrit, red and considerit, wer deliverit to Mr. Secretary, in quhais handis thay remane.

Efter quhilk probatioun led, the saidis commissioneris for the Quenis Majestie of England allow'd of our proceidingis, declarand, that we had done the dewty of honest men ; and that hir Hienes wald mantene the Kingis state and our caus, till she should understand the contrary.

And hereupon we returnit into Scotland by hir Majestie's permissioun and gude favour, and since have done nathing, which, we traist, sould ony wayis alter hir Majestie's gude will and favour towardis us : nor zit have we got ony knawledge that hir Majestie has understuid ony thing of the said Quene, to the contrary of that quhilk we alledgit and pruvit at our being in Ingland.

And gif furder pruif be requirit, we have sent with zow the depositiounis of Nicholas Hubert, alias Paris, a Frenchman, one that was present at the committing of the said murder, and of late execute to the deith for the samin.***

THE CONFESSIONS OF JOHN HEPBURN, YOUNG HAY OF TALLA,
DAGLEISH AND PARIS, UPON WHOM WAS JUSTICE EXECUTED
THE THIRD OF JANUARY, THE YEAR OF GOD, 1567.

John Bowton confessed, that nine was at the deed doing, my
Lord Bothwel, the Lord of Ormiston, Hob Ormiston, himself,
Talla, Daglish, Wilson, Pourie, and French Paris, and that he saw
no more, nor knew of no other companies.

Item, He knows no other but that, that he was blown in the air,
for he was handled with no mens' hands as he saw; and if it was, it
was with others, and not with them.

Item, As touching Sir James Balfour, he saw not his subscription; but I warrant you he was the principal counsellor and deviser.

Item, He said, I confess that it is the very providence of God that
has brought me to his judgment, for I am led to it as an horse to
the stall; for I had ships provided to fly, but could not escape.

Item, He said, let no man do evil for counsel of great men, or
their masters, thinking they shall save them; for surely I thought
that night that the deed was done, that although-knowledge should
be got, no man durst have said it was evil done, seeing the *hand
writ*, and acknowledging the QUEEN's *mind thereto*.

Item, Speaking of the Queen in the tolebooth, he said, God make
all well; but the longer the dirt is hidden, it is the stronger. Who
lives, our deaths will be thought no news.

Item, In the conclusion he confessed, he was one of the principal
doers of the death, and therefore was justly worthy of death; but
he was assured of the mercy of God, who called him to repentance.

Item, Talla confessed, *ut supra*, agreeing in all points as concerning the persons, number, and blowing up into the air.

Item, He affirmed, that in Seton my Lord Bothwel called on him,
and said, What thought you when you saw him blown in the air?
Who answered, Alas, my Lord, why speak you that? for whenever
I hear such a thing, the words wound me to death, as they ought to
do you.

Item, That same time he saw Sir James Balfour put in his own
name and his brother's unto my Lord Bothwell's remission.

Item, He knew of the deed doing three or four days ere it was
done, or thereabout.

Item, He said, After that I came to the court I left the reading of God's word, and embraced vanity, and therefore has God justly brought this on me.

Wherefore let all men shun evil company, and to trust not in men, for ready are we to embrace evil, as ready as tinder to receive fire. And further, in the tolebooth he required John Brand, minister of the congregation, to pass to my Lord Lindsey, and say, My Lord, heartily I forgive your Lordship, and also my Lord Regent, and all others, but specially them that betrayed me to you; for I know if you could have saved me you would, desiring as ye will answer before God at the latter day to do your diligence to bring the rest who were the beginners of this work to justice, as ye have done to me; for ye know it was not begun in my head : but yet he praises God that his justice has begun at me, by the which he has called me to repentance.

Item, Dagleish * said, As God shall be my judge, I knew nothing of the King's death before it was done; for my Lord Bothwel going to his bed, after the taking off of his hose, which was stocked with velvet, French Paris came and spake with him, and after that he tarried on me for other hose and cloaths, and his riding cloak and sword, which I gave him, and after that came up to the gate to the Lord Ormiston's lodging, and tarried for him, and thereafter that he passed to a place beside the Black Friers, and came to the slope of the dyke, where he bid me stand still; and as God shall be my judge, I knew nothing while I heard the blast of powder; and after this he came home, lay down in his bed, while Mr. George Hacket came and knocked at the door; and if I die for this, the which God· judge me if I knew more, what shall be done to the devisers, counsellors, subscribers, and fortifiers of it?

Amias, my most faithful and careful servant—God reward thee trebblefold in the double, for the most troublesome charge so well discharged. If you knew, my Amias, how kindly, beside most dutifully, my grateful heart accepts and praiseth your spotless endeavours

* This is the valet of Bothwell, upon whom the casket .and letters were found.

and faithful actions, your wise orders and safe regard performed in
so dangerous and crafty a charge, it would ease your travail and rejoyce your heart: in which I charge you carry this most instant
thought, that I cannot balance in any weight of my judgment, the
value that I prize you at, and suppose no treasure can countervail
such a faith, and shall condemn me in that fault, that yet I never
committed, if I reward not such desert; yet, let me lack, when I
most need it, if I acknowledge not such a merit, *non omnibus da-
tum.* Let your wicked murdress know, how with hearty sorrow
her vile desert compels these orders, and bid her from me ask God
forgiveness for her treacherous dealing towards the saver of her life,
many a year to the intollerable peril of her own: and yet not content
with so many forgivenesses, must fall again to so horrible surpass-
ing a woman's thoughts, much less a princess, instead of excusing
whereof, not yet being so plainly confess'd by the author of my
guiltless death. Let repentance take place, and let not the fiend
possess her so as better part be lost; for which I pray with hands
lifted up to him that may both save and spill. With my loving
adue and prayers for thy long life.

Your most assured and loving Sovereign, as
thereto by good desert induced,
E. REGINA.

To my loving Amias.

THE END.

T. DOLBY, Printer, 17, Catherine-Street, Strand.